Ride Pennsylvania Horse Trails- Part II

The *Western* Half of Pennsylvania

40+ Equestrian & Shared Use Trails

Includes Hiking, Bike, Snowmobile, X-C Ski, Carriage,
and Camping Destinations

By
Carolyn B. Cook

Hit The Trail Publications, LLC
Pennsylvania

Ride Pennsylvania Horse Trails- Part II
The *Western* Half of Pennsylvania
40+ Equestrian & Shared Use Trails
Includes Hiking, Bike, Snowmobile, X-C Ski, Carriage, and Camping Destinations

By Carolyn B. Cook

Copyright © 2005

Note to the Reader: Trails and environmental conditions are always changing. If you find any of the described trails have significantly changed or new trails have opened, please notify the publisher and author at the below address. Any comments will be considered in the future editions of this book and are appreciated.

Published by:
Hit The Trail Publications, LLC
P.O. Box 970
Cherryville, PA 18035

Editor: Connie Bloss
Contributing Editors: John Spotts, Barbara Cook, Thomas Cook

ISBN 0-9729080-1-3
Library of Congress Control Number 2004114846
Cover photos: John Spotts at Moshannon State Forest, Black Moshannon region (top), Jan Huffman at Elk State Forest (bottom)
Back photos: Bull elk by the Thunder Mountain Equestrian Campground (top), John Spotts and Jan Huffman entering the Thunder Mountain Equestrian Trail Campground (bottom)
Other photo courtesies: Larry Bloss and Connie Bloss (wedding photo), Stephanie Ewing (editor photo)

Additional courtesies: listed in individual chapters

Website: www.ridepennsylvania.com OR www.patrail.com

DISCLAIMER!
READ AND UNDERSTAND PRIOR TO USING THIS BOOK!

Please note: This book is a reference source and information book only. The author, publisher, and all others, directly or indirectly associated with this book, do not make any recommendations or guarantees regarding any place, person, animals, service, business, ad, directions, conditions, environment, or other items mentioned in this book, nor are they responsible for any errors in this book. This book is not all-inclusive. The author may indicate a good personal experience or a favorite personal preference but that does not mean the reader or user of the information in this book will have the same positive experience upon their visit to the location or use of the facilities or services.

Horses (mules included) and horseback riding can be, and is, a dangerous sport. Trail riding can present all sorts of unpredictable or predictable hazards and risks. Circumstances, obstacles, weather, terrain, places, people, attitudes, equines, behavior, trails, traffic, crowds, animals including wildlife, experiences, multiple-uses, hunting seasons, legalities, permitted uses, improper usage, safety factors, surroundings, etc. change. Call the trail administrator in advance; check on the conditions of the trails, changes in the trails, relocation of camping locales, obstacles, concerns, or any other info that the office or source of information on the trail can provide. Even if no fees or permits are listed, check for changes or exceptions, such as for large, organized group rides. Obtain maps; ask for recommendations and comments. If water is listed as accessible on a trail, check that the water quality is good and that horses are permitted to drink from the water source. Check if camp fires are permitted; consider weather and environmental conditions including nearby natural gas sites. Owners of large rigs should check accessibility and grade. Use common sense and caution. Bring a cell phone, first-aid kit, and be prepared in the event of an emergency.

The reader or user of information in this book assumes their own risks and agrees the reader or user of information in this book is responsible for their own health and safety. The author, publisher, and all others, directly or indirectly associated with this book, expressly disclaim any and all liability against any and all claims, causes of action, liabilities of any nature, damages, costs and expenses, including, without limitation, attorney fees arising because of any alleged personal injury, property damage, death, nuisance, loss of business or otherwise, by the reader or user arising from or in any way connected to the information contained in this book.

Table of Contents

Table of Contents

Introduction

This book is the second of two books that I have written on equestrian and shared use trails in Pennsylvania. I started my first book as a result of hearing of trail closings, and set out to find where equestrians could still ride with the goal of telling everyone about those trails so that they would be used, preserved, and not lost from lack of information or communication. As indicated in my first book, we found so many trails open to equestrians; we could not cover the state in just one book. So, I divided the state down the middle and covered the eastern half in Part I. This is Part II, which covers trails in the western half of Pennsylvania, embracing trails from the center of the state to the western border of the state. Like the first book, I have structured Part II to be a lightweight, soft cover that is a practical size so it can be carried in a saddlebag.

Before I began my quest to locate trails open to equestrians in Pennsylvania, I was under the mistaken impression that Pennsylvania did not have many trails to offer equine enthusiasts. Fortunately, I was wrong and I discovered a whole new world of wonderful destinations. I have spent years exploring Pennsylvania's National Forest region, State Forests, State Parks, County Parks, Rail-Trails, U.S. Army Corps of Engineers land, and others that are open to equines, and still could spend several more. As a result of my travels, I bring to you good news of new trails and trail development. The last several months have been very encouraging as I spoke with representatives of numerous locations that told me they were developing new trails and/or expanding current ones with multiple-use, including equestrian, in mind! Some doors have been closed to us but now new ones have been opened. Nor does it mean the old doors cannot be reopened; I have also been hearing about some good progress in that area. But we need all equine enthusiasts contributing. A "little" from each individual goes a long way; and "a lot" multiplies itself several times over. Take the initiative, lead these new opportunities, volunteer and set a positive example, attend meetings and influence the outcome…and (then) we shouldn't need to worry or complain about the closing of trails.

Just as with my first book, I have ridden each of the trails covered in this book that are detailed in the chapters; the last chapter includes a brief mention of a variety of trails, some of which we could not ride due to weather, construction, etc. Our travels and the book are not all-inclusive of every trail mile and detail within a trail system; that would be nearly impossible to do as the trails are extensive and always changing. Nor does this book include every trail in western Pennsylvania; rather this is a selection of a variety of trails for equestrians to try and explore. Just as in my first book, it is my intention to give readers a reference point for an assortment of trails (instead of riding or wearing out that "same old trail"), to provide information about the trails as I or we experienced them, and to encourage equestrians to have fun exploring.

One of the most challenging aspects of researching the trails for this book was inconsistent or lack of information. Although the various official sources of information were well intended, often I was provided different information by another source or representative, sometimes from the same office. This can be due to lack of communication, unfamiliarity with equestrians, changes in management, interpretation of policy, weather damage, and other factors. Frequently, staff didn't know if there were trails equestrians were permitted on, where we could ride, where to recommend for parking rigs, what roads to approach on, suitability of sites for camping, etc. This was more the norm than the exception. I had to be unrelenting in my pursuit of information and be careful to double and triple check as much information as possible. Sometimes the misinformation came from other equestrians. One clear instance was when we were told a trail was very good from what we thought was a very reliable source. We tried it; it was dangerous so much so that John's horse almost toppled head first with him down a steep decline (fortunately, he pulled the horse's head back and instead remained in the saddle as the horse slid down on his hindquarters) only to learn later that these folks had not ridden this trail in some time nor were they very familiar with it or what a "good" trail should be. Also, what is a "good" trail to some is not always what is acceptable to us and others (and vice versa I am sure). In addition, western Pennsylvania was experiencing two years of severe weather consisting of heavy rains, micro bursts, hurricane remnants, and even tornadoes. These occurred before, during, and after our visits. I know much terrain may have been altered dramatically after we covered certain trails. All these inconsistencies, different perceptions, and shifting factors combined made it hard to write about or provide precise information, rules, description, etc. of a locale. We were pursuing fast moving targets. This was just the reality of the situation as there were and are numerous factors at large. Through patience and persistence I put this together; it is written as we experienced it at the time of our stay. You will not find everything the same. Prior to your visit, check with the office as to any developments, changes, and recommendations. If the individual sounds unfamiliar with equestrian trails or camping sites, elevate it and politely ask to speak to someone who is familiar with the lay of the land and equestrians' interests, perhaps a senior ranger. Please consider their perspective; they may be short on personnel, new on the job, may have never been to the locations you are inquiring about, may never had inquiries from other equestrians, or may feel the need to try to provide an answer even though they aren't sure. And I do not mean this as a negative; most everyone I communicated with really tried to get me to the right place or the best source of information. And once I provided clarity, guidance, and feedback, most were wonderfully responsive and helpful. I have tried to do the foundation for you. But I ask that you help me by continuing to build upon it. If we equestrians become more involved and more visible, good information and increased options will be more readily and easily available. Provide feedback to the office. Not every employee can cover all the ground that we do or understand our needs. After visiting a site, where necessary, try to offer

vii

constructive recommendations to the staff so they will have better information for the next equestrian who comes along. And don't forget to share what you did like!

As with the first book, I have not stayed at or visited the "nearby stables" or used the farriers and vets listed at the end of the chapters unless indicated otherwise. Farriers, veterinarians, and nearby stables are listed for the reader's convenience for information purposes or in the event of an emergency. I have found local stables are an excellent resource in helping contact a vet or farrier; usually they can get hold of one quicker than someone who is not a regular customer. They may also be able to accommodate you if you need emergency overnight stabling, or hay if you run short while traveling, or they may offer overnight stabling or trail rides in their regular course of business. Regarding maps, I do not include copies of maps in the book as I found most do not reproduce well when shrinking down to the size of the book, making it difficult to see detail. (In fact, sometimes I have had to enlarge the originals in order to read them!) I thought it much more useful to list where you can obtain a full size map of the area. Most land management provides these for free and will promptly mail them to you. Often, you can obtain them online. *I prefer to have them mailed as they are frequently very large, provide more information and detail, and are of better quality.*

At this writing, it has only been a year and a half since my first book came out. My life and John's have been very hectic since this undertaking. For those of you who know a little bit about us from Part I, John and I somehow managed to find time to plan a wedding while releasing our first book and researching for the second! We had a wonderful wedding on horseback (of course) at Green Lane County Park in Montgomery County. People say that their wedding date was one of their most momentous; well, I was completely swept away at mine. Not only was I moved that John personally organized the wedding (how many men would do that!), but also our friends and family came from far and wide to join us. Our families lovingly added so many special touches and our friends were amazing at helping, especially coming to our rescue when one normally well-behaved horse suddenly decided he didn't want to partake in the wedding party if his equine best buddy wasn't invited (oops!). The caring and warmth that we felt was so important to us and will be a memory we will always treasure. We are blessed to have such good family and friends. After the wedding, we set off for our honeymoon. And yes, you guessed it; we took the horses and immediately began researching trails in western Pennsylvania. There was much new territory for us to explore, but that never stopped us before as we enjoy making new discoveries and new friends. Well we did find some gems, in fact numerous treasures that we are anxious to share with you. I hope you like them as much as we did. And please help us to remain welcome on these trails. Enjoy, share, and preserve!

See you on the trail, Carolyn

The Author

Carolyn Cook has had a life-long love for travel, exploring trails, and horses. From the start, it seemed inevitable that these passions would come together and result in the research and promotion of equestrian trails. While taking a break from her long distance travels covering the trails in the western half of Pennsylvania, the author (above) visits one of her favorite destinations in the eastern half of Pennsylvania at Gettysburg National Military Park.

Carolyn and her husband, John Spotts, reside in Pennsylvania with their menagerie of horses, dogs, cats, and even a few chickens.

Dedication and Thanks

There have been so many wonderful people to thank. I would like to begin by thanking my husband and best friend, John Spotts, who accompanied me to every destination and shared both the challenges of this research and the rewards of the new, fantastic discoveries along the way. Thank you to our horses Tabasco, Bonanza ('Bo'), and Moonshine for faithfully carrying us up and down the mountains of western Pennsylvania; you elevate the phrase "trail horse" and stand above the rest. Thank you to my caring parents Barbara and Ed Cook, my family, and my friends for their unrelenting support and understanding, especially when I could not be around to share in gatherings due to travel for this book. My deepest gratitude to my editor and dear friend, Connie Bloss. Connie, thank you so much for your continued patience, encouragement, and enthusiasm for this project; I am fortunate to have a friend like you.

I also want to thank all those that helped make this book possible by contributing in their way, whether it was providing guidance in our research, helping keep our horses healthy, taking care of our other animals as we traveled, promoting these writings so people know about the trails, or just being amazing in their support of our endeavors. I would like to thank Cylia Allison, Sue Arnold, the folks at Artillery Ridge Campground (Gettysburg), Dr. Balliet, Karl and Kristen Barndt, Dr. Bateman, Matt Beaver, Annette Bishop, Cindy and Gene Brandner, Thomas Cook, Lisa Doubleday, Kim Douglas, Dominic Farole (Esq.), Connie Fenner, Kathy Grube and Janice Martin (Lehigh Valley Horse Council), Jan Huffman, Julie Hussmann, Brenda Imus, Howard Josephs and the Sheridan Printing Company, Marc and Ann Konchinsky, Stephanie Lawson, John Little, Steve Luoni, Jill and Kenny Martin, Sue and Dick McCoy and Willow Brook Farms, Pete Pizzo and Ronald Ahlbrandt of the County of Montgomery office, Denise Parsons, Teresa Proctor, Garth and Kathy Rumsmoke, Smucker's Harness Shop, Ellie Snyder, the Walls (a very special thank you to Wendy, Wayne, Christopher and Nicholas), Bud and Gwen Wills and the Pennsylvania Equine Council, Heather Volkar, Sally Wood, our local riding buddies (Katherine, Woody, Pat, Ray, Cheryl, Ray Jr., Monica, Dale, Lori), and all the other individuals, groups, tack shops, publications, clubs, and organizations that have supported us in this endeavor. Also, I can't express enough my gratitude to all those who established these trails, preserve them, maintain them, promote them, and manage them for all to enjoy. Without you there would be nowhere to ride. Thank you to all those who were so helpful in sharing information on these trails including DCNR (Bureau of Forestry and Bureau of State Parks), the U.S. Forest Service, the U.S. Army Corps of Engineers, the County Parks, the Rails-to-Trails groups, the Pennsylvania State Game Commission, and all the other public and private organizations. I have met many new friends along the way. And most of all, thank you God for giving me the wonderful gift of trail riding and for allowing me to enjoy the beauty and serenity that the great outdoors has to offer.

What is the difference between National Forests, State Forests, State Parks, State Gamelands, etc.?

In Ride Pennsylvania Horse Trails-Part I, The Eastern Half of Pennsylvania, I included some of the following information. I am again including this, with updates, as it is important for trail enthusiasts to understand the difference between the various types of land ownership and the effects on the use of these lands.

We have been asked many times, what the difference is between the types of areas in regard to equestrian and other uses. It is significant as to who oversees the land and the laws under which its use was created, as both will also affect what is permitted within the lands and what types of facilities are available. Each category has their own set of rules and regulations, and even the same kind may differ depending on the region and other factors. The following is based on our own observations derived from our experiences, and also from information obtained from the officials of the various trail systems. Further information, including contacts, is listed in the related chapters.

National Forests: Administered by the U.S. Forest Service of the U.S. Department of Agriculture, the National Forests are regulated on a Federal level and are distinct and separate from local State and County jurisdictions. The Allegheny National Forest (ANF) is a Federal supervised National Forest located within the state of Pennsylvania. The Allegheny National Forest permits horseback riding and dispersed equestrian camping throughout with certain limitations. Certain areas are closed to horses such as hiking (only) trails or cross-country ski trails. Most camping is primitive, although there are some developed locations, such as Kelly Pines, that have facilities. Other locales have nearby commercial operations offering convenient access to ANF trails. There is no fee or permit required for camping on ANF land; camping is on a first come, first served basis.

State Forests: State Forests are administered by the Department of Conservation & Natural Resources (DCNR) Bureau of Forestry (BOF). Along with other purposes, these lands are intended to be left in mostly an undeveloped, primitive, and natural state. Also, importantly, one of the established purposes of the State Forests is to provide outdoor recreation to the public in a manner that is consistent with the above goals. In keeping with "a natural state," the roads within the forest are often of dirt or gravel surface, and the trails are not as well defined. Generally, horseback riding is permitted throughout the State Forest's trails and roads, except for areas specifically prohibiting horses such as Natural

Areas or designated hiking (only) trails. Equestrians have 1.9 million acres of State Forest land, much of which is open to horseback riding! Often, the Bureau of Forestry and the local trail and equestrian groups perform the maintenance on the trails. So, equestrians can influence the establishment and assist in the maintenance of these trails. Check first with the local State Forest office as rules can differ among separate districts. Ask for information, guidelines, and restrictions, and then get out there and explore! Carriage drivers should check with the individual district office as to which State Forest roads permit and are suitable for carriage driving, as some State Forest roads are of good grade and excellent surface. We have experienced Pennsylvania State Forests to be wonderful places to visit, with endless possibilities. This is a very good area for equestrians to be effective and make a positive difference. Ask the district office if volunteers are needed; help support our State Forest trail systems!

In addition to trail riding, State Forests permit primitive and motorized camping. Primitive (non-motorized) equestrian and non-equestrian camping is allowed and is free. Permits are not required if not camping more than one night in one place. In the past and still at some locations, motorized non-equestrian and equestrian camping have been allowed on the sides of the State Forest roads, pull-off areas, and sometimes at designated locations. However, a recent trend is heading toward allowing motorized camping at designated sites only. Motorized camping is also free, but a permit is required. Frequently, water is not available (so bring water). Comfort stations or restrooms are limited or nonexistent. Usually, there is a State Park or two within the State Forest where facilities are accessible. Other special rules and limitations apply, and can be obtained from the local State Forest district office.

U.S. Army Corps of Engineers: The U.S. Army Corps of Engineers also manages land that may be open to the public and horseback riders. They have numerous important functions, some of which include managing water resources, maintaining navigation areas, providing aid under national emergencies (including natural disasters), engineering shoreline protection, and other coastal projects. The permitted use of the land may vary in accordance with the intended purpose and function of the land.

State Parks: Pennsylvania's State Park system is one of our country's largest. The DCNR Bureau of State Parks manages these parks. The purpose of State Parks has evolved over the years and, today, one of their key functions is to provide outdoor recreation for the general public in natural settings. They typically have accommodations including comfort stations, picnic areas, pavilions, water, paved parking, etc. Usually, the park's grounds are maintained and groomed. The State Parks have designated central recreational areas (i.e., picnic areas) where, generally, horses are not permitted. Often, they do not permit horses or have more restrictions and limitations if they do. Usually, equestrian camping is not offered, although there may be exceptions such as at Kettle Creek State Park. Fees may be charged for camping in the State Parks. In general, trails are well defined. If horses are accepted, they may be directed to travel in the outlying or surrounding areas. Sometimes, equestrian trails in the State Park serve as links to other trails, and that is why they exist.

We have found Pennsylvania's State Parks to be great places to ride with many excellent, well maintained, and beautiful trail systems. But, State Parks are an area where equestrians need to be especially sensitive, aware, and considerate of other users, as the parks are more central and heavily used by a variety of visitors, many of which are unfamiliar and sometimes not in favor of horses. Please keep in mind that cleaning up in the parking lots or the scattering of manure in popular and well traveled areas will help keep these locales open to riders.

County Parks: The local counties administer the County Parks. It is up to the individual county and location of the park as to whether equestrian day use or camping is permitted. Many County Parks are smaller or are located in congested areas, so equestrian use is not appropriate. Other County Parks, such as Two Mile Run, have horseback riding. Two Mile Run is also considering horse camping. Comfort facilities, recreational grounds, and picnic areas are usually available. While researching trails in Pennsylvania, we noticed an increase in permitted equestrian use in County Parks and these parks had awesome trail systems. Do not overlook the County Parks! Equestrians, especially local riding groups, should support and stay active with the County Parks to help ensure that equestrians remain welcome and to retain a positive presence.

Rail-Trails: Rail-trail lands can be owned or managed by rail-to-trail organizations, the county, the Pennsylvania Game Commission, and others. A rail-trail can travel through different land ownership with dissimilar authorized uses. Riders need to know who owns the rail-trail land and if they permit horseback riders.

Comfort facilities are not always available, but may be available at central locations or at historic attractions. The tendency seems to be the addition of restrooms or portajohns at various intervals along the trails. The good, durable surface of the rail-trails has kept many of these trails open to horses and mountain bikes. Sometimes, only certain sections are or can be open to equestrians due to congested areas or paved surfaces. There has been an increase of rail-trail conversion in recent years, and much is still being defined. The trend currently seems to be that equestrians are being considered and permitted on many new rail-trails. The rail-trails offer some fantastic travels along the corridors of our nation's history; this is another area where equestrians should volunteer, join the organizations, and be actively involved in order to keep rail-trails open to them in the future.

State Gamelands: Pennsylvania State Gamelands are administered by the Pennsylvania Game Commission. These lands have been designated for a specific purpose. Each gameland may differ as to its permitted use. Check the Pennsylvania Game Commission rules and regulations prior to riding on State Gamelands. See the State Gamelands Trail Information chapter for additional detail, contacts, and information. The State Gamelands' settings are primitive and normally do not have comfort stations.

Courtesy: I would like to thank Matt Beaver for his input regarding sections of the above.

Example of an excellent equestrian facility at Kelly Pines,
Allegheny National Forest

A Message from the Pennsylvania Equine Council (PEC)

The following is provided courtesy of Bud Wills, State Trail Chair of the Pennsylvania Equine Council.

Pennsylvania is one of the most beautiful states to see from the back of a horse or mule, largely do to the diversity of the terrain as well as the flora and fauna. You can be riding in the shade of an old growth forest in the morning, then hop in the truck and by mid-afternoon be riding sandy, flat lands. We have been spoiled for the most part because we have been accustomed to riding anytime and anywhere we wanted. Shrinking landmass, due to a growing population, is concentrating more equestrians on less land. As a result, user conflict may begin to take its toll.

Agriculture is still the largest industry in Pennsylvania, and the equine related portion is rapidly becoming the largest segment. Recently, reports have indicated that the equine industry is larger than the beef industry, and nearing, if not already, passing the dairy industry. Trail riding is the fastest growing segment of the equine industry nationwide.

Because of the free-spirited nature of horse folks, individual specialized breed and discipline groups, and simply the hours spent caring for our four legged friends, our time and energies have not been directed in areas of organization for the overall good of the equine industry. Other user groups, such as hikers and bikers, have pockets of organized groups and have for the most part done a better job of educating their members on land use ethics, construction, and maintenance of sustainable trails for their user group's needs. In order for the equine community to continue to have access to public and other land that we have enjoyed in the past, we must become organized, educated, and involved. We can no longer assume that, because we have had access to public lands for years, it will continue. Most agencies, such as DCNR (State Forest and State Parks) and the Allegheny National Forest, have suffered budget cuts and greatly appreciate trained volunteer groups' assistance. The Pennsylvania Game Commission, because of its legislated mandate, has not had funding for recreational trails. Recently, there have been developments to allow for some access on sustainable designated trails to lands they own for non-motorized users in a compatible manner. Clearly, it is time for equestrians to step up to the plate and assume some responsibility for keeping ourselves informed on all issues related to the industry, as well as assist agencies as needed on public lands.

The Pennsylvania Equine Council (PEC) was formed in 1988 and is the only statewide equine organization addressing issues that affect every equine owner, regardless of with what breed or discipline they are associated. The Council's purposes are: to promote and protect the common interest of all people involved with equines, and to broaden the scope of understanding and knowledge in all areas of equine ownership and management through education.

The PEC Trail Committee, in early 2002, set on a course to provide a three phase educational program to provide a coordinated effort to agencies and the existing trail users of today (whether hikers, bikers, or equestrians), and to reach out to the equine community particularly those who may be the trail riders of the future. Step one, through a 3-day training program, assists agencies by providing sound trail layout, design, and maintenance education to agency personnel and also equestrian, biking, and hiking volunteers who coordinate efforts statewide to meet the need for sustainable trails in Pennsylvania. Step two, via a 1-day training program, trains agencies and local stewardship groups in the best-accepted practices for trail construction and maintenance work. Trainings in the safe packing of tools and materials on stock are also being offered. Step three is an outreach program and is offered to all equine related groups. The PEC offers many programs, including Trail and Outdoor Ethics courses such as "Leave No Trace," and "Barn and Trailer Safety." The PEC feels confident that its efforts can keep Pennsylvania's trails open and, through educating our equestrians in best practices, can create a friendly shared-use environment.

Visit us online at www.pennsylvaniaequinecouncil.com or call toll free 888-304-0281 and help us help you.

Pennsylvania Equine Council
State Trail Chair
Bud Wills

My editor, Connie Bloss with her Icelandic Horse, Thor (top); and our wedding party, Jan Huffman, Steve Luoni, John and I, and Lynda Mouton-Smith (bottom)

Ride Pennsylvania

The *Western* Half of Pennsylvania

Not Drawn to Scale

1 The Thunder Mountain Equestrian Trail System & Elk State Forest	12 Keystone Mountain Country Shared Use Trail
2 Quehanna Region	13 Blue Knob State Park
3 Black Moshannon	14 The Lower Trail
4 Cook Forest State Park	15 Canoe Creek State Park
5 The Allegheny River Tract	16 Ohiopyle State Park
6 Two Mile Run County Park	17 The Laurel Highlands Trail System & The PW&S Trails
7 Tidioute & The Hickory Creek Wilderness Region	18 Mountain Streams Trail System
8 Kellettville Region	19 Trough Creek
9 Kelly Pines & The Duhring (Marienville) Region	20 Brush Ridge & The Northern Tract
10 Kettle Creek State Park	21 The Old Logging Trail
11 The Eagleton Mine Camp Trail	22 Sideling Hill
	23 The Broad Mountain Tract & The Bear Valley Forest Division

Horse Trails–Part II

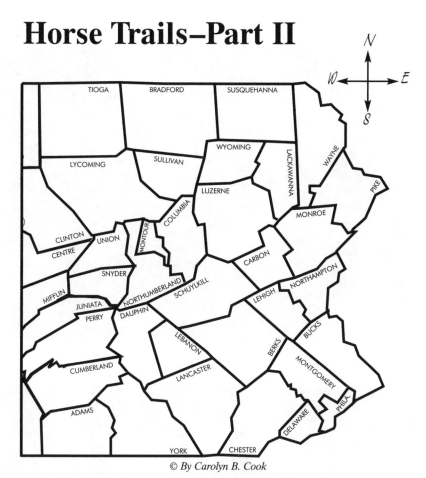

© By Carolyn B. Cook

24 Northmoreland County Park
25 South Park
26 Round Hill Park
27 Deer Lakes Park
28 Hartwood Acres
29 Harrison Hills
30 Mingo Creek Park
31 Brady's Run Park
32 Raccoon Creek State Park
33 Hillman State Park
34 Bear Run
35 Swamp Run
36 The Babcock Division
37a Hell's Hollow
37b Brush Creek Park

37c North Park
37d The Allegheny Passage
37e Rock Run
37f Susquehannock State Forest, northwest section
37g Settler's Cabin

*See **Ride Pennsylvania Horse Trails – Part I** for trails in the eastern half of Pennsylvania.

1. The Thunder Mountain Equestrian Trail System (TMET) & Surrounding Areas
Elk State Forest
BOF-DCNR
(Bureau of Forestry/Department of Conservation & Natural Resources)

Lasting Impression: Four Spur Award! The sight of herds of elk, majestic bulls with colossal racks, and the sound of a lonely bull bugling to his potential mate is an absolutely awesome experience! The landscape of the country and the wildlife are reminiscent of my travels out west. This region is one of my absolute personal favorites to enjoy on horseback, especially in the fall.

Location: The Elk State Forest is located in Elk, Cameron, Clinton, Potter, and McKean Counties.

Length: *Day Ride, Weekend, or Week-long Destination*- Visit for a couple to several days and explore! There are many miles (100+) of trails and forest roads in these 200,000 acres of State Forest that permit riding. The Thunder Mountain Equestrian Trail (TMET) is a designated and maintained equestrian trail within Elk State Forest and is about 26 miles in length with the possibility of additional trails being developed. Horses are also permitted on the State Forest roads which are open to public travel. Horses are not permitted to ride designated hiking trails including the Elk Trail. Check the latest regulations at the time of your visit.

Level of Difficulty: The Thunder Mountain Equestrian Trail and surrounding area trails can vary from easy to difficult (some steep sections), but usually are of a moderate level of difficulty. We did not encounter any extreme or impassable sections while riding the TMET trail or surrounding trails. Most TMET trails use switchbacks to minimize the climb or descent. Sometimes sections were eroded due to weather but alternate inland trails were available. The TMET is mostly easy to follow with the help of the map, and is well marked with blue blazes or blue horseshoes and small brown equestrian signs. Some intersections are not as easy to follow. Surrounding areas can be more difficult, so bring the Elk State Forest Public Use Map (green) along with the TMET Map.

Terrain: The area is full of peaks and valleys through open fields and thick forests. The surface is dirt, grass, or gravel State Forest roads. Except for a few low lying areas, we did not find the trails to be rocky. With increased usage, a few areas will come to need small bridges or fill to link ravines.

Horse Camping: Yes

Non-horse Camping: Yes

Carriage Potential: Yes, Elk State Forest has lots of level State Forest roads which consist of gravel or dirt surface and should be excellent for carriage driving. The camping area has plenty of room for carts and so do the roads

1

leading directly out of camp. Carriage enthusiasts will need to contact the office to introduce their user group, as carriage driving has not been common (yet) to State Forests nor did we see any evidence of carriage driving at any of the destinations that we visited.

Maps and Info: Thunder Mountain Equestrian Trail (and camping information) & Elk State Forest, DCNR, Elk State Forest, 258 Sizerville Road, Emporium, PA 15834, (814) 486-3353, email: FD13@.state.pa.us. Ask for the Thunder Mountain Equestrian Trail Map and the Elk State Forest Public Use Map. Information on State Gamelands can be obtained by contacting the Pennsylvania Game Commission, Harrisburg, (717) 787-9612 or (717) 783-8164, website: www.pgc.state.pa.us. For the northwest region call (877) 877-0299. The Big Elk Lick campground is located in Benezette and can be reached at (814) 787-4656.

Activities: Hiking, Horseback Riding Trails, and Camping. *Note: exercise caution as there is extensive hunting in this vicinity and many State Gamelands surround the TMET system and adjoining or nearby trails. The TMET system permits year round riding and does not close to equestrians during hunting season.*

Fees for Trail Use: None

Permits for Day Trail Use: None

Permits Required for Overnight Camping: Yes, permits are required for overnight, motorized camping.

Fees for Overnight Camping: No fee is charged for the permit to camp at the Bureau of Forestry DCNR Thunder Mountain Equestrian Trail Campground.

Comfort Station: There are no facilities. Group rides may be required to rent a portajohn; check with the DCNR office for the latest rules and regulations. Bring water.

DIRECTIONS:

To Benezette: From I-80, take Exit 111 Penfield (Route 153). Take Route 153 north for 8 miles to the light at Junction 255. Make a right and head north on Route 255. Take Route 255 north for 6.4 miles into the town of Force and (just after) look for Route 555. Bear right onto Route 555. Take Route 555 (passing the towns of Weedville, Caledonia, & Medix Run) for about 8.3 miles and you will see signs on the left for The Big Elk Lick campground. Make a left into the campground entrance if that is your destination. To travel to the town of Benezette, continue on Route 555 for another mile. To reach the public elk viewing sights at Winslow Hill (without hauling), make a left at the Benezette General Store onto Front Street and follow signs.

Thunder Mountain Equestrian Trail Campgrounds: To reach the Elk State Forest Thunder Mountain Equestrian Trail campgrounds continue on Route 555, past Benezette, for another 8 miles into the town of Dents Run (you will see a small town sign; slow down to look for the turn) and make a left onto Dents Run Road. (It is a total of 17.3 miles on Route 555, from the junction of Route 255, to the

2

left turn onto Dents Run Road.) Travel on Dents Run Road, continue straight, pass a bridge on the left, still continue straight, go past the first entrance to Bell Draft Road on the right, continue straight, go past Porcupine Bridge, and again continue straight. While you are hoping for no oncoming traffic (the road was narrow during our visit), be careful to stay on Dents Run Road! After a total of 5.5 miles on Dents Run Road (an easy way to remember is "5.5 miles from Route 555"), look for a right onto the second Bell Draft Road. Travel about 1.8 miles on Bell Draft Road. Shortly after the pipeline right-of-way and the cabin (opposite this cabin is a spring with running water), look for a right onto a dirt road which travels a short distance into the Dark Hollow equestrian camping area. There is a sign "TMET Camping." *Note: plan your approach to these campgrounds at a time when it is unlikely that you will encounter road travel, especially trailers, on Bell Draft or Dents Run. The roads are two-way but of 1½ lane width. We kept hoping no oncoming traffic would appear and fortunately it did not. However, during our most recent visit, work was in progress to widen the roads and this may not be an issue in the future.* To reach the second campground, the Gas Well site, continue for about another half mile and make a left onto a dirt road that travels uphill. The Gas Well site has a steep entrance for a short distance; this approach is longer and steeper than the Dark Hollow site approach. If your truck has trouble hauling uphill, you may want to request the Dark Hollow site. However, the Gas Well site's entrance is doable and we did see many trucks of various sizes having no problem. Once you enter either of the camping areas, there is lots of room to turn around and park as both are open areas surrounded by the forest. However, the Gas Well site would likely offer more shade in the hot weather. The Dark Hollow site is larger and can accommodate bigger groups and easily park 20+ big rigs with plenty of turn around and pull through room. The Gas Well site is also a nice size and, if you don't mind the climb, you could fit a group of 15+ large rigs. Both locations have trees to tie line to and easy access to the trails. In addition, the State Forest roads are of dirt and gravel surface and we found them quiet and pleasurable to ride when we connected between trails. In fact, we encountered more riders on the roads than on the trails during our visit. (Quite a few were lost so do bring that map!)

Thunder Mountain Equestrian Trail Day Parking: To reach the TMET day parking which is at a different location from the camping area: (*Note: during our visit we felt the bridge on the approach road, plus the parking at the trailhead, were not wide or long enough for large living quarter type rigs. Only 2-horse bumper pull or small rigs should attempt to park at this location.*) Follow the above directions but do not turn off of Route 555 onto Dents Run Road, instead continue .8 miles past Dents Run Road (about a total of 18 miles on Route 555). Make a left onto Hicks Run Road. Follow signs to East Hicks Run Road (bearing right). You will cross a bridge that (the turn) could be too tight for larger living quarter type rigs. Like Dents Run Road and Bell Draft Road, this road has some narrow sections. Travel about 3.7 miles. You will see a cleared area on the right with a sign "Day Use Only"; park there. The actual trailhead is just a short distance down the road on the left side through the pine trees. There is a brown equestrian sign plus blue horseshoes on the trees. If you choose to ride the TMET from this end, or really any end, be careful to watch the directions of the blue horseshoes and also to read the TMET State Forest trail description on the reverse side of the map. Even though the trails are well marked, both are helpful to keep you on course when you come to the many crossroads.

Possible additional day parking: We inquired as to where equestrians could park in addition to the Hicks Run location so that they could access trails from a different location. We were told that equestrians sometimes park off of Porcupine Road. (Check this locale without hauling to see if it is suitable for your trailer, as it is not large and requires backing to turn around.) To reach this spot, take the main entrance to the Winslow Hill viewing area opposite the Benezette Store (and behind the Benezette Post Office) on Route 555. Follow Winslow Hill Road. Watch for a left onto Porcupine Road. Take Porcupine Road and come to a State Forest and State Gamelands gated intersection. There is a small pull-off area on the left which allows access into the State Forest, which leads to the equestrian trail and also to a State Gamelands dirt road on the left that was indicated as open to riding. We checked out the lot which could accommodate at most a 2-horse, possibly 3-horse, trailer if the driver is comfortable backing to turn around. It is small but with the adjoining forest roads there is enough room to turn a small rig around. We visited this location but did not ride from this parking lot. (We rode from The Big Elk Lick campground, the TMET campground, and the Hicks Run day area.) *Note: while calling for information regarding the area, we were told of day parking at the far end of Front Street (Front Street is opposite the Benezette Store at the Winslow Hill access). We do not recommend this location. Unless the area is expanded, we found the lot and turning area much too small for rigs, including 2-horse trailers, plus the access road is narrow.* We found the best way to familiarize oneself with this large area (after we got lost while riding) and to assess hauling destinations was to camp at one of the equestrian campgrounds and take a drive (without the trailer) to judge the lay of the land and the day parking areas. Do this before you head out on the trail!

THE TRAILS:
This area is one of our most loved; the surrounding mountains and State Forest land offer countless trails to explore, many that are formal designated trails and many that have been established over the years by locals, visitors, logging equipment, and mining operations. Besides the wonderful beauty of the area, the thrill of seeing elk while on horseback, especially a big bull, is breathtaking.

If you stay at one of the DCNR Bureau of Forestry State Forest campgrounds, which are at the heart of the TMET trail system, you have direct access to the equestrian trails and can ride out from camp. We stayed at the Dark Hollow site and accessed the trails a few different ways. You can ride out of the entrance to camp, make a left and ride the short distance down Bell Draft Road (this was a quiet dirt/gravel forest road during our visit), and pick up the pipeline right-of-way, making either a left or a right, to intersect with the trails. The pipelines have nice mowed areas and can be very easy and scenic to ride, but they can also be very steep. To avoid the road, you can also head out along the fenced area adjoining the camping area and access the gas line. On one of our many trips, we rode down Bell Draft Road for about a mile where the TMET intersected with Bell Draft Road. There were brown equestrian markers on both sides of the road. We made a right, and began a ride of the central loop in the direction of markers 12 to 11 (some climbs and rocks), to 11 and 10 (a bit rough due to wet areas but passable), and then picked up 7 to 6 (nice, high, and dry). We completed the loop to 5, 4, 13, and somewhere around 12 we took a wrong turn and used Bell Draft Road to return to camp. It is tricky when you are riding from the map location number 11 to 10; you must make a right on the road by 10 and look for the continuation of the trail. At this point you can also continue straight to the connector trail to the lower loop of the TMET. **Our favorite part** is the TMET lower loop, especially between numbers 8 and 9 on the TMET map, as it offers overlooks and views of the surrounding mountains and valleys.

Horseback riding is permitted on the Thunder Mountain Equestrian Trail system, the pipelines (which are wonderfully well-maintained, green stretches of land), the State Forest roads, and many other areas of the State Forest. You will probably see many of the folks staying at the Gas Well site ride through the Dark Hollow site to connect to the trails. You can also easily access the trails from the Gas Well site by riding the dirt road out of camp (in the direction away from or opposite the entrance) to link up with the pipeline right-of-ways. Designated hiking trails in Pennsylvania's State Forests are off limits to horses. During our visit, the ranger mentioned that some rerouting would be done due to the Elk Trail, a hiking (only) trail, traveling through the center of the Gas Well equestrian camp, resulting in equestrians unknowingly riding that trail. This section will be rerouted to prevent misinterpretation and riders will be asked to stay off of it. *Note: sometimes this can be confusing because the TMET, marked by blue blazes, often intersects or joins the Elk Trail, marked by orange blazes. Just try to follow and keep to the equestrian designated area and the blue blazes or blue horseshoes.* Also, State Gamelands border the State Forest. Utilize the Elk State Forest Public Use Map to determine land ownership, watch for signs indicating where equestrian use is and is not permitted, and check the Pennsylvania State Gamelands website for permitted uses and more information.

If you stay at The Big Elk Lick campground, you can ride many of the trails that lead directly out of camp or you can ride about an hour and a half to pick up the Thunder Mountain Equestrian Trail lower (southwest) loop, one of the most scenic sections of the TMET. Before departing for the trails, it is important to check with the folks who run The Big Elk Lick campground to see if any areas are off limits and to confirm which are open to riders. Some private lands permit riders and others do not. Also, check the latest Bureau of Forestry and State Gamelands information as to any limitations or changes in policy regarding the surrounding areas. To reach the campground's adjoining trails, ride up the back of the campground to the top, and follow the hoof prints out from the back of camp a short distance onto a dirt road. Many trails lead from there. We made a right on the dirt road, came to a high summit with a great overlook, and rode to the right which eventually led to a wooded area. This is an old shale/mining area and the trails head in many directions and offer hours of leisurely riding with the possibility of seeing elk. Also, from The Big Elk Lick locale, you can ride on the opposite side of Route 555. To access this, follow the path from the front of camp, travel behind the office and across the open lawn, pick up a trail through the woods and head toward the road, cross the road, and meet up with the path which is to the right of a tree. Yes, there are many trees so it is worthwhile to take a moment and check out the entrance beforehand as you will want to minimize your time spent on horseback near Route 555. The road is heavily traveled and vehicles travel very fast. Exercise extreme <u>caution</u>. Once on the other side, you'll come to an old railroad grade which travels down to the town of Medix Run and back. This is a nice, easy, and scenic ride. Watch for elk and have your camera ready. Look in the brush in the lowland to the right and in the woods on the left. We saw many elk along this route, probably attracted by the salt licks left out by residents to draw them. You can cross to the other side of the river. There are various locations to traverse the river and pick up the trail on the opposite side. Wanting to cross, we followed hoof prints to the river and hoof prints from the river on the opposite side. We continued riding south and came to a really neat stone tunnel with shallow water running through it. We crossed through the tunnel. (Some horses will not be comfortable with this; surprisingly, ours did not hesitate, but just make sure a train or rail patrol vehicle is not going overhead or within hearing distance. We did not see any trains during our ride on this section of trails, but we did see an SUV, which was converted to rail, patrol the tracks!) After the tunnel, there are a few trails leading in different directions. We picked up a trail to the left. This paralleled the railroad tracks and climbed to a high point overlooking Benezette. We enjoyed the gorgeous view, then turned around and backtracked back to camp. We were later told that we could have continued along that mountain dirt road/trail, crossed back over the river and back down to Benezette, traveled down Front Street, across Trout Run and back to camp.

To ride to the Thunder Mountain Equestrian Trail from the Big Elk Lick campground, you can take the long loop out of the back of camp to Gray Hill Road and proceed at the gate as described below (a long ride). Some equestrians ride the short distance on the shoulder of busy Route 555, make a left on Gray Hill Road, and make a right at the yellow and black gated entrance to the right. (We do not recommend riding Route 555. During the time of our visit, the folks at The Big Elk Lick campground indicated they were working toward obtaining permission to access the yellow gate via a short distance of State Gamelands dirt road which would allow riders to avoid Route 555. Hopefully, that will occur. Check with the campground before departing for developments and how to proceed via these or any of the surrounding trails and access points.) Take the road behind the gate to the top, look for a trail to the right (or you can take the road all the way around if you pass it), ride down the dirt (rocky but passable), mountainside trail to the cluster of cabins and past the white blazes and State Forestry silver markers. Continue riding (upstream direction) down the old dirt road alongside the Trout Run River. Watch for equestrian hoof prints to the right. Look for a shallow, safe crossing and cross the river and pick up the trail on the opposite side. (It greatly helps to have someone from the campground, who is familiar with the trails, to show you the route first time out.) Ride the trail up the mountain to a dirt road and make a left on the dirt road. (You should see orange blazes indicating the Elk Trail also passes through this section. Avoid this hiking [only] trail.) Follow the road all the way past an open field to the Thunder Mountain Equestrian Trail system evidenced by brown markers and blue blazes. (From Gray Hill Road, it's about an hour and a half ride to link with the lower loop of the Thunder Mountain Equestrian Trail system.) After the field and to the left leads to what we feel is one of the most scenic trail sections as it offers beautiful views of the surrounding landscape, a must do on our list. This section is part of the TMET, travels along a ridge, and is one fabulous view after another. *Note: for those who don't like "on the edge" trail riding, there is more than one path to take through this section.* It appeared that the outer most path, which sometimes is eroded, was replaced by an alternate path. The alternate path is also marked by blue horseshoes and is less close to the edge and much more comfortable for folks like myself who do not want to be at the absolute edge of the mountainside. So look to the inside, you will see an inner trail for the Elk Trail (orange blazes) and two parallel trails for the TMET (blue blazes). My first time out, I did not see the inner, blue trail and was pretty nervous near the edge on horseback but didn't want to miss seeing the beauty the trail offered. I felt much better on the return trip when I saw and was able to ride the inner trail which offered just as much of a view. Also, be careful near the fence that surrounds certain protected growth areas as it is electric. If you are forced to deviate from the designated trail, let the office know there is a problem so that they can consider re-engineering the trail. The office was very considerate of concerns during our visit and also appreciative when we notified them of problems on the trail, including two downed trees that fell through the electric fencing allowing wildlife access to the sensitive seedlings in the protected area. The lower or smaller loop continues into a scenic forested area offering wonderful riding. This lower or smaller circle of the equestrian trail was easy to ride in that the surface was good, with minimal rocks, and of moderate level of difficulty. Still, horses need to be fit due to the many uphill and downhill climbs; it is a workout for them. We also rode the connector trail to the big loop which travels through forested areas. *Note: to pick up the bigger loop from the connector where 7 and 10 meet, if traveling from marker 11 to 10 on Dents Run Road, one entrance to the lower loop is to the left as you ride out of the connector onto Dents Run Road and the continuation of the bigger loop is down Dents Run Road (up) to the right.* We found the connector trail and a portion of the bigger loop (between 12 and 7) to have some steeper, rocky or muddy areas, and more challenging sections than the lower loop (7, 8, 9). There are also many areas to water the horses along the trails. The lower section or smaller loop of the TMET has numerous opportunities for the horses to drink. This section offered some very nice riding which we plan to return to and explore.

Along with wonderful trails and awesome views, there is the possibility of seeing herds of elk throughout the trail systems. Often massive bull elk accompany these herds. Those not as accustomed to people seem to hide in the background, are usually the last ones to be seen, and remain the most elusive of the herd. In the fall, these bulls have a rack of antlers; the older ones have more points. When they finally make their appearance, it is breathtaking and the epitome of nature's beauty. We saw many herds standing or laying in high places looking down on us as we rode by. They are not as shy as deer and tend to linger as we watched them. The bulls seemed to know everyone was looking for or at them as they usually disappeared before the rest of the herd.

Mining is common to the area; avoid any blast areas labeled as such. We did not see any mining near the TMET, just in outlying access areas. But still, use good judgment and steer clear. The TMET is very well marked with blue markers, horseshoe signs, and small brown equestrian signs but the intersections can be confusing. Other trails in the surrounding area are difficult to determine which are okay to ride and which are not. White markers represent both State Gamelands and the Bureau of Forestry (DCNR) boundaries. Look for an additional marker accompanying the white blaze to indicate the landowner. When you are looking at the blaze or sign, that is the land that the marker applies to. Again, check with officials and use good judgment. Also, look to see where the main, well-worn paths are. Basically we asked "regulars" to show us and we also followed the hoof prints. This is an excellent equestrian destination, one to take extra care to stay on the right trails and one to keep good relations with the local landowners and, especially, the DCNR Bureau of Forestry who created this fantastic trail for equestrians and for future generations to enjoy.

<u>Where to find the elk:</u> Elk can be viewed at many locations and by just driving around. We saw numerous sightings by auto in the early morning and early evening. We viewed our first herd, escorted by a large male, on Gray Hill Road and Mt. Zion Road in the vicinity behind The Big Elk Lick campground. Other elk often come right into town along Front Street in Benezette and dine on apples in the locals' yards. Sometimes you just listen for the bugles and look in that direction. (Male or "bull" elk call out or "bugle" to their potential mates during the fall mating season.) During the fall and peak viewing times, most visitors travel by vehicle to the elk viewing areas at Winslow Hill which are reached by taking Front Street (by the Benezette General Store and Benezette Post Office) to Winslow Hill Road and following the signs. You'll know by the backed up traffic if you have arrived near an elk sighting. *It's just like out west; if you have ever visited Yellowstone National Park, you'll know what I mean.* Of course we wanted to see the elk while on horseback and in a more remote location. We did see quite a few while riding along the rail-trail to Medix Run. We also saw elk on many occasions while riding the TMET and surrounding areas. The elk head for the feed lots that surround the TMET camping area in the early morning or evening. I saw these elk by walking the grassy stretch out the back of the TMET Dark Hollow camp (located opposite the entrance to camp) which leads to a large, open feed lot. I viewed these elk at about 6:00 pm in mid October. *Note: if driving, do not stop in the middle of the road or trespass. Besides the road danger, you can get fined. And whether in the car, on horse, or on foot, leave some space and be careful. Although the elk appear peaceful, they are wild animals that can weigh up to 1,000 pounds, and can do serious damage.*

EQUESTRIAN CAMPING:
We stayed at two different campgrounds plus private rides during our many visits to Benezette. We stayed at the DCNR Bureau of Forestry Thunder Mountain Equestrian Trail Campground (no fee) in the State Forest, and The Big Elk Lick campground (commercial, nominal fee).

<u>Thunder Mountain Equestrian Trail campgrounds:</u> There is quite a long dirt access road (7.5 miles) to reach the campgrounds but well worth it. You are in elk country; check out all those big hoof prints around camp! Once there, you will find two large, high and dry, open and roomy campgrounds: the Dark Hollow site and the Gas Well site. Both are managed by the Bureau of Forestry. Each campground has bordering trees to tie line between, room for groups of campers, and a large central area with plenty of room to turn around without backing. The Dark Hollow site is the first on the right as you travel on Bell Draft Road (per the above directions) and is the larger of the two. The Gas Well site is a short distance from the Dark Hollow site and is on the left side of the road.

One of the advantages to staying at the DCNR Bureau of Forestry camping areas is that the equestrian camps have ideal locations central to the TMET system. To access the trails, just ride from camp. Both are primitive and you need to bring either a camper with bathroom facilities or arrange for a portajohn. There is no water at camp; you need to bring your own water. But, there are many stream crossings on trails and there is a spring opposite the small cabin on Bell Draft Road just before the entrance to the campgrounds. We found the campgrounds very clean and in an ideal and relaxing setting. They are also well patrolled and monitored by rangers, which likely explains why they are in such excellent condition. And at night, the area is quiet (except for that lonely bugling elk), serene, and covered with a blanket of stars. Our good friend, Jan Huffman, had the foresight to bring his digital telescope so we could view the stars. Absolutely awesome!

The Big Elk Lick campground: The Big Elk Lick is more centrally located near the town of Benezette on Route 555. For folks who like to be near a main road and have electric hookups, a shower, and water, this may be the place for you. Each camping area offers different access to the trails, allowing for a variety of riding. If you grow tired of one camping location; try the other. Both have unique trails. The Big Elk Lick is run by Sandy and Bert and is an old time favorite for many equestrian travelers. This is a good size camping area and there are a variety of settings for camping, including field and wooded sites. There are level areas close to the entrance for larger rigs (electric hookups); a big, open field (where the elk like to cross) for group camping (primitive); along with many other wooded sites in the rear of camp (mostly primitive) which individuals or small groups may use. It is wise, if you are not familiar with the campground layout, to first check out (by foot or without hauling) access to the rear primitive sites to see if you feel comfortable maneuvering. Lots of big rigs camp up top, but backing is necessary to exit. The open areas near the camp entrance are more suitable for folks who aren't confident backing their trailers or for those with very large rigs. We like camping up front which, if you are lucky, offers a view of elk walking down the middle of the field in the early evening or morning. *We had one large bull bugle right outside our camper at 6:00 in the morning for two mornings in a row. That was a different kind of alarm sound!* Equestrians must tie line, use portable corrals, or electric fence. One of the many advantages to this campground is that it is at a convenient location just off of Route 555, making it easy to get to. It also has convenient access to a main road to go elk sighting, to get fuel and groceries, and to visit nearby restaurants. There is one hitch to this location: if you are looking to ride the TMET, the current approach by many equestrians is to ride along active Route 555 for a very short distance. Route 555 is a very busy road (with truck traffic due to mining operations), plus it takes over an hour to reach the lower loop. One option is to day trailer to the day parking area at Hicks Run (tight for turning very large living quarter rigs). Or, instead, try the many wonderful trails directly joining The Big Elk Lick. This campground adjoins some very nice trails and remains a favorite of regulars.

During each visit we have seen elk while either riding the nearby trails or while camping at this locale, plus we have always enjoyed our stays.

There are also many other fun trail rides, sponsored by individuals and outfitters local to the area, usually at their properties. Watch The Paper Horse (out of Mifflin, PA) and other equestrian publications for information regarding these rides.

HISTORICAL INFORMATION:

At one time, elk were indigenous to all of Pennsylvania and abundant in this area, thus the name Elk County. Unfortunately, it was reported that by the late 1860s, the last native Pennsylvania eastern elk was killed. In the early 1900s, the Pennsylvania Game Commission brought in Rocky Mountain elk from a variety of areas, including South Dakota and Yellowstone, to Pennsylvania. At first the herds thrived but legal hunting in the 1920s and 1930s significantly decreased the number of elk. Hunting became prohibited in the 1930s until recent years. Hunting has again been permitted as the herd sizes have increased dramatically. As this is the only region in Pennsylvania or nearby that has Rocky Mountain elk in the wild, tourists flock from all over to Benezette and the surrounding communities to enjoy sightings of the elk.

During the early years of settlement in this area, white pine was abundant and one of the first types of trees to be logged. Once cut, these trees were often used as ship masts. Most of the area's other trees were harvested and the old forest ceased to exist. By the early 1900s, purchases of land to set aside as State Forest began to occur with the goal of restoring the forests. Over time, the area also became popular for gas well drilling, timber, and coal strip mining. Many of the local trails were once old wagon trails, logging trails, and gas well access points, and have been preserved over the years.

COURTESIES:

I am so impressed with this region of Pennsylvania that I want to immediately thank all those (especially the Bureau of Forestry-DCNR) who have established equestrian trail systems for enjoying this gorgeous area on horseback. Thank you to Rangers Jeanne Wambaugh and Jim Degler for sharing information about the area and answering my many questions. Also, thanks to the Pennsylvania Game Commission, the Rocky Mountain Elk Foundation, and other organizations, corporations, and individuals for their many contributions, especially for their role in reintroducing elk to the area and for preserving the future of the elk in the area. Thank you to Ray and Sandy Wood and Clayton Fox for sharing information regarding these trails. And, I know many horse folk will join me in expressing a very special thanks to Sandy and Bert at The Big Elk Lick for welcoming equestrians. And also our gratitude goes to a local equestrian, Betty Ragan (we did not meet Betty but we were told she is well known for helping maintain the TMET trails), along with other volunteers, individuals and groups who contribute to these wonderful trails. Thank you to Grant Hagan, a local farrier, for shoeing our horse at last minute notice and saving us from missing two great days of riding. Thank you to Joan and Karen for showing us access routes to these trails and also for sharing the pleasure of your company. And last but not least, thank you to our first guide, "Woody" (Don Wood), for introducing us to this area.

THINGS WE LEARNED THIS RIDE:

- There are rattlesnakes in this area, even well after the first frost, and both sightings and encounters are not that infrequent. We were riding along the old railroad grade near map location 6. There was a large rock on the trail that I was trying to navigate and my focus was on that. As I began to pass the rock, luckily, I was still looking at the ground and my horse's footing. There lay a large rattlesnake curled and ready to strike. He blended into the fall leaves perfectly and was difficult to see, almost impossible until it was too late. As soon as I saw him, I pivoted my horse so quickly my horse never even saw or yet heard him. That was sooo close! My horse would have definitely gotten struck as we were about to pass right over him or on him. John estimated he was about 5 foot in length with a 4 inch girth. He had many rattles! And this bugger wouldn't move. Five horses passed him (later and at a safe distance) and he would still not budge other than raising his head and rattling his tail. *Also, there are lots of ticks in the area; take precaution. I had three on me all in one ride and in spite of using spray.*

- I was reminded how unpredictable wildlife can be. I had taken an October early evening walk with my dog out the back of the TMET campground along the fence row to the feed lot. I had brought my new digital camera and came upon a herd of 26 elk accompanied by one impressive, huge bull elk. I cautiously kept my distance, my dog didn't make a sound, and we witnessed a wonderful site of this large herd grazing. Upon seeing us, there was the loud sound of a large stampede as they headed for and disappeared into the thick forested area. Sometime during this, I also heard a bull bugle. I knew it wasn't the one I just saw as he already had quite a harem and had moved them away. I didn't give it further thought. As quiet settled on the large, open area I sat to enjoy the beauty of the colorful fall scenery for a moment, took some photos, then rose and turned to head back to camp as it would soon get dark. Much to my surprise, there stood a large bull, six points each side, just staring at me from the edge of the woods. He was in the direction that I needed to go. I couldn't make out his expression which was either one of curiosity or displeasure for my being on what he viewed as his turf. He continued to walk cautiously toward me and studied me with each step. And foolishly (and knowingly foolish), I did take some photos (see the photo on the back cover). It was hard not to be mesmerized by his presence. Soon I became quite concerned as he kept walking toward me and that this could possibly result in an unfriendly encounter. There was no cover to seek as I was in an open field. All I could think of was past readings of natural horsemanship books about herd animals; I decided to turn my shoulder to him and not stare at him directly as if he were prey or as if to challenge. Instead I bent over a bit and picked the grass and gave a chewing effect (no I didn't eat it) as if I too was a grazing animal, passive, and no threat. I kid you not; at that point, the elk stopped walking toward me. He instead walked around me, still looking, but passing me. I actually have digital shots of all this. He slowly moved off in the opposite direction of where the large herd had run to, all the time proceeding carefully while keeping one eye on me until he finally disappeared into the woods. After saying a prayer of thanks, I ran back to camp to download my pictures on my laptop to show my husband what he missed. What an exciting experience! Of course, when I told my friends about this they commented that he was likely the lonely bull who I heard bugling earlier, and there I was pretending to be a herd animal! Hmmm, I didn't even think of that at the time!

NEARBY EQUESTRIAN CAMPING AND OTHER:
- The Big Elk Lick (equestrian campground with electric hookups, shower and toilet facility, gift shop), Benezette (814) 787-4656
- Hicks Run Outfitters (guided tours, possible equestrian camping, maps, trail info), Driftwood (814) 787-4287, email: hicksrunoutfitters@yahoo.com

NEARBY AND SURROUNDING AREA VET SERVICES:
- Dr. Wise, Troutville (814) 427-2424

NEARBY AND SURROUNDING AREA FARRIERS:
- G. Hagan, St. Mary's (814) 834-6376
- D. Bloom, Grampian (814) 236-0514

2. Quehanna Region
Moshannon State Forest
BOF-DCNR
(Bureau of Forestry/Department of Conservation & Natural Resources)

Lasting Impression: This Quehanna Region of Moshannon State Forest is a big, beautiful, undeveloped area, one which hopefully remains as it was during our visit, unstructured and wide open for all to enjoy. This area is an explorer's or trail blazer's paradise. It is special in that it is an expansive area where equestrians and other users are still free to explore throughout the State Forest and discover new trails. Other than the Quehanna Hiking Trail, there is no defined or established trail system; there are only State Forest roads, old logging or fire roads, and deer and elk paths. After visiting this area and seeing the miles of forest along with the abundance of wildlife (this is bear and elk country), it seems only appropriate that it remain just this way, wild, untamed, primitive, and thus unspoiled. Explore and enjoy this one in its natural setting!

Location: Moshannon State Forest is comprised of two separate blocks of land. One, adjoining and including portions of the Quehanna Wild Area, is mostly north of Interstate 80 in Elk, Cameron, and Clearfield Counties. The other is located south of Interstate 80 in Centre County and surrounds the Black Moshannon State Park. For simplicity, I will refer to one as the Quehanna tract and the other as the Black Moshannon tract. This chapter pertains to the Quehanna tract or region.

Length: *Day Ride, Weekend, or Week-long Destination*- Moshannon State Forest consists of approximately 185,000 acres. There are no designated equestrian trails but there are days of riding as horses are permitted on all State Forest trails and roads, except for those specifically closed to horses such as Natural Areas and hiking (only) trails. The designated hiking (only) trail in this section of Moshannon State Forest is the Quehanna Trail. Equestrians may ride Moshannon State Forest's cross-country ski trails, snowmobile trails, and power and pipeline right-of-ways. *In regard to extending one's ride and traveling the trails in the nearby Elk State Forest section of the Quehanna region, please note they are currently under review for suitability for equestrian travel. Check with the Elk State Forest district office as to the latest information at the time of your visit.*

Level of Difficulty: Easy to moderate

Terrain: The trails that we rode were single and double dirt tracts (not rocky), grass paths, old mountain roads, and dirt or gravel State Forest roads.

Horse Camping: Yes

Non-horse Camping: Yes

Carriage Potential: Due to the many miles of level rural roads, and old logging and railroad paths which consist of gravel or dirt surface, this should be excellent for carriage driving. Carriage enthusiasts would need to contact the office for more information.

Maps and Info: Maps and information can be obtained from the District Forester, Forest District Headquarters, Moshannon State Forest, 3372 State Park Road, Penfield, PA 15849, (814) 765-0821, email: fd09@state.pa.us or contact the Department of Conservation & Natural Resources (DCNR) website: www.dcnr.state.pa.us. For nearby State Park information and maps, contact Parker Dam State Park, RR1, Box 165, Penfield, PA 15849-9799, (814) 765-0630 or S.B. Elliott State Park c/o Parker Dam State Park. The DCNR flyers/maps and the snowmobile maps for both of these parks are useful if you are planning to camp or ride the State Forest land surrounding either of these parks.

Activities: Hiking, Biking, Horseback Riding Trails, Picnicking, Fishing, Camping, X-C Skiing, Snowmobiling, and Hunting

Fees for Trail Use: None

Permits for Day Trail Use: None

Permits/Fees Required for Overnight Camping: Permits (no fee) are required for overnight, motorized camping. There are no designated camping areas; however, there are some suitable areas that are level and open which are conducive to horse camping (see below). Also, you can camp where you choose if it is within the guidelines set by the Forest District. Camping is not permitted in the Quehanna Wild Area.

Comfort Station: There are no comfort facilities on the State Forest land, but there are facilities at nearby Parker Dam State Park and S.B. Elliott State Park.

DIRECTIONS:

The following represents what we think will be suitable for day parking or camping. You can use other areas that you consider appropriate. At the time of our visit, there weren't "designated motorized sites" at Moshannon State Forest. We have presented the following to provide a selection of destinations for those who are unfamiliar with the area and may not have the opportunity to scout it out in advance. Please be careful when exploring these roads in the Moshannon State Forest with large rigs. Due to variations in grade, width, turning radius, overhead clearance, etc., this is one area where you need to know where to go. Usually official "State Forest" roads are good, but sometimes they enter another jurisdiction and can change radically. "Access" or "unimproved roads" are unpredictable and often not suitable for hauling, but can make nice riding trails. We spent extensive time at this location to determine routes which large rigs could travel on, and where they could park or camp. Do not attempt traveling these roads without the Moshannon State Forest Public Use Map. However, once you get the lay of the land, it's an area that's wide open to possibilities. Sites are primitive with no facilities; you need to bring water and can refill at the spring described below.

From I-80, take Exit #111 Penfield (Route 153). Take Route 153 north for 8 miles to the light at Junction 255. Make a right and head north on Route 255. Take Route 255 north for 6.4 miles into the town of Force and look for Route 555. Bear right onto Route 555. Take Route 555 (passing the towns of Weedville and Caledonia) for about 5 to 6 miles. Watch for a sign indicating the town of Medix Run. Then slow down and look for a right turn onto Quehanna Highway between a small corner store and a restaurant (Medix Run Hotel). Make a right onto the Quehanna Highway (paved).

FYI: to reach the nearby town of Benezette and the Rocky Mountain elk viewing areas, return to Route 555 and continue north into the town of Benezette, then follow the signs to Winslow Hill. More detail is provided in the Elk State Forest chapter.

Easy on/easy off day parking: Take Quehanna Highway from the town of Medix Run. After a few miles you will begin to see clearings or pull-off areas on the right where you can day park. Some of these are at the entrance to State Forest roads which have signs. You can park at these and ride the dirt State Forest roads into the heart of Quehanna State Forest. From there you can connect to a multitude of dirt forest roads, connectors, access roads, and trails. There is no designated trail system or loop.

One roomy pull-off area where equestrians do park is located alongside Quehanna Highway at Sullivan Trail and just before Jack Dent Road (about 4 to 5 miles from Medix Run on Quehanna Highway). It is easy to see as you pass by. There are dirt roads which lead into the State Forest such as Sullivan Road and Jack Dent Road. The access roads also provide access on horseback. (Again, do not haul via access roads, these are not maintained and may be rough or impassable with a rig.) The large lots on the right are easy on, easy off so some riders like these. We instead preferred to haul into the State Forest to get off of the highway. We found the following to be suitable as described. These would serve as both day parking and camping locales. *Note: before proceeding to any of the following, check with the State Forest office and ask if any bridges are being replaced. Periodically, bridges are replaced and a main road will be closed. (If they are unfamiliar with your request, ask for Wade Dixon who works out of the Quehanna Highway office and is most familiar with this area; he will be able to tell you if a road is closed or if there are obstacles.)*

Jack Dent Road day parking or campsite locale: From Route 555 in Medix Run, take Quehanna Highway for 5.3 miles. Make a right onto Jack Dent Road. There are two roads at this turn so follow the sign to Jack Dent Road. Immediately you can see a clearing on the left to pull off. This is a short distance from Quehanna Highway. A few rigs can park here. Upon departure, turn around to leave the same way you came in. *If you decide to continue straight, Jack Dent Road is a good State Forest road. You can drive or ride Jack Dent Road into the core of the State Forest. However, for hauling purposes, Jack Dent Road does have some narrow bridges (but passable with a large rig) and a tight left turn at the end. If you decide to proceed hauling on Jack Dent Road, continue until you reach Medix Grade Road which is just after a bridge, and there is a sign. You can turn right (plenty of room) and take that road back to Medix Run.*

Most of the main State Forest roads in this section are good but best explored without the rig. State Forest roads usually have a graded surface with gravel covering. The problem is it's hard to tell when you have ventured off a main road or off the State Forest road. (This is evident with Caledonia Road which is a partially maintained, gravel State Forest road and suddenly becomes a very rough dirt road when it enters the county's jurisdiction.)

Merrill Road sites day parking or campsite locale: This is one of our preferred sites for day parking which would also serve as a camping locale (room for long rigs) with easy access to main roads and the center of the Quehanna area. This is along a dirt forest road (in regard to camping sites, we usually prefer to be a little farther off of any road for privacy, safety, and security) but this and all of the forest roads within this section appeared to be very quiet roads. To reach this, take Quehanna Highway from Medix Run for 5.4 miles to Ardell Road. This is the road just past Jack Dent Road. Make a right onto Ardell Road (dirt); there is a sign. Take Ardell Road; you will pass a State Gamelands sign. (This section of main road travels through a short stretch of State Gamelands which adjoins the State Forest land. Do not ride on State Gamelands unless indicated otherwise.) Ardell Road becomes Merrill Road. After clocking 4.6 miles on Ardell/Merrill Road there will be a large, open area on both sides of the road. This section can fit numerous rigs (15-20+). Good tie or high line trees are limited, but portable corrals and electric fence will work. Stay clear of any cabins and at least 200 feet from any stream. Farther down on Ardell/Merrill Road, at a total of 5.3 miles, there is a nice open area on the left (one of John's picks). There are plenty of trees to tie line to and room for about 3-4 rigs. Up to this point Ardell/Merrill Road is an easy, level, wide dirt road with no bridges. At about 7 miles, Ardell/Merrill Road will make a sharp right (by a white cabin with the name Trappers Shanty). The road then gets hilly and narrower but is passable. At 7.7 miles ("Gifford Run"), there is a good place on the right to fill the water containers. You will see a white pipe with water flowing from it. You will cross a bridge that is wide enough for rigs. We drove a total of 8.4 miles on Ardell/Merrill Road to an intersection at Caledonia Pike (this section of Caledonia Pike is of good grade). If you passed your site earlier, you can use the intersection to back and turn around.

Shaggers Inn Road day parking or campsite locale: This is one of our preferred locations for either day parking, to access some of the trails in the State Forest which surrounds Parker Dam State Park, or for camping. This is particularly nice for camping as it is on a back State Forest road and is at a scenic locale. The following approach (until the 2 mile point on Shaggers Inn Road) is an easy grade of gravel State Forest road, level, wide, has no sharp turns or steep climbs, has good clearance, and is suitable for large rigs. However, you need to be proficient in backing your rig. This approach is not out of Medix Run like the above destinations. Rather, take I-80 to Exit #111 Route 153 north. Travel about 1 mile (pass the State Forest district office; continue on Route 153). Make a right at the entrance to S.B. Elliott State Park, but immediately bear left onto Four Mile Road; there is a sign. Take Four Mile Road for 4 miles following signs to Caledonia Pike. You will come to McGeorge Road. Bear left on McGeorge Road (do not go right). You will pass a "Wallace Sphagnum Bog" sign. Take McGeorge Road for 4.7 miles to a stop sign. Make a right (do not go to left; see Note below) on Caledonia Pike. Take Caledonia Pike .3 miles and make a left onto a dirt/stone road. This is Shaggers Inn Road. We didn't see a sign for Shaggers Inn Road, but if you see a lake on the left, you just missed it and will need to back the short distance. (On Shaggers Inn Road, you will pass a gate to the right and parking area on the lake side; but you cannot camp there. During our discussions with a ranger, he indicated equestrians are requested to stay clear of the lakeside on horseback; please respect this and do not bring the horses to drink at the lake. The view of the lake can be enjoyed on horseback from a respectable distance at various neighboring vantage points.) Take Shaggers Inn Road for .4 miles. There will be an area on the left which offers sufficient room for day parking or camping and has space for a few rigs, including large rigs. It is a grassy area on the side of this back road, mostly level, may be a little soft at the entrance during wet weather, is in a nice setting with some backing needed, and has lots of tie line area. There is another location a short distance down the road at a total of .7 miles and is on the left side also. It can accommodate 2-3 large rigs; some backing is needed. There is also a clearing at 2 miles but it is uneven and rough (has potential if portions are graded and leveled). Do not go past this point at 2 miles on Shaggers Inn Road as the road begins to narrow to a single lane and travels down hill. Instead, use the cleared areas to back and return the way you came in. *Note: had you made a left instead of a right on Caledonia Pike you would have seen wide open, grassy shoulders where you could camp or park, and where groups of rigs could fit. It is not yet suitable to tie lines due to young trees but is suitable for electric fencing or portable corrals. But you do not want to continue down Caledonia Pike as it turns into a rough road once it heads into county jurisdiction and is no longer a State Forest road. You can set up camp along this open section but will need to back, turn around, and head out the way you came in.*

Shale Pit (on Medix Grade Road) day parking or campsite locale: The entrance needs some trimming (bring your clippers) but this could be an excellent and fun group camping locale. There are a couple of secluded acres to camp in at this location. *This is one area where a club could volunteer to do some lightweight work, such as trimming, and have a nice large area to hold numerous campers. I checked with the local forest office and they said volunteers are welcome. However, it's always best to coordinate and check with the office before doing any maintenance or volunteer work even if it is just trimming.* This approach was of level grade and without sharp turns. To reach this location, travel north on Route 555 to Medix Run. From Medix Run, make a right onto Quehanna Highway. Take Quehanna Highway for 1.6 miles. Make a right onto Medix Grade Road (dirt). There is a sign for Medix Grade Road. Take Medix Grade Road for 5.8 miles. (On Medix Grade Road you will pass Jack Dent Bridge on the left, the steep end of Shaggers Inn Road [described above] on the right, and Wilson Switch Road on the left. The turn is .4 miles past the turn for Wilson Switch Road.) Upon clocking a total of 5.8 miles on Medix Grade Road, make a right onto a gravel/stone road. There is no sign, but the turn is just before a gray cabin. There is a single lane, two-way entrance leading into the large loop which is the shale pit. This is a spacious, open area that can fit 15+ rigs including long ones. It is not all level but there is room to move about and plenty of room to back and turn around. Since this is off the road and may require some maintenance, we suggest you scout it out **before** planning to stay at this location.

Note: while traveling the State Forest roads you will cross a few short bridges. We checked with the ranger and he indicated they would hold large campers or horse trailers. He also mentioned that some were being rebuilt and will be able to accommodate even heavier weight. We found there was sufficient room to accommodate a dually and large trailer even on the older bridges that we crossed on this road.

THE TRAILS:
Elk may be viewed in the northern areas of Moshannon State Forest, more likely within the State Forest situated north and east of the Caledonia Pike. We didn't see elk within Moshannon State Forest during our visit, but we did see many signs of elk, including hoof prints.

As this area is undeveloped, we just headed out and tried different trails, mountain roads or paths that spun off of the forest roads. Sometimes there will be names at the end; other times they are unnamed. Usually, if there is a sign with a number, that means there is a cabin at the end of the road. But sometimes you can start out on a double tract and it may go to a cabin or it may head into the woods for an interesting trail ride. There are the main State Forest roads and connectors that are reflected on the map, but there are also many other paths which are not on the map. I wanted to head into the Quehanna Wild Area so we rode the path as follows. *Equestrians are permitted to ride the dirt/gravel State Forest road through the Quehanna Wild Area. The Public Use Map reflects all boundaries.* To reach this area, we rode along Caledonia Pike to Lost Run Road (dirt). We traveled along Lost Run Road, let the horses have a drink, crossed the bridge, and headed up the mountain into the Quehanna Wild Area along the dirt/gravel road. Although a dirt road, this was a nice, scenic ride surrounded by forest. We rode into a section of the Quehanna Wild Area which rises high above the surrounding area. We didn't see a soul the whole ride. We then turned around and were going to try riding the power line, but it began to rain and I wasn't going to ride under high power electric wires in the rain. So we decided to return via some paths that we passed earlier that spun off of Lost Run Road. We went back to a trail that was to our right as we headed back in the direction of Caledonia Pike. The trail we picked up was a grassy, double tract, and looked like an old mountain road that had returned to a grass surface. This was a beautiful trail that gradually climbed up the mountain and passed through forest land with a view of a stream to the right. *The stream plus the onset of rain must have muffled the sound of our horses approaching. As we looked to the left side of the trail, immediately to the side of us, there was a coal black bear eating what looked like berries. His reaction was comical. He was as surprised as we were; he had not heard us nor had we seen him until we were all looking at each other face to face. There is a saying for the look on his face and ours! He totally didn't expect to see us, looked like he couldn't quite figure us out, stood up for a second, and then turned and ran. He backed off so quickly the horses didn't even flinch; they just watched. Not what I would have thought would occur! But when he ran, it looked like something out of a cartoon. He sort of boomeranged through the forest, running one way, then running another, and back and forth for a couple of minutes until he finally ran across the trail (in front of us) and off in the other direction. During this, we just rode quietly and observed his behavior. What was really great was that the wildlife was really wild here. He didn't know what to make of us! It was pretty exciting for us too as not only was it unusual to see a bear, but to be so close. Usually, we see signs of bear in the area such as footprints or even bear droppings. One time, the droppings were hot off the presses so the bear was very near but never face to face such as this! I always wondered and perhaps dreaded what the horses would do. But, fortunately, it was the bear that took off. This must have been our week because this was our second sighting of bear. The other time we were still in the truck driving to a trailhead.*

We continued our ride meandering through State Forest roads and connectors. Throughout our whole ride we didn't see any people, cars, hikers, mountain bikers, or equestrians and had the place to ourselves. In fact, although the area does get visitors, the only activity we saw during our visit was people going to and from their cabins, and that was minimal. We did, however, cover this area during the week. We saw that a few camping areas had been used (non-equestrians), so weekends will likely have more activity. Even still, this is a vast area and not as well known as neighboring Elk State Forest, so consequently there is much less activity. Although we didn't see any vehicles while we were riding, the dirt roads that we rode and also those that we drove had plenty of shoulder to move onto in the event of an oncoming vehicle. During our visit, we focused on the area between Quehanna Highway and Caledonia Pike; there are also many square miles of State Forest between Caledonia Pike all the way to south of Route 80 plus much State Forest north of the Quehanna Highway. *Note: this is really a huge area where you can spend weeks riding throughout and seeking your favorite location. There are clusters of snowmobile trails in different locations throughout the Moshannon State Forest. Ask for the snowmobile maps for each section because those will likely offer a nice variation from riding the dirt roads. In hindsight, I would have liked to explore some of the area north of the Quehanna Highway. As that approaches the Benezette area, it is more likely an area to see elk. We were told many riders explore that section and camp or day park by just pulling off of Deible Road (just down the road from the Deible Road ranger office on Quehanna Highway). We took a drive on Deible Road; these sites weren't large or obvious but basically just offered, at most, some room for one vehicle to pull off. Probably, beyond Deible Road, there are better or roomier sites similar to the ones we explored more thoroughly in the section between Quehanna Highway and Caledonia Pike.*

You can explore this area for days or longer. Just pick one of the parking or camping locations mentioned and head out on the State Forest road or its connectors. Bring the Public Use Map along with a topographical map and a GPS, if you have one. Some trails are marked on the Public Use Map, but many are not. If you don't mind riding some stretches of dirt/gravel State Forest roads or connectors (mostly very quiet) and like trail blazing and exploring in an unstructured, natural environment, you should have fun here. (There are some ideal areas to gait too if you have gaited horses! I would also think this area is excellent for carriage driving.) If you prefer structured, marked trails with a corresponding map to follow, you may want to head a little farther up Route 555 and try the Thunder Mountain Equestrian Trail system in Elk State Forest. See that chapter for more information.

EQUESTRIAN CAMPING:
Descriptions of a selection of camping locales are provided above. At the time of our visit, you could park or camp almost anywhere (within certain State Forest regulations) that you found suitable. At first it wasn't easy to find camping locales. Fortunately, Ranger Wade Dixon was kind enough to help guide us and lead us to the sites described above. And even once we knew where they were, John and I spent a whole day checking out approaches to these and other sites for hauling horse trailers and campers. Within, the State Forest land consists of State Forest dirt roads and limited maintenance roads. They can be unpredictable in terrain, grade, width, and turning radius. It's great that they are dirt roads and undeveloped (that's what makes State Forests special) but it takes time to travel their course. *This was the longest research time we ever needed to spend on just*

21

getting equestrians to a place to park or camp. The area, at first, is overwhelming. But once you become familiar with the lay of the land, it becomes much more manageable to maneuver throughout. And we are sure there are many more parking and camping locales in the other sections that we did not visit. Sites are primitive and without water; so bring water. As indicated, you can fill your water containers along Merrill Road just north of Caledonia Pike; exact mileage is provided above. The office asks that if you choose an area to camp, be careful not to position horses near a feed lot area and do not tie horses where they have access to do damage to trees. At the time of our visit, equestrians were not permitted on the State Gamelands. You can use the map to determine what areas to avoid.

HISTORICAL INFORMATION:

Long before this area was settled and the forests stripped of their lumber, the trees were so tall and dense that sunlight could barely reach the base of the forests. These forests consisted of a variety of trees, including chestnut, maple, cherry, oak, hickory, hemlock, pine, and others. In the mid 1800s to early 1900s, Moshannon State Forest was logged extensively. The area soon became barren and devoid of its former beauty. By the early 1900s, the need to restore this land became recognized and the state proceeded to acquire large tracts with the goal of restoration and preservation. In the 1930s, CCC camps were established to build roads and trails. Some of the old logging roads, fire roads, and railroad tracts have become the trails and connectors used today.

Areas of interest in the Moshannon State Forest region are the Black Moshannon State Park (roughly 3,400 acres), S.B. Elliott State Park (318 acres), Parker Dam State Park (968 acres), the Marlon Brooks Natural Area, and the Quehanna Wild Area. This area once contained native chestnut trees which were lost to disease in the early 1900s. Chestnut plantings have been made with the hope of restoring chestnut to this locale. Horses are not permitted in the Natural Areas.

COURTESIES:

Thank you to Matt Beaver, Wayne Wynick, and Phil Day for helping me obtain information on this area. Thank you to Jodie Gribik for your professionalism and willingness to work with me. Jodie was very helpful in providing useful documentation along with an outline of the area so that I had a base to work with. I would also like to express a very special thank you to Wade Dixon, who has a wealth of knowledge about this State Forest, and was willing to answer my very many questions, plus share information on the lay of the land, road access, and potential parking and camping areas. I learned much from Wade and I am very grateful to have met him. His passion and concern for this wonderful, wild, and beautiful locale shine through. Also, thank you to Don Coine of nearby Parker Dam State Park for answering my inquiries regarding the surrounding area.

22

THINGS WE LEARNED THIS RIDE:

- When I am inquiring regarding trails and camping, I always ask if there is a designated equestrian trail system. I ask this so I can get right to where management would like us to ride and to stay clear of where they don't, and to see what information is already available. However, I have become aware that the perception that I sometimes generate is that I want a designated trail system and only that. Actually, I like the best of both worlds, I like a marked trail system that makes for leisurely riding but I also love the freedom to deviate and explore adjoining areas or other trails at a particular destination. Unmarked trails offer the fantastic element of surprise as one can encounter their own discoveries. I learned that rather than both occurring together, usually one comes at the sacrifice of the other. That shouldn't have to be but often is. I was also reminded that marked trails can equal high impact; unmarked trails can equal low impact. There is a value at certain types of destinations, especially those smaller in size, to having marked trails; many riders prefer this. In general and in many areas, there is a trend toward designating trails and limiting where you can ride; it is becoming less flexible. But at this spacious destination, other than the Quehanna Hiking Trail, there is no designated trail. Equestrians have the freedom to explore and share the area throughout, resulting in low impact to any one area. As this is special and becoming less common, hopefully this wonderful locale can preserve this for years to come. Pennsylvania is very fortunate to have both types of destinations, mapped and unmapped.

- Western Pennsylvania has an abundance of active and closed gas well sites. This particular area was once one of the biggest gas operations. While discussing potential parking or camping sites with the local ranger, I learned to pay serious attention as to whether a site is an active gas well site or an official closed site. Often established equestrian camping areas are on old gas sites. Gas sites are attractive to equestrians because they are usually cleared and of firm ground which can support trucks. Sometimes it is hard to tell what may be totally closed and what may not. Plus, untreated gas does not have an odor. Up to now, I hadn't given it much thought, but I learned it is critical not to park or camp near a site that may still be active and emit gas. Light a camp fire, barbeque, or cigarette in the wrong place…well, you can imagine. Steer clear of active areas; if unsure, check with the land management that the site has been properly closed.

- Do not make a campfire or light a barbeque, etc. near a pine plantation. Pine needles are particularly susceptible to igniting and starting fires. (We did not camp near any pine environments, but conversations with the ranger reminded me that extra caution is needed near pine trees.)

- If one is planning a large group ride, the local office (off of Quehanna Highway on Deible Road) can open a gated site or special area to accommodate the group. Often these gated areas are closed well sites and may be groomed and quite conducive to equestrian camping.

23

- The future trend of State Forest destinations may be online reservations with a choice of designated motorized sites. There's the advantage of knowing you have a reserved site in more limited locales. One of the disadvantages, especially in a larger location such as this, is that you are limited to the choices listed. And if you have other preferences, you will have to pursue a change, let the management know, and wait until or if an online revision is made. I suggest larger locations list available sites and have an "other" box where applicants can write in their preference and submit for approval.
- I learned to stay off of "limited access roads" or "minimum maintenance" roads with a rig. State Forest roads are usually better roads that are graded and maintained. Many are sufficient for hauling. "Limited access roads" are often not suited for hauling and sometimes not for driving.
- Most of the cabins on the State Forest land are leases. In some cases cabins can be rebuilt at existing sites. In other instances, a trade of one site for another can be made, and a new cabin built on the new location. Currently, in this area, new leases are not being issued.

NEARBY EQUESTRIAN CAMPING AND OTHER:
- The Big Elk Lick (horse and non-horse campground with electric hookups, shower and toilet facility, gift shop), Benezette (814) 787-4656
- Hicks Run Outfitters (guided tours, possible equestrian camping, maps, trail info), Driftwood (814) 787-4287, email: hicksrunoutfitters@yahoo.com
- Wapiti Woods, cabin rental (may be able to accommodate horses), website: www.wapitiwoods.com

NEARBY AND SURROUNDING AREA VET SERVICES:
- Dr. Wise, Troutville (814) 427-2424

NEARBY AND SURROUNDING AREA FARRIERS:
- G. Hagan, St. Mary's (814) 834-6376
- D. Bloom, Grampian (814) 236-0514

3. Black Moshannon
Moshannon State Forest
BOF-DCNR
(Bureau of Forestry/Department of Conservation & Natural Resources)

Lasting Impression: Absolutely fabulous trails! The trails seem almost hidden; but once you link up with them you can ride for hours or days enjoying wide grass stretches through diverse forest land and wonderful vistas. Somehow I never heard about this trail system; it must have been a well-kept secret.

Location: The Black Moshannon tract of Moshannon State Forest is located south of Interstate 80 in Centre County, just east of Philipsburg.

Length: *Day Ride or Extended Weekend Destination*- Go for at least a weekend! Black Moshannon is part of Moshannon State Forest. This individual tract consists of about 43,000 acres and surrounds Black Moshannon State Park. There are numerous miles (easily 50+ miles) of trails, State Forest roads, and pipeline right-of-ways to ride on Black Moshannon State Forest land. Horses are permitted on all State Forest trails and roads, except for those specifically closed to horses such as Natural Areas and designated hiking (only) paths. The designated hiking path in this vicinity is the Allegheny Front Trail (AFT). Horses are not permitted in Black Moshannon State Park.

Level of Difficulty: Easy to moderate

Terrain: Overall good terrain and maintained trails of mowed grass paths, dirt tracts, old mountain roads, dirt or gravel State Forest roads, with minimal if any rocks

Horse Camping: Yes, camping is permitted. Large groups should contact the office for special arrangements.

Non-horse Camping: Yes

Carriage Potential: Yes, there is much carriage potential on some of these State Forest roads and trails due to the many logging and access roads, and double width paths. Contact the office for more information.

Maps and Info: Maps and information can be obtained from the District Forester, Forest District Headquarters, Moshannon State Forest, 3372 State Park Road, Penfield, PA 15849, (814) 765-0821, email: fd09@state.pa.us or contact the Department of Conservation & Natural Resources (DCNR) website: www.dcnr.state.pa.us. Ask for the Black Moshannon Snowmobile Trail Map (very useful for a close-up of the immediate area and reference points, and it depicts the area where you can ride and some of the areas you can't). Also request the Moshannon State Forest Public Use Map (pertains to all of Moshannon State Forest, a large scale representation), and the Rock Run Trails Cross-Country Skiing Map (useful in determining, north of Route 504, which areas are the AFT trails to avoid). If you need a contact, ask for Jodie Gribik,

Recreation Forester or Ranger Stacey Flick. Both are extremely knowledgeable, friendly, and helpful. For information regarding nearby Black Moshannon State Park, contact Black Moshannon State Park, 4216 Beaver Road, Philipsburg, PA 16866-9519, (814) 342-5960, email: blackmoshannonsp@state.pa.us or the Pennsylvania Bureau of State Parks (888) PA-PARKS.

Activities: Hiking, Biking, Horseback Riding Trails, Picnicking, Swimming, Fishing, Camping, X-C Skiing, Snowmobiling, and Hunting

Fees for Trail Use: None

Permits for Day Trail Use: None

Permits/Fees Required for Overnight Camping: Permits (no fee) are required for overnight motorized camping. There are no formerly designated camping areas; however, there are some level, open areas which are suitable to equestrian camping (see below).

Comfort Station: There are no restrooms but there are facilities at nearby Black Moshannon State Park.

DIRECTIONS:

Black Moshannon State Forest is located south of I-80 and west of Route 220, near State College. You can reach it from several directions. We were told to avoid Route 504 between Route 220 and Black Moshannon State Forest. We agreed it was much too steep with tight turns for hauling. Rather, the route that was recommended to us and the one we took was I-80 to Exit #158 Route 220 south. Travel 10.5 miles on Route 220 south and prepare to slow down. You will be entering the town of Julian and looking for a right onto Beaver Road (formerly known as Julian Pike). Clocking from the end of the I-80 eastbound ramp, you should see the turn at 10.9 miles. Take Beaver Road for 5 miles to the top of the mountain. This is a climb, but we did not find it excessive nor were there sharp turns.

Day parking- Beaver Road and Underwood Road intersection: After traveling 5 miles on Beaver Road, there is a large gravel lot on the right at the corner of Beaver Road and Underwood Road. This is a medium size, level lot which can fit about 4 to 7 rigs depending on the size of the trailer. Very large rigs can fit and there is pull through space without backing. There is a possibility that this lot may be enlarged in the future. The trailhead is across the street from the lot and also to the rear of the lot. *If you visit this lot or any lot, please clean up your horse's manure before heading for the trail and also upon leaving the lot. We had just departed from our campsite, and had made the usual extra effort to leave it clean, when we passed this very visible and multiple-use parking lot and saw, for the second day in a row, that a day rider had not cleaned up their horse's manure. We have seen this on numerous occasions at various locales; mounds of manure are left in plain sight of all that pass by. I've seen a trend in the increase of signs at day parking lots telling equestrians to clean up manure, bedding, and straw and take it with them. We shouldn't need signs to tell us to clean up after our horse; this is common courtesy. Leaving piles of manure can quickly make us unwelcome with many other trail users and land management. In day parking areas, please take the manure out with you. Certainly do not clean your trailer out at these multiple-use locales (we've seen day riders dump out both shavings and manure at central lots). In camping areas, where riders do need to dispose of manure, scatter any manure (unless directed otherwise); do not leave mounds. If we, as a group, are considerate of others and practice good public relations, we stand a much better chance of remaining accepted at these beautiful destinations.*

Camping Site- Benner Run Road Site #1: From the intersection of Beaver Road and Underwood Road, make a right onto Underwood Road. Underwood Road is a level, wide, gravel road of good surface. Take Underwood Road for 3.5 miles. Make a left onto Route 504. Go .6 miles on Route 504. Make a right onto Benner Run Road which is of a gravel/dirt surface, also of good terrain. The Benner Run Road sign is set back so you almost have to turn onto it to see it. *Why do they do that?* Take Benner Run Road for .3 miles and make a left into a medium size gravel lot. This lot will fit at least 2-3 large rigs or about 4 smaller rigs. Some backing will be necessary. At the time of our visit, this lot was a plain gravel lot surrounded by small shrub-like trees. There were a few trees to tie line to and not many immediately surrounding the lot. Plans are for this lot to be enlarged and improved. We will need to suggest tie poles for high lines as that would be useful at this location. To reach the trails, ride out either way on Benner Run Road and pick up either the pipeline (which parallels Route 504 for a distance and provides access to many trails), Smays Run Trail (via the trailhead opposite the entrance to Benner Run Road off of Route 504), head northwest via Benner Run Road or the pipeline toward North Run Trail, or pick up the trail out of the back of Benner Run Road Site #2. See the map for more information or just ride down the road and sample the many assorted trails. *Note: there is a gated dirt road at this site; this is not a trail but rather an access road to the Penn State Observatory and the Doppler Radar Dome (which looks like a giant soccer ball).* This site has also been used for equestrian day parking; however, day parking may interfere with equestrians, especially larger rigs, arriving to enter the lot for camping. If possible, leave room for others. Once the lot is enlarged, this may no longer be an issue.

Camping site- Benner Run Road Site #2: From Benner Run Road Site #1 above, continue on Benner Run Road for another .3 miles (a total of .6 miles from Route 504). There is a clearing on the right. Although this is along the side of Benner Run Road, we liked this site as it is an attractive grass covered camping area (vs. gravel parking lot) with plenty of trees to tie line to. This clearing is the smaller of the two and could fit about 2 large to 3 medium size rigs; rigs will need to back into the site. There is a good surface for portable corrals; but will be tight for electric fencing. Trails can be accessed by riding out Benner Run Road as detailed above. There was also a trail directly out of the back of this camping locale but we did not explore that one.

Camping site or large group site- gated Old Gas Well Site (gas well site now closed) North Run Road: To reach this take Beaver Road to Underwood Road. You will see the day parking area. If coming from Route 220, make a right onto Underwood Road and travel about 1.5 miles to the triangle intersection. Make a left onto North Run Road. Travel on North Run Road for .6 miles. You will see a yellow gate at the right; the site is at the top of the long grass entrance. At the time of our visit, this was considered only for larger groups, and required permission from the office and arrangement for the gate to be unlocked. *Note: we wondered why some open areas are gated. We found there are many reasons, but one positive result is that it keeps unauthorized users from misusing the area and, thus, it is kept clean from littering, broken bottles, etc.* This site has a long entrance of uphill grade for roughly 250 feet; the wide entrance is of solid terrain and two lane width (although some small bushes were planted lining one side which may eventually limit the width to one or one and a half lanes). This approach was once an access road where heavy duty trucks drove to the gas well site, so it was meant to hold big rigs and to be of good terrain. The lengthy approach leads to an ideal area for horse camping. This is our favorite site and where we would most like to camp. There's lots of room here! It is a very large, grass covered, open area that can easily fit 20+ very large rigs, along with electric fence corrals and portable corrals. There are also plenty of tie line trees. No backing is necessary; there is ample pull through room. It is maintained, mowed twice a year, remote, high, dry, central to trails, and is away from any roads, cabins, or park activity. Thus it is ideal for horse camping. Use of this camping site along with the wonderful trails that are available to explore earn this our "Four Spur Award!"

Camping or group site- Dug Road: This locale is in the southwest section of the Black Moshannon Snowmobile Trail Map and is west of Beaver Road. Dug Road is reflected on the map as a connector between Shirk State Road and Strawband Beaver Road. To reach it, follow the directions to the day parking area at Beaver Road and Underwood Road as described above. Continue on Beaver Road past the parking area and make a left onto Strawband Beaver Road. (The turn leads to a fork in the road; bear left to pick up Strawband Beaver Road and bear right to pick up Shirks State Road fork.) Take Strawband Beaver Road to Dug Road, make a right onto Dug Road and the open area will be on the left side of Dug Road. During our visit, one of the access roads was closed due to road improvements in process, plus both the roads and the camping site were still too rough for hauling so we did not clock it. Subsequent to our visit we were told improvements were in the works for both the roads and the campsite. Watch for this locale to be another option in the future.

Other: This area is just becoming better known as a good riding destination. The rangers that I met and spoke with at this State Forest office were wonderfully open and responsive to new ideas and suggestions. As equestrian interest increases, watch for lot improvements, enlargements, changes, or additional lots to be added. We were also told of another parking area suitable for trailers which would access the western part of the trail system. However, we did not visit or assess this site which is located just off of Route 322 before the intersection of Hannah Furnace Road and Horse Hollow Road. This parking area is labeled with a 'P' on the Black Moshannon Snowmobile Trail Map.

Water: There is plenty of water in this area, especially along the trail. Bring 5-gallon water jugs to fill at either of the following two sites. From Route 504, take Benner Run Road for 2.0 miles (this is past the two Benner Run campsites described above). There is spring water on the left across from a small cabin with a small pull-off area (go without the trailer). There is also water on Route 504, just south of Benner Run Road and the Tram Road trailhead. To reach this from Beaver Road, take Underwood Road to Route 504, make a right off of Underwood Road onto Route 504. Travel 1.5 miles and you'll see white pipes on the left side of Route 504. Or you can reach this from Benner Run Road by traveling east on Route 504 (in the direction of Underwood Road) for 2 miles and you will see it on the left.

THE TRAILS:
Equestrians can have a field day (literally) here. As with the Quehanna section of Moshannon State Forest, it's an explorer's paradise. Blaze your own trail (but practice "leave no trace" impact); it's wide open. Have fun exploring! There are no designated equestrian trails but equestrians can ride within the State Forest, except for a few exclusions such as hiking (only) trails. And these are not just State Forest roads. Look closer; there are trails, old mountain roads, logging paths, former railroad tracts, and groomed pipeline right-of-ways. Head out and ride for hours. Some may have a sign with their name, a white sign indicating permitted usage, an orange diamond indicating snowmobile trails, a blue blaze indicating Rock Run Trails, an orange rectangle blaze indicating the hiking (only) Allegheny Front Trail (AFT), or may be totally unmarked and not on the map. (The AFT can be viewed on the maps so you know where to avoid and also usually have trailhead markings indicating "AFT" along with an orange rectangle blaze. *Sometimes it can be confusing as the snowmobile paths, indicated by orange **diamond** markers, are usually okay to ride; but the AFT, designated by orange **rectangle** markers, is not to be ridden.*) Equestrians are permitted on most of the other trails in the State Forest. Equestrians should refer to the map and not ride within the boundaries of Black Moshannon State Park (a designated Natural Area) and State Gamelands (use the green Moshannon State Forest Public Use Map as a reference) unless indicated otherwise.

For those who prefer a marked trail, there are established multiple-use trails which you can follow. These are marked at the intersections, and the main trails and connectors are reflected on the Black Moshannon Snowmobile Trail Map, an 8.5" x 11" black and white map. It's the best of all worlds because you have a choice of both marked and unmarked trails. This area is best described as being composed of three sections, and thinking of it this way helps you navigate through the trail system. There is the area north of Route 504, the section between Route 504 and Beaver Road, and the area between Beaver Road and Route 322 (the section west and southwest of Beaver Road). We rode a sampling of all three sections.

You can ride small loops or big loops; there are many connectors and extenders. On our first day's ride we were out for about 7 hours and took Underwood Road to North Run Road (gravel), made a right onto North Run Trail, crossed Route 504, and continued straight crossing the pipeline right-of-way. We continued in the direction of Benner Run Road (gravel & dirt) and came to a new growth area. The change in the landscape was dramatic and the color was very picturesque where you cross from the older woods to the new growth. The path throughout remained wide, easy, and of excellent terrain. We headed into the forest of young saplings and reached a section that had springs generating water in the vicinity. This was the only wet section that we encountered in the area north of Route 504 (may be due to the recent storms). We came to the yellow gate on Benner Run Road and made a right and then another right in the direction we just came from. We decided to backtrack, but avoided the wet section by riding to an old, open logging area and following an old skid loader path to the right. We then returned the way we came in and took the pipeline path. We made a right onto the pipeline right-of-way (in the direction of the State Park) which was a beautiful, maintained, wide, grass stretch of good terrain. We took the pipeline path and explored various offshoots along the way. Throughout, the paths were of good surface, had minimal rocks (if any), and the overhead clearance was good. At this point, the path we followed is indicated as Dry Hollow Road on the map. We explored some of Dry Hollow Road (dirt) along with offshoots, took the Short Cut Trail (a connector) to Benner Run Road, made a right on Benner Run Road, made another right back toward the pipeline path, and made a left on the pipeline tract. During this stretch we ran into two other equestrians from a local stable that frequent this area. These were the only people we ran into on horse, foot, or bike during our first day's ride. We then headed east along the nice, long stretch of pipeline that parallels the northeast side of Route 504; we made a left and rode into what was to be **my favorite section**. This turn lead to a large, open, scenic area with a vista of the surrounding landscape. There is a fenced protected area to one side and a view of the surrounding area to the other. It is a gradual approach. At first we ended up below the fenced area, and the orange diamond markers seemed to head into an overgrown or unused area. So we turned around and rode a path up along the fencing for the protected area. When we arrived at the top there were a series of nice, wide trails that offered great views including those of the Doppler Radar and Penn State Observatory buildings. (Actually, at this location, you are on the mountain behind the Benner Run Road Site #1 looking toward the Benner Run Road Site #1. This location can be seen if you walk out the back from the camping area.) We rode these high trails for a bit and then headed back in the direction of Route 504.

Our intention was to cross Route 504 and pick up Smays Run Trail and take that back to Underwood or North Run Roads. However, we crossed Route 504 and impulsively picked up what we thought was a shortcut trail. This is where we learned that what may appear like a trail may actually be a logging site which travels in circles or dead ends. The roads can act as reference points, but perhaps give you a false sense of security because you can still get turned around in some sections. We experienced just that. We hadn't brought a GPS so we decided to use our horse's internal GPS. Our one horse has a good sense of direction, plus we knew he was tired and would be anxious to get back. So John dropped the reins and let him go. And he did! It was amazing how this non-gaited horse transformed his usual Quarter Horse crawl into a running walk as he navigated through the woods in the exact direction of where we were parked. If you or your horse have a good sense of direction, the terrain is ideal (hardly any rocks, good surface) for trail blazing.

The next day we decided to try some of the trails in the central part of the trail system, along with areas between Route 322 and Beaver Road. We left Underwood Road and took North Run Road and made a left on Smays Run Trail. Smays Run Trail is a very scenic, wide path. As this area approaches the locale of Black Moshannon State Park, we did see some hikers and mountain bikers as we traveled its course. As you venture away from the park borders, any activity quickly decreases. *There was lots of room to share the trails throughout and the folks that we encountered were very friendly. There were groups of young boys, perhaps scout groups, having a great time and it was nice seeing them play in the river, having friendly water fights with the ice cold water, and just having a good time outdoors.* Smays Run Trail has many stretches of excellent terrain and has beautiful scenery throughout as it travels through rolling and diverse landscapes. However, there are some wet areas along Smays Run Trail (wet sections may be temporary and exist as a result of the recent storms). We found all passable and usually of a durable surface, as many of these paths have also sufficed as old logging or mountain roads or access roads for cabins. We continued in the direction of Beaver Road, crossed, and rode a dirt and grass path that paralleled Strawband Beaver Road. It was a nice path but there were some connectors and adjoining sections that had wet areas. Where it was wet usually had a tough surface, and the water just seemed to flow past it and did not soften the turf. Actually, after the recent remnants of Hurricane Frances, it was amazing that there weren't more wet areas. *Although being on the top of a plateau helped greatly. When we were traveling to this locale, we passed nearby valleys which were in sad shape with much flooding.* For the most part, we only had to bypass a couple of spots, but still, overall, it was exceptional especially considering the previous weather.

Many of these dirt road connectors also served as an entry to cabins. We took a dirt road to the right, linked with Strawband Beaver Road, made another right when the next dirt road presented itself and headed back into the woods. We explored this area for a while and then headed back in the direction of Beaver Road. It should be noted that there is a small but active airport on the north side of Shirk State Road, and is reflected on the Black Moshannon Snowmobile Trail Map. We did not approach it but riders may want to avoid the immediate area; there are other alternatives to choose. Subsequently we traveled to the parking area at the corner of Underwood Road and Beaver Road and picked up the trail that links with Smays Run Trail. We continued in the direction of North Run Road. Just past North Run Road we encountered a stretch of wet area along Smays Run Trail. This seemed to be an area that had a lot of cabin or small scale logging traffic, and just needed some hard-wearing stone dust fill as the trail also served as an access road. Soon the trail improved and we followed Smays Run Trail all the way to the end, and then headed back along Underwood Road to where we were parked.

There are so many dirt roads and trails to explore that are not reflected on the map. Using the roads as a reference, it is nice to combine riding the established trails with exploring offshoots. Overall, the trails were of very good quality and exceptional beauty. We found the ones north of Route 504 to be mostly dry and the ones between Route 504 and Route 322 to vary from dry to wet. Nonetheless, we did not encounter much soft ground; rather the surface was durable. This is probably due to both being at the top of the mountain and due to fill being brought in over time to maintain the mountain roads. *We did note that this land management was continuously making improvements, appeared to stay on top of their maintenance, and they probably already have these few inferior areas included in their maintenance plans.* There are plenty of streams to water the horses along the way. Most of the woods are not dense so you can see much while traveling the trails; the good visibility seems to enhance the beauty and enjoyment of the trail. The main trails are marked at the intersections with roads; explore an off trail and you are on your own (although, it is fun to see where you come out). This is a good place to play an orienteering game. At the time of our visit, it appeared that the area was being visited by equestrians but not receiving heavy use (we hardly saw any hoof prints on the trail). Probably, a lot of equestrians were not aware of these nice trails.

EQUESTRIAN CAMPING:

The camping areas are described above under "Directions." Camping is primitive. Spring water is located just a quick drive from each of the camping areas, so bring containers. The demand for equestrian camping didn't seem to have presented itself prior to our arrival. We know there wasn't much equestrian camping in the past as when we contacted the office, they weren't sure where to recommend we set up camp. Nonetheless, everyone tried to be very helpful and, ultimately, I was able to reach some rangers who could guide us. One ranger we spoke with has horses and was very familiar with equestrians needs. *Especially because we are a unique user group, it's always great to have a fellow equestrian in the office!*

HISTORICAL INFORMATION:

This area was once the home of the Seneca Indians. The European settlers arrived, and by the early 1800s the Philadelphia-Erie Pike was constructed opening the area for settlement. Today this road is Route 504. Stone markers still exist along the road today marking mileage along the pike. We were told this was a toll road and that the road that is now Underwood Road was built by individuals wanting to avoid the toll. By the late 1800s to early 1900s, lumber companies stripped the once dense woods of its timber. Many of the trails and roads in the area today were once either logging roads or railroad paths used to transport the lumber. In the 1900s, the state assessed the logging damage and began to purchase these lands with the goal of re-establishing the forests.

Today, the woodlands have been restored and preserved for the public to enjoy. Welcoming an assortment of outdoor activities, Black Moshannon is a destination many should enjoy. This destination is not only diverse in its landscape; it is unique in that it is situated on the Allegheny Plateau, high above the surrounding areas. The elevation of 2,000+ feet offers cooler temperatures in the summer and conditions conducive to a variety of winter sports. This is a good place to visit on those hot summer days; it is shaded and cooler than the valleys below.

COURTESIES:

Thank you to Wayne Wynick for following up on my correspondence, for answering my many questions, and for putting me in contact with Jodie Gribik. I would like to express my profound gratitude to Jodie Gribik, the Recreation Forester at Moshannon State Forest, for taking the time to provide the right maps and outline recommended routes, for being so pleasant and patient through my many calls, and supporting us in our endeavor to explore and enjoy both the Quehanna and Black Moshannon sections of Moshannon State Forest. Thank you to Ranger Stacey Flick who, on his way home from work on a Friday night, stopped by to say hello and to talk with us. I very much enjoyed my conversation with Ranger Flick who is also an equestrian and shared much useful and needed information including some of the nice vistas and camping locales. Stacey, we will definitely be revisiting Black Moshannon State Forest as we really enjoyed it; we hope you can join us on a trail ride next time. What a great group of friendly and professional staff we had the pleasure of communicating with regarding Moshannon State Forest! Thank you for making us feel so welcome.

THINGS WE LEARNED THIS RIDE:
Don't head out near dark on "unmaintained roads" in unfamiliar territory. We had a long day of riding and we left the horses tied and decided to head out to clock mileage for places to obtain spring water. It was early evening, shortly before dusk, and I impulsively said to John, "Let's take a ride down the Tram Road," as the sign indicated it was open to motorized vehicles. I figured this would give us a good reference for where we might ride the next day or in the future. I had previously been cautioned by a ranger for the Quehanna section of this State Forest that "unmaintained roads" are just that and can be rough and unpredictable, even impassable. But my sense of adventure got the better of me even though I know better than to head out at dusk. (I was lost at age 10 with my brother in the Canadian Rockies by doing just that.) But we were in our 4-WD truck with plenty of gas; that was all we needed right? Well, it's amazing how long it can take to go 9 miles in the dark on a rugged, jagged road with little clearance on all sides and nowhere to turn around. It started off beautiful and inviting. We saw two large bucks and were enjoying the ride; but the sun soon went down, and various dirt roads spun off in different directions which were unmarked and not on the map. We weren't sure if we were on the Tram Road or some side mountain road that came to an impassable point. How would we return as we couldn't turn and the roads were too rough for backing, plus we couldn't see behind us? We kept heading up the mountain hoping to hook up with a good road. We did catch an awesome sunset ("red sky at night, sailor's delight"), but the road kept deteriorating. Do we continue, which should be a shorter distance than where we came from? Did we turn in the right direction at the last intersection? The road was getting so narrow that the trees on the side were barely clearing our truck. Thank goodness we didn't bring the dually! Finally, we decided to turn around as the truck had been bouncing along the rocky surface so much so that it felt like an amusement park ride. But we had to wait for a small clearing to turn. By the time we came to one, it was pitch black as there was no moon visible. I got out to feel the surrounding turf with my feet and to determine if the uneven ground would support turning the truck. It was doable, so we turned with some effort and back we went. We managed to backtrack without catching a sidewall of a tire on some of the serrated rocks as we headed back to camp. We had been out on this dirt road for hours! John's last remark was something like, "Whose idea was this anyway?" (as I looked sheepishly away). But in hindsight, once I knew my truck was coming back in one piece, it was kind of fun! Maybe we'll do it again... but in John's truck.

NEARBY AND SURROUNDING AREA STABLES:
- Benner's Boarding Stables (boarding, hauling services), Bellefonte (814) 355-2911
- Eastwood Farms (boarding, lessons), Bellefonte (814) 355-4523
- Telicks Queens Three Farm (boarding, lessons), Bellefonte (814) 383-4781
- Hoof N Paws (boarding, overnight stabling), Bellefonte (814) 359-2693

NEARBY AND SURROUNDING AREA VET SERVICES:
- Centre Equine Practice, Centre Hall (814) 364-1921
- S. McAllister, Centre Hall (814) 234-7415

NEARBY AND SURROUNDING AREA FARRIERS:
- Scott Sims, Julian (near Port Matilda) (814) 353-1511
- A. Barnett, Phillipsburg (814) 342-5548
- T. Siegenthaler, Spring Mills (814) 364-9534

4. Cook Forest State Park
DCNR
(Department of Conservation & Natural Resources)

Lasting Impression: This is worth the trip just for a day ride; make time for it if you are passing through the area onto other trails! Delight in a ride through rows of majestic pine, hemlock, and oak forests along a well maintained grass trail, or enjoy the durable surface of the woodland trails that wind under the canopy of towering trees. Although the equestrian and multiple-use trails travel outside of the protected growth timber area, "Forest Cathedral," you are still surrounded by enormous trees along the trail. It's hard to imagine that even taller, wider, and older trees exist along the hiking paths in the Forest Cathedral area which is a designated National Natural Landmark.

Location: Cook Forest State Park is located in northwest Pennsylvania where Forest, Clarion, and Jefferson Counties meet. There are other well known, privately owned equestrian destinations in this region, but this chapter pertains to the public State Park.

Length: *Day Ride Destination*- The park consists of almost 7,200 acres and there is roughly 10 miles of riding plus adjoining dirt roads. There is the possibility that the current trail system will be expanded and links completed, which will increase the length. Either way, visit this one for the beauty and not the length.

Level of Difficulty: These trails were mainly easy and leisurely, only one short section was more challenging and can be avoided (see below).

Terrain: The terrain was mostly wide, gradual, gravel/dirt double tract paths, wonderfully groomed grass stretches, and dirt roads. There are some (sometimes busy) road connectors which can be avoided by backtracking. If loops on the State Forest land are established, this will not be an issue.

Horse Camping: None

Non-horse Camping: Yes

Maps and Info: DCNR, Cook Forest State Park, P.O. Box 120, Cooksburg, PA 16217-0120, (814) 744-8407, website: www.dcnr.state.pa.us, email: cookforestsp@state.pa.us. To reserve cabins or picnic areas, or for disability information, contact the Pennsylvania Bureau of State Parks, (888) PA-PARKS. The equestrian trail is reflected on the State Park map by a horse symbol.

Activities: Hiking, Biking, Horseback Riding Trails, Guided Trail Rides, Picnicking, Swimming, Tubing, Fishing, Canoeing, Ice-Skating, Sledding, X-C Skiing, Cabin Rentals, Tenting, Camping, Snowmobiling, and Hunting

Fees for Trail Use: None

Permits for Day Trail Use: None

Comfort Station: Yes

DIRECTIONS:
The park can be reached from many directions via Route 36, or by taking Route 66 or Route 68 to Route 36. To approach from Route 68, take I-80 to Exit #62 Route 68 north. Take Route 68 north for 13.5 miles to the intersection of Route 36. Make a right onto Route 36. Take Route 36 for 3 miles. Make a sharp left onto SR (State Route) 1015. It is sharp but there is extended pavement and sufficient width for a large rig. You'll see a sign for the Silver Stallion Stables at the turn. Go .8 miles on SR 1015, cross a stone bridge and you'll see the lot on the left. (Do not take the rigs or horses to the lot on the right of SR 1015, by the Log Cabin Inn, as that is the parking lot for access to the trails in the Forest Cathedral [old growth] viewing area. That section is a National Natural Landmark and is protected; so it's hiking only.) Make a left into the lot which is a nice size loop with pull through room without backing. You can see this location on the map indicated by a loop and near shelter #2. There is room for several rigs including large rigs. But due to limited access and to remain welcome at this shared, central, and convenient parking area, this is probably a more appropriate destination for smaller groups (4 rigs or less) or individual units, not large groups.

Equestrians should park away from the picnic tables and pavilions. Please keep horses away from the picnic area and pick up all droppings in the lot (do not leave it there all day until you return to load up). We also made sure there was no manure left in this shared use lot for the short distance from the trailer to the trailhead so as not to alienate other visitors, again with the goal of remaining welcome. To reach the trailhead, we rode down the stone parking area in the direction toward the picnic pavilion. You can see the wide, gravel, gated trail on your right starting at the end of the picnic grounds. Before reaching the pavilion site, we traveled a short distance under the pine trees where the ground was firm to connect with the trail. We avoided crossing immediately in the vicinity of where we parked as there is some low lying area which may have been soft. We then connected with the trail which you can clearly see and it is marked. We made a left and proceeded down the trail. Remember not to ride the opposite side of the road from where you entered the parking lot as that is the hiking (only) trail through the protected area mentioned above; neither equestrians nor bikes are permitted due to the delicate environment. *If you can, have a friend watch your horse, it's about a 20 minute walk up into the forest taking the trail behind the Log Cabin Inn. By walking the short distance, you can see the virgin forests.* Shortly after beginning our ride, we encountered a place to water the horses. The ground was good and firm, even along the stream, and it provided easy access.

THE TRAILS:
The trails, which equestrians are permitted to ride, are multiple-use trails. We arrived on a Sunday morning and had the woods to ourselves. By the afternoon, there was light activity, both in the parking area and on the trail. It was very

37

relaxing on the trails and they did not feel congested, probably due to the nice, wide width of the trails leaving plenty of room to share. The multiple-use area that permits equestrians travels the outside perimeter of the old growth sections. There is a Cook Forest State Park Trail Guide flyer that is available from the office which describes in detail the many hiking paths and attractions within the State Park, and also mentions the Bridle Trail.

There are two sections of trails which connect at the Hefren Run Trail and at the Tom's Run Trail, just a short distance from the parking area. We rode the trails accessed via the Hefren Run Trail. We traveled out from the lot, picked up the end of the trail behind the gate, traveled a short distance, crossed a small stream, and made a right onto the Hefren Run Trail. From the moment we set out and throughout most of the trail, the surface was of dirt, pebble, and fine stone dust, an excellent terrain for both drainage and durability. It was perfect for standing up to heavy, multiple-use traffic including horses and bikes. The trails along Hefren Run are gorgeous; the base of the forest is not dense as it is surrounded by a variety of tall trees shielding the lower areas from thick growth. Thus you can see far into the forests and you'll find yourself looking up, up, and up to see the tops of the trees. There are many trails and connectors spinning off in different directions. We headed straight and stayed with the Hefren Run Trail. When we came to the Deer Meadow Trail sign, we made a right and continued on Hefren Run toward SR 1015. Numerous trees had fallen in the forest; this is likely due to this season's heavy storms. Nonetheless, the trail paths were cleared and perfectly maintained.

We took the Hefren Run Trail to SR 1015 and crossed to the one-way dirt road on the other side. SR 1015 is sometimes a busy road (two lane paved), but we did not have any problem crossing it. There is a small parking area on the right, and as you ride the dirt road entrance you will see a single path aside the road to the right and/or left which is used by local stables and riders. The dirt road, which leads into the pine forest, was very quiet on the weekend when we visited. We only saw one maintenance vehicle pass. We followed this dirt road and passed a gate to the left. We came to the Bridle Trail sign and followed the series of signs. There were also orange diamonds indicating a snowmobile path. The Bridle Trail turned into a stretch that was **our most favorite section.** It was a straight, mowed grass path down the middle of rows of tall pines of pole type appearance (see photo). This section was pristine and amazing in its beauty. *But the towering pines do creak almost continuously as they move slightly in the breeze. After having had a large tree fall dangerously near my path while on horseback (at another destination), I found this a bit unsettling.*

We continued following the signs for the Bridle Trail to a section where the trail traveled uphill. Up until now the trail was very level and easy. At the top of the knoll, there is a sign directing the Bridle Trail to the left and the Joyce Kilmer

Trail to the right. Initially, we made the left and followed a section of trail which was a steep descent onto Cemetery Road (paved). Use caution if you choose this route. The trail drops you onto the road without much shoulder. Don't pile down, but rather proceed cautiously in the event of traffic. We were later told that riders could make a left on Cemetery Road and head down to Troutman Run Road, explore portions of Coleman Road, head back on Forest Drive, and enjoy some nice portions of trail. (Per the map and the office, these three are dirt roads.) We didn't ride Cemetery Road; instead we decided to take a different route. Being confused at this intersection and not seeing any additional signs by the road, we turned around. The short connector that we chose to return on we later discovered may be considered part of the hiking path (see below). It can be confusing at this intersection even with the map. *In hindsight, if we had tried the left on Cemetery Road and concluded it was unsuitable or unsafe, we could have backtracked along the Bridle Trail and hooked up with Forest Drive and then headed northeast to sample some of the riding along the dirt roads or just headed back and rode Browns Run and Toms Run trails. Otherwise, if we had found Cemetery Road to be safe enough to travel, we could have used it to connect to some of the dirt roads and return via Forest Drive.* Our alternate path brought us back to Forest Drive and we returned to the parking area via the same route we took in.

We explored the eastern section of trails but from what we could see, the western section of Cook Forest State Park, which included Toms Run Road and the Browns Run Trail, looked like it also offered the same wonderful, wide, solid surface to travel on. In regard to these two trails, the suggested route provided to me reflects the end connector to form a loop at Lencer's Drive (dirt and paved) and a small portion of SR 1015 (paved). Rather than have riders approach SR 1015, I am hoping an inland link will be established on the State Park land between the end of Toms Run Road (dirt/gravel) and the Browns Run Trail (dirt/gravel).

This was a delight to visit. We shared our positive feedback and praise of the trails with the office. We also asked if there was the possibility of one section of the hiking loop at the Old Logging Road and Joyce Kilmer Trail to be open to horses. The section we refer to is a durable, short section of trail that is not near the core of the Forest Cathedral but rather outside of the main part of the park and the protected areas. The office was wonderfully receptive and agreed that this would appear a more favorable option than riding a trail out onto a paved and possibly active road. Plus a loop provides low impact vs. backtracking which provides high impact. The office did say they will look into that option. They also explained that, if it is determined by their office to be feasible and they confirm it is a sufficient distance from the Forest Cathedral section, approval from Harrisburg must be sought and received. Once, and if, that occurs equestrians will be able to share in the usage of the short connecting loop. If you are local, please try to help facilitate this process and work with the office. This will be even more of a spectacular day ride if the two connectors, one at the east end and one at the west end, are established.

Contact the office to obtain a map. At the time of your request, ask if the loop has been established permitting this described portion of the Joyce Kilmer Trail to be ridden in order to link back with the Old Logging Road. *Note: if you look at the map, it is easy to tell which portion I am talking about. The desired section of trail, indicated by #1 between Cemetery Road and the Old Logging Road, is the area that lies on the border of the light green, no hunting area and the darker green area. This is **not** the section within the lighter green shading which includes the Forest Cathedral protected area and adjacent trails.*

Even though this is a significant distance from our home, when we are passing in the area we plan to revisit these trails. They are unique in their outstanding beauty and excellent maintenance. Plus they should be a very nice ride in the hot weather due to the forest canopy, and they offer good wildlife sightings. During our visit, we saw two large bucks and a mother bear and her cub. *Of course I knew this would be a fun destination, just by the name!*

HISTORICAL INFORMATION:
Cook Forest State Park is well known for its dark, dense forests and, like the Tiadaghton State Forest region, has been called the "Black Forest." Beautiful clusters of giant hemlocks and mature white pines have earned it our nation's Natural Landmark status. At one time, this was Seneca Nation territory. Ultimately, the land was acquired by the English, and farming and logging operations were begun. One of the first settlers was John Cook, and thus the name of today's State Park. Descendants of the Cook family remained in this region for generations to come and some still reside in the area today. In the 1800s, like many other forests in Pennsylvania, this area was extensively logged and stripped of timber. The Clarion River was used to transport the logs to Pittsburgh, and once had so many logs and debris that it was called "Stump Creek." The runoff from the logging also contributed to another name for the creek, "Mud" or "Muddy River." However, fortunately, some sections of forests were saved from the saw mill thanks to emerging conservation interests in the early 1900s.

In the 1900s, various concerned individuals and groups created the Cook Forest Association with the goal of preserving the dwindling and remaining virgin forest segments of the Cook Forest region. These old growth clusters can be seen today at the Forest Cathedral, Seneca, and Swamp Area locations. These untouched woods consist of oak, black cherry, beech, maple, white pine, hemlock, and many other varieties, along with the remains of American chestnut trees which were destroyed during a blight in the early 1900s. Some of these trees that can be viewed are hundreds of years old. The Forest Cathedral section, near the Log Cabin Visitor Center (accessed via the Longfellow Hiking [only] Trail), is one of Pennsylvania's largest clusters of virgin forest with trees up to 400 years old, 5 feet in diameter, and up to 200 feet high. These old growth tracts offer a beautiful sight to behold.

By the late 1920s, the land known today as Cook Forest was purchased by the state of Pennsylvania and preserved for all to enjoy. The park was further developed in the 1930s by the Civilian Conservation Corps (CCC). The CCC, formed by President Franklin D. Roosevelt during the Great Depression, was intended to provide jobs during this difficult time in our nation's history along with preserving natural resources and improving them so that the public could access and enjoy them. In fact, the Log Cabin Inn, which houses the environmental learning center, was constructed by the CCC. This area also once had natural mineral springs which attracted visitors from far and wide in the early 1900s. Its waters were considered to have healing ability and benefits. If you have the opportunity, visit the Log Cabin Inn historical room which offers information regarding the history of the area and displays historical artifacts of the region.

COURTESIES:
There is a great group of folks at this State Park office! Thank you to Marsha Gordon who just recently joined this office. I mentioned my recommendations as described above, and Marsha listened attentively and discussed the options and possibilities with me. Marsha, who is also an equestrian, told me she will follow up regarding the connection of loops as described above. Thank you so much, Marsha, for being so responsive and concerned! Also, thank you to Dorothy Rodgers and Ranger Stephen Mazik for answering my many questions, and thank you to DCNR and all those who allow us to enjoy this State Park on horseback and for constructing trails of excellent surface that are ideal for horse and multiple-use traffic.

NEARBY:
- Cook Forest Area Vacation Bureau, Cooksburg (814) 849-9377
- Wild West Tack Shop (located conveniently in the heart of Clarion), (814) 223-3484

NEARBY AND SURROUNDING AREA STABLES:
- Pine Crest Cabins & Stables (guided trail rides, non-horse camping, possible emergency overnight stabling, and many other family activities), Cook Forest, Clarington (814) 752-2200, website: www.cooksforest.com
- Silver Stallion Stables (guided trail rides through Cook Forest State Park), Cooksburg (814) 927-6636

NEARBY AND SURROUNDING AREA VET SERVICES:
- Dr. Turner, Marley Veterinary Clinic, Titusville (814) 827-1778
- P. Farrell, Russell Veterinary Clinic (need to trailer to), Russell (814) 757-5440
- S. Gavin, Seneca (814) 676-8470

NEARBY AND SURROUNDING AREA FARRIERS:
- R. Knight, Tidioute (814) 484-3347
- D. Bentrem, Burgettstown (at times may also be available in Marienville area) (724) 947-3411, (412) 580-4458 cell
- P. Neill Jr., member PPFA, Sigel (814) 752-2989
- J. Bailey, Tionesta (814) 676-0135

5. The Allegheny River Tract
Clear Creek State Forest
(a.k.a. the "Kennerdell Trails" or "Dennison Run")
BOF-DCNR
(Bureau of Forestry/Department of Conservation & Natural Resources)

Lasting Impression: I loved the views! Kudos to the Bureau of Forestry. The Allegheny River Tract is beautiful, remote, and well marked especially at the intersections! A nice destination, particularly when the fall foliage is in full color.

Location: Clear Creek State Forest consists of over 13,000 acres and it spans Jefferson County (9,000+ acres), Venango County (3,100+ acres), and Forest County (1,000+ acres). The Allegheny River Tract is in Venango County.

Length: *Day Ride or Weekend Destination*- This chapter covers trails in the Venango County section of Clear Creek State Forest along the Allegheny River Tract. There are over 3,100 acres in Venango County with over 22 miles of designated multiple-use and equestrian trails, plus numerous miles of State Forest roads, pipeline connectors, and adjoining trails. Trails and roads in the State Forest are open to horseback riders unless specifically designated as closed.

Level of Difficulty: The designated trails that we rode were mostly moderate with some challenging sections due to rocks or steep trails.

Terrain: Most trails were of good terrain and consisted of dirt or grass surface. Horses should have shoes as some logging roads may have ballast. Avoid Bear Wallow Trail during wet conditions. Most trails were not rocky except in the higher elevation of the Blunder Trail.

Horse Camping: Yes

Non-horse Camping: Yes

Maps and Info: Bureau of Forestry, 158 South Second Ave., Clarion, PA 16214, (814) 226-1901 or contact the Department of Conservation & Natural Resources at www.dcnr.state.pa.us. Ask the office for the Allegheny River Tract map/brochure which has a listing of the various trails, their length, and difficulty.

Activities: Hiking, Biking, Horseback Riding Trails, Fishing, Boating, X-C Skiing, and Hunting

Fees for Trail Use: None

Permits for Day Trail Use: None

Permits/Fees Required for Overnight Camping: A permit is required for motorized overnight camping (no fee).

Comfort Station: None

DIRECTIONS:

To reach the Allegheny River Tract of Clear Creek State Forest parking and camping area, take I-80 to Exit #29 Route 8 north. Travel about 4.8 miles on Route 8, and watch for signs to Route 308 south. Get off at Route 308 south but head in the direction of Route 308 <u>north.</u> (We missed this first try; Route 308 actually ends here so you need to get off and travel the few hundred feet, in a northerly direction, to the end. In other words, if you are traveling north on Route 8, make a left at the end of the Route 308 ramp. If you are heading south on Route 8, make a right after getting off the Route 308 ramp.) Just after turning onto Route 308, the road splits. Take the right at the 'Y' and go to a stop sign. Make a right onto Old Route 8 north. Take Old Route 8 north for 2.2 miles and make a right onto Twin Oaks Road. (Note: after traveling .3 miles on Twin Oaks Road, you will come to a 'Y'; bear left and stay on Twin Oaks Road. Do not make a right onto Bullion Road.) Travel a total of 1.7 miles on Twin Oaks Road (a bit rough, but passable) to the intersection with Dennison Road. Make a right onto Dennison Road. Travel .2 miles on Dennison Road; you will see the Five Points lot which is the first gravel lot on the left. You can park there for day parking or for camping (with permit). There is another, smaller parking lot just down the road a short distance which is also on the left side (a good overflow lot). The Five Points lot is a big gravel lot (15+ horse trailers can fit, including several large living quarter types) with plenty of turn around and pull through room. At the lot is the brown, covered sign/billboard with a map of the trails (but do bring your own map as we did not see any stocked at the trailhead). There is a yellow gate marking the trailhead. The lot has a durable surface of gravel with a matt foundation. The lot is located directly next to Dennison Road which is mostly a gravel surface.

THE TRAILS:

The Allegheny River Tract map provided by the Clear Creek State Forest office is very helpful and provides detail as to the types of trails, boundaries, connecting pipelines, etc. Horses are permitted on all trails except hiking (only) trails such as the Ho Ya Neh, Goat, and mid portion of the River Trail. Equestrians should not ride on the nearby State Gamelands (unless permitted specifically by the State Gamelands). In the vicinity of the Allegheny River Tract, horses aren't permitted south of Dennison Run.

During our visit, we rode from the Five Points lot, traveled through the yellow gate and down the Pipeline Trail which is an easy, wide, dirt and gravel access road. This leads to other trails. Orange blazes mark the Bureau of Forestry's trails indicating they are maintained by the Bureau of Forestry. Follow the orange blazes; if you don't see them, retrace your steps and glance around. Sometimes the blaze is at the far end of a clearing. We rode the Stripmine Trail (nice, flat, easy) to the Fisherman Cove Trail (steeper but still very nice, moderate) to the River Trail (easy, just watch the pipes, gorgeous views). We then proceeded back via the Ho Ya Neh trail (we didn't know we were on this trail as the marker was down; later we learned this is not a horse trail). This trail makes a right up the hill by the river; there is a post which probably once held the signs. Avoid the Ho Ya Neh Trail since this trail is not designated for horses on the map. When we realized we should not have gone up that way, we then wondered how equestrians were to return back up the trail without backtracking. Without Ho Ya Neh there is nowhere to make a loop when you come out this trail. (We didn't find it to be extreme; it was just rougher than the other trails due to some rocky sections and steep grade. Local equestrians may want to contact the State Forest office to obtain permission to use that trail or find an alternate so as to complete a loop vs. backtrack.) We continued to the Bear Wallow Trail (avoid this as it is challenging due to very wet conditions) then to the Rock Oak Trail (a level logging road laid with fresh ballast at the time of our visit) and back to the Pipeline Trail (easy, level, logging or access road). One of the great things about riding the Allegheny River Tract in Clear Creek State Forest is that the intersections have signs. Plus, there are the orange blazes on the trees to guide you (which are needed as there are dozens of branches off the trails and it can be challenging to stay on course if it were not for the blazes). We were thrilled to see the excellent signs.

There had been an unusual amount of rain prior to our visit, but most trails had very good drainage. Only one trail, the Bear Wallow Trail, was extremely wet and would likely hold water after rainy periods. This was the only difficult trail that we encountered due to its wet pockets, plus many trees had fallen across the trail. However, we were able to go around the trees. The rest of the trail system was very well maintained. The downed trees that we encountered were probably temporary and likely recent due to extreme storms in the area. We also rode the Rock Oak Trail. We kidded that Rock Oak was rocks between oaks, but actually it was a recently laid ballast road and rough to ride. Once the ballast sinks in, it should be better. Most of the trails were not rocky. This area once had many oil wells and some remnants still remain. There is much history along these trails but one also needs to watch the occasional pipes along the trail. The only one that concerned us was an exposed broken pipe on the River Trail, just below Ho Ya Neh. It was located within close distance of an abandoned oil well (due to the nice views of the Allegheny River at this location it is easy to be distracted from watching your footing).

On our second day of riding, we left the lot along the Pipeline Trail (easy), made a left off of the Pipeline Trail to the Window Trail (gradual climb to a high area, gorgeous views but more suitable for advanced trail riders due to the elevation and single trail path that travels close to the edge of the overlook). If you don't like heights, the Window Trail may not be for you. However, what is nice about the Window Trail is that there is lots of land to the right of the path, farther inland, which you can ride and still enjoy the view. *Guess where I chose to ride!*

If you do ride the outer most ridge path, keep an eye out for spots where the trail can present a hazard such as eroded sections leaving a gap or weakness in the trail, roots to trip over, etc. I like hugging the inland side as there is more room for error if my horse spooks, plus I did not have to be as concerned with watching my footing, leaving more time to look around and enjoy the beauty along this trail. This portion of the trail was a wonderful surprise and I found it to be delightful and a "**don't miss**" section. Even though there are trees that block some of the view, you can still take in the scenery at several intervals. It must be even more awesome when the leaves are off the trees.

After the Window Trail, we made a left on the Ridge Trail. We hesitated, thinking by the name that it may be too steep or close to the edge. The beginning of the trail was very rocky, but it quickly changed to a much better surface. *Occasionally there will be clusters of rocks on the trail. Often when we encountered this, we could take an alternate path to the side. Watch for the hoof prints where others have bypassed the bad spots.* The Ridge Trail turned into a very nice inland trail of gradual slope. We then rode to the River Trail which also serves as a motorized access trail. It is of dirt and gravel and offers a leisurely ride along the Allegheny River with a view of the Kennerdell Bridge. There are many photo-ops along this trail and at other locations on the Allegheny River Tract so bring your camera. There is a gate by the bridge where we turned around as the trail for equestrians ends at this point. We backtracked and picked up the Blunder Trail. At first, we particularly loved this wide trail as it gradually climbs back up the mountain to the top, while providing a wonderful view of the valley below along with a cooling breeze coming down the path. This must have been an old mountain road at one time. But, unfortunately, this trail soon became extremely rugged and rocky due to years of erosion along its path. The rocks went on for quite a distance and we had to proceed very carefully. We then came to the top and followed the Pipeline Trail back to the lot.

There are underground pipeline right-of-ways that the trails pass which we also found very pleasant to ride. They often have mowed stretches making for nice riding. On the designated trails, we encountered trees that had fallen but had been recently cleared, so it appeared the trails were being maintained. There were a few places where smaller trees were lying on the trail, but they were easy to go over (may have been the reason for not removing them). We really enjoyed the beauty of these trails. Next trip, we would like to explore the trails north of where we rode as we were told there is more to ride.

EQUESTRIAN CAMPING:
Equestrians are permitted to camp at various locations within the Clear Creek State Forest, but a permit is required. All locations are in a primitive setting. The office recommended the Five Points Parking Lot (for the Allegheny River Tract) which is a roomy gravel lot with direct access to the trails. This location can

easily accommodate a group of equestrian campers. We didn't see any evidence of equestrian campers but this should make a good camping spot. There are plenty of trees in the woods to tie line to. It does adjoin a dirt/gravel road, but we didn't have a problem with that as the road is mostly quiet and the horses could be tied a safe distance from the road. However, we did note that one disadvantage to this locale is that the parking/camping area is used by other trail users and other vehicles may come and go. As a result, we would not leave any horses unattended if we camp there. On the weekend, there were several rigs (day riders) and vehicles in the lot. During the week, we had the lot and trails to ourselves.

HISTORICAL INFORMATION:
The Allegheny River Tract is located in the vicinity of the Oil Heritage Region. Early inhabitants were the Seneca Indians. One of their great chiefs, Chief Cornplanter, has become legendary; the Cornplanter State Forest and other areas carry his name to this day. This ideal locale offered river transportation which brought an influx of settlers to this area. Early inhabitants were of French origin. Other Europeans also made it their home. Unfortunately and sadly, the arrival of settlers also brought disease which spread throughout the Indian villages in this region, ultimately resulting in most of the native populations dying off.

Clear Creek State Forest derives its name from the clear river that runs through the Jefferson County portion of the State Forest. As with many of the areas in northwest Pennsylvania, in the mid to late 1800s until shortly after the turn of the 20th century, this area was cleared of timber. Lumber was transported by the waterways and railroads or used in iron furnaces after being converted into charcoal. One could imagine how much forest was stripped of its timber as the nearby Bullion Run Iron Furnace would use the timber of approximately one acre of forest per day to be burned for fuel to run its operations. Interestingly, the furnaces ceased operations in the summer months so its employees could tend to the area's farms.

In the late 1850s, the first lucrative oil well was dug in this area. This ignited the oil boom heyday in Pennsylvania and changed the landscape radically. Word spread far and wide as people flocked to this region; towns grew over night. Prosperity in the region resulted. But also contamination wreaked havoc on the landscape. Much of the area's surfaces had a deep blend of mud mixed with oil resulting in impassable roads. The environment was full of the sight and smell of oil. By the 1870s, production declined as the oil supply became depleted. Many residents moved on to new oil discoveries elsewhere. There is still evidence of this flourishing time in the beautiful, ornate architecture (see www.victorianregion.com), which can be enjoyed via an auto tour around the towns of this region. By the early 1900s, the state began acquiring parcels of land from the logging companies with the goal of restoring and preserving this region's natural beauty for future generations.

From the south to the north, many trails of different names connect and were once a continuous part of the same rail corridor. The Pennsylvania Railroad had run along this route connecting the cities of Pittsburgh and Buffalo. Today, there is the Allegheny River Tract (Kennerdell to Brandon), the Allegheny River Trail (Brandon to Franklin), and the Samuel Justus Recreation Trail (Franklin to Oil City). The trail in the section from Brandon to Oil City is paved with a dirt shoulder which horses can ride on. (We did not ride north of Brandon. If you decide to ride that section, prior to your visit, you may want to assess which sections are horse friendly especially in regard to any long bridges and tunnels along the path.) There is also the Sandy Creek Trail (Van and Belmar Village) where horses are not permitted as this trail travels through some extremely long tunnels and high, lengthy bridges. The Sandy Creek Trail connects to the Allegheny River Trail. There are also many adjoining branches which may be ridden. This whole area is a beautiful section of Pennsylvania and there are so many areas to explore.

COURTESIES:
Thank you to Matt Beaver, PA Department of Recreation, for putting me in contact with the right people. Matt, you are always so helpful and I remain grateful. Thank you to Bill Slippey, Gary Frank, and Joanna and Veronica at the State Forest office for patiently answering all my questions and providing many useful materials. Amy Culp of the Franklin Chamber of Commerce was also very supportive and provided much information on this region. And thank you to everyone who helped make these trails available for equestrians to enjoy; this is a great destination, one I am very excited to add to my list of favorite places.

When we came to the intersection with Bullion Road, we were unsure as to how to find the trailhead and pulled over for a moment. (We didn't want to head down the wrong road with a large trailer in tow. We learned our lesson from one time when we had to back all the way down a mountain because a road just continued to narrow with nowhere to turn a trailer around.) Out of nowhere came our trail guardian angel "Ken" who saw the "Ride Pennsylvania Horse Trails" signs on our truck, took the initiative to walk up to us to tell us how to proceed to the parking area, and enthusiastically shared information regarding how nice the trails are. We then knew we were on the right track both on the road and with our choice of riding destinations. Thank you Ken for your kind help; your timing was perfect!

THINGS WE LEARNED THIS RIDE:
I learned not to pack all the food and drink in one horn bag and I learned to secure the horn bag with a backup leather string so as not to lose it. On a nice,

straight stretch on the trail, John and I were playing with our horses to see who had the faster trot, and who had the faster canter. Sometime during this, my horn bag popped off. How that bag full of drinks, snacks, and a tape recorder (it's much easier than writing all this while riding) came off without my knowing or hearing it still baffles me. Well, we learned to keep a backup snack or two along with extra water in our saddlebags as we got hungry out on trail about lunch time.

NEARBY:
- Oil Heritage Region Tourist Promotion Agency, Oil City (814) 677-3152 Ext. 18, (800) 483-6264, website: www.oilregiontourist.com
- Drake Well Museum, Titusville (814) 827-2797
- Oil Creek and Titusville Railroad (tour rides), Titusville (814) 676-1733
- Venango County Historical Society, Franklin (814) 437-2275
- Franklin Chamber of Commerce, Franklin (814) 432-5823

NEARBY AND SURROUNDING AREA STABLES:
- Knapping Knapp Farm (guided horseback trail rides, Country B&B, overnight stabling), Titusville (814) 827-1092, email: Knapping@csonline.net

NEARBY AND SURROUNDING AREA VET SERVICES:
- S. Gavin, Seneca (814) 676-8470
- Dr. Turner, Marley Veterinary Clinic, Titusville (814) 827-1778

NEARBY AND SURROUNDING AREA FARRIERS:
- D. Myers, Hermitage (412) 347-5903 or 0362
- R. Wright, Greenville (724) 475-4644, (724) 699-4831
- J. Bailey, Tionesta (814) 676-0135

6. Two Mile Run County Park
Venango County Park

Lasting Impression: After hearing much about the tornado type activity and subsequent bad weather that had befallen this park and western Pennsylvania over a period of two years, we expected to find trails that would be challenging to ride. Instead, we found a gorgeous, well maintained park, with numerous wonderful stretches of enjoyable trails in very good condition.

Location: Two Mile Run County Park is located in northwest Pennsylvania between Franklin and Titusville in Venango County.

Length: *Day Ride Destination (weekend destination if horse camping is established)*- Two Mile Run County Park is roughly 2,700 acres. There are hours of leisurely riding available at this park. Prior to the micro burst and heavy rains, the trail mileage was estimated to be about 26+ miles of equestrian and multiple-use trails, plus adjoining trails. At the time of our visit a few southern sections below the lake were closed due to storm damage; however, we found plenty of riding in the northern portion of the park and the construction of new trails.

Level of Difficulty: Easy to moderate

Terrain: Most of the terrain we rode was either grass or dirt surface and consisted of leisurely single tracts, double tracts, logging roads, gas well access roads, and old forest roads through woodlands along rolling terrain. Except for one section (see below), the trails weren't rocky. Logging operations may put temporary obstacles along or near the trail path.

Horse Camping: Horse camping was not permitted at the time of our visit. Subsequent to our visit, I checked with the park management and they said they do plan to research the effect and feasibility of equestrian camping in the near future.

Non-horse Camping: Yes

Carriage Potential: Watch for carriage potential at this park as it redefines and expands its trails. The Orange Trail already has nice, double width tracts, dirt access roads, and logging roads. Contact the office for more information.

Maps and Info: Two Mile Run County Park, 471 Beach Road, Franklin, PA 16323, (814) 676-6116, website: www.twomile.org. A new map is supposed to be in the works. If not yet available, ask for both the beige pamphlet and the black and white map with the equestrian trail highlighted. The copy that I received reflected the bridle trail manually highlighted in one color, the road system in another, and the hiking in its own color. This helped us find our way through the park as you will likely need a map to orient yourself. Since the trails are in the process of being restructured, designated uses will likely change.

Activities: Hiking, Biking, Horseback Riding Trails, Camping, Cottage Rentals, Picnicking, Swimming, Fishing, Boating, Canoe and Rowboat Rentals, X-C Skiing, and more. Exercise caution during hunting seasons.
Fees for Trail Use: None
Permits for Day Trail Use: None
Comfort Station: Yes, near the picnic areas

DIRECTIONS:

Two Mile Run County Park can be approached from several directions via Route 417 north of the city of Franklin. We traveled from I-80 to Route 66 and Route 322. To use this approach, take I-80 to Exit #60 Route 66 north to Route 322 west. Take Route 322 west for 26 miles to the north end of the town of Franklin. Just after the second bridge crossing, pick up Route 417 north. (Depending on where you are traveling from, a more direct approach may be to take I-80 to Exit #29 Route 8 north to Franklin. Many roads merge in Franklin; watch for signs to Route 417 north, and proceed as follows.) Take Route 417 north from Franklin for 6.5 miles and you will see a small Two Mile Run County Park sign on the right. Make a right onto Baker Road. Travel 1 mile on Baker Road and come to a stop sign. Make a left at the stop sign; you are now on Cherry Tree Road. Proceed about .5 miles and make a right onto Beach Road. Immediately after, make a left into the open grass field called Pioneer Flats. There is a sign at the entrance, along with plenty of room for parking numerous rigs (20+) including large living quarter types. Minimal if any backing is necessary. Watch for low lying or soft areas; there looked like there could be some at a few spots. *Please keep us welcome by maintaining plenty of distance from the picnic grounds. We are hoping the upper area, just above Pioneer Flats, is opened to equestrians. You can see it from the lot or access it by continuing down Beach Road and looking for the turn to the left. Although Pioneer Flats has room for many rigs and is a quality parking area, the above area is more secluded and would direct equestrians away from the picnic area. Plus the ground is even better on higher ground and this locale has direct access to some of the trails without riding the main park roads. The lower grounds at Pioneer Flats could be used for overflow.*

THE TRAILS:

At the time of our visit, there were two different types of maps for the park. One is on the back of the beige flyer which provides general information about the park. We did not find this one sufficiently detailed to follow the trails. There is another map that was sent to us which is just a black and white copy of the park. This map was highlighted for us as to where the main equestrian trails were. Over a year's time, we received two different highlighted versions of this same map. One reflected the equestrian Orange Trail highlighted in a complete circle around the park. This reflected the original trail system prior to the onset of storm damage. The second map reflected a much shorter trail system, basically just the trails in the northern section of the park. *Based on this, we weren't sure how much trail was left and whether there was still sufficient riding. We were glad we decided to check the trails out. We found there was plenty of riding available and on good trails. This park is already a gem, plus it has even more potential as additional trails are being added.* Neither map is sufficiently detailed. A trail map is needed but it may be a while before a new map is made since the trail usage is being redefined and new trails are being established. However, the black and white map is still useful for getting a feel for the lay of the land and for a general sense of direction; we were able to get to where we needed to go with the use of it.

As indicated, the trail used to be a large loop around the outlying areas of the park, and is indicated by orange blazes. A significant portion of the multiple-use and equestrian trail system in the southern portions of the park was recently closed due to two years of extreme weather conditions. This may be re-opened or different trails may be established of more solid terrain. However, the trails in the northern section of the park were open to multiple-use and equestrians during our visit. Equestrians are directed to the outer most loop of the trails. The trails are not well marked so it can be tricky, but not difficult, to link to the outer loop or the Orange Trail. There are blazes on the trees which are very helpful; once you see orange blazes you will know you have reached the outer trail. There are numerous, suitable and excellent trails on the outskirts of the park. Once you link up with them you will not want to depart from them. There are also many places to water your horse along the way. The network of trails is gorgeous and makes for a nice ride. We had delayed our visit to allow the trails time to recover from the extensive rains they had suffered and were told some areas had still not recovered. We expected the worst. Reflecting some of the extent of damage, we did see many locations where trees had been cleared off of the trail and the work had already been done. However, what amazed us is that we found the outer trails of the middle to northern section to be in superb shape and of tough surface. These were ideal for horses and would appear to hold up well even under extreme circumstances. We concluded the park had done a fabulous job of clearing downed trees and other obstacles. Much of these trails had groomed paths when they connected through the fields and woods. I was thrilled at the quality of these trails.

We began our ride following the highlighted map provided to us using the path suggested to link with the outer most "Orange Trail." We took Beach Road, made a left on Cherry Tree Road (paved), traveled along Cherry Tree Road, and made a right onto a single tract trail marked by a yellow blaze. The trail is just before where Cherry Tree Road meets with Baker Road. *On the holiday weekend when we visited, Cherry Tree Road was an active road. There is some shoulder but not much. It is a short stretch but we would prefer to see a trail link put in to reach it. As we rode, we saw there was an ideal locale and terrain just to the left of the Cherry Tree Road which wouldn't take much to clear a path. We will suggest this to the park office as this would be a much safer alternative than riding the road.* After making a right onto the trail, it took some looking to see where the trail continued due to recent logging operations (likely a clean up of storm damage). However, we followed the blazes and very quickly were back on the trail. This section has some significant rock clusters for a short distance. We took our time and allowed the horses to pick their way through. About the time I was deciding if I wanted to discontinue riding this trail due to rocks, the trail quickly improved and became very nice to ride. *That section had the only rocky patches that we encountered. We did find it passable with care and in the overall picture did not consider it an issue. Horses should have shoes if you choose this link.* We followed the single path, crossed a dirt logging or access road, came to another dirt road, and made a right. We passed an old bridle trail sign. We came to a gas well and continued straight, bearing slightly to the left. This section was particularly inviting as the path was a nice, wide single tract (about the width of a four wheeler) of mowed grass through the woods and connecting fields. We came across a sign that said "White Tail Trail" and an open field. We followed the mowed path; we were glad it was mowed as it would have been hard or impossible to tell where to proceed in the high grass. As you travel, step carefully around the drainage pipes which can have sharp ends. We crossed a paved road and traveled straight and connected with a dirt road. We then encountered a trail to the right which had a few markings, including a blue blaze. We thought we were supposed to turn (later we came across it from the opposite direction, and realized the Orange Trail did continue past this point and we didn't need to turn off). This is where the detailed maps or signs will come in handy. The section we entered had two long bridges which were too springy for horse crossing. One was easy to bypass; the other required crossing a short distance of deep mud to avoid it. I tested the second bridge on foot and then guided my horse across. These bridges were of sturdy material but needed additional supports, such as telephone poles, to be able to support weight. Seek alternatives rather than crossing any bridges of a long span, or any length, that may be questionable. Also, such bridges may be an indication that you have wandered off the equestrian trail and onto a trail more suited to foot or bike traffic. We returned back to the parking area and traveled in the direction of the lake.

We did not approach the area immediately surrounding the lake or the southern area since we had been told that some areas were still being repaired. We instead followed a trail which was on the east side of the lake and near Beach Road. There were new ribbon markers along with newly cleared paths. This stretch traveled along Beach Road, not on the road, but a high, dry, durable, wooded path that paralleled the road on both sides. This was a very nice path, ideal for horses. We made a left and picked up an access (dirt) road connector. We wanted to return to the Orange Trail in the eastern section of the park so we headed in that direction. We reached the Orange Trail and then proceeded north. There were numerous old forest roads, farm roads, logging roads, single and double tracts in all directions. This was **our favorite section**. The trails were great! Ultimately we found a single tract path which led directly into the back of the parking area by the upper area of the Pioneer Flats. This avoided all paved road riding and was ideal in that you could connect directly with the parking area. There were two or three small ravines. These were not difficult but, if there was a high level of equestrian activity, they would be sensitive to heavy use. A short bridge to cross these ravines and some scattering of stone dust in a few places would quickly resolve this and make this an ideal alternate or spur, allowing riders to avoid road riding.

Note: the above was written based on our understanding of what we were told of the lay of the trails, and related blazes implied during the planning stages for our visit. Subsequently, I rechecked with the office for clarification regarding the significance of the blazes, mainly the yellow and blue, because I wasn't sure to what extent equestrians were permitted on these. I know some of them were quite suitable and others were needed to link with the outermost Orange Trail. I could logically conclude to avoid any trails immediately surrounding the lake or of sensitive terrain, but was unsure about the outer areas of the park or some trails that followed along side roads and already served as multiple-use. The office indicated that, due to the trail system being in the process of total redefinition and redesign, the blazes at the time of our discussion did not have exact significance. They recommend equestrians contact the office at the time of their visit and inquire as to the latest structure of the trails. *Equestrians, please note: while equestrian usage is under review, this would be an excellent time to get involved, volunteer, and provide your input to positively influence the outcome!*

HISTORICAL INFORMATION:
There is much history to this region which was first extensively settled and developed during the oil boom period of the 1800s. More information, including a detail of the history of the surrounding area, is provided in the Clear Creek State Forest Chapter. Two Mile Run County Park, itself, is a result of the hard work of many individuals, groups, and organizations including the County Commissioners, Planning Committees, County employees and representatives, other elected officials, and volunteers who worked tirelessly to establish this park. This was not an easy endeavor but rather a complex process. Written from the perspective of a county participant in the early, decisive days of the park formation, visit www.twomile.org/history for the details, obstacles, influencing personalities, contributors, and political dynamics of how the park came to be. Various significant funding projects also contributed to this successful outcome including the Federal Open Space and Project 70 undertaking. Much of the foundation of this park project was assembled and completed in the 1960s and 1970s.

The typical oil towns in northwest Pennsylvania contain an array of interesting historic architecture dating from the heyday of oil and lumber in this region. Many of these homes are very well preserved. Also typical of the time is a town park situated at a central location. One place to view these homes is the town of Warren where there are many blocks of these remarkable homes.

In July of 2003, a micro burst (which is just short of a tornado) descended on the park and devastated much of the trail system, leaving fallen trees in its path. One section lost 15 acres of trees. The park managers had their work cut out for them. Throughout 2003 and 2004, heavy rains also pounded the terrain. Knowing all that had occurred we postponed our visit to this destination until the end of our research to allow recovery time. Fortunately, and thanks to the folks who did the maintenance to restore it to its former beauty, a significant portion is again in fine shape and they are working on completing the remainder.

Two Mile County Park is unique from the other destinations that we have visited in that the management of the park is outsourced to an outside organization. We found this interesting as this was the first we heard of this type of arrangement within a park system.

COURTESIES:
Thank you to the many devoted groups, individuals, and the early county and planning individuals whose unrelenting dedication resulted in this wonderful park. Its planners had many challenges and complicating factors including compliance with various sources of funding and related shortfalls, land negotiations, utility right-of-ways, land acquisitions, mineral rights considerations, and even condemnations. All these had to be overcome with perseverance, creative thinking, and team work in order for the park to finally become a reality and the beautiful destination you see today.

A personal thank you to Dave Pieper who shared his enthusiasm about these trails; this motivated us to put them on our list of trails to cover for this book. Until recently, Dave operated the riding stable (rentals) at Two Mile Run County Park. As well, I would like to express my utmost appreciation to Judy Downs, Beverly Hart, and Jeremy Phillips in the Two Mile Run County Park office. My many calls and inquiries were always received and responded to patiently, pleasantly, and professionally. Thank you for remembering equestrians and allowing visitors to enjoy Two Mile Run County Park on horseback!

THINGS WE LEARNED THIS RIDE:
- I learned that the oil industry actually started in Pennsylvania, not out west in Texas or elsewhere.
- From the park documentation, I learned that trees may be more inclined to fall after a region is hit with a powerful storm such as a micro burst or

tornado. I tended to think when the storm left, so did the danger. However, trees can still fall well after a storm has passed. If winds pick up, weakened areas can remain dangerous. Besides time for clean up, this factor contributed to why some of the trails needed to be closed for extended periods until damage was assessed and the area stabilized.

NEARBY:

- Oil Heritage Region Tourist Promotion Agency, Inc. (800) 483-6264, website: www.oilregion.org

NEARBY OR SURROUNDING AREA STABLES:

- Knapping Knapp Farm (guided horseback trail rides, Country B&B, overnight stabling), Titusville (814) 827-1092, email: Knapping@csonline.net
- Hickory Creek Wilderness Ranch (guided trail rides, equestrian camping, camping with hookups or primitive, stall rentals, cabin rentals, summer youth camp, rodeo events), Tidioute (814) 484-7520, website: www.hickorycreekranch.com
- Flying W Ranch (guided trail rides, rodeos, equestrian camping, stall rentals, cabin rentals, camping with hookups or primitive), Kellettville (814) 463-7663, website: www.theflyingwranch.com

NEARBY AND SURROUNDING AREA VET SERVICES:

- S. Gavin, Seneca (814) 676-8470
- Dr. Turner, Marley Veterinary Clinic, Titusville (814) 827-1778
- P. Farrell, Russell Veterinary Clinic (need to trailer to), Russell (814) 757-5440

NEARBY AND SURROUNDING AREA FARRIERS:

- Steve Wilson, Sugar Grove (814) 489-3051
- R. Wright, Greenville (724) 475-4644, (724) 699-4831
- J. Bailey, Tionesta (814) 676-0135

7. Tidioute &
The Hickory Creek Wilderness Region
The Allegheny National Forest (ANF)
U.S. Forest Service

Lasting Impression: Upon our first visit, we knew we would return in the near future. There are wonderful, easy trails through forest land with a convenient, nearby equestrian campground (commercial) located with direct access to the trails. Kick back and relax at this one.

Location: These trails are located in the western section of the Allegheny National Forest near Tidioute and link with the Hickory Creek Wilderness area in Warren County.

Length: *Day Ride or Long Weekend Destination (or stay for a week and visit other nearby ANF destinations)*- The Allegheny National Forest is huge and permits horseback riding on hundreds of miles of trails. Plus the bordering Hickory Creek Wilderness consists of almost 8,700 acres. Horses and pack animals are permitted in the Hickory Creek Wilderness but they are not allowed on the hiking (only) trails such as the Hickory Creek Trail which is marked with pale yellow blazes. We did not find any exact estimate of trail miles in this region but there are many hours and days of exploring on horseback.

Level of Difficulty: The trails we rode were easy to moderate.

Terrain: Very good trails, maintained, grass or dirt surface, little if any rocks, gradual climbs, outlying areas may vary

Horse Camping: The Allegheny National Forest permits dispersed camping on a first come, first served basis. There is no permit or fee for "dispersed camping." We visited some of the recommended sites that are located throughout the ANF. A few were not suitable to large equestrian rigs, a few were spacious but were already full with non-equestrian campers occupying the sites, and one, Kelly Pines, was excellent for equestrians (see the Kelly Pines chapter). In this sector of the ANF, we decided to stay at a nearby privately owned facility (open to the public), the Hickory Creek Wilderness Ranch, to be assured a reserved site. The Hickory Creek Wilderness Ranch offers both horse camping and non-horse camping.

Non-horse Camping: Yes

Carriage Potential: There are many dirt roads and double width paths (may be gated) in the area which may be suitable for carriage driving. Check with the ANF to discuss carriage driving within the ANF.

Maps and Info: Information, topographic maps (nominal fee), and Allegheny National Forest (ANF) maps are available at the following ANF offices: ANF Headquarters in Warren (814) 723-5150; Marienville Ranger Station in

Marienville (814) 927-6628; and the Bradford Ranger Station in Bradford (814) 362-4613. You can also write to Allegheny National Forest, P.O. Box 847, Warren, PA 16365 or via their website: www.fs.fed.us/r9/forests/allegheny. Ask for the large ANF Region map which depicts the snowmobile paths in the Allegheny National Forest. This is very helpful for exploring this area as equestrians share many of the snowmobile trails. To contact the Hickory Creek Wilderness Ranch in Tidioute, call (814) 484-7520 or write to Hickory Creek Wilderness Ranch, P.O. Box 93, Tidioute, PA 16351, or visit website: www.hickorycreekranch.com, email: info@hickorycreekranch.com.
Activities: Hiking, Biking, Horseback Riding Trails, Picnicking, Snowmobiling, and Hunting (in certain areas)
Fees for Trail Use: None
Permits for Day Trail Use: None
Permits/Fees Required for Overnight Camping: Neither are required within the ANF. There is a fee at the nearby commercial camping facility.
Comfort Station: No, but there are facilities at the nearby commercial campground.

DIRECTIONS:
To reach the Tidioute and Hickory Creek Wilderness region of the Allegheny National Forest, including the Hickory Creek Wilderness Ranch, proceed as follows: From the south or southeast: take I-80 to Exit 60 which is Route 66 north. Take Route 66 north for about 15 miles and look for Route 36. Take Route 36 north for 13.8 miles into Tionesta. Route 36 merges with Route 62. Take Route 62 to Tidioute for approximately 14 miles. Just before the bridge (which is on the left) in Tidioute, make a right onto Route 337/SR 3005. (From the west you can take I-80 directly to Route 62; from the north access via Route 62 and turn onto Route 337/SR 3005, continuing as indicated below.) Follow the Hickory Creek Wilderness Ranch signs which will bring you to both the ranch and the heart of many of the trails. There is a pretty steep uphill climb after making the right on SR 3005. Travel about 4 miles on SR 3005 and look for the entrance to the campground on Economite Road on the right. You can continue straight to reach the trails but finding sufficient room to pull off with a horse trailer can be challenging. Instead, for day parking, you may want to contact the campground to see if they can accommodate you. There may be a nominal fee but they have a nice location, and a big field opposite the rodeo grounds that has plenty of room for large rigs, and has direct access to the trails (head in the direction to the top of the field opposite the rodeo grounds). To reach the camping area, pass the rodeo entrance, and take the second entrance to the right and through the arch. This is a tight turn so prepare to swing wide. We took our large rig with living quarters and were able to get the rig in without a problem, but it is tight. There is quite a climb, although a short one, up to the campground. As there is only width sufficient for one vehicle at a time, you will want to make sure the path is clear before proceeding. Once at the top of the hill, just follow

the road to the camping sites. There are sites with hookups along the road in wooded settings and also in the lower field. There is additional primitive camping in the outlying areas.

The trails can be accessed by various surrounding roads by hauling via Route 337/SR 3005 to SR 3018 and making a right toward the forest and wilderness area, or directly out of camp from a few locations. Within the camp there are orange markers and poles below the open back field leading both to the snowmobile trails and non-motorized trails. (To reach this field, pass the pool and stables on the main camp road. Make a left and head down to the open field.) Trails can also be accessed via the fields opposite the rodeo grounds. You will need to ride in the direction away from the rodeo grounds, up the open field hillside to the edge of the woods. Look for the trail of hoof prints leading into the forested area.

THE TRAILS: We were not familiar with this campground as it was still relatively new, and we had not heard much about these trails. We were pleasantly surprised on both accounts. Both this section of the Allegheny National Forest and this campground are likely to be very popular destinations as word gets out.

The trails were a pleasure. We did not get as much riding in as we had liked due to some bad weather; but of what we rode, about 8 hours, we very much enjoyed them. The trails vary from wide, grassy paths to old logging or woodland roads, to dirt trails crisscrossing through the woods. There are many loops that can keep you going in circles. We did not find it difficult to find our way back but we did find it helpful to drive the parameters the evening before. Since maps weren't available at the campground and there were no distance or distinguishing markers, it helped to know the lay of the roads to have as a point of reference. We have been doing this on many of the western Pennsylvania trails due to there being minimal markers. Also, there are topographic maps for this region which can be purchased from the ANF office for a nominal fee. These provide additional information on this area and can be helpful in locating areas to ride and explore.

We rode out from camp from the back of the open field following the orange markers and poles. The trail forks and we followed the snowmobile marker to the left which leads to an intersection with many signs, including a number 5 marker. We used this as our central point of reference. From there we continued straight through the woods and hooked up with various trails marked by gates. The trails behind these gates were wide grass stretches and well maintained. The second day we did not make a left at the snowmobile sign but instead rode to the right (where it said no snowmobiles). This too was an excellent trail that traveled through thick forests full of deer and other wildlife. There were many clusters of mature pine forests that smelled heavenly as you passed by. We very much enjoyed this ride but were turned around due to a bad thunder storm. We took a shortcut back to camp and later resumed our ride when the weather improved. However, this time we headed out from the field opposite the rodeo grounds. This offered some leisurely woodland riding which eventually linked in with the grass loops and gated areas that are near State Route 3018, and ultimately return back to intersection #5. Throughout, the terrain remained very gradual, easy, and relaxing. Where there was variation, switchbacks were created to help avoid erosion. At the time of our visit, these trails were still relatively new and not overly used. Even with the recent rain, the trail terrain held up to the traffic. Of course there are a few spots where they were muddy but, due to the gentle grade of much of the trails, those spots looked easy to reroute. One of the things that impressed us the most was that these trails were well kept. The numerous wide grass stretches were mowed, overhead brush was cleared, and downed trees were removed from the trail.

EQUESTRIAN CAMPING:
When we visited these trails, we stayed at Hickory Creek Wilderness Ranch. We found this to be a top quality facility for both the design of the camping area and the trails that adjoin, and it was obvious that much time and thought was invested in making this campground a wonderful equestrian camping destination with excellent accommodations and trails for horse campers. The owner's devotion, perseverance, and hard work in putting together this campground in this choice location are evident as soon as you arrive and soak in your surroundings.

This campground is in a great setting. There are both wooded sites, and sites in a large, open field which are ideal for group camping. Many sections of the field had clusters of trees offering shade in the hot weather. Electric and water hookups are available at many of the wooded and field sites. Primitive camping is also available. This campground is large with plenty of room for large rigs and many visitors. Although, you may want to time your arrival and departure for off-peak hours of the day as all visitors enter and exit through the same road, which is about a one and a half lane width. The main road does have a large area (past the stables) to turn around. There is a water spigot at the horse barn, and a trailer with a large container of water was brought to the outlying primitive area for the convenience of the campers at some of the back sites. There are also showers and toilets by the front entrance, and chemical toilets placed in the rear camping area. During our visit there was some construction underway and some sites were not leveled yet, but it was great that all these improvements were being made, and we look forward to seeing this progress. We picked a site situated in the wooded section just before the newly constructed stables. (Equestrians have a choice of tie lining their horses or keeping them in the stable of 10' x 10' stalls.)

The campground is also scenic, from the large, open fields by the rodeo entrance to the great view at the top of the main entrance near the pool area. There is no need to ride main roads to access the trails; the trails lead directly out from camp. There is some forest (dirt) road riding but these roads we found to be quiet and actually quite pleasurable to ride. (Due to an onset of a sudden series of thunder storms, we rode one of these for a shortcut back to camp, and we encountered only two vehicles which traveled slowly due to the dirt and gravel terrain. There was sufficient shoulder to pass.) The nice trails and campground made for a relaxing weekend and we are looking forward to returning in the near future.

HISTORICAL INFORMATION:
This area was settled in the early 19th century. Early pioneers cut the trees to build homes and barns. Once cleared, some of the area was converted to farmland. By the mid 1800s, large scale lumbering operations took hold. About this same time, the bark of hemlock began to be used to cure leather, and tanning became a thriving industry. By the end of the 1800s, lumber increased in demand to meet a variety of uses including building materials for growing cities and industry. The progression of railroads which could climb steep, mountainous terrain and transport lumber facilitated this demand. Other industries such as wood alcohol and coal utilized most every type of wood and its by-products, resulting in this region being fully stripped of timber. Once the land was no longer productive, it was often deserted. By the early 1900s, seeing what was happening to the forests in the east, the federal government interceded. Recognizing the need to preserve land and re-establish forests, it acquired this land and began a process of reforestation. In the 1920s, the federal government established the Allegheny National Forest with the goal of restoration and preservation for future generations to enjoy.

Within the Allegheny National Forest is the Hickory Creek Wilderness. This select locale was determined by Congress to be a "Wilderness Area" with the goal of preserving this section so that it remains in its natural state, unspoiled, and unaffected by mankind. As a result, motorized equipment or vehicles cannot be used within its borders.

COURTESIES:
I would like to thank Don Clymer, who I was told does the trail maintenance at Hickory Creek and other areas of the Allegheny National Forest. We were amazed how quickly the storm damage was repaired in the Hickory Creek Wilderness area and how nice the trails are maintained. Also, thank you to the folks at Hickory Creek Wilderness Ranch for putting such a nice campground together; we really enjoyed our stay.

NEARBY AND SURROUNDING AREA EQUESTRIAN CAMPING AND OTHER:
- Hickory Creek Wilderness Ranch (guided trail rides, equestrian camping, camping with hookups or primitive, stall rentals, cabin rentals, summer

youth camp, rodeo events), Tidioute (814) 484-7520, website: www.hickorycreekranch.com
- If you would like to visit other sections of the Allegheny National Forest or surrounding areas, there are many additional areas to ride in this region. See the map in the front section of this book for nearby trail systems.
- Y-Bar-U Saddle Club, RR 1, Box 1384, Russell, PA 16345. Y-Bar-U Saddle Club offers organized group trail rides that tour the west side of the Kinzua Dam and Reservoir. I have ridden with this fun group and they cover some scenic areas with beautiful vistas. For more information and membership, contact the club at the above address.

NEARBY AND SURROUNDING AREA VET SERVICES:
- Dr. Turner, Marley Veterinary Clinic, Titusville (814) 827-1778
- P. Farrell, Russell Veterinary Clinic (need to trailer to), Russell (814) 757-5440
- S. Gavin, Seneca (814) 676-8470

NEARBY AND SURROUNDING AREA FARRIERS:
- Steve Wilson, Sugar Grove (814) 489-3051
- R. Knight, Tidioute (814) 484-3347
- P. Neill Jr., member PPFA, Sigel (814) 752 2989
- J. Bailey, Tionesta (814) 676-0135

8. Kellettville Region
Allegheny National Forest
U.S. Forest Service

Lasting Impression: There are many interesting areas to explore in this rural region of wide open spaces and mountainous country that surround the scenic Tionesta River.

Location: This chapter visits the trails in the Allegheny National Forest (ANF) region near Kellettville in Forest County in northwestern Pennsylvania.

Length: *Day Ride or Weekend Destination*- Exact trail miles are not available but you can come for a weekend or longer and ride many different trails.

Level of Difficulty: Moderate to difficult

Terrain: This is mountainous country with many climbs and descents, and the terrain is diverse in both surface and grade. Some surfaces are of a good, tough texture, not rocky, and are leisurely to ride. As elsewhere in this region, the trails can vary quickly from moderate to difficult. Some can be challenging due to steepness, rocks, erosion, or mud. The surrounding area has some very nice trails, but you need to know how and where to find them as there are no detailed equestrian trail maps, and minimal if any markers to provide guidance. Available from the ANF office, for a nominal fee, are maps which provide additional information and reflect old railroad grades, dirt roads, etc. These are helpful for navigation and are recommended. However, they do not provide specifics as to level of difficulty, terrain conditions, accessibility, or recommended routes as there are no "designated trails." The snowmobile trails are a good bet as they are usually nicely maintained, easy to moderate in terrain, and have periodic markers. We have some favorite sections and describe them below to help introduce you to the area.

Horse Camping: The ANF permits dispersed camping. Some equestrians prefer to scout out camping or day parking locations on ANF land for access to the trails. Subsequent to our visit, we were told by a few equestrians that they like to camp on Forest Road #159 which is off of Route 666. Forest Road #159 is reflected on the Allegheny National Forest Region map (to obtain, see below). As with other locations within the ANF, sites are first come, first served. Maps can be obtained by calling the offices below. Check the locations in advance to determine if they are suitable to your rig size. Since we were traveling a distance, wanted to be assured a camping locale, and also enjoy the amenities, we made reservations at the Flying W Ranch, a privately owned facility open to the public.

Non-horse Camping: Yes

Maps and Info: Information, topographic maps (fee), and ANF maps are available at the following ANF offices: ANF Headquarters in Warren (814) 723-

5150; Marienville Ranger Station in Marienville (814) 927-6628; and the Bradford Ranger Station in Bradford (814) 362-4613. For information, you can write the Allegheny National Forest office at P.O. Box 847, Warren, PA 16365 or visit their website: www.fs.fed.us/r9/forests/allegheny. Ask for the large Allegheny National Forest Region map which depicts the snowmobile paths in the ANF region. (There are two region maps; this is the map with the Allegheny Region Recreation Table.) This is helpful for exploring this area as equestrians share many of the snowmobile trails and they are clearly reflected on the map. These maps are good for following the snowmobile trails but do not reflect all of the other trail detail or information in the area. Snowmobile maps can be obtained in the winter (and sometimes off season) at the Whig Hill General Store just off of Route 666, or you can contact the local snowmobile groups at (814) 463-5019. The snowmobile groups have contributed much to the establishment and maintenance of nice trails in this area. Nearby camping is available at the Flying W Ranch (814) 463-7663; information can also be obtained via their website: www.theflyingwranch.com.

Activities: Horseback Riding Trails, Hiking, Biking, and Snowmobiling. Exercise caution during hunting season as areas may permit hunting.

Fees for Trail Use: None

Permits/Fees Required for Overnight Camping: Neither are required within the ANF. There is a fee for camping at the nearby commercial campground.

Comfort Station: No, but there are facilities and hookups at the nearby commercial campground.

DIRECTIONS:
There a few ways to get there. We took I-80 to Exit #60 Route 66 north toward Shippenville. Take 66 north for 15 miles to the light at Route 36. Make a left onto Route 36 north. Follow signs for Route 36 north for 13.8 miles to Tionesta. In Tionesta continue straight and pick up Route 62 north. (If traveling from the west, you can also take I-80 to Route 62 north to reach this point.) Take Route 62 north from Tionesta for 7 miles; make a right onto Route 666 (there is a sign for the Flying W Ranch). *Note: at the turn onto Route 666, the road immediately splits. Bear left and stay on Route 666. Travel 7.6 miles and you will see the Flying W Ranch on the right. If your destination is the ranch, be careful not to make a right by the first set of signs which look like the turn, instead pass the Whig Hill General Store and take the paved road to the right by the pale blue Flying W sign. Follow the road to a large open area. The road passes through the center of the ranch.* The ANF trails covered in this chapter will be described from this point as the Flying W Ranch is central to the trails described.

THE TRAILS:
This area has much undeveloped land with forests, dirt roads, streams, and open fields. Many sections permit riding. This is an area where it is hard to tell which is private land and which is land that is open to the public. As we have found in

many locations in this part of Pennsylvania, you are more or less on your own to sort out where to ride and what to ride. One can leave with many different impressions as the trails are diverse and, like so many other places, it depends on which trail you ride and recent weather conditions. Basically, the trails that we enjoy riding are at two different locations. One is the loop of snowmobile trails which can be accessed off of Route 666, just west of Whig Hill and are indicated by markers number 2 and 21 on the snowmobile map. We accessed these by riding out of the Flying W Ranch entrance road, made a left on Route 666 (there is lots of shoulder; however, proceed with caution as this road does have traffic), passed the Whig Hill General Store and picked up the snowmobile trail to the right. The trail is not hard to find and is marked, but it is helpful to observe it first while driving past it. (In fact we recommend driving the area first, without a trailer, to get your bearings especially in the vicinity of Tionesta Creek.) If you have trouble locating the snowmobile trails, you can contact the host snowmobile house at the below number. Make sure you obtain the "Allegheny National Forest Region" snowmobile map before heading out on these trails as it is helpful because it reflects the trail numbers which correspond to those you see on the snowmobile paths, along with information on the connector routes and dead ends (sometimes the trails are interrupted due to private property and can be confusing). The nice thing about the snowmobile trails is that we found them well groomed, marked at intervals, and easy to ride. You can spend several pleasant hours (or days if extending into adjoining regions of the ANF) exploring these snowmobile trails which travel in a rural setting.

We have visited this locale on numerous occasions. Our other preferred section to ride is on the opposite side of the Tionesta Creek. When rains had not been heavy, we crossed the Tionesta Creek (which is a significant river) and rode on the other side of the creek which offers some challenging but beautiful trails with nice views. Although unmarked and rugged, we have enjoyed exploring this sector of the Allegheny National Forest as it is very picturesque. On one of our first visits to the area, we did not even know about these trails. We ran into another rider who told us about them and we were thankful to her for introducing us to them. To cross the river, we rode (in the direction opposite Route 666) down the main dirt road that passes the Flying W Ranch grounds toward the direction of the river. This road leads to another dirt road which parallels the river. We made a right onto this road. We then traveled along the road and downhill to where you can easily access the river. There is a short path which descends to the river on the left and is opposite a dirt road to the right with a blue and yellow pipeline marker at the end. After you go down this brief path, you cross to the island in the middle, go around it, and cross to the other side. Be cautious and assess the river flow. If it is high or strong, it can affect a horse's equilibrium. Horses need to be comfortable with crossing a wide and possibly deep river to reach the other side. We do not cross the Tionesta Creek after heavy rains as the current can be fast and the water can be deep. But if the rainfall has not been significant and we can see the river's bottom, we have found it easy to traverse. At these times the river is at its most beautiful as it is very blue. You may feel more comfortable traveling with someone who is familiar with these trails the first time out.

We crossed the river and initially rode to the left along an old railroad corridor, but the grade by the river was soft and eroded so we did not proceed farther. We, instead, headed up one of the many paths up the side of the mountain. The paths were pretty worn so it was easy to see which were used regularly, so we followed them. We did not encounter any significant "on the edge" trails but it is mountainous so horse and rider need to be fit and experienced with this type of terrain. On the far side of the river, you can ride for several hours and explore. These trails are not maintained nor is there anything to tell you the condition of the trails, level of difficulty, or if they are dead ends or solid loops. We explored and found many fun, wide trails that traveled up the side of the mountain in numerous directions. We have brought various groups of friends to this section and together we have continued to enjoy exploring. Over time, we have seen quite a few other equestrians on the trail in this vicinity so this is likely a popular destination for locals and visitors. Many of the branches of trails lead to a main double tract section at the top of the mountain and provide a nice overlook of the valley below. You can venture past this point or travel back down the mountain and try different branches.

Rather than making a left and traveling across the river, we have tried some other trails by traveling down the dirt road and heading to the right and connecting back to camp. There can be some very pretty paths but also there are some very rough and rugged tracts so we prefer to circumvent that section. Instead, we ride the snowmobile trails and those described above on the opposite side of the Tionesta Creek.

We really enjoy our visits to this region and plan to revisit in the future. We like to stay at Flying W Ranch because it offers a variety of camping locales in a scenic setting, a choice of amenities or primitive camping, fun rodeo and equestrian events, and informative clinics such as the trail stewardship presentations by the Pennsylvania Equine Council. *If you attend one of these, look for the Stagecoach West vendor stand (800-648-1121). They cater to the trail rider. This is one of my favorite booths for picking up unique and useful trail supplies.* For folks who like to meander around camp on their horse, the spacious 500+ acres of grounds and surrounding fields offer a nice, leisurely ride in a family atmosphere. We found it quite enjoyable to watch the parade of horses go by while we relaxed at our campsite. During some of our visits, we saw riders enjoying the arena which offered them a nice place to exercise their horses. There is primitive, wooded camping at the top of the hill opposite the main grounds (shaded and cooler in warm weather, but can retain moisture after wet weather, and big rigs can fit but must be able to maneuver and back) and camping with hookups near the buildings in the open field (room for big rigs, warmer in hot weather, dryer after rainy weather, and in convenient proximity to the rodeo grounds, other campers, stables, restaurant, saloon, and facilities). If you camp at the top, bring water containers to fill up by the barns in the lower areas. This can be a popular destination especially during special events; reservations are recommended.

COURTESIES:
A very special thank you to Bob and Darla Wood. Bob is the snowmobile guru of the Allegheny National Forest region in the vicinity of Tionesta and Tidioute. He is a snowmobile host and works on these trails extensively. Bob and Darla graciously invited us to their home (served some wonderful fresh baked cookies too!) and showed us the vast network of snowmobile trails in this region. Bob and Darla are snowmobile enthusiasts yet made us, equestrians, feel so welcome to explore the trails that they work so hard to maintain. We hope to visit with them again and maybe tour this region on a snowmobile!

THINGS WE LEARNED THIS RIDE:
I learned how important it is for equestrians to work with the local snowmobile groups and other trail users. We can all share an abundance of information and help each other. After this trip, I developed quite a respect for the work that these folks do and also an interest in checking these trails out from the back of a snowmobile.

NEARBY AND SURROUNDING AREA:
• Flying W Ranch (guided trail rides, hay rides, summer camp, cabin rentals, equestrian and non-equestrian campground, stall rentals, camping with hookups or primitive, rodeos, restaurant and tack/gift shop on premises), Kellettville (814) 463-7663, website: www.theflyingwranch.com
• Local Snowmobile Host, The Woods (814) 463-5019

NEARBY AND SURROUNDING VET SERVICES:
• Dr. Turner, Marley Veterinary Clinic, Titusville (814) 827-1778
• P. Farrell, Russell Veterinary Clinic (trailer to), Russell (814) 757-5440
• S. Gavin, Seneca (814) 676-8470

NEARBY AND SURROUNDING AREA FARRIERS:
• Steve Wilson, Sugar Grove (814) 489-3051
• R. Knight, Tidioute (814) 484-3347
• P. Neill Jr., member PPFA, Sigel (814) 752 2989
• J. Bailey, Tionesta (814) 676-0135

9. Kelly Pines &
The Duhring (Marienville) Region
Allegheny National Forest
U.S. Forest Service

Lasting Impression: This is an old time favorite and well known destination for equestrians and equestrian campers from far and near.

Location: These trails are located in the southern section of the Allegheny National Forest in Forest County, in the town of Duhring, near Marienville.

Length: *Day Ride or Weekend Destination (or combine with other locales and make it a week-long tour of the Allegheny National Forest)*- Allegheny National Forest is over 513,000 acres sprawling over the counties of Elk, Warren, Forest, and McKean. Exact trail mileage is not available; however, this location has access to many days of riding. At this writing, within the Allegheny National Forest, equestrians are permitted to ride in most areas except for certain sensitive areas, and hiking and cross-country ski trails. Those trails are indicated by yellow paint, gray markers, and blue and white diamonds.

Level of Difficulty: Easy to difficult

Terrain: The surface is diverse and includes single dirt tracts winding through mountainous country, trails that pass interesting rock formations and old quarries, double tract logging roads, and old railroad grades of dirt or fine stone dust surface. There are many nice sections but there are also old, exposed, and sometimes broken pipelines in this area, so riders need to proceed with caution. The terrain can vary from easy to extremely rugged and rocky in sections.

Horse Camping: Yes

Non-horse Camping: Yes

Maps and Info: Information, topographic maps (these are available for a small fee and are helpful), and Allegheny National Forest (ANF) maps are available at the following ANF offices: ANF Headquarters in Warren (814) 723-5150; Marienville Ranger Station in Marienville (814) 927-6628; and the Bradford Ranger Station in Bradford (814) 362-4613. You can also write to Allegheny National Forest, P.O. Box 847, Warren, PA 16365. Ask for the large Allegheny National Forest Region map which depicts the snowmobile paths and the Allegheny Region Recreation table. This is very helpful for exploring this area as equestrians share many of the snowmobile trails. Information can also be obtained via the ANF website: www.fs.fed.us/r9/forests/allegheny. For information regarding Kelly Pines or the trails in the Marienville area, contact the Marienville office. You can reach Summers Campground, a privately owned facility, open to the public, which offers equestrian camping (fee), at (814) 927-8318 or (814) 927-6710.

Activities: Hiking, Biking, Horseback Riding Trails, Picnicking, Swimming, Fishing, Camping, Snowmobiling, X-C Skiing, and Hunting (in certain areas)
Fees for Trail Use: None
Permits for Day Trail Use: None
Permits/Fees Required for Overnight Camping: We were surprised when we were told that permits and reservations are not needed for camping at Kelly Pines and the other "dispersed" camping areas within the Allegheny National Forest (different from State Forests that require permits). The sites are first come, first served. There are obvious advantages to not having to make advance reservations but you also take a chance that no one else will be occupying the site upon your arrival. This would be significant for folks traveling a distance to this area and not being assured a camping location. If traveling a distance, you may want to plan your arrival during the week. Also, check with the office as to any changes in policy. There is a fee for camping at the nearby commercial campground.
Comfort Station: Yes

DIRECTIONS:
To the Allegheny National Forest Kelly Pines Campground and the trails: Take I-80 to the Shippenville Exit #60 to Route 66 north. Travel 32 miles (you will pass the town of Marienville) on Route 66. Just after passing the intersection of Route 666 and the railroad crossing, look for Duhring Road and signs for the Allegheny Trail Ride. Make a right onto Duhring Road. Travel a total of 5.6 miles on Duhring Road. There is a large, brown sign at the entrance. Make a left. The bridge is tight but we were able to cross it with our long horse trailer. The area is generously proportioned with individual camping slabs and plenty of pull through room. You should be able to pull through even if others are camping there (assuming they are not blocking the main road which they shouldn't be). The constructors of this site did a great job as it is rig and horse friendly.

There are other "dispersed" camping locations within Allegheny National Forest which are listed in the package the office sends and also on the website. As indicated, we had checked several sites and they were either too small for large equestrian rigs, near a main road, or others (non-equestrians) were already camping at those locations. However, we found the Kelly Pines locale to be ideal and the most suitable and equestrian friendly of the ANF site locales that we visited.

To reach Summers Campground: You can also camp at nearby Summers Campground which is a privately owned equestrian campground that is open to the public. Summers Campground, like Kelly Pines, has direct access to the trails in this region. Travel as you would to Kelly Pines, but only travel a total of 3 miles on Duhring Road (from Route 66). Look for the Allegheny Trail Ride sign. Make a left onto a dirt road and cross a bridge. Look for an old trail ride sign on the left; make another left. This was a rough dirt road during our visit, so take it slow. You will pass a popular equestrian camping site to the right which is part of the Allegheny National Forest (also an option for camping). Continue straight to the old barracks and CCC camp. Stalls are on the left and camping is behind the stalls and along the entrance.

THE TRAILS:
Whether you stay at Kelly Pines or at the nearby Summers Campground, just head out and follow the hoof prints and the many branches of the trails. From Kelly Pines, you can pick up a trail on the opposite side of the river to the rear of the camping area as you enter. There are numerous loops that travel the mountainside. You can eventually link in with the old railroad corridor which returns to both Kelly Pines and Summers Campground on the side of the entrance just before crossing the bridges. The rail-trail is a nice, easy ride and passes many homes in a rural setting along its path. As this tract is so popular with equestrians, the occupants along its route are used to the sight of horses.

To reach the mountainside single paths from Summers Campground, ride out of the front of camp, make a left, travel in the direction away from the entrance and bridge, look for a trail to the right, and connect there. There are so many regulars who are familiar with the trails at Summers Campground; if you are uncertain where to go, you can ask them. The mountainous terrain offers a more challenging landscape with some steep and sometimes difficult sections. There are also some dramatic rock formations and picturesque terrain to view along the path. The rail-trail presents a gentler alternative. To reach the rail-trail from Summers Campground, you can either cross the stream or cross the bridge in the direction from which you entered and make a left onto the rail-trail. At various locations along the trail and at intersections you may see orange markers or diamonds. These identify the snowmobile path and can be helpful for navigation.

The trails head in many different directions, you can't miss them due to the worn paths. The terrain is mostly dirt with some rocky patches. Except for the rail-trail, the ride is mostly shaded as it travels through the woods and pine forests. There is some very beautiful scenery in this area offering many hours of enjoyable riding. But, over the years, natural gas and oil have been prevalent in this region. As a result, unfortunately, there are some sections of unsightly old or abandoned pipelines in the area. Some of these are near portions of the trail, especially near the rail-trail, and have the strong smell of fumes along with the site of related equipment. Not within the control of the ANF, these lines usually belong to private interests who own the oil and gas rights. In such a wonderful wilderness region, hopefully, obsolete lines will be removed and active lines placed underground or out of sight in the future.

After years of heavy use, there has been a proposal to re-engineer and reroute the trails in the high traffic areas to a designated equestrian trail system and retain the freedom to explore in outlying areas. You may see various markers or fluorescent pink ribbons throughout indicating possible or proposed routes.

EQUESTRIAN CAMPING:
Kelly Pines has been a popular Allegheny National Forest equestrian camping destination for decades. As a result of its popularity, Kelly Pines was showing the wear and tear. This camping locale had become in need of attention and also redesign to avoid horses being tied near sensitive areas, such as the river and trees, and overall to minimize their effect on the environment. Consequently, and thanks to the cooperative joint effort of many individuals and groups, the camping area got a wonderful facelift. Covered tie stalls were constructed, the area was made level with large camping sites of a fine stone surface, and a nice entrance and exit loop was built to accommodate those traveling with horses. There are both single sites and double sites, and plenty of length for long rigs. Well water and toilets were also added. Everything was precisely planned, beautifully constructed, and clearly marked. We give this refurbished campground a "Four Spur Award" for smart layout and design. We visited this site at an early stage of research for this book, when it was brand new. We hope equestrians are taking good care of it, keeping it clean, and appreciating the hard work that went into it.

Summers Campground has been in existence for generations. This is a rustic campground but a popular one. Camping is mostly primitive; however, there are bathrooms, showers, and water available. Summers Campground has a few organized group rides each year and riders can also camp at off-peak times. We found it interesting that Summers Campground was one of the first CCC camps and also a locale that housed German prisoners during WWII. We were told of the German U-Boat officers that were detained there. (When sitting around the campfire, ask if anyone is familiar with some of the stories of the camp; you may hear some interesting ones.) Currently, there are equestrian stalls in some of these buildings but you can still visualize what they looked like then. *Some of the stalls have drywall with wooden floors. I have never seen stalls that had both wooden floors and drywall; I would be concerned that my horse would either try to chew the drywall or put his hoof through it!* Summers Campground is one that many regulars frequent and can be full. If so, there are other nearby areas that you can try, such as the ANF area you passed on the right (mentioned above) as you drove the entrance road to the Summers Campground or nearby Kelly Pines.

HISTORICAL INFORMATION:
Northwestern Pennsylvania is where the oil and lumber industries once dominated and where the trails still show many signs of the effects of those industries, especially oil. In the 1920s, the Allegheny National Forest region of Pennsylvania was declared National Forest Land. This is the only designated National Forest in the state of Pennsylvania and includes Pennsylvania's only federal wilderness area, Hickory Creek. Today, Marienville is known by many as

the snowmobile capital of the state. Snowmobiles are even permitted on many of Marienville's main streets. Horseback riders benefit in this region and throughout a significant portion of Pennsylvania from the sharing of the snowmobile trails. If you are planning a winter visit to this area, you may want to time your stay for the Marienville Winter Festival where winter sports enthusiasts gather and share in their enjoyment of these activities.

COURTESIES:
I would like to thank the Pennsylvania Equine Council, Joe Langianese, Brenda Adams-Weyant, and the many others whose work influenced and contributed to the newly renovated Kelly Pines equestrian camping area. Thank you to the Allegheny National Forest for allowing this destination to be enjoyed on horseback. Please continue to allow equestrians the freedom to explore throughout. Also, I would like to personally thank John Stear and the folks from Ohio for showing us some of the Allegheny National Forest trails and for also inviting us to that tasty fish-fry.

NEARBY EQUESTRIAN CAMPING AND OTHER:
- Summers Campground (equestrian camping), HC #2, Box 50, Marienville (814) 927-8318 or (814) 927-6710
- Forest County Tourism, Brookville (800) 348-9393
- Kelly's Hotel, near the train station in Marienville (814) 927-6652 (stop by Friday night for their fish-fry)

NEARBY AND SURROUNDING AREA VET SERVICES:
- Dr. Turner, Marley Veterinary Clinic, Titusville (814) 827-1778
- P. Farrell, Russell Veterinary Clinic (need to trailer to), Russell (814) 757-5440
- S. Gavin, Seneca (814) 676-8470

NEARBY AND SURROUNDING AREA FARRIERS:
- R. Knight, Tidioute (814) 484-3347
- D. Bentrem, Burgettstown (at times may also be available in Marienville area) (724) 947-3411, (412) 580-4458 cell
- P. Neill Jr., member PPFA, Sigel (814) 752 2989
- J. Bailey, Tionesta (814) 676-0135
- Steve Wilson, Sugar Grove (814) 489-3051

10. Kettle Creek State Park
DCNR
(Department of Conservation & Natural Resources)

Lasting Impression: I fell in love with this area upon arrival at Kettle Creek's remote and beautiful equestrian campground. The camping area is in a peaceful setting surrounded by large, mowed fields, tall pines, a convenient nearby stream, and occasional herds of deer grazing in adjoining fields. This is a big, scenic, diverse, and sometimes challenging area to ride and explore. We plan to return in the fall as the scenery must be very colorful due to the abundance of birch trees.

Location: Kettle Creek State Park is located just north of Westport in northcentral Pennsylvania in Clinton County.

Length: *Day Ride or Weekend Destination (or longer)*- Kettle Creek State Park consists of approximately 1,800 acres and adjoins Sproul State Forest which, in total, has over 292,000 acres. This is an extensive wilderness area. There is a designated 22 mile multiple-use and equestrian trail which travels in the vicinity of the Kettle Creek State Park and parts of the neighboring Sproul State Forest, plus there are many adjoining trails. In nearby Sproul State Forest, riding is permitted on the State Forest roads and most trails except for hiking (only) designated trails such as the Donut Hole Trail.

Level of Difficulty: Moderate to challenging (due to some steep climbs)

Terrain: Generally good, durable, dry surface of dirt or grass, not rocky

Horse Camping: Yes

Non-horse Camping: Yes

Maps and Info: DCNR, Kettle Creek State Park, HCR 62, Box 96, Renovo, PA 17764, (570) 923-6004, website: www.dcnr.state.pa.us, or www.state.pa.us; or Sproul State Forest, 15187 Renovo Road, Renovo, PA 17764, (570) 923-6011. Permit, fee, and an application are required for the equestrian camping area at Kettle Creek State Park and can be obtained at the Kettle Creek State Park office on Kettle Creek Road (you will pass it on your way to the equestrian campground and trailhead) or by calling the above number. Maps can also be obtained from the State Park office. There are three maps which will be useful. Obtain the DCNR Kettle Creek State Park recreational (green) guide and map, the Sproul State Forest/Kettle Creek State Park Equestrian Trail Map (we were given a black & white copy), and the DCNR Public Use Map (also a green cover) for Sproul State Forest. For disability information, contact the Pennsylvania Bureau of State Parks (888) PA-PARKS.

Activities: Hiking, Biking, Horseback Riding Trails, Picnicking, Swimming, Fishing, X-C Skiing, Sledding, Ice Skating, Snowmobiling, Camping, and Hunting

Fees for Trail Use: None

Permits for Day Trail Use: None
Permits/Fees Required for Overnight Camping: Yes, to camp at the Kettle Creek State Park campground, a permit and application are required. There is a fee as this is managed by a State Park and some facilities are provided.
Comfort Station: There is a toilet at the trailhead at the equestrian campground. There are also toilets located at other campgrounds in the State Park. There is a dump station available in both State Park non-equestrian campgrounds, but take a drive without the rig to see if it is accessible with your size trailer. We were told that there are plans for showers to be located in the Lower Campground (non-equestrian). We were also told that come the time, equestrians (with a permit to camp at the Kettle Creek State Park equestrian campground) will be permitted to use the bath houses at the Lower Campground (located along SR 4001/Kettle Creek Road south of the Alvin Bush Dam).

DIRECTIONS:
Take I-80 to Exit #178; follow Route 220 north (toward Lock Haven). Travel approximately 7 miles on Route 220 north. Get off the exit for Route 120 and follow signs for Route 120 west. (The road will wind through Lock Haven; be careful to follow the signs, especially the sharp left by the concrete bridge.) Continue on Route 120 west for a total of about 34 miles to the town of Westport (just past Renovo). In Westport, make a right onto Kettle Creek Road, which is SR 4001. There is a sign that says "Kettle Creek State Park 8 miles." Travel a total of 10 miles (2 miles past the core of the park while passing the Alvin Bush Dam and the State Park office) on Kettle Creek Road and follow the brown equestrian trailhead signs. After traveling the 10 miles, there is an equestrian trailhead sign and a sign for Beaverdam Road. Make a left on Beaverdam Road. This equestrian trailhead is clearly marked on the map. At the trailhead, you will see a small area (covered with ballast at the time of our visit) to the right. That is the day parking area. It wasn't very large, but if there is no room due to other vehicles there is plenty of room to turn around in the adjoining field area. Immediately after the clearing, make a right onto the large, grassy area with pine trees. (Do not continue down Beaverdam Road! During our visit, it was a narrow road of a rough surface, little shoulder, low clearance, and not suitable for hauling. If it looks like it has changed, disconnect the truck and explore without the trailer. But even without the trailer, we found it too narrow for a two-way road. We were later told that there are plans to improve Beaverdam Road, so there is a possibility that it may be better by the time of your visit.) Drive toward the grass field and head to the left by the pine trees and picnic tables. You'll wonder if you are in the right place as the camping area isn't marked or structured. But, just pull in and choose where to stop the rig. That is the camping area. The area is large with plenty of pull through room and turnaround space.

THE TRAILS:
There is some really nice riding in and around Kettle Creek State Park. Much of the designated equestrian trail travels through Sproul State Forest. Before heading out on the trail, bring the Kettle Creek State Park (green) brochure map, the Sproul State Forest/Kettle Creek State Park Equestrian Trail brown (or black) and white map, along with the Sproul State Forest Public Use Map. You should be able to obtain these from the State Park office before your visit. This is a very large area so you'll want to look at the lay of the land on the maps including available topographic maps. As you travel, keep an eye out for elk. An elk sighting is a possibility in this vicinity.

We rode these trails in mid May before the Memorial Day weekend. Although the weather was great, we had both the campground and the trails completely to ourselves. We didn't see any hikers, bikers, or horseback riders. We didn't even run into any vehicles along Beaverdam Road. The site was quiet, peaceful, and relaxing. We just rode out from camp, down Beaverdam Road, and started exploring. From Beaverdam Road, there are paths branching out throughout the trail system. Some of these lead to gas well sites and abruptly end at those sites. That could be frustrating as often we thought we were starting on a new trail only to find that it was a pipeline access road, basically a dead end, very similar to riding to a feed lot. Others are trails or connecting forest or logging roads. Many cleared pipeline access paths crisscross the trails as well. We found that, initially, there are equestrian signs to guide you. Periodically, there will be additional signs throughout many parts of the trail system but they are not frequent. The trails do have markings but, due to the vast network of trails and many opportunities to deviate from the main trails, the maps, a GPS, and someone with a good sense of direction are needed.

Of the trails we rode, the trail surface consisted of dirt or grass and they were not rocky. In fact, except for the new ballast on some roads, the surface was very nice. The paths are mostly wide; many are logging roads or maintenance access roads. Although we found the surface to be good, much of this trail system is not an easy ride due to the mountainous terrain. Consider your horse's ability. There are some very steep climbs and descents in this range of mountains and valleys. Just check out some of the pipeline paths that intersect with the trail system; they are off the scale! Endurance enthusiasts should love some of those. *We were trying to figure how they could cut the grass at that angle without toppling over!* But, don't let the climbs deter you. Other than a few of the pipeline right-of-ways, which can be extreme but are easy to avoid, most of the trails are wide allowing for plenty of breaks, can be taken in moderation, and are not "on the edge."

From camp, we headed up Beaverdam Road (the road that runs along the campground area) in the direction away from Kettle Creek Road. You will see the brown sign for the horse trail. The dirt road forks; bear left and head up the mountain. *If you bear right, you can ride the dirt road which leads you into the Sproul State Forest. During our visit there were large chunks of newly laid ballast that would have been rough on our horses' feet. Once the ballast sinks into the dirt, it may not be too bad. We turned around. We later traveled down this road in a vehicle for a few miles. This is when we noted that there were various branches off of this road which may allow for additional exploring.* Although a wide dirt path with ample room for breathers, the left of the fork leads to a rigorous climb up the mountainside. Time this for a cool time of the day. It is a workout for the horses so they should be in decent shape. If taken slowly and with breaks, we found it doable and not stressful to the horses. At the top of the dirt road, there will be a gate. Going left will bring you to an array of trails with varying degrees of difficulty from easy to very challenging. Some of the trails travel through the valleys and do not require much physical exertion. We accessed a nice valley trail by heading up the road, making the left at the gate, coming to another intersection and making a left, crossed a bridge (be careful of holes that have formed where the bridge concrete meets the dirt at the entrance and exit) and proceeded down a nice, level, leisurely path that led to the State Park office. We backtracked via this trail and hooked up with a trail at the bottom by the Beaverdam Brook on the opposite side. (This trail is on the map and has post markers.) From here, we rode back up to the gate and made a right to head down the dirt road to return to camp. This offered a nice, easy ride.

On another ride, we traveled to the top of the dirt road, made a right at the gate, and then a left and rode up the pipeline right-of-way to the top (past the orange snow fencing) where we connected with Montour Road. This is an open area along the pipeline which can be hot on a summer's day. *Note: the trail actually travels along Beaverdam Road to the top of the mountain, instead of the pipeline. But due to Beaverdam Road having the large chunks of ballast during our visit, we took this approach.* From the pipeline path at the top, we continued on the marked trail and rode along Montour Road which was a nice, quiet, scenic dirt road. We made a left on Sugar Camp Road, which was also attractive and leisurely. We made the first left off of Sugar Camp Road and encountered an extremely steep trail. Although the entrance to this trail had a horse sign, it was hard to follow, had fallen trees at the entrance, and appeared not to receive much use (assuming we had the correct path; hard to tell at this location). The trail that we attempted to continue along was too steep to descend. Instead we returned to Sugar Camp Road and came to a sharp left turn (there is a multiple-use sign). We took this trail and headed in the direction of the State Park office following the orange snowmobile blazes. We have found that snowmobile trails are usually excellent trails and gradual, unlike the non-snowmobile trail we just encountered. At that point we came across a porcupine standing in the middle of the trail facing us. He stood for a few minutes just looking at us (I think we were as surprised as he was) and wouldn't budge. We had to make a lot of loud noises to get him to move out of our way! At the top of the mountain, at an equestrian sign, the trail makes a left and forms a switchback down the mountainside. From Sugar Camp Road to the State Park office, the trail was absolutely gorgeous. Now this was riding! The path remained a wide trail of logging type (so although it looks down a deep wooded embankment, it didn't have that "on the edge" feel). *Throughout our ride, in spite of the climbs, we did not find any narrow, cliffside trails; all were pretty wide.* This was **our favorite portion of the trail** and we wished we had time to explore more of it. However, it was getting dark so we headed back to camp along Kettle Creek Road (paved). (You do not need to ride the road to return. You can bear left at the fork by the ranger station, head up that trail, over the bridge, to an intersection [passed earlier], and make a right heading down the steep dirt road and back to camp.)

This is an area where you can ride as much as it suits you and choose the level of challenge you aspire to. If your horse has too much energy, you should be able to find a trail that will calm him down nicely! Overall, there are some, but not a lot, of signs or markers throughout the trail system so bring your map. And there are trails everywhere. We did not have the opportunity to ride the southern end of the trail system near Cooks Run and are looking forward to returning and trying that portion of the trail. In the evenings, we returned to camp to later unhook the rig and take a drive north along Kettle Creek Road to view the large herds of deer in the fields. We were hoping to catch a glimpse of an elk but we did not see any during our visit.

EQUESTRIAN CAMPING:
We visited Kettle Creek on our honeymoon in the month of May. We had plans to visit a few places and had only a few days to stay at Kettle Creek State Park. We wish we could have spent more time as the beauty of the camping area was a delightful surprise. We had not heard much if anything about this camping area until our visit. This seemed to be another well kept secret. Our stay was during the week and we had the campground to ourselves; but were told that the campground did get lots of use. It certainly didn't look that way as it was in pristine condition. It appeared that both the campers and the park were taking good care. It appeared so unaffected that we weren't even sure it was the camping area and we had to ask a maintenance employee and the office if we were in the right place. It also got a little confusing as to whether we were in Sproul State Forest or Kettle Creek State Park, as each has different camping requirements and regulations. We checked with the Kettle Creek State Park office, and were told the campground as described in this chapter is within the Kettle Creek State Park jurisdiction.

The campground is large and spacious. There is ample room for groups of rigs (estimate 20). Some of the turf in the rear of the camping area was softer than the solid ground toward the entrance to the field. We pulled in with our rig and first tested the surface on foot before driving farther. We had had a very wet winter and spring and wanted to check the ground before settling in. Most of the area was ideal and we had no difficulty. Near the camping area is a creek which is great for watering the horses. Be cautious, however, of old pipes that you must pass on your way to the river. Many are exposed and lying on the surface. They may be brittle and sharp if broken, so be careful to avoid them. (We did not find these to be a problem, just a word of warning.) Pipes or pipelines like these are common in this part of Pennsylvania and in the vicinity of the Allegheny National Forest. Although we saw these at the edge of camp near the stream, we did not see any pipes on the trails described in this chapter.

The campground setting offers plenty of shade for hot days. Horses can be tie lined; there are numerous trees to tie line to on nice, level ground. Be careful not to tie directly to a tree where the horses could damage one of these beautiful old pines. Wrapping the tree with burlap or some other appropriate protection is well advised. However, there is lots of room to tie line and to space the horses in the center of two trees where they cannot spoil the surroundings. Electric fencing is also an option as there is much open grazing area. And don't forget the bug spray for the horses; you will likely need it! There are picnic tables and fire rings in the camping area. As with most destinations and environmental conditions, check with the office beforehand as to whether fires are permitted during your stay. We found the river to be the only source of water at the equestrian camping site during the time of our visit. The river water appeared to be of good quality and at a convenient location to water the horses. You may want to check with the office as to the current quality or consider bringing your own. Water is available to equestrian and non-equestrian campers (camping with a State Park permit) at the non-equestrian Upper and Lower Campgrounds. The locations are marked on the Kettle Creek State Park map.

It was mentioned to us during conversations with other equestrians that frequent the area that once, after they had left the campground, someone else had come and left it in bad condition. They were mistakenly contacted as being the perpetrators and were understandably upset as being incorrectly identified. They had left it in good order but it appeared that after their departure, some others had visited the site and abused it. Since so many equestrian camping destinations are remote from the main grounds and may not be easily monitored or frequently inspected, this kind of mistaken identity could occur. We have seen where these outlying locations had been visited by non-campers or intruders and used as a dumping ground. To avoid this unwanted but possible misunderstanding, equestrians (especially groups) may be well advised to be proactive. Report any findings upon arrival, and consider asking the office to take a look at the grounds before you depart. This should help avoid any misinterpretation and keep good relations. In addition, on occasion, we have found equestrians were the offenders and did not always leave the area in good condition. Individual standards will vary and this is a personal decision call, but we have often tidied up for others as we did not want the office to have to deal with those that were not the best representatives of our interest group. A little effort on our part could keep them from ruining it for the rest of us. Unfortunately, there are always some abusers but at least we made a good contribution to minimize their effect.

HISTORICAL INFORMATION:
There is a legend of an old farmer who lived in this region and believed natural gas was in the area. He had a drilling rig which broke down. He drilled where it stood and found a wealth of natural gas! Some of the surrounding areas, such as those near the Kettle Creek equestrian campground, were also found to be rich in natural gas. As a result, pipelines and gas well sites can be seen at various locations. The railroad industry was also significant to this region; at one time over 1,000 men were employed building steam locomotives in nearby Renovo. At the time of our visit, there was talk of a historical attraction being constructed to commemorate this time in Renovo's history.

In the 1930s, the CCC (Civilian Conservation Corps) was instrumental in the construction of portions of the park. In the 1960s, the Alvin R. Bush dam was constructed for flood control, an undertaking by the U.S. Army Corps of Engineers, with assistance from the DER (Department of Environmental Resources). Combining the attraction of the area's natural beauty plus the newly created water shoreline, this locale was transformed into a popular recreation destination. Now offering a wide and diverse assortment of fun activities, the Kettle Creek State Park is overseen by the DCNR's Bureau of State Parks. Nearby, the surrounding Sproul State Forest is supervised by DCNR's Bureau of Forestry.

COURTESIES:
Our thanks to Mary Hirst and the park personnel who provided useful information regarding the campground, to the friendly maintenance folks who came to visit and who help keep the camp so attractive, to the considerate equestrians who have taken good care of the campground sites, and to the helpful camp host at the Lower Campground for sharing information on the area. Thank you to the Bureau of State Parks and the U.S. Army Corps of Engineers for welcoming equestrians at this wonderful campground.

THINGS WE LEARNED THIS RIDE:
- Upon visiting the park office, we learned the horse camp is actually in a flood zone (however, during our visit, we found the camping area to be lowland but not wetland) owned by the U.S. Army Corps of Engineers and is leased to the State Park. The equestrian camping area is experimental. We certainly want to take good care of our relations with the folks running this

campground so that equestrians remain welcome, especially as they are doing a great job making this a wonderful destination.

- We were reminded to check out forest dirt roads in advance of hauling a rig on them. Even without the rig, they can be too narrow. We had headed down Beaverdam Road with the dually, only to have quite a bit of difficulty turning around due to the narrow width of the road and lack of shoulder. Upon turning, the soft shoulder was giving way under our rear tires! I think we need to haul a small jeep or our dune buggy for these explorations.
- In some sections of the park, they cannot drill for water due to the gas lines.
- Forty elk were transferred here from Elk County; so seeing elk is a very real possibility.
- When you stay at this lovely remote setting, you awake to the gobble of turkeys, and persistent deer coming into camp to join the horses. My idea of a romantic honeymoon!

NEARBY:

- Yesterday's Restaurant, Renovo (570) 923-2642 (There are not many nearby places to eat out, so bring plenty of food for the camper. But if you want to head out for something to eat, there is a nice, little nostalgic place in Renovo where you can get a burger, shake, fries, homemade pies, or various other dishes in a 1950s casual decor.)

NEARBY AND SURROUNDING AREA STABLES:

- Pagerun Rangerbreds (breeding and sales of Colorado Rangerbred/Appaloosa horses, boarding, overnight stabling), website: www.pagerun.com, Renovo (570) 923-1464, email: prranger@ultraisp.com

NEARBY AND SURROUNDING AREA VET SERVICES:

- Centre Equine Practice, Centre Hall (814) 364-1921
- S. McAllister, Centre Hall (814) 234-7415
- Lewis Vet Clinic, Linden (570) 398-2729
- Laurel Highland Farm & Equine Services LLC, E. Early, Williamsport (570) 326-1134

NEARBY AND SURROUNDING AREA FARRIERS:

- G. Hagan, St. Mary's (814) 834-6376
- J. Bodle Shoeing, Mill Hall (570) 726-6969
- M. Seybold, Lock Haven (570) 769-7857
- A. Barnett, Phillipsburg (814) 342-5548
- Scott Sims, Julian (near Port Matilda) (814) 353-1511

Note: in this chapter and many of the other chapters, I have intentionally included an extensive range for farriers and vets. This is due to remote areas having limited access and availability to these services.

11. The Eagleton Mine Camp Trail
& Sproul State Forest
BOF-DCNR
(Bureau of Forestry/Department of Conservation & Natural Resources)

Lasting Impression: Sproul State Forest is vast and remote with several locations to camp and ride. Travel for hours on trail and not see a soul! The new Eagleton Mine Camp Trail is a very enjoyable, diverse, and sometimes challenging trail system. Ride and play a fun game of find the red blazes (once you ride it, you will know what I mean). I believe the Eagleton Mine Camp Trail will soon become a very popular new equestrian and multiple-use trail destination. Worth the road trip!

Location: Sproul State Forest is located in central Pennsylvania and sprawls across Clinton, Cameron, and Centre Counties. Although there are many trails in Sproul State Forest, three designated multiple-use trails that travel through portions of Sproul State Forest are covered in this book: the Kettle Creek Trail (located in northwest Sproul State Forest, northwest of Renovo), the Eagleton Mine Camp Trail (based in southeast Sproul State Forest, northwest of Lock Haven), and the Keystone Mountain Country Shared Use Trail (sections of which are located in northeast Sproul State Forest). Since Kettle Creek extends into both State Forest and State Park jurisdiction, it is covered in the Kettle Creek State Park chapter. The Keystone Mountain Country Shared Use Trail travels through the eastern portions of Sproul State Forest and other State Forest jurisdictions. It is covered in the Susquehannock State Forest chapter. The Eagleton Mine Camp Trail is the focus of this chapter.

Length: *Day Ride or Weekend Destination (visit the Eagleton Mine Camp Trail for a weekend and Sproul State Forest for a week)*- Sproul State Forest consists of 292,000 acres and, interestingly, includes a tract of about 450 square miles where there are no permanent homes or electric service! Within the Forest, there are over 300 miles of State Forest roads (of limestone and natural surface) and numerous trails. Equestrians are permitted to ride both the State Forest roads and the trails, unless it is otherwise indicated. The Eagleton Mine Camp Trail system is approximately 20 miles in length plus there are numerous miles of additional adjoining trails and State Forest roads to explore.

Level of Difficulty: Moderate to difficult

Terrain: The Sproul State Forest landscape, as a whole, is diverse and full of mountains, valleys, flat open areas, water crossings, dense woods, and sometimes very steep terrain. This is no different at the Eagleton Mine Camp Trail locale. The terrain was mostly of dry, solid footing consisting of dirt, grass, sand, some rocky sections (but not overall rocky and were passable), dirt forest roads, and some bridge crossings.

Horse Camping: Yes

Non-horse Camping: Yes

Carriage Potential: The Eagleton Mine Camp Trail system is not suited to carriage driving; however, Sproul State Forest has many other sections with miles of dirt State Forest roads which may be suitable. Contact the office to obtain recommendations and for more information.

Maps and Info: To obtain maps, information, camping permit application, and reservations for Sproul State Forest, call (570) 923-6011 or write Forest District Headquarters, District Forester, Sproul State Forest, HCR 62, Box 90, Renovo, PA 17764. You can also visit the office at 15187 Renovo Road in Renovo or email: fd10@state.pa.us. More information can be viewed at the DCNR website: www.dcnr.state.pa.us or by contacting the Department of Conservation & Natural Resources, Bureau of Forestry, P.O. Box 8552, Harrisburg, PA 17105-8552. When calling the Sproul State Forest office, ask for the Public Use Map for Sproul State Forest, and the Eagleton Mine Camp Trail map along with any additional maps that may be available. Ask for Lin Greenaway, a Forester (and one time equestrian), or Ranger Rich Kugel (who is a fellow equestrian); both are very helpful and knowledgeable.

Activities: Hiking, Biking, Horseback Riding Trails, Picnicking, Fishing, Boating, Canoe Rentals, X-C Skiing, Camping, Snowmobile Trails, ATV Trails (designated area), and Hunting. Canoeing is popular along the Susquehanna River in the vicinity between Keating and Karthaus as the river travels through scenic and secluded canyons.

Fees for Trail Use: None

Permits for Day Trail Use: None

Permits/Fees Required for Overnight Camping: Permits are required for overnight motorized camping (no fee).

Comfort Station: None

DIRECTIONS:

The Eagleton Mine Camp Trail is in the southeast section of Sproul State Forest. There are two designated parking areas at this location, one at the east end (near Route 120 and marker #1) and one at the west end (at marker #4) on the map. We preferred the west end site #4 for camping, as the other site #1 is on an active road. There are a few ways to reach the west end site with both advantages and disadvantages.

Eagleton Road- To approach from Route 150 southwest of Lock Haven: (The advantage to this approach is that there are less climbs and less tight turns. The disadvantage is a lengthy approach on a gravel road with potholes. If the potholes are filled, this would easily be the better of the two due to the more gradual approach.) Take I-80 to Exit #178 at Lock Haven. Pick up Route 220 north for 5 miles to Route 150 Mill Hall exit. Get off the exit ramp, proceed .5 miles and come to a light (by the shopping center). Follow signs to Route 150 south. Take Route 150 south for 6.6 miles. Before the iron/steel bridge that crosses Beech Creek, make a right onto Monument-Orviston Road (it is the last road on the right before the bridge and just after Harrison Road). This is a local, winding road that initially travels past clusters of homes. We had been told to look for Beech Creek Road at the turn but, at this point, we only saw signs for Monument-Orviston Road. Follow Monument-Orviston Road for 2.4 miles. (The road twists and turns but, with two wide and long 50+ foot rigs, we had sufficient room.) This part can be confusing, so take this slow. Before the concrete bridge, you will come to a fork where the roads head in three different directions. Do not go to the left over the concrete bridge. Instead, bear right, but do not make a right onto Falls Road. Take the middle road of the three and pass an old white schoolhouse on your right. The key is to pass the old schoolhouse on the right. This is Martins Grove Road. Take Martins Grove for .5 miles and it becomes a gravel road called Beech Creek (Mountain) Road. Take Beech Creek Road for 8.3 miles. The negative to this approach is that Beech Creek Road is a somewhat narrow, two-way gravel road that had numerous potholes during our visit. You will climb up the side of the mountain. Traveling over 8 miles on this rough surface seemed to take forever as you need to proceed very carefully and take it slow. (Even though this was a lengthy approach we still found the trip very worthwhile. And when we knew where we were going, it didn't seem so bad. You'll notice lots of locals don't seem to mind it either as there are many cabins in the area.) After traveling the 8.3 miles, make a right onto Eagleton Road. Eagleton Road is also a gravel road but did not have the potholes. Take Eagleton Road for about 1.4 miles and make a right into the camping or parking area. There is a West Branch Eagleton Mine Camp Trailhead sign at the entrance. The lot is a medium size gravel lot with one outlet serving as an entrance and exit, so you need to be able to back your trailer. There is open area surrounding the gravel lot which helps but it was overgrown with vegetation. However, there is plenty of existing open space with a solid surface to expand the lot if interest increases and also room to travel off the gravel, if needed, when turning. Approximately 4 living quarter type rigs could fit comfortably, or several smaller trailers. It would take cooperation among those sharing the site. We visited this site with a friend who also has a 50+ foot rig. We took the horses out before turning around, and then John and our friend, Jan, maneuvered the rigs so they knew they could get them out. If the lot is empty, a good driver should be able to do it without difficulty. No one else was at the lot throughout the holiday weekend when we visited. John and Jan managed to turn the large rigs without a problem, but having goosenecks helped handle the tight turning radius. If the driver can back a rig, smaller rigs should have no problem.

There is another parking area 6.6 miles farther down the road. It is at a trailhead and is situated under electrical wires. That will work for day parking but we did not feel it was preferable for camping as you are directly alongside the road. We liked the first area by #4 on the map for camping. It could be a little bigger or at least have an exit lane but it's surrounded by greenery, sufficiently away from the road, and the trail leads directly out of camp. The trees are set back and some are on unleveled ground, so it takes some looking to find a suitable tie area. But there are plenty of trees. We tie lined our horses to a row of trees to the right of the entrance which worked out well. Bring a long rope.

Eagleton Road- To approach from Route 120 northwest of Lock Haven, south of Glen Union: (The advantage is you avoid the potholes on Beech Creek Road; the disadvantage is this approach has some significant climbs and tight turns on Eagleton Road. It also has a few steep grades along Route 120 coming out of Lock Haven.) From Lock Haven, at Lock Haven University, take Route 120 northwest for 7 miles. (Along the way, you will pass a large area of cut rock and also a Boy Scout camp.) Make a left onto Eagleton Road. *John and Jan both agreed that the long living quarter trailers could be hauled up this road with a heavy duty rig in 4WD; however, they felt the other approach from Beech Creek Road was better, all things considered.* This road, like the other, is two-way but narrow. If you choose this route, you will need to use much of the road for the bends. Proceed cautiously. On Eagleton Road, travel 2.4 miles and you will see a day parking area on the right or north side of Eagleton Road, below the electric lines. (Again, this can also suffice for camping; however, we did not consider this desirable as it was actually on Eagleton Road, which does get traffic, and also is located directly under power lines.) The trailhead at this location is clearly marked. To continue to where we camped at lot #4 and the location we preferred, continue another 6.6 miles on Eagleton Road. The entrance to the lot is on the left; you will see the sign. We did feel the turn from this direction was tight for very large rigs due to a small drain area on the side. If you have trouble turning, you can travel past the entrance a hundred or so feet to the wide and spacious gas well access road, back and turn around, and enter from the other side. The approach to these locations can be seen on the Sproul State Forest Public Use Map. A map of the Eagleton Mine Camp Trail, which leads from camp, can be obtained from the Sproul State Forest office; do ask for the map to help get a lay of the land and how the loop travels. You will see the red trail markers on the trees as you enter this location.

THE TRAILS:
Seasoned trail riders who like a little challenge should enjoy this one. This is no cushy bridle path, but rather a real trail in its natural state of uneven terrain, varying degrees of difficulty, and wonderful paths that travel through some majestic, pristine wilderness. The scenery and the trails are varied. At one stretch, they can be easy; turn the bend and they can dramatically change to moderate or difficult.

In Sproul State Forest, there are many State Forest (dirt/gravel) roads, old CCC trails built as fire trails, logging roads, former railroad corridors, and an assortment of other trails throughout. The Eagleton Mine Camp Trail is a new shared trail system which is a combination of all of the above. The trails are nicely marked with dark red painted rectangles on the trees indicating the main trail system, and dark red painted circles on the trees indicating connector trails. Periodically, there are triangle multiple-use plaques on the trail. A change in direction is signaled by the direction of the paint markers on the trees. This is very well done; just about when you are wondering where the trail continues, you can look around and find a red marker. There are some road markers also but it is helpful to get the Eagleton Mine Camp Trail map for an overall picture of the trails. We found the map simple and accurate to follow. However, without the markers, it would be easy to get lost as the trail zigzags through dense forests. Although this new trail system had not been used much prior to the time of our visit, at times the trail path was detectable. It had been cleared at an early stage of its development and, mostly, it had not yet become overgrown. Other times, ferns had already overtaken the path. Due to the sectors of indistinguishable paths and growing greenery, especially in the middle of the woods, you really need to keep your eyes open for the red blazes indicating where to continue. And be alert for tilted blazes or two blazes indicating a change in direction of the trail (which is very helpful as you will see).

We took our trail rides on absolutely gorgeous days over Memorial Day weekend. Up to this point the weather had been unseasonably hot; however, this weekend it was sunny, dry, and in the 70s. Just perfect! We departed from our campsite at the west end of Eagleton Road via the back of the open gravel parking/camping area. The trail is indicated by the deep red marker on a tree at the edge of the woods to the far right side of the lot as you enter. There are some low lying tree branches blocking it, but with some looking you can see it. Once in the woods, the trail path was clear and the markers were plentiful. This is Shear Trap Trail. Shear Trap Trail starts as a nice, easy, single path through the woods. Unfortunately, shortly after beginning our ride, we encountered downed trees. This made an easy to moderate path sometimes quite difficult as we maneuvered around them. (With a little trail work, this should be an easy fix.) Most of the downed trees that we encountered during our stay were on the Shear Trap Trail. It made for a challenging start as the trees were large. There are also several bridges on this section of the trail system. We found them to be strong enough to hold a horse; however, someone had laid rocks at the bridge entrance and exit to provide ramps for bikes. That works for hikers and bikers, but not horses. As the rocks were not secure, I needed to dismount to check the footing before asking my horse to cross (leaving a safety distance in case he decided to jump over them, which he did). At some spots you can bypass this and cross over the river, at others it may take some time looking. There were a few stream crossings that required stepping carefully due to rocks or soft ground. We just took our time and worked through these. Later on, in another section of the trail near Boiler Run Trail, near a cabin, we noticed that someone filled the rock gaps with stone dust. This made an excellent bridge approach and exit for horses and all users, and a much safer one. Maybe this will be done on the other bridges also. But out of the 6 or 7 hours that we rode on the first day, only this section presented these challenges. And the obstacles on this one tract are easily fixable. (Do not let this deter you, the makers of this trail system did a good job and the area is wonderful. Although, I wouldn't consider this a trail for beginners as the terrain is diverse and requires rider and horse to be confident and experienced. Most seasoned trail riders will probably consider these to be insignificant obstacles.)

We continued our ride by turning left onto Slaughtering Ground Trail. Contrary to the sound of its name, this was a beautiful trail with mostly easy or moderate riding. We connected onto Scalded Meadows Trail which was also gorgeous and not difficult. A deer surprised us at the meadow where we decided to stop and take lunch on a convenient natural bench of a fallen tree. We then continued toward a switchback (watch the markers in this section as you twist and turn) in the region of the Left Branch Boiler Run Trail. This switchback is steep in sections and is more suitable for experienced trail riders who are used to mountainous terrain. Some equestrians may prefer the more gentle terrain of other portions of the trail system. On the other hand, the footing was solid and the side of the mountain had lots of trees as a buffer. The trail then travels through the valley. This section is very picturesque but also is somewhat rocky and rutted in sections. This required some ducking and diving around recent growth so, hopefully, this won't soon become completely overgrown. As this section was more demanding, we took our time picking through; however, we still found it very enjoyable. We then came to a bridge (this one was horse friendly with stone dust fill at the ends of the bridge). We crossed the bridge by the cabin, passed some signs with arrows (but did not enter the woods), and picked up an access dirt road to the left (there will be a red marker on the tree) and continued on the dirt road. This is Boiler Run Trail. We took Boiler Run Trail and made a left onto Eagleton Road (in the event of traffic, most of this road had plenty of shoulder if needed) and returned to camp. We really enjoyed our ride and it traveled through some very beautiful areas. We felt the trail was well thought out and with just a few small improvements, would be very horse friendly throughout. (Local riding clubs, please note: here is your chance to volunteer. This is a very nice one; let's take good care of it!)

Along the ride, there were many areas to water the horses. There are several small water crossings and, although not wide, they can be tricky. Sometimes you can choose an alternate crossing, other times you are limited. We did need to be cautious at some of the crossings. Also, be careful of holes. On either the first or second bridge that we encountered on Shear Trap Trail, just before the bridge, one of the horses sank and lost his balance for a moment. Watch for soft ground. During the time of our visit, this trail did not show a lot of use so it may have not yet been tried and tested thoroughly by equestrians. So proceed with caution.

On the second day, another perfect weather day, we rode the northern section. We proceeded out of camp (at the western lot), rode east down Eagleton Road (gravel), and made a left at the gate where there is a large, wide path of white sand mixed with soil and some rock. We rode past an area on the left which contained open areas and reforestation. This was an excellent area to see deer. We continued to follow the red rectangles and multiple-use signs. We made a right into the woods following the red markers. The ferns made it almost impossible to see the path (this shouldn't be an issue once the trail becomes better known). Initially, there was water along the way. As we traveled along the stretch of trail north of Eagleton Road to the switchback section by Eagleton Railroad marker #1 on the map, we saw less water so give your horses a drink where you can. Water will be again available in the valley after the switchback trail where the map indicates the Eagleton Railroad. (From map markers #2 to #3 to #4 we encountered plenty of opportunities to water the horses.) We rode the full length of the trail in an easterly direction; throughout it varied greatly from easy, wide grassy stretches, to challenging climbs and descents, to leisurely wooded paths and old logging roads. You will again pass a reforestation area fenced to keep local wildlife out. The trail will also turn and travel through a beautiful section of an old forest road now covered in grass and framed by a canopy of mature trees. This was one of **our favorite sections** as the fresh spring grass made this section look very inviting. You ride through a stretch of this gorgeous terrain and then return into the woods. That previous section was so attractive; we found it hard to leave it. Once back into the woods, you play the game of who can spot the red marker. At certain points the trail crisscrosses Eagleton Road. (We did not find it difficult to cross even though this gravel road can be active.) We encountered one section, just after the road, which looked like the rocks made it impassable. However, by just traveling to the left of the rocks, it was easy to continue along the trail. If something looks rough, do look around for a better way. Most areas had room for alternative bypasses. Particularly in this section of the woods, if it wasn't for the red blazes, we would not have been able to follow the trail. Ferns covered whatever path there was. Scan the woods and "find the blaze;" more than one person looking is helpful. We continued in a clockwise direction following the trail as shown on the map.

Soon, again, the terrain varied greatly. We crossed over Eagleton Road and entered an interesting area of old railroad switchbacks. The terrain was quite out of the ordinary; we needed to be careful of knee knockers where the trees were close together and also had to pass through them to continue on the narrow trail. This was fun but we had to pay attention. There also was some low hanging branches as we departed the switchback (maintenance was needed in this section). We then went down the side of a mountain on a narrow path. It was well marked but it was quite challenging as it was rugged, narrow, and required passing between trees with little leg room on each side. I felt like I was in a pole bending competition. Plus it was steep. *Please note: this section, which is located* *between markers #1 and #2 on the map, is <u>not</u> for inexperienced trail riders as it is demanding and/or difficult in certain locations. However, endurance riders may enjoy this as it is an advanced course. We have since been told that some of this may be rerouted or improved.* We then continued down the mountain to the valley and stream below. We crossed a bridge which gladly didn't have the rocks piled against it, but had a step and the horses needed to be comfortable with stepping up on it and down off of it. Ours were uneasy yet crossed it. At this point, the trail climbed back up the mountain and resumed its path back to marker #2 on the map. We returned via Boiler Run Trail and encountered some hikers. It was a nice surprise to meet this friendly group as we hadn't seen anyone using these trails. We returned via Eagleton Road back to camp.

Although there are gas lines and wells, the effect on the area appeared to be minimal. You see pump stations at various intervals but we did not feel they interfered with the enjoyment or beauty of the ride as the trails seem to detour around them. Bikers and horseback riders share the trails, so exercise caution around blind turns and locations with poor visibility.

EQUESTRIAN CAMPING:

Camping is primitive; there are no facilities. Bring your own water. There are special motorized camping guidelines issued by the Bureau of Forestry that apply and can be obtained when requesting the permit and maps from the district office. Horses are not permitted to be tied where they can have access to trees, and manure should be picked up or spread out a minimum of 100 feet from the campsite.

We camped at the west end lot which turned out to be a very nice campground. It was simply a gravel lot in a primitive setting, but once we found trees to tie line to, we set up camp and it was very comfortable. Other than an occasional vehicle on Eagleton Road, we didn't hear anything except for one lonely and persistent whip-poor-will who loudly serenaded us every evening. During the day we enjoyed riding and exploring this new trail system, and on the clear, starry nights we shared our friend Jan's high powered telescope to view the moon and the stars. It doesn't get any better than this!

HISTORICAL INFORMATION:

Pennsylvania's State Forests comprise over 2 million acres. At .3 million acres, Sproul State Forest is one of Pennsylvania's largest. The history of Sproul State Forest reflects its abundant wealth in natural woodlands and water resources. Before the Europeans settled in this region, this area still contained pristine forests which were hundreds of years old. Unfortunately, most of this was cleared for lumber by the end of the 1800s. In addition, mining took its toll on the land. By the mid 1800s, towns such as Eagleton sprung up as coal and iron mining prospered. During this time the Eagleton Railroad transported coal and iron from these mines over various railroad corridors built for this purpose. However, eventually, mining operations ceased. By the 1900s, new plant growth had begun to cover the old scars, and eventually the forests recovered much of their former beauty. In the 1980s, gas wells were constructed, the proceeds of which went toward the preservation and conservation of this area. Today, portions of the Eagleton Mine Camp Trail travel over the same tracts that the Eagleton Railroad once traveled.

Also of interest, Sproul State Forest contains the following Natural and Wild areas. Burns Run Wild Area is known for its native trout and clusters of mature white pine trees, and for its secluded setting without any roads passing through it. The Old Growth Forest Area has been identified as a managed forest development area. Two areas that include watersheds are the Fish Dam Wild Area and the Maurice K. Goddard Wild Area. The State Forest also includes four Natural Areas: Cranberry Swamp, Tamarack Swamp, East Branch Swamp, and Bucktail State Park.

COURTESIES:
We were very fortunate while researching Sproul State Forest to meet and correspond with fellow equestrians who were employed by the Bureau of Forestry and were familiar with the area from an equestrian perspective. I would like to express my gratitude to Rich Kugel and Lin Greenaway for their patience and assistance in answering all my questions, and for providing so much useful information. Lin, a very special thank you for your many notes and sharing of enthusiasm for these trails! Also, thank you to the friendly folks in the town of Monument who helped get our convoy back on track when we took a wrong turn trying to find Beech Creek Road. (If you end up in Monument, you missed your turn!)

THINGS WE LEARNED THIS RIDE:
- We were reminded that new trails are still being formed. Everyone thinks trails are only being closed, but our friends in the Bureau of Forestry and DCNR have stepped up to the plate and are making new trails. The new Eagleton Mine Camp Trail is an example of a newly created, fun trail system that has horse camping too!
- We should have known this one. On Memorial Day, if you don't head home early you may not be able to travel through towns due to parades. On more than one occasion we have had to wait for a parade to complete its course before traffic was permitted to proceed. I also learned that Memorial Day began in Pennsylvania in the 1860s when women began the tradition of placing flowers on the graves of Civil War soldiers.

NEARBY AND SURROUNDING AREA STABLES:
- Apple Tree Stables (boarding, training, and sales), Mill Hall (570) 726-7589

NEARBY AND SURROUNDING AREA VET SERVICES:
- Lewis Vet Clinic, Linden (570) 398-2729
- Laurel Highland Farm & Equine Services LLC, E. Early, Williamsport (570) 326-1134
- S. McAllister, Centre Hall (814) 234-7415
- Centre Equine Practice, Centre Hall (814) 364-1921

NEARBY AND SURROUNDING AREA FARRIERS:
- J. Bodle Shoeing, Mill Hall (570) 726-6969
- M. Seybold, Lock Haven (570) 769-7857
- Brian Montei, Salladasburg (570) 398-1320

12. The Keystone Mountain Country Shared Use Trail System
& Susquehannock State Forest
BOF-DCNR
(Bureau of Forestry/Department of Conservation & Natural Resources)

Lasting Impression: Well done! The Susquehannock State Forest has added many new equestrian and multiple-use camping sites. Plus, the extensive trail network of the Keystone Mountain Country Shared Use Trail System is a wonderful new feature of our state, one that its creators should be very proud of. Pennsylvania is so fortunate to have folks like the Bureau of Forestry who recognize the need and thus provide excellent locations for diverse multiple users to enjoy the beautiful outdoors the state has to offer. This location has many trails and camping destinations to choose from, all marked on a map which can be used as reference. An awesome bonus is that we were told another trail system is in the works for the northwest corner of Susquehannock State Forest!

Location: The Susquehannock State Forest is located in northcentral Pennsylvania and is located mostly in Potter County. Some sections extend into McKean and Clinton Counties. The Keystone Mountain Country Shared Use Trail System travels through Susquehannock, Tioga, Tiadaghton, and Sproul State Forests. We camped and rode from the trailhead located in Susquehannock State Forest.

Length: *Day Ride, Weekend Destination, or Week-long Destination*- Susquehannock State Forest consists of 265,000 acres; horses are permitted on the Keystone Mountain Country Shared Use Trail System and throughout the Susquehannock State Forest trails, pipeline paths, logging roads, and adjoining State Forest roads totaling 100+ miles. However, horses are not permitted on hiking (only) paths such as the 85 mile Susquehannock Trail System (marked by orange rectangle blazes along the trail and indicated by "STS" on the Public Use Map).

Level of Difficulty: Easy to moderate (other equestrians informed us that there are some difficult areas but we did not encounter them during our visit)

Terrain: The trails are diverse and consist of dirt, grass, gravel roads, gradual grades, hilly sections, flat tracts, and mountainous terrain. The trails remain interesting as the surrounding landscape changes frequently and varies from open areas to dense wooded "black forests" of pine and fir. Except for the lower section of the Pipeline Trail, the trails weren't rocky and were of good terrain.

Horse Camping: Yes

Non-horse Camping: Yes

Carriage Potential: Carriage enthusiasts may want to assess this location as the many State Forest and access dirt roads appear well suited for carriage driving.

91

Maps and Info: To obtain maps, information, camping permit, and reservations for Susquehannock State Forest, call (814) 274-3600 or contact Susquehannock State Forest, 3150 East Second Street, PO Box 673, Coudersport, PA 16915-0673, or email: fd15@state.pa.us. More information can be viewed at the DCNR website: www.dcnr.state.pa.us or by contacting the Department of Conservation & Natural Resources, Bureau of Forestry, P.O. Box 8552, Harrisburg, PA 17105-8552. Ask for the Public Use Map (green map), the Keystone Mountain Country Shared Use Trail System Map, and the North Central Snowmobile Trails Map. We did not see maps at the equestrian camping areas, so call for maps in advance. A map will be helpful for following the trail and road systems.

Activities: Hiking, Biking, Horseback Riding Trails, Picnicking, Swimming, Fishing, Camping, X-C Skiing, Downhill Skiing, Snowmobiling, Hunting, and ATVs in the northeast section of the State Forest and the Lyman Run State Park location. The area that we visited and covered in this chapter is multiple-use but does not permit ATVs.

Fees for Trail Use: None

Permits for Day Trail Use: None

Permits/Fees Required for Overnight Camping: A permit is required (no fee). Large groups should check with the office if special permits are needed and to verify the number of trailers permitted in a lot.

Comfort Station: None

DIRECTIONS:

There are many different camping or parking areas to access the Keystone Mountain Country Shared Use Trail System. The various camping areas can be seen on the Keystone Mountain Country Shared Use Trail System Map provided by the Bureau of Forestry. The following are some of the camping locations that we visited.

To reach the Dyer Road lot: Take Route 220 to the town of Jersey Shore. From Jersey Shore, take Route 44 north (Pine Creek State Park exit). Take Route 44 north for 17 miles to Haneyville. Route 44 is a winding road and has some significant climbs. Come to a 'T' in Haneyville. Make a right at the stop sign. Stay on Route 44. From Haneyville, continue another 19 miles and look for a road on the left. Turn left onto a road that is trimmed with a stone entrance. There is a sign that says Dyer Road. Travel down Dyer Road for about .5 miles and you will see the entrance to the right. There is a sign that says Dyer Road CCC Campsite. The entrance is a bit tight and larger rigs may have a problem. Some big rigs do get in here, but we felt you may want to check it out first without the rig to see if you are comfortable with your size rig and ability. If you do choose the Dyer Road site, there is adequate room for smaller and medium size rigs. About a maximum of 10 rigs can fit but backing is required. Different from the large gravel Twelve Mile Run lot, this is a grassy, irregular shaped area with uneven terrain in a scenic setting of a pine forest and open fields. There are places to tie line including in the cluster of pines which are on the left as you enter the lot. In regard to the area under the pine trees, we heard that it can be a slippery surface if it rains. Regarding camp fires or stoves, exercise caution during dry weather. You may want to consider the weather forecast before choosing this location.

To reach the Twelve Mile Road lot also known as the Pine Mountain Campsite and snowmobile parking area: Continue on Route 44 for an additional 2 miles past Dyer Road (a total of 38 miles on Route 44 from Jersey Shore) and look for a left onto Twelve Mile Road. There is a sign and it is well marked. The lot is on the left and easy to see as it is a very large gravel lot (could fit 15+ large rigs, but check with the office for maximum permitted) with boulders trimming its entrance. *John always comments that there will be a nice oversized lot to accommodate large rigs but then someone will make the entrance narrow by putting rocks, a gate, or some other barrier which limits the turning radius into that area. When he sees this at the entrance, he always remarks that it wasn't people who were familiar with hauling or big rigs who built the lot. The narrow entrance almost defeats the purpose of having the large lot! But even still, this lot had sufficient width of entrance for our larger rig.*

To reach the Rauch Road Gas Well site: Continue for another .2 miles past the turn for the Twelve Mile Road lot. From Route 44, make a right onto Rauch Road. Travel 1.5 miles on Rauch Road (you will pass Randall Road to the right; just continue straight). There is a grass lot on the left. This is a nice location in a remote setting. It is smaller than the Twelve Mile Road lot but is more scenic and could fit at least 5 sizable rigs. There is more open space to turn a rig around at this location vs. the Dyer Road lot. The Dyer Road lot offers shade in the pine forest but there are also trees surrounding the area at the Rauch Road Gas Well site. In summary, the largest of the three lots that we visited was the Twelve Mile Road lot. Although it is a gravel lot, it is quite functional, level, easy in, easy out, very central (to the trails), and overall a nice lot. The Dyer Road site is harder to get into with a big rig but has a pretty pine area (however, slippery in wet weather) in a remote setting, and many people like this lot for its greenery, privacy, and good access to trails. The Rauch Road Gas Well lot is farther off of the main road (1.5 miles of dirt road) but is located a quiet distance from Route 44 and is a nice, open, private, grass surface, with plenty of pull through space without backing. However, we were told some traffic does travel down Rauch Road. In regard to trails, Rauch Road may not be as centrally located as the Dyer Road or Twelve Mile Road lots, but we were told some of the trails out of the Rauch Road Gas Well site heading in the direction of Twelve Mile Road are very nice. We did speak with quite a few equestrians and each seemed to have tried or visited the three lots and all had different preferences. It's nice to have a choice of a few good lots, all with trails nearby!

Note: we were told that it was not recommended to travel south from Route 6 on Route 44 or Route 144 to access these camping areas due to steep, rough, and winding roads. *Just email Garth and Kathy Rumsmoke (Trail Rider magazine feature writers) if you need detail or verification. You can reach them via their website: www.garthandkathy.com.*

THE TRAILS:
The Susquehannock State Forest and its neighboring State Forests are massive, undeveloped, natural areas, where one could spend weeks riding different trails. This whole region is a super equestrian and multiple-use destination where there are multitudes of trails and an abundance of wildlife. There are bear in the area (just check out the prints in the wet areas) and elk sightings are becoming more common. (This is not far from Elk County and the elk may have expanded their territory or been relocated.) During our stay, we decided to visit the southeast section of the Susquehannock State Forest and ride some of the newly completed Keystone Mountain Country Shared Use Trail System which is the result of a cooperative effort between Tiadaghton, Sproul, Susquehannock, and Tioga State Forests to link numerous trail systems into a long, continuous one. We were also anxious to check out the various camping areas, as each of these State Forests have designated camping locales, including newly created ones, within close proximity to portions of this trail system. The southern portions of this trail network are in the Tiadaghton/Black Forest vicinity and are trails that have been in use for some time. We visited much of this during the research for Ride Pennsylvania Horse Trails- Part I. The Black Forest/Tiadaghton trail system has now been greatly enlarged, connected to previously separate trails, and extended so that it travels through adjoining State Forest districts making for a long trail network and a fun equestrian riding, multiple-use, and camping destination!

The Keystone Mountain Country Shared Use Trail System structure consists of various size loops, portions of which are actual trails and other sections are really connectors that travel along paved roads (such as Route 44) or dirt/gravel State Forest roads. *I found the State Forest dirt/gravel roads to be very remote, quiet, and leisurely, and it didn't feel like I was riding a "road." Plus, the State Forest roads that I traveled had ample shoulder room and often few, if any, vehicles traveled their course. Some are closed to public motorized use. Nonetheless, riders should remain alert as cabin occupants may use these to access their cabins.* The Keystone Mountain Country Shared Use Trail System started out like a nice, wide grass path through the woods directly out of our camp. The sections that are cut through the woods are wonderful to ride. But there are also some sections that travel along Route 44 which is a well traveled, two lane, paved road. Although there is a very wide stretch of grass to the side of the road, the connector trails are still next to and within hearing and sight distance of loud trucks, motorcycles, etc. In fact, one section (near the Twelve Mile Road lot) travels on ground below the road resulting in intensifying the effect. Riding along

94

Route 44, horse and rider need to be comfortable if loud vehicles pass. Crossing Route 44 we found to be easier as there were breaks in traffic. When we did need to ride along or near a main road, we tried to ride in the early morning when the road was quieter. Trail riders do not have to ride along the road to have a lengthy and enjoyable ride. If you want to ride the whole Keystone Mountain Country Shared Use Trail System, occasionally you will have to ride the side of a paved road. But if you are just looking for some quiet back country and good trails to ride, there is a great deal of that without traveling along the paved road. There are many trail loops, dirt road connectors, and fabulous riding located both west and east of Route 44. It just takes a little scouting but it is there. It does help to become familiar with where the actual trails are so you don't miss the really good ones.

The trails are a variety of terrain; comprised of old logging roads, single paths, double tracts, old railroad routes, pipeline right-of-ways, and State Forest access roads. The map is useful as it provides the mileage of some of the loops. Also, to help guide you, the trail system is marked at various intervals with red rectangles and brown triangles indicating the trail is a multiple-use trail. However, even with the map and periodic markers, first time visitors may find this trail system confusing. There are sections, such as that at the Twelve Mile Road lot, where the trailheads are well marked and it is easy to see where the trail begins. However, once farther down the trail, there are gaps in markers and it can become difficult to know where to proceed. On our first day, we got off course quite a few times. We checked with several other riders and they had experienced the same.

As we headed out on trail from the Twelve Mile Road lot, there were red rectangles on the trees along with the triangle markers. Many sections are effectively marked and we thought we could just follow these nice, wide paths. Traveling the spacious path in the direction toward Route 44, we planned on riding a clockwise loop. But once we hit Route 44, it did not stay a trail through the woods. Instead, the path traveled the wide grass berm along the road for a significant distance before we could link with other trails. *This stretch, beside the road, is actually a snowmobile path that now serves as the link between the trails. For horseback riding, some distance between the road and the trail would be a safety buffer, more scenic, and thus more pleasurable. It appeared it wouldn't take much to move the path a short distance inland, away from the road as the surrounding terrain is ideal for a trail. Hopefully, as the trail system is refined, inland paths will be established.* Shortly after traveling along Route 44, the markers seemed to fall off and we weren't sure if we were still on the multiple-use trail. The surface was solid but the grass was high and there were no markers in sight. Just past Lebo Road, we decided to cross back over the road and pick up the pipeline right-of-way. The wide grass pipeline stretch was actually very nice and scenic as we found most of the pipeline paths in this area.

We then picked up Lebo Road and made a left. Lebo Road was a quiet dirt road on the holiday weekend when we visited, and was scenic to ride as it traveled past a variety of terrain and only an occasional cabin. From Lebo Road, we made a right onto a trail labeled "Big Trestle Trail." It actually looked like a narrow footpath climbing upgrade onto the mountainside. We weren't sure if it was suitable for horses but looked like a shared use trail and there was no indication otherwise. (After looking at the map, we do believe there may have been a wider trail off of Lebo Road, just past this, but we did not take that path. We concluded this as we later saw another trail merge with our trail and it had red markers on it.) The path that we chose was actually extraordinary and we were glad we selected it. However, it is not a beginner's trail and riders will need to be comfortable with heights. The beginning of this trail travels somewhat "on the edge" for a stretch and may be too steep for some riders. Farther down along the path, the trail widens. The grass became high and, along with a lapse in markers, it became hard to tell where to proceed. However, we soon joined the wider trail which had the red blazes. This section was very easy to ride and leisurely. We were now into some gorgeous rolling landscape, with a more gentle terrain, and loving it. We passed a cabin ("Camp David") located dead center in the middle of the trail and met some very friendly folks from the Philadelphia area. They told us the story of how the Big Trestle Loop got its name. We also saw many equestrians along this route who were riding the trails. Lots of horseback riders travel by the front porch of "Camp David" and it must be quite interesting for the residents to sit and watch.

After passing the cabin, we continued toward the Twelve Mile Road direction and the east side of the Big Trestle Loop. The Big Trestle Loop area has many different branches of trail but the main path is a horseshoe shape. Once, a narrow gauge railroad moved lumber over its course and crossed the gorge via a trestle, and thus the name of this area. You can ride some of the old railroad grade which is mostly of good surface and travels through some absolutely beautiful areas. This is where we came upon an outstanding trail. To reach this, look for a 'T' intersection near where Big Trestle Road and the gas line access road meet. Looking at the Keystone Mountain Country Shared Use Trail System Map, this area is in the northwest section of the map near where the "water" arrow (the arrow farthest to the left of the map) is. Look for some large gas well apparatus at the intersection. If traveling from the lowland at the bottom of the Big Trestle Loop, head up the hill along the dirt road with the pumps to your left. There will be a sign on the dirt road indicating you are on the shared use trail. You can see that you can continue along the dirt road straight ahead or to the left. However, look to the edge of the woods (past the open, grass area) on the right side for the trail. There isn't a sign at the entrance and its entrance is partially camouflaged by an overgrown tree limb and flora. Thanks to a fellow equestrian we met on trail, we knew to look beyond the hidden entrance. You can barely see a small opening into the woods. Once you are past the curtain of greenery, the trail opens and it is very well marked. This trail is gorgeous and follows the old Big Trestle Loop where the narrow gauge railroad once traveled. The trail is of good surface, is wide (I did not feel it was "on the edge"), and looks down over the canyon along the train's former path. I found this to be a "**must see**" trail. This travels a distance along the gorge and connects into various sections of the Big Trestle Loop. We rode this back to Lebo Road and Route 44, and then back to camp.

As we became more familiar with these trails, we quickly found that they were sometimes well marked, and at other times the red markers and signs were sparse or nonexistent in many sections. We concluded that there were many markers in the close vicinity of the campgrounds. The outer areas seem to vary from marked to unmarked. Often there was a sign at the end of a trail but, once within, it became hard to tell where to proceed. Other times a red blaze had become hidden under overgrowth; there are also many trails and roads not on the map. Nonetheless, don't let the irregular markings interfere with your enjoyment. Just allow time, bring the two maps, and enjoy the exploration and new discoveries along the way. With each additional day of our stay we were enjoying this locale more and more.

On the second day, we decided to try some trails east of Route 44. We headed out early from the Twelve Mile Road campsite (to avoid the possibility of traffic), followed the path along Route 44, made a left onto Francis Road (a dirt and gravel road), rode Francis Road for a significant distance, and made a right onto the Pipeline Trail. When we came to the intersection with the Pipeline Trail, we weren't sure if we were traveling on the correct trail as there had been no signs or markers for quite some time, or at the entrance to the trail. Also, at first, the trail was rugged to travel due to some rocky sections. The Pipeline Trail is a wide path in a striking setting framed in greenery. It starts in a valley, along lowland by a small stream, and climbs to higher elevations up the side of the mountain. Although rough at first, it gets much better and becomes quite exceptional. Ultimately, the trail linked with other trails which did have markers. At that point there were signs and we now knew we were finally heading in the right direction. *I especially liked the upper trails in this section that zigzagged around the mountain, and I decided to return in the future to explore this area further. Except next time, I would approach from the opposite direction, from the Dyer Road Trail, and forgo riding Route 44 to Francis Road. Francis Road permits motorized traffic and you can encounter vehicles. One word of caution: just before passing a downed tree, I (unknowingly) encountered nettle plants. My horse started acting very strange, tossing his head, trying to bite his legs, and pawing at the ground. Fortunately, once we convinced him to move on, the irritation and his frightening behavior subsided. I subsequently learned that once the animal is moved out of the area of the plant, the irritation should diminish quickly. Some animals do not even react to it. This plant usually grows in wetlands and along streams, and is quite common. Watch out for this plant in*

97

the lowlands just before you climb the mountain; other plant growth is high through many sections of the lower trail and visibility of the nettle plant can be limited. The trail begins to enter a very beautiful area winding up the mountainside. At the top, there is a fork. We made a right onto the Big Dam Hollow Road. The trail remained remarkable throughout the high sections as they formed a switchback up the mountainside. We took Big Dam Hollow Road to Route 44.

After crossing Route 44, we picked up the Dyer Road loop and headed to the right. We came to the lower or rear site at the Dyer Road equestrian camping area (you'll see tie rails), made a left, and traveled through a wonderful pine forest. I called this the "jagged pine forest" as the trees were quite unique with their multiple limbs, odd shape, and pointy trunks. We then came upon an interesting work of art. It was probably from the days of the CCC camps. On the side of the trail, there is what looks like a small Eskimo round hut made out of tiers of flat stone in a circular shape, encircling a natural spring. The stone work and precision is amazing. We stopped to take lunch at this spot so we could look at this closer and take some pictures. We then continued on the Dyer Road Loop and came to Robinson Road. We made a right onto Robinson Road. We headed down Robinson Road and made a left onto Cutoff Road which is well labeled and has snowmobile signs. We came to Lebo Road, made a left on Lebo Road, and then made a right onto Whitman Road. We took Whitman to the pipeline right-of-way where the red markers and multiple-use triangles pointed to the trail along the pipeline tract on the right. We made the right and took the pipeline path back to the Twelve Mile Road lot. I found our second day's ride to be very enjoyable, except for the long stretch on Francis Road. Although it seemed to be a quiet, dirt road, it still was riding a road that had a lack of shoulder and could be tight if traffic came through. To really relax, I much prefer a trail. To the contrary, the "guys" (John and our friend Jan) enjoyed it and didn't mind riding Francis Road to link up with the trail.

Our favorite trails: We really enjoyed the Big Trestle Loop and the North Link Trail where the narrow gauge railroad once traveled (marked by NLT on posts at various intervals along its route). Another favorite (on the east side of Route 44) was the high end of the Pipeline Trail and the Big Dam Hollow Road which are old logging or access mountain roads of grass surface.

After our second day's ride, we started to get a good feel for the lay of the land and the trails. We then felt much more comfortable finding our way around and also finding ways to avoid the paved roads and travel the more scenic routes. If you are visiting this area for the first time, get a copy of the maps mentioned above and drive the dirt roads around your camping area, such as Twelve Mile Road and Lebo Road, to get your bearings. Consider doing this prior to setting out for trail and you should find it helpful if you get disoriented. We rode first but, after taking a drive, we found it was helpful to clarify the location of key intersections and connector trails and roads. We also were amazed at the many miles of dirt roads with numerous trails heading in different directions. There is so much to discover. In all, once you get a few days of riding here and talk with other riders, it becomes much less confusing. After getting a baseline, you should be able to comfortably explore as there are so many hidden gems within this State Forest and its surrounding area.

EQUESTRIAN CAMPING:
The map of the Keystone Mountain Country Shared Use Trail System indicates camping and parking locations. All lots are primitive with no water or toilet facilities. Bring lots of water. We have been told that equestrians in the area have been able to obtain water at the Black Forest Campground located on Route 44, just south of Twelve Mile Road and Dyer Road. Fin, Fur, and Feather in Haneyville has graciously helped us out in the past. Usually, campgrounds or other stables will provide water; sometimes for a fee. The map shows where water can be obtained for the horses while on trail, but these places are infrequent so make sure the horses have water upon departure and return. The following areas have been designated for equestrian camping with access to the Keystone Mountain Country Shared Use Trail System and the locations are reflected on the map. These are Dyer Road CCC and Rauch Road Gas Well campsites located in Susquehannock State Forest (both covered in this chapter), Bear Run Gas Well campsite in Tioga State Forest (not covered), Pump Station Gas Well campsite (I encompass this in Ride Pennsylvania Horse Trails- Part I under the Tiadaghton/Black Forest Chapter), and the Robbins Run and Left Branch Hyner campsites in Sproul State Forest (not covered). A recent addition is the Twelve Mile Road site located in Susquehannock State Forest (described in this chapter).

Twelve Mile Road parking/camping area: We stayed at this location during our visit. An immediate advantage to this location is that it is near Route 44 and very easy to get to (no traveling for miles down a bumpy, dirt road). But the corresponding disadvantage, although we did not find it to be a problem, is that sometimes you can hear vehicles on Route 44. However, this was mainly during the day and it was mostly quiet at night. But still, the lot has the feel of a remote setting as you cannot see Route 44 from the lot, and it is surrounded by woods providing a buffer between the camping area and tie area, and also between any of the roads. Near the camping/parking area is Twelve Mile Road. This is a lightly used dirt road which travels past the far end of the camping/parking lot and is traveled mostly by people who have cabins near its path. Since the lot is so large, there is quite a bit of distance from the dirt road. We visited on the 4th of July weekend and only saw a few vehicles traveling down this road in the course of the day.

During our visit, the lot was brand new and spotless. An excellent job was done grading it and it is a high, dry, and level surface. It would make a nice destination for a large group of riders as there is plenty of room to park and many trees to tie line to. We chose to tie line our horses at the far end of the lot (from where you drive in), behind some bulldozed tree trunks. We walked our horses past these and there was a flat, shaded area which had room to tie line many horses. We intentionally kept the horses away from the mountain laurel which can irritate a horse if they ingest it. The lot is in an open area and not shaded; however, the surrounding trees provide shade at various times of the day. You'll notice that saplings were planted around the border of the lot which was a nice touch and will help provide a scenic camping area once grown. There is no water at the lot so bring water with you. The trailheads are at the lot and well marked with signs, red rectangle blazes, and triangle brown emblems indicating it is a multiple-use trail. We very much liked the Twelve Mile Road for both parking and camping. Plus, the lot is ideal in that it is central to the trails. We considered the Twelve Mile Road lot to be the best pick in the event of wet weather as it is high and dry and, with the thick gravel surface, would be less messy and vehicles should have no trouble getting in or out.

HISTORICAL INFORMATION:
The Susquehannock Indian Tribe once occupied and hunted these lands. Later, the land was settled by the Europeans. At one time, the forests were so thick with pine and hemlock in many sections and neighboring areas that the light never penetrated the cover of trees resulting in the name "black forest" being used to describe this type of dense woods. However, by the end of the 19th century, the area was heavily logged, and its natural resources depleted. By the beginning of the 20th century, land acquisitions began to be made with the goal of creating the Susquehannock State Forest. Trails, roads, and other improvements were constructed by the Civilian Conservation Corps (CCC) in the 1930s. Today's Susquehannock State Forest includes six State Parks, one Wild Area, and a Natural Area.

Many of the cabins in this area are owned by the occupants but the land is actually State Forest land. They have a lease which must be renewed periodically. The folks at "Camp David" explained that these are usually grandfathered. We were also told that at one time, in the early 1900s, leasing the property was initiated as a revenue generator. At that time, people could build the cabins, own the cabin but not the land, and had the right to sell the cabins or pass them on to future generations if they chose. Some of these cabin owners are fortunate to have locales which are in very scenic portions of the State Forest.

COURTESIES:
Thank you to Tom Wallace, District Forester, for being so helpful and for telling us about the new trail system planned for the northwest section. Thank you to

Justin Shaffer, Forester at Susquehannock State Forest, for providing information on this region and the new Keystone Mountain Country Shared Use Trail System. I knew this trail system was in the works but I was delighted to see the map of the trails and the many choices of equestrian camping areas. I would like to express my appreciation to Thankful Batterson for answering my many questions. Thankful indicated that many enhancements are in the works for the camping sites and the trails in this area, so expect to see changes and improvements. My deepest gratitude to all those who worked so hard to establish this extensive trail system and additional camping areas, notably Jim Hyland, DCNR and the Bureau of Forestry, the rangers, the individuals, the groups, clubs, organizations, and all others whose cooperative and ambitious effort made this a reality; you have made such a positive difference. With good reason, I know this has already become a popular equestrian camping and riding destination.

THINGS WE LEARNED THIS RIDE:

- I learned about stinging nettles the hard way.
- Susquehannock State Forest is constructing another multiple-use trail in the northwest section of the State Forest.

NEARBY AND SURROUNDING AREA STABLES:

- Fin, Fur, and Feather (guided trail rides, emergency overnight stabling, general store, various local items of interest, souvenirs), Haneyville (570) 769-6620, website: www.finfurandfeather.com

NEARBY AND SURROUNDING AREA VET SERVICES:

- Lewis Vet Clinic, Linden (570) 398-2729
- Laurel Highland Farm & Equine Services LLC, E. Early, Williamsport (570) 326-1134
- Troy Veterinary Clinic, Troy (570) 673-3181

NEARBY AND SURROUNDING AREA FARRIERS:

- Brian Montei, Salladasburg (570) 398-1320
- T. Andrews, Cogan Station (570) 326-3807
- M. Seybold, Lock Haven (570) 769-7857
- J. Bodle Shoeing, Mill Hall (570) 726-6969
- D. Saunders, Mansfield (570) 662-7524

13. Blue Knob State Park
DCNR
(Department of Conservation & Natural Resources)

Lasting Impression: The trails are nice, wide, gentle, and leisurely with a good, durable surface, and travel through scenic woodlands.

Location: Blue Knob State Park is located near Altoona in northwest Bedford County in southcentral Pennsylvania.

Length: *Day Ride Destination*- There are over 5,600 acres and 9 miles of designated trails in Blue Knob State Park. Horseback riding is also allowed on the side of the park roads.

Level of Difficulty: Easy to moderate

Terrain: The majority of the trail surface was a stone dust type covering and provided good drainage and footing. There were very little, if any, rocks on most of the trail.

Horse Camping: None

Non-horse Camping: Yes

Maps and Info: DCNR, Blue Knob State Park, 124 Park Road, Imler, PA 16655-9207, (814) 276-3576, website: www.dcnr.state.pa.us, email: blueknobsp@state.pa.us. We did not see maps at the parking area, so call for maps in advance. For disability or other information, contact the Pennsylvania Bureau of State Parks (888) PA-PARKS.

Activities: Hiking, Biking, Horseback Riding Trails, Picnicking, Swimming, Fishing, Camping, Hunting, and Skiing

Fees for Trail Use: None

Permits for Day Trail Use: None

Comfort Station: We did not see restrooms at the trailhead but there are restrooms at a few locations in the park, including the picnic area.

DIRECTIONS:

Take the Pennsylvania Turnpike I-76 to Exit #146 at Bedford; follow signs to I-99 north and Blue Knob State Park. Take I-99 north about 6 miles to Exit #7 for Osterburg and Route 869. Take Route 869 west for about 9 miles to Pavia. Route 869 has many 'S' turns but is passable; continue to follow signs for Route 869 west. In Pavia, cross a small bridge. Make a right on Pavia Road. See the Blue Knob State Park sign. Follow Pavia Road for 2.9 miles up the mountain. This is a steep road with one narrow turn. We were able to bring our big rig with living quarters up this mountain, but do not attempt it if your truck has marginal pulling power. Follow signs to the park. At the top of the mountain there is a large, open field on the right (opposite the Blue Knob Campground) with a small gravel turn around area. This is called Chappell's Field. Due to the size of the surrounding area, you can pull off of the gravel onto the grass and there is plenty of room for large rigs or group of rigs.

You can also approach this lot from the rear or north of the park by taking Route 220/I-99 to Route 164. Be careful to follow signs to Route 164 west. Travel about 9 miles on Route 164 west. Trucks will need to handle a long climb. (If you can, pull over to a parking area and check out the gorgeous view as you travel up the mountain.) There will be a brown sign on the left saying Blue Knob State Park 5 miles. There is a landscape place on the right (with a statue of liberty holding a light) and a sign for Moss Creek. This is SR 3003. Make a left onto SR 3003. This is not as steep but was a bit rough during our visit due to patched pavement. After traveling 4.4 miles on SR 3003, come to a fork and a turning loop on the right along with a large Blue Knob State Park sign. Bear right and go into the park. There is a sign for Route 869 just after this turn. After traveling a total of 5 miles on SR 3003, you will come to the large field called Chappell's Field. From this direction, parking is on the left. There are trailheads in both directions from this lot. Each approach passes at least one of them. The trails are also reflected on the map. The trails lead in different directions off of this access road and are marked with white posts where they intersect with the road.

THE TRAILS:
The Blue Knob State Park overlooks a surrounding landscape of rolling countryside and a multitude of knobs or curved mountain tops. This is gorgeous country. We loved the overlook while driving south from SR 3003 and Route 164. You can look down and enjoy a wonderful view of mountains, valleys, and streams. The rounded mountaintops and landscape reminded me of some sections of the Shenandoah Valley in Virginia. Since this park is high in elevation, bring layers of clothing as the temperatures are cooler than at lower elevations and can change more dramatically depending on the time of day or change in weather conditions. (Typical snowfall in this location is about 12 feet of snow per year!) The trails are mostly wide, mowed grass or dirt trails traveling through forested land. Often, they switch back on the side of the mountains, and many sit high overlooking the valley below. These were not "on the edge" trails; I did not find any of those here. Rather, I found these wide, gradual trails to be leisurely and relaxing. And there are many very pretty and scenic sections. When the leaves are off the trees, it must be even more breathtaking. At the areas where the trails intersect with the park roads, the trails are clearly marked with white poles and the trail names. Different trails have different color blazes which correspond to the trail. The map is also very useful in that it tells the length of the trails. The challenge was following the right trail at a fork or intersection. We found it hard, sometimes, to tell where equestrians should or could proceed. One trail, the Homestead Trail, had large trees down across the trail and required navigating around them. Luckily, the surrounding land was suitable to bypass the obstacles. Hopefully, it was just due to that season's heavy spring storms and that, normally,

fallen trees are quickly cleared. During almost the whole riding season, including the day of our visit, we couldn't escape the rain. It seemed to follow us. *We were hoping to have a nice day but as we returned from our ride, it began to pour heavily. We had to rush back to our trailers to peel off our wet tack and clothing. Still, in spite of the onset of heavy rain, we had enjoyed our visit to Blue Knob State Park.*

We rode out from Chappell's Field, picking up the trail entrance at the location of the white post that we passed just before the parking area (we were traveling from the main park entrance on the Pavia side and the marker was on our right just before we arrived at the parking field.) Shortly after departing the Chappell's Field parking area, I realized the designated horse trail travels along a narrow, paved road and links up with the paved Tower Road before connecting with the Three Springs Trail. I am hoping that a path can be cut so that equestrians can avoid any paved road connectors, especially narrow ones such as this, and enjoy continuous loops. Also, the section by Whysong Road appears to necessitate backtracking. However, there is a nice link nearby which would complete a loop that is already cleared but wasn't indicated as being open to multiple-use, and looked like it was being used for storage. This would link Whysong Road and Saw Mill Trail and make for a nice connector. Hopefully, local riding groups can work with the State Park to connect the trails off road. Not only are connecting loops nicer to ride, they have much less impact on the environment. This is one worth working on as this trail system has many beautiful sections.

We took Chappell's Field Trail to the paved road and made a left. At the intersection with Tower Road, we made a sharp right, traveled up Tower Road to the Three Springs Trail, rode the Three Springs Trail (a delightful trail), and continued past the Willow Springs picnic area. (To pick up the trail below the picnic area, look for the white post indicating the trail.) We then picked up the Homestead Trail. On this section, we needed to be careful not to lose the trail due to some downed trees across it. Look for the ruins of an old homestead along the path. After the Homestead Trail, we picked up the Saw Mill Trail to the left. We passed cabins, some of which were part of the old CCC camp. We continued on the Saw Mill Trail and headed back to the Chappell's Field Trail, and ultimately returned to the parking area.

A note of caution on the trail: sometimes there are manhole covers which cover water lines. During our ride, not all the covers were on, so do glance down at the trail periodically to make sure you are not about to step into a hole. Overall, other than the one stretch of road riding and section of storm damage, these trails are excellent. The park is clean, well kept, and has a great, durable ground surface with little or no rocks.

HISTORICAL INFORMATION:
This area was settled in the mid 1700s. The Indians drove the first settlers out and later, when the forts were built, the settlers returned. This region is in close proximity to the Lincoln Highway or Route 30. Originally an Indian trail, it was expanded to accommodate settlers' wagons. Once the road was widened, the area was quickly settled. Due to the fact that at that time it was the only road linking eastern Pennsylvania with Ohio and beyond, taverns opened and thrived. Legend has it that every third home was once a tavern along what is now Route 30. As a result, a lot of history occurred in these inns and in this vicinity. The nearby Jean Bonnet Tavern, built by an Indian trader and associate of George Washington, later became the scene of a liberty pole raised in protest during the Whiskey Rebellion years in the late 1700s. It is now a restaurant and B&B, and open for your viewing. See contact information in this chapter to learn more about the area or to obtain a visitor's guide.

In the 1930s and 1940s, the Blue Knob State Park was first identified as an area to be preserved as a park. The National Park Service and the Civilian Conservation Corps (CCC) played a vital role in the park's early development years. By the 1940s, after World War II, the state of Pennsylvania acquired the land and it became a State Park. Blue Knob State Park obtained its name from its quartzite summit and the appearance of a blue mist that is often seen embracing the mountain. It is the second highest peak in Pennsylvania, a height exceeding sea level by 3,100 feet. The highest is Mount Davis which is almost 70 feet higher.

COURTESIES:
Both John and I would like to personally thank Nancy Gable for her wonderful hospitality, for allowing us to camp on her property while we rode the nearby trails, for sharing her wealth of knowledge on these trails, and for joining us to cover some of the nearby trails. Nancy, we really enjoyed our visit, you're an excellent trail guide, a gracious hostess, and you also pick great restaurants! I had told Nancy how I love to dine at old historic inns and asked her if she knew of any good ones nearby. Well she brought us to the Jean Bonnet Tavern. Built in the 1700s, it is a lovely old historic inn, just the kind I like. During our visit, we dined in the rustic atmosphere of candlelight in the basement of the inn. Unknown to any of us that they would be dining nearby, a very large party of historic re-enactors in 19th century garb filled the restaurant. The atmosphere was complete. Without missing a beat, Nancy turned to me and said, "Is this historic enough for you?" After we laughed at the coincidence and Nancy's perfectly timed statement, we enjoyed a charming dining experience that truly felt like a step back in time.

I would like to thank Ron Bhrem (now retired) who shoed my horse at a moment's notice. My horse pulled a shoe while unloading upon arrival. Ron was very accommodating and came to our rescue so that we would not lose any time covering the trails in the area. Along with DCNR, we would also like to thank all other individuals and groups who contribute to these nice trails.

THINGS WE LEARNED THIS RIDE:

• The "Lost Turkey Trail" is near this trail system. While riding we came upon a picnic area labeled "Turkey Roast." Sounds like we know what happened to the turkey!

• Paint the easy boot a bright color so, when it falls off, you can find it! (Thanks, Nancy!)

• Covered bridges were usually named after nearby mills.

NEARBY AND SURROUNDING AREA:

• TJ's (Transfer Junction) Tack & Western, Altoona (814) 942-4434

• Bedford County Covered Bridges, c/o Bedford County Visitors Bureau (800) 765-3331, website: www.bedfordcounty.net/bridges

• Old Bedford Village (historic village and re-enactments), (814) 623-1156, (800) 238-4347, website: www.oldbedfordvillage.org

• Lincoln Caverns, Huntingdon (814) 643-0268, website: www.lincolncaverns.com

• Jean Bonnet Tavern, Bedford (814) 623-2250, website: www.jeanbonnettavern.com (We really enjoyed our visit to this historic inn; ask for the basement dining area if you like a rustic and period atmosphere.)

• The Silver Stirrup tack store (tack and trail items), off Route 764 in Duncansville (814) 695-4530

• Watch for information on local club trail rides published in The Paper Horse (717) 436-8893.

NEARBY AND SURROUNDING AREA VET SERVICES:

• Dr. Knepper, Windswept Equine Center, Berlin (814) 267-5617

• M. James, Martinsburg (814) 793-3566 (use (814) 793-9226 only if he can't be reached at other number)

• E. Bracken, Williamsburg (814) 832-2313, (814) 932-6893 cell

NEARBY AND SURROUNDING AREA FARRIERS:

• T. Awckland, New Paris (814) 733-4996

Ride Pennsylvania Horse Trails- Part II

14. The Lower Trail
Rails-To-Trails of Central Pennsylvania

Lasting Impression: Through woodlands and past farms, this is a very nice, leisurely rail-trail with a remote feel.
Location: The Lower Trail is located in Blair and Huntingdon Counties in central Pennsylvania and runs from Williamsburg to Alfarata. This is close to Canoe Creek State Park and should be connected to Canoe Creek by the time this goes to print.
Length: *Day Ride Destination*- This rail-trail is 17 miles long (one way) plus additional miles will be available upon the completion of the planned link to nearby Canoe Creek State Park trails.
Level of Difficulty: We found this trail to be easy. There are some bridges that horses will need to be comfortable with crossing. However, we found the bridges to be of good width and structure; consequently our horses did not hesitate to cross them.
Terrain: Hikers and bikers are permitted on the main rail-trail which is stone dust. Equestrians are not permitted on the central path, but are permitted to ride the wide grass stretches on the side of the rail-trail. This surface was of good terrain and solid ground. It was also mowed and well maintained.
Horse Camping: None
Non-horse Camping: None
Maps and Info: Rails-To-Trails of Central Pennsylvania, P.O. Box 592, Hollidaysburg, PA 16648-0592, (814) 832-2400; Rails-To-Trails Conservancy, website: www.railtrails.org. Trail information was also available at the Williamsburg lot during our visit.
Activities: Hiking, Biking, Horseback Riding Trails, Fishing, X-C Skiing, and Wheelchair Accessible (Although hunting is not stated as an authorized use, always exercise caution during hunting season as adjoining sections may have hunting.)
Fees for Trail Use: None
Permits for Day Trail Use: None
Comfort Station: There is a bathroom at Canoe Creek State Park, and also a chemical toilet at the Williamsburg trailhead.

DIRECTIONS:
We parked at the Williamsburg lot. Take I-99 to Route 36 to Route 22 Hollidaysburg. From Hollidaysburg, take Route 22 east for about 9 miles (you will pass the Canoe Creek State Park entrance). Watch for signs for Route 866. Take Route 866 into Williamsburg. (Route 866 will change to First Street.) Travel 3.5 miles on Route 866 to the lot. The Lower Trail parking area is on the

left. (Also, you will see the Past to Present ice cream store and bike rental where you can get a treat before or after your departure.) The lot is a medium to large area which has ample space, if others aren't also using the lot. We brought our larger rig and, probably due to marginal weather, we had all the room we needed. However, at this central location, weekdays or off-peak times may be a better choice if you are seeking solitude and guaranteed parking room with a big rig. If your horses are acclimated to multiple-use activity and your rig is a smaller trailer (2-horse type) the lot should be suitable and have sufficient space on the weekends. There is a hitching rail by the lot. There is also a sign which indicates where equestrians are permitted and where they are not.

THE TRAILS:
This rail-trail travels through some very pretty and scenic countryside. The trail is of a wide width and has a gravel or stone dust surface, and attractive, manicured grass borders the main route. Upon our arrival, we noticed the sign that indicates equestrians must stay on the grass area or they will not be allowed on the rail-trail. We complied but sometimes this was hard to do as the normally wide shoulder of the rail-trail was narrow in certain sections due to some unfinished trail maintenance. The rail-trail was very well groomed at the time of our visit, but we must have visited while maintenance was in process. At numerous intervals there were piles of brush which blocked the grass area forcing the horses to walk close to the edge of the trail. Probably a storm had come and the maintenance crews were unable to finish their work to gather or set aside the cuttings. We had to be careful to steer clear of the main path; a few times this was challenging due to these obstacles. However, we were very grateful to the maintenance crews who were doing such a nice job keeping the trail in excellent shape.

There are mile markers to judge your distance and signs explaining the historical significance of locations throughout the trail. Sometimes the markers become confusing because different numbers have been placed by alternate sources over time. We found the map useful and interesting, identifying various points along the trail. We also enjoyed the lovely patches of gardens that dot the landscape of the trail. Many are dedicated to departed ones and are often maintained by volunteers. Stretches of interesting rock walls line the sections of trail on one side. On the other side is the Juniata River, offering a contrast in scenery, all adding to the beauty of the surroundings. The river was quite a site during our visit as it was full, flowing quickly, and had many rapids due to recent record rains. Except for a surprised grouse and a big snapping turtle, we had the trails to ourselves. We had ridden from the Williamsburg lot to Mt. Etna and back and, throughout, our ride was leisurely and the terrain was easy. Due to the onset of a storm, we had to turn back just short of the Mt. Etna Mill Race covered bridge. We had wanted to visit the covered bridge and will have to return to see it. In fact, it began raining heavily as we headed back from covering this trail. But in spite of the weather, this rail-trail's simple splendor was apparent, resulting in a very enjoyable ride.

HISTORICAL INFORMATION:
There is much historical significance of the Lower Trail and its story reflects the various phases of our nation's history. This path was significant to travelers over time as it presented a more feasible route, traveling along the river versus over the mountains. The Indians used this route and the settlers traveled along its path. Later, it was converted to a canal path, then to a railroad corridor, and in current times to a recreation trail.

During the early 1800s, the passageway was a canal path (a.k.a. the Pennsylvania Canal) and served as a travel route between Philadelphia and Pittsburgh. Local commerce thrived during this early development phase and remains of some of the businesses, such as iron ore, can still be seen along its route. Of special interest is the section where canal boats were transported over the Allegheny Mountains to the community of Johnstown. They were moved via incline planes and flat cars over the mountains!

By the mid 1800s, the more efficient railroads replaced the use of canals for transporting cargo. The canal path was acquired by the railroad industry, rails were laid, and the Pennsylvania Railroad operated along its route. The railroads operated along this corridor for a long time but, ultimately, their heyday also passed. By the late 1970s and early 1980s, the railroads ceased operations and abandoned its use. In the 1990s, the rail-trail was acquired for purposes of converting this passageway to a multiple-use recreation trail, to both preserve this important phase of our nation's history and to provide a form of recreation for all to enjoy.

Both on the map and along various locations on the trail, there are signs indicating the historical significance of sites or the identity of the remains of industries which once thrived along this route.

At this writing, plans are under way to link the Lower Trail rail-trail to Canoe Creek State Park. There may even be an underpass built to travel under the highway. If they are able to link the two trail systems (and if it is decided equestrians will be permitted throughout), there will be a significant increase in total trail mileage available to ride.

COURTESIES:
Many thanks to the Rails-To-Trails of Central Pennsylvania, to Mr. T. Dean Lower, and to the other individuals, groups, and organizations who recognized this as a trail that should be preserved, who have contributed so much to the establishment of this wonderful recreation trail, and for welcoming equestrians.

Also, thank you to the folks at the Past to Present ice cream shop, who were very friendly and helpful in sharing information about the rail-trail during our visit.

THINGS WE LEARNED THIS RIDE:
- I learned, during the onset of rain, how hard it is to take notes when the paper is wet!
- Importantly, I was reminded to support the local rails-to-trails groups through memberships, contributions, or assistance as they are preserving an important part of our nation's history for so many to enjoy, and allowing equestrians to enjoy it on horseback.

NEARBY AND SURROUNDING AREA VET SERVICES:
- E. Bracken, Williamsburg (814) 832-2313, (814) 932-6893 cell
- M. James, Martinsburg (814) 793-3566 (use (814) 793-9226 only if he can't be reached at other number)

NEARBY AND SURROUNDING AREA FARRIERS:
- Chester Horton Horseshoeing, Alexandria (800) 993-SHOE, (814) 669-4652

15. Canoe Creek State Park
DCNR
(Department of Conservation & Natural Resources)

Lasting Impression: What a picturesque setting with Canoe Creek nestled in the surrounding mountainous terrain! This is a lovely area to meander throughout and enjoy the beautiful views.

Location: Hollidaysburg (near Altoona) in Blair County

Length: *Day Ride Destination*- There are several miles of trails and adjoining dirt access roads on almost 1,000 acres of land, plus there are plans to link Canoe Creek State Park with the nearby Lower Trail resulting in additional trail miles.

Level of Difficulty: Mostly easy to moderate; some sections are more challenging

Terrain: The terrain varied from flat dirt roads, to rolling hills, to mountainous terrain. Overall, the trails were of good surface. Some of the lowland trails may retain moisture after periods of rain but can be bypassed.

Horse Camping: None

Non-horse Camping: Cabins are available for rental.

Maps and Info: DCNR, Canoe Creek State Park, RR2, Box 560, Hollidaysburg, PA 16648-9752, (814) 695-6807, website: www.dcnr.state.pa.us. To reserve cabins or picnic areas, call (888) PA-PARKS. Maps are available at the Visitor Center; but in the event the center is closed, it is best to obtain a map via mail or online before your arrival. For disability information, contact the Pennsylvania Bureau of State Parks (888) PA-PARKS.

Activities: Hiking, Biking, Horseback Riding Trails, Picnicking, Boating, Swimming, Fishing, Cabin Rental, Sledding, Ice Fishing, Ice Skating, Ice Boating, X-C Skiing, and Hunting

Fees for Trail Use: None

Permits for Day Trail Use: None

Comfort Station: Yes, see the park map for locations.

DIRECTIONS:
Take I-99 to Route 22 east toward Hollidaysburg. Or, to avoid traffic, take I-99 to Exit #23 and pick up Route 36 north, following signs for Route 36 north to Hollidaysburg. (It is 5 miles on Route 36 from the exit to Hollidaysburg and Route 22.) Make a right on Route 22. From Hollidaysburg, travel 7 miles on Route 22 east. Look for Turkey Valley Road to the left. (Note: there are 2 lefts onto Turkey Valley Road. Pass the first one which occurs about 3 miles east of Hollidaysburg. Instead, continue the full 7 miles on Route 22 east to make the left onto Turkey Valley Road.) There will be a Canoe Creek State Park sign at the entrance.

Take Turkey Valley Road for about .6 miles. Make a right into the park through the gates. Travel 1 mile on the main park road and make a left at the sign for the Visitor Center. Equestrian parking is on the mowed shoulder of the road, on the edge of a field, just before the Visitor Center. *Note: when we called the park office we were told that if there was a possibility of rainy weather we could park in the large paved lots just below the road for the Visitor Center (behind the first stop sign on the main park road). If you are traveling with a large trailer, the turning radius will be too tight in those parking lots. However, a standard 2-horse trailer or small gooseneck should have no problem turning within the lots, if other vehicles are not blocking their path. If there is the possibility of rain, larger rigs will likely have to park in the usual designated location by the Visitor Center and exercise extra care to avoid impact if the ground becomes wet and vulnerable.*

THE TRAILS:
During our visit, we parked on the side of the road just before the Visitor Center. We arrived on a Friday in June and saddled up and headed out early. We rode past the Visitor Center toward the eastern section of the park and lake. Our morning began dry but, later, a light rain started as we were returning to the lot. Rain was frequent this riding season and we couldn't seem to escape from it. Since it was a weekday with marginal weather, we had the place to ourselves. The area felt wonderfully remote and peaceful, and the abundance of deer, including fawns, and other wildlife that we encountered reflected the unspoiled fields and forests within and surrounding the park. As we rode, there were numerous areas where the grass was flattened as herds of deer had bedded down. We surprised quite a few that "were sleeping in" as we traveled the trails.

Many sections of the trails provide a scenic vista of the 155 acre Canoe Creek Lake. The equestrian trails are in the northern section of the park and some are reflected on the DCNR map. There are many trails that branch off that are not on the map. Even though the main trail on the map looked easy to follow, we were unsure where to proceed due to many offshoots and lack of markers. When we spoke with the Visitor Center, they explained they prefer not to put up too many signs as some folks prefer the natural, unmarked look to the trails. We very much appreciated this and their flexibility. However, we also expressed that a disadvantage to not having at least some signs or guidance, is that it is hard to determine where equestrians are permitted or prohibited from riding. And we did not want to wear out our welcome by traveling on the wrong path, nor did we want to miss any interesting trails such as those leading to the Kilns.

We rode in a loop, first heading down a dirt road which connected with a dirt trail that traveled along Canoe Lake and then aside Canoe Creek. We weren't certain how to head up the mountain until we saw an equestrian sign. At this point the trail climbed up the side of the mountain and unexpectedly became more challenging and difficult. We were wondering if there was a more gradual approach up the side of the mountain. If so, we didn't see it. Once we were at the top, we took a trail that passed various old mine sites which now serve as homes for a variety of bats (see photo). As you ride, watch for bats as Canoe Creek State Park is known for having one of the biggest bat communities in the east! We continued in this counter clockwise direction, passed the mines, and followed a narrow trail on the north side of the mountain. At first it was very pleasant and scenic, but then it became too narrow for our comfort level and we speculated that we had wandered off course. The trail was quickly becoming challenging to ride so we got off the trail and blazed cross country to the open fields on the south side of the mountain. This section offered terrific views of the lake, and many knobs of rolling landscape of high grass terrain to ride. This was my **most favorite portion** of the park as it is absolutely beautiful. But watch that high grass! Wildlife is hidden in the high grass; fawns pop up like a jack-in-the-box and then bolt. The horses really loved that! We then linked in with another trail, explored various connecting trails, and ultimately headed back in the direction of the Visitor Center. During the last stretch of our ride we had wanted to visit the Blair Limestone Co. Kilns. We weren't sure if equestrians were permitted in that vicinity so we did not approach the area on horseback. We later checked at the Visitor Center and they indicated there is a trail that we could have taken to the historic site. We will have to see that attraction on our next visit.

HISTORICAL INFORMATION:
Limestone was abundant in the area resulting in nearby quarries being established in the early 1900s. Limestone was used in the steel, iron, and other industries. Remains of some of these quarries and limekilns still exist, are reflected on the park map, and can be viewed while visiting the park. Later, Project 70 contributed to the creation of this park. In the late 1970s, the park was officially opened.

Near this trail system is the Allegheny Plateau in the region of Indiana to Altoona. This is the home of the Horseshoe Curve. Built in the mid 1800s, it allowed trains to cross the Allegheny Mountains via rail. This passageway was so critical and strategic that, during World War II, it was on Hitler's list of targets to attack and destroy. Fortunately, that never occurred.

COURTESIES:
I would like to express my gratitude to Heidi Boyle and Russ Wade at the Canoe Creek Visitor Center who were very interested in hearing our suggestions regarding the addition of trail markers on some of the equestrian trails, and who also made us feel very welcome. It was a pleasure to speak with them. Do stop by the Visitor Center where Heidi, Russ, and the other friendly folks at the center share information on the area and local wildlife, along with maps and interesting historical and environmental displays. They have an excellent model of the area

which you may want to view before departing on the trail to help you get the lay of the land. Don't forget to thank the rangers at the Visitor Center for allowing equestrians to enjoy this attractive park on horseback.

NEARBY:
* The Silver Stirrup tack store (if you forget something for your trip, these nice folks have a good stock of tack and trail items), Duncansville (814) 695-4530

NEARBY AND SURROUNDING AREA VET SERVICES:
* E. Bracken, Williamsburg (814) 832-2313, (814) 932-6893 cell
* M. James, Martinsburg (814) 793-3566 (use (814) 793-9226 only if he can't be reached at other number)

NEARBY AND SURROUNDING AREA FARRIERS:
* Chester Horton Horseshoeing, Alexandria (800) 993-SHOE, (814) 669-4652

16. Ohiopyle State Park
DCNR
(Department of Conservation & Natural Resources)

Lasting Impression: This is a nice, leisurely day ride which has many nearby trails to explore and interesting areas to visit.

Location: Ohiopyle State Park is located mostly in Fayette County in southwest Pennsylvania. The Youghiogheny River winds through the interior of the park offering some wonderful views of waterfalls and its banks. There are fantastic river sights but they must be viewed on foot or bike. The equestrian trails are located in the south and eastern sections of the park. Although the equestrian trails do not travel near the river, they are also scenic and a pleasant ride.

Length: *Day Ride Destination*- Ohiopyle State Park consists of over 19,000 acres. Estimates range from 9 to 12 miles of horseback riding trails, 13 miles of biking trails, and over 79 miles of hiking trails. The park also includes the Youghiogheny River Trail, a rail-trail which is 27 miles in length and is open to hiking and biking, and is part of the planned Great Allegheny Passage. The passage will be 152 miles in length (plus a 52 mile branch), once completed, connecting Cumberland, MD to Pittsburgh, PA. Equestrians are permitted on certain sections of this trail and those sections are indicated on the "Great Allegheny Passage" map available at the Visitor Center (in the train station building) in Ohiopyle, or from the contacts indicated below.

Level of Difficulty: The equestrian trails vary from easy to moderate.

Terrain: Overall, good surface with minimal rocks

Horse Camping: There is no horse camping at Ohiopyle State Park. But, there are facilities, a short drive from the trails, at the nearby Nemacolin Woodlands Equestrian Center (724) 329-6961, ext 1.

Non-horse Camping: Yes

Carriage Potential: There is carriage potential at Ohiopyle State Park due to the miles of double width paths. Carriage enthusiasts would need to check out the lay of the land, access, and parking to determine if suitable. Also check in advance to confirm the paths have been cleared of downed trees.

Maps and Info: DCNR, Ohiopyle State Park, P.O. Box 105, Ohiopyle, PA 15470-0105, (724) 329-8591, email: ohiopyle@state.pa.us, website: www.dcnr.state.pa.us. Handicapped information can be obtained by calling (888) PA-PARKS. Arrange for a map in advance or pick one up at the Visitor Center; there weren't any maps at the equestrian trailhead at the time of our visit. As the equestrian area is quite a distance from the Visitor Center, it is more convenient to obtain one in advance. Regarding information on the Great Allegheny Passage, a map can be obtained from the Allegheny Trail Alliance (888) 282-

115

2453, via email: atamail@atatrail.org or website: www.atatrail.org, or stop at the Visitor Center in Ohiopyle.
Activities: Hiking, Biking, Horseback Riding Trails, Picnicking, Rafting, Canoeing, Whitewater Boating, Guided Raft Trips, Fishing, Camping, Sledding, Snowmobiling, X-C Skiing, and Hunting. The nearby Youghiogheny River Trail is handicap accessible. And, Ohiopyle State Park even has natural waterslides! The waterslides are located in Meadow Run and can be accessed by parking by the Route 381 bridge (which crosses Meadow Run) and following the path which is located at the rear of the parking lot, or by following signs to the Meadow Run Trail.
Fees for Trail Use: None
Permits for Day Trail Use: None
Comfort Station: None

DIRECTIONS:
There are many ways to reach the Ohiopyle State Park equestrian trailhead. The trailhead can be accessed off of Route 40, near the town of Farmington, east of where Route 381 intersects with Route 40. Take Route 40 east from the Route 381 intersection and make a left onto Dinnerbell Road and continue as indicated below. (Dinnerbell Road is about a mile east of the Nemacolin Woodlands Resort and Equestrian Center.)

Or, if traveling from the north, take the Pennsylvania Turnpike to Exit #110, the Somerset exit. Follow signs for Route 281 south. *Route 281 has many bends; be sure to watch for signs especially in the towns where there can be sudden and sharp turns.* Travel on Route 281 south for about 24 miles to the town of Confluence and Route 523. *Do not continue on Route 281 as Route 281 is very steep between Confluence and Route 40. In Confluence, be sure to take the first left, not the one at the stop sign.* Take Route 523 south for 6 miles to Route 40. Make a right onto Route 40 and travel toward Farmington. Route 40, between Routes 281 and 381, has some climbs; trucks should have adequate pulling power. Travel about 11 miles and begin looking for Dinnerbell Road (there is a road sign) on the right. From this direction, if you see the Nemacolin Woodlands Equestrian Center, you have passed the turn.

Travel on Dinnerbell Road for 4.8 miles and make a right onto Grover Road (dirt/gravel). Go 1 mile and look for the left to the equestrian parking area. There is a sign where to turn. The lot is of medium size with pull through room. Even though it is a designated equestrian lot, it had cement place holders arranged in a manner more suited to vehicles, but not trucks with horse trailers as we had to maneuver to get around them. But still, this lot was nice and secluded, offered sufficient room to pull through the loop, and you could park on the side and avoid the cement blocks. Only if the lot was crowded, would this be an issue. There is also plenty of open surrounding area to accommodate overflow. There is

116

a small corral at the lot for equestrians to let their horses stretch if they choose. Water is indicated on the map, but it is best to bring your own as it is a hand pump and is a distance from the parking area. This location appears to be an ideal location for primitive equestrian camping (hint, hint) as there is plenty of room and a very low level of activity. Unfortunately, equestrian camping was not permitted at the time of our visit.

To reach Ohiopyle and to view the non-equestrian attractions, take Route 381 directly into the middle of the town. If traveling from the south, take Route 40 to Route 381 north. There are signs along the way indicating where each attraction is. The Ohiopyle State Park map is helpful.

To reach the Equestrian Center at Nemacolin Woodlands, head east of Route 381 on Route 40. The facility is located on the north side of Route 40 in Farmington.

THE TRAILS:
Ohiopyle is a lovely area on the southern tip of Pennsylvania where people come from all over, including the neighboring states of Maryland and West Virginia, to enjoy the area's many attractions. People bring their family and friends (and even their dogs) to wade in the water and to enjoy the beautiful surrounding scenery of the river. This is a major mecca for kayaking, mountain biking, and hiking. When you come to visit the trails, do take a visit to the town of Ohiopyle. This central area is where the Youghiogheny River Trail passes through the heart of this town. This section has some of the prettiest scenery in the area but, because it is so popular and crowded, horses are not permitted in this vicinity. The more remote sections of the trail on the grass section between Boston and Connellsville (Yough Trail section) and on the grass section between Rockwood and Garrett (Allegheny Highlands Trail section) permit horses. See the Great Allegheny Passage map available at the Visitor Center for more information.

Regarding the Ohiopyle area, the Ohiopyle State Park has set aside a network of trails in the Sugarloaf Snowmobile and Mountain Bike Area (southeast section) where horses are permitted. This is far removed from the nucleus of activity above, and is located in a quiet, remote, high, and dry area. The advantage is you can ride for hours and not see a soul. The disadvantage is that the designated equestrian trails do not provide views of the various waterways of the area and little of the scenery that Ohiopyle is famous for. However, these trails still offer some very picturesque vistas and offer many hours of enjoyable riding through woodlands and over rolling hills in a relaxing setting.

The equestrian lot is tucked away in the southern section of the park. It was a Saturday on a holiday weekend, yet we had the lot and trails to ourselves. We departed the lot, making a left out of the lot (away from the entrance) and headed down the gravel road in the direction of the trails. Just before the sign for water, we made a right onto a wide grass tract. (We checked out the water thinking we could give the horses a drink; however, this was a hand pump and we would actually have had to carry a bucket a significant distance to the pump in order for the horses to drink. We passed on that and suggest folks bring their own water.) Before turning onto the grass trail to the right, we rode toward the water pump and took in the vista of the surrounding mountain range. This area was one of the prettier parts of the trail as it offered a good view of the neighboring countryside. We did not travel farther down this section but it looked like a good area to explore or to extend one's ride. (Check for restrictions prior to exploring this area.)

We headed down the grass path and came to a four-way intersection. At first we had quite a bit of trouble connecting in with the main network of trails. It gets confusing. Although there are markers, they are not numbered in a manner corresponding to the map. Plus it was hard to follow the map because there were breaks in trail links and they did not always line up exactly. You needed to know to travel farther down the road before you could connect with the next section and continue on the trail. Once we figured this out, it became easy (after about an hour of riding in unintentional circles). So, hopefully, we can save you that, or maybe it was us because we didn't get much sleep due to the fireworks the evening before (see below).

We came to the first intersection, made a right, then a left onto Grover Road (dirt/gravel). We traveled a short distance down Grover Road (this road was quiet during our visit) and made a right onto the trail (just before the next paved road). Someone, like us, must have missed this same entrance as a ribbon was placed there to mark it. We took this trail, crossed another dirt road, and continued following the trail markers. There was an opportunity to go to the left and cross the road, but we decided to bear right. That was the right choice as the trail lead to open meadows and eventually to the sledding area. Once in the vicinity of the sledding area, just before the snowmobile parking lot, look for markers to the right which lead into the wooded area. *There is a helicopter landing strip with overhead electric wires. How did that happen? We are hoping someone will move those wires underground or move the landing strip!* This is where there are various loops of trails. We made the right and then made a left and headed up an incline which overlooks the sledding area. There are some climbs but we found them gradual and not difficult. Once at the top, the trail continues through the woods in loops and there are opportunities to cut the loops short. We chose to do so at one point by following a mowed stretch which offered a shortcut.

Throughout the trail system, the trails are either wide dirt or grass stretches. These types of trails are conducive for riding side by side. Although this is a nice trail system, most of the trails in this section travel straight and are of farm lane or

118

logging road width. Some riders may prefer a single lane width trail that winds through the woods. If so, this would not be the trail system for them. However, we did find this to be an easy trail system to ride; and as the trails are mostly shaded, they offered a cool escape from the July heat. This would probably be a good trail system to train trail horses as there seems to be very little, if any, activity. Rocks are minimal and the surface was very good. The trails were clean and most of the trails were well maintained until we reached the outer loops of the trail. In the outer sections, we ran into downed trees lying across the trails along with low hanging brush. We were still on the equestrian trail per the map but this section needed to be cleared. From what we could see, this locale could still be ridden as the land around the downed trees was usually passable and of level ground. You just had to watch rocky clusters that were often on the side of the trail. We had already been out for many hours and, with the possibility of a thunder storm looming, we instead decided to take one of the cross cuts to pick up the return loop. As you return, there are alternate loops leading back to the sledding area. Most are marked at the end points but occasionally we saw a post with no signs. They had been shot off. The naked posts are hard to see and it can be easy to miss a turn. We returned to the sledding area. As you return to the top of the hill by the sledding area, be sure to notice the view. Going back offers a different perspective of this section of the trail, with a better vista of the surrounding knolls of mountains. We then followed the trail back and returned to the day parking area.

There is a lot more to do in this area. After riding the equestrian trails, visit the Youghiogheny River Trail which provides an opportunity to hike or bike the trail or, on a hot day, wade in the water below the bridge (you will know "the bridge" when you see it) at the center of Ohiopyle, or enjoy traveling in a raft or canoe along the river and rapids. *Note: the levels of difficulty range from class I to class IV which requires experienced whitewater boaters to navigate. Check the rating in advance and seek guidance as to a suitable level. Family rafting or beginning levels are designated in the Middle Yough near the Ramcat Put-in (Confluence) where class I and class II rapids can be enjoyed. Challenging sections are described in the area below the Ohiopyle Falls, and it is depicted as one of the most active whitewater areas east of the Mississippi. Levels of difficulty will vary due to environmental factors and weather.* Three waterfalls, Cucumber Falls, Jonathan Run Falls, and Cascades can also be seen in other sections of the park.

HISTORICAL INFORMATION:
The early history of this area is interesting. Legend states that at about the time of the arrival of Europeans, the Monongahela People, who were originally native to this area and whose settlements ranged from the Mississippi River to its branches, vanished without evidence as to why or where. Various American Indian tribes and Europeans settled in this region including the Delaware, Shawnee, and

119

Iroquois. Conflicts continued to arise between the Indians, the French, and the British. At one point, the land was declared Indian territory, but the declaration was ignored and settlers stayed. And, even Pennsylvania and Virginia conflicted as to who had rightful claim to the territory. So many significant events in history were a part of this area. The Whiskey Rebellion ran strong in these parts. Eventually the disputes diminished, and by the early 1800s, the National Road opened these parts to travel and lumbering. The railroad industries increased development and prosperity. By the 1870s, railroads, including the Baltimore and Ohio Railroad and later the Western Maryland Railroad, were a major form of transportation to Ohiopyle. The lumbering industry along with local communities thrived. Tourists also arrived via railroad. The 1880s brought hotels to the area, including the Ferncliff Hotel, featuring dance pavilions, boardwalks, tennis, bowling alleys, and various other popular recreation of the time.

When the automobile became commonplace and interstate roads were built, the popularity of these resorts declined as tourists hit the road for new and different destinations. Over the years the region changed dramatically. The town of Ohiopyle reflected this as its name changed from Pyle or Pile City in the 1850s, to Falls City in the 1870s, to Ohiopyle (believed to be from the Indian language meaning white, frothy water) in the 1880s. Ultimately, the Western Pennsylvania Conservancy acquired the land to protect it. By the 1960s, the Commonwealth of Pennsylvania purchased this land with the goal of preserving it for future generations to enjoy.

COURTESIES:
Thank you to Dan Bickle of the office of DCNR at Ohiopyle for returning our call, telling us about the equestrian trails along with sending us information on the area, and for making us feel welcome. Also, thank you to Debbie at the DCNR office who nicely referred us to the Tall Oaks Campground so we had a place nearby to camp overnight. Thank you also to the very friendly and helpful folks at the Tall Oaks Campground for referring us to Nemacolin Woodlands so that we could learn about their unique resort and equestrian facilities.

THINGS WE LEARNED THIS RIDE:
We probably were taught one of our strongest lessons this trail ride. Due to the 4th of July falling on a Friday, we had the opportunity to take a long weekend and travel to Ohiopyle. Since there were no equestrian campgrounds in the Ohiopyle vicinity that we yet knew of, we had decided to stay at a non-equestrian campground. I gave consideration to fireworks and checked if any were planned. None were in store and so I felt it would be a safe destination for our horses to camp while we covered Ohiopyle. Plus, I figured we would be in a back field away from any activity so it should be a quiet location. What we learned: Unknown to the campground, everyone else planned to go to that same remote

location and set up their own personal fireworks show. Certainly not anyone's fault or wrong as it was the 4th of July, but not the place to be with horses. Next time we will pass on traveling with horses around the 4th of July unless we are familiar with our destination. Both of us had our hands full with two horses tie lined while all sorts of explosions and squealing sounds blasted directly over their heads and in the fields all around them. It was so bad that debris and casing landed in the horse buckets. I also learned not to stand close to the horses as they would whirl around when additional explosions sounded almost trampling my body in the process. It was too late to leave that evening but we knew we couldn't stay at the same location the next night. Explaining the horses' reaction, I went from group to group asking if they could please hold off the fireworks until the next evening when we wouldn't be there; they kindly obliged. The next morning we pulled out. To our rescue, came the nice folks at the Nemacolin Woodlands Equestrian Center who allowed us to board our horses in their wonderful facility with clean, airy, roomy stalls and also allowed us to stay in our camper at their show and vendor lot. We then could cover Ohiopyle, have a secure place for the horses, and have a chance to relax and explore the surrounding attractions. Our many thanks to Sheryl, Cassie, and everyone at Nemacolin!

NEARBY ATTRACTION:
Nemacolin Woodlands Resort and Equestrian Center is a unique resort and an upscale destination. You can see the elegant hotel from many surrounding locations as it sits high and overlooks the area below. It is plush and reminds us of a modern version of the old Mohonk Mountain House in New York State, and is even equipped with its own landing strip directly behind the hotel. It also has some wonderful dining and shops to appeal to a variety of tastes and budgets, and is open to the public. Equestrians and other visitors should enjoy the Nemacolin Woodlands Store located east of Route 381 (indicated on the Great Allegheny Passage map) on Route 40. It has a fun assortment of outdoor goods, attractions, and a combo museum and store experience. Check out the store's center piece! It is an awesome mountain with an array of animals (taxidermy exhibit) positioned in a natural setting. My favorite part was walking through the mountain and enjoying the display of poisonous snakes (live). I was wondering how one managed to maintain their cages without getting bitten. Not a job that I would want!

We also took the advice of the folks at the Nemacolin Equestrian Center and tried the Tavern for dinner, which is on the hotel complex. The food was reasonably priced, the meals were delicious, and the atmosphere was less formal than the other attractions. Our table was near an enormous aquarium. It was entertaining watching these huge fish swim in this gigantic tank. (There is some magnification in the walls of the tank, but still these were big fish.) Don't miss checking out the gold piece at the bottom of the tank salvaged from a ship wreck that occurred in the 1600s.

And of course, do take a visit to the Nemacolin Woodlands Equestrian Center. The Center has an array of activities including carriage rides, sleigh rides, guided trail rides, natural horsemanship training, shows, etc. During our visit, the Nemacolin Woodlands Equestrian Center was currently working on establishing a direct link from their facility to the Ohiopyle equestrian trail system, making for a nice long trail ride. However, the equestrian center is part of the Nemacolin Woodlands complex and some activities may not be for those on a limited budget. Even if that is the case, everyone is welcome to visit and check out their facility. This is a warm and friendly staff that will provide you with information on local happenings and current events at the center. The equestrian center also offers overnight boarding in their 46 stall event barn. We particularly enjoyed boarding our horses there allowing us the freedom to explore the surrounding area without having to watch our horses. This is a nice place to indulge yourself and your horse. Fee for board ($25 per night during our visit) includes 12' X 12' stalls, hay (just give them feed instructions and they'll feed for you), stall cleaning, use of a wash stall, and use of the indoor and outdoor arenas, including the round pen. We found this to be an excellent layover and a reasonably priced boarding destination, all things considered, as you could not only board your horse but you could exercise your horse in an excellent facility with even an adjoining polo field that riders can enjoy. And, perhaps, if you need an addition to your family, check out their puppies and kittens for adoption.

NEARBY:
- Laurel Highlands Visitors Bureau, Ohiopyle & Somerset (800) 333-5661, website: www.laurelhighlands.org
- The Great Allegheny Passage (rail-trail), Allegheny Trail Alliance (see Chapter 37), (888) 282-2453, website: www.atatrail.org, email: atamail@atatrail.org
- Fort Necessity National Battlefield, Farmington (724) 329-5512, website: www.nps.gov/fone
- Frank Lloyd Wright's Fallingwater, Mill Run (724) 329-8601, website: www.paconserv.org
- Nemacolin Woodlands Resort & Spa, Farmington (724) 329-8555
- Guided Whitewater/Raft Tours, Ohiopyle (800) 4-RAFTIN, (800) WWA-RAFT, (888) 644-6795
- Tall Oaks Campground (a full service, non-equestrian campground which has graciously accommodated overnight equestrian campers in a remote, open field setting; check with the office first), Farmington (724) 329-4777

NEARBY AND SURROUNDING AREA STABLES:

- Equestrian Center at Nemacolin Woodlands in close proximity to the Ohiopyle State Park equestrian trails (accommodations for overnight stabling, boarding, guided trail rides on rented horses, and lots of other fun equestrian activities and events), Farmington (724) 329-6961 ext. 1, website: www.nemacolin.com
- Deerfield Stables (boarding), Uniontown (724) 438-1681
- Seven Springs Mountain Resort (guided trail rides, sleigh rides), Champion (800) 452-2223
- Camp Soles (guided trail rides, summer equestrian camp), Rockwood (814) 352-7217

NEARBY AND SURROUNDNG AREA VET SERVICES:

- Camelot Vet Clinic, Uniontown (724) 437-7838
- Dr. Knepper, Windswept Equine Center, Berlin (814) 267-5617
- Laurel Highlands Animal Hospital, Somerset (814) 445-8971
- J. Sacksen, Somerset (814) 352-7515

NEARBY AND SURROUNDING AREA FARRIERS:

- J. Zundel, Vanderbilt (724) 529-0525

17. The Laurel Highlands Trail System & The PW&S Trails
Forbes State Forest
BOF-DCNR
(Bureau of Forestry/Department of Conservation & Natural Resources)

Lasting Impression: Four Spur Award to these new trails, detailed DCNR map, and corresponding markers! Just from the excellent maps provided by the Forbes State Forest District office, and hearing word of new trails and a recently constructed motorized camping area, I couldn't wait to ride these trails. The location, trails, and superb trail markings far exceeded my expectations. Well worth the trip!

Location: Located in southwest Pennsylvania, there is the Forbes Forest District and the Forbes State Forest. The Forbes Forest District covers a larger territory and includes additional counties. However, Forbes State Forest, consisting of roughly 60,000 acres, has numerous separate tracts sprawling over Westmoreland, Fayette, and Somerset counties. This chapter focuses on the Laurel Highlands Trail System and the PW&S trails which are located northwest of the town of Somerset, south of Route 30, and north of I-76.

Length: *Day Ride, Weekend (or longer if you choose to ride nearby areas)*- As a whole, Forbes State Forest has almost 200 miles of trails considered suitable for horseback riding. There are additional trails but these may have low clearance or insufficient width for horses. In regard to the Laurel Highlands Trail System (north side of I-76), a total mileage estimate is not provided; however, there are days of riding and exploring the trails in this area. There are additional trails nearby (you'll need to trailer as I-76 interrupts any equestrian trail link) at Mountain Streams Trail System (see that chapter) or other nearby sections of Forbes State Forest. Horses are permitted on all trails and State Forest roads unless specifically designated as closed to horses. Horses are not permitted on the Laurel Highlands Hiking Trail, the Roaring Run Natural Area, and Mt. Davis Natural Area. Horses are permitted on Linn Run Road in the vicinity of Linn Run State Park (do not approach the picnic areas).

Level of Difficulty: The trails that we rode were easy to moderate. There are also more challenging or difficult ones which we chose not to ride.

Terrain: There are double tracts, old logging roads, old railroad passageways, single dirt paths, snowmobile trails, cross-country ski trails, and dirt forest roads all on a mountain plateau. The terrain is mostly very good. It is also diverse and consists of dirt, grass, fine stone, possible ballast around fresh logging or low lying areas, some rocky patches (but passable), and some mud (minimal) at high traffic intersections. Horses should have shoes.

Ride Pennsylvania Horse Trails – Part II

Cook Forest State Park (top) and
Moraine State Park (bottom)

Ride Pennsylvania Horse Trails – Part II

The Allegheny River Tract (top & bottom)

Ride Pennsylvania Horse Trails – Part II

Round Hill Park (top & bottom)

Ride Pennsylvania Horse Trails – Part II

John Spotts and Jan Huffman at The Keystone Mountain
Country Shared Use Trail System (top & bottom)

Ride Pennsylvania Horse Trails – Part II

Brush Ridge (top) and
Trough Creek (bottom)

Ride Pennsylvania Horse Trails – Part II

Laverne Shearer & Heather Volkar at Raccoon Creek State Park (top) and
Hillman State Park (bottom)

Ride Pennsylvania Horse Trails – Part II

Riding with Cindy Bowser and Diane Hensel at
Deer Lakes Park (top & bottom)

Ride Pennsylvania Horse Trails – Part II

The Eagleton Mine Camp Trail (top) and campsite (bottom)

Ride Pennsylvania Horse Trails – Part II

Morning at Sideling Hill (top) and
dusk at Sideling Hill (bottom)

Ride Pennsylvania Horse Trails – Part II

The cave and rock formations along the Laurel Highlands
Trail System (top & bottom)

Ride Pennsylvania Horse Trails – Part II

Elk herd (top) and the Dark Hollow site (bottom) at the
Thunder Mountain Equestrian Trail System

Ride Pennsylvania Horse Trails – Part II

Elk State Forest (top and bottom)

Ride Pennsylvania Horse Trails – Part II

Mansion at Hartwood Acres (top) and
stable complex at Hartwood Acres (bottom)

Ride Pennsylvania Horse Trails – Part II

Flora along the trail (top & bottom)

Ride Pennsylvania Horse Trails – Part II

View along the trail at Harrison Hills (top) and
Susquehannock State Forest (bottom)

Ride Pennsylvania Horse Trails – Part II

Black Moshannon State Forest (top) and
the author at home with Tabasco (bottom)

Horse Camping: Yes
Non-horse Camping: Yes
Carriage Potential: There is carriage potential on some of these State Forest roads and trails. Contact the office for more information including access to gated roads.
Maps and Info: To obtain maps, information, and a permit for Forbes State Forest, call (724) 238-1200 or write Forest District Headquarters, Bureau of Forestry, Forbes Forest District 4, 1291 Route 30 East or P.O. Box 519, Laughlintown, PA 15655-0519, email: fd04@state.pa.us. More information can be viewed at the DCNR website: www.dcnr.state.pa.us or by contacting the Bureau of Forestry, DCNR, P.O. Box 8552, Harrisburg, PA 17105-8552. We did not see pamphlet maps at the parking area. When calling, ask for the Forbes State Forest Public Use Map (green cover), the Snowmobile Map, the Mountain Streams Trail System Map (if you decide to ride that trail system also), the colored PW&S Trail Map (a busy but fun and excellent map), and the Forbes State Forest "Designated Motorized Camping Site" flyer (which includes directions to camping areas for motorized vehicles).
Activities: Activities include Hiking, Biking, Horseback Riding Trails, Picnicking, Swimming, Fishing, Bird Watching, X-C Skiing, Downhill Skiing, Snowmobiling, Camping, and Hunting (ATVs are not permitted)
Fees for Trail Use: None
Permits for Day Trail Use: None
Permits/Fees Required for Overnight Camping: A permit must be obtained for all motorized camping (no fee). Site #1 is gated; confirm in advance that the gate will be unlocked.
Comfort Station: Camping is primitive with no facilities. There are facilities at various locations indicated on the trail map including by the Warming Hut.

DIRECTIONS:
Locally, you can reach this locale by taking Route 30 to Laurel Summit Road south or by taking Route 381 to Rector, turning east onto Linn Run Road through Linn Run State Park, and then making a left or heading north on Laurel Summit Road. There are many long distance approaches to reach this area but the following was the one recommended to us as it was gradual. If using another approach, check out the road conditions and grade in advance as you are traveling in mountainous country. To reach the Laurel Highlands Trail System and PW&S trails north of the Pennsylvania Turnpike, or to reach motorized camping Site #1, take the Pennsylvania Turnpike I-76 to Exit #110 Somerset. Once you exit the turnpike, you will enter a hub of roads and businesses. Follow signs to Route 219 north and be alert for turns. Travel 2.4 miles from the toll booth and you will see a sign for Route 219 north; travel up the ramp and you will be on Route 219 (exclusively). Travel another 7 miles on Route 219 north to Route 30. Make a left onto Route 30 west and travel 7.2 miles west to the top of the mountain. *Even though there were truck warning signs, we found the stretch leading to*

Laurel Summit Road to be a gradual approach and not steep. We found it more steep west of Laurel Summit Road, between Laurel Summit Road and Route 381, but still doable. If your rig has marginal pulling power, avoid heading west of the intersection of Laurel Summit Road and Route 30. Also, we hauled as far as Route 381 but we did not travel west of Route 381 along Route 30. That portion of Route 30 may be even more precipitous. Slow down when you see the Walots sign on the left. Just after Walots, look for a left onto Laurel Summit Road. The turn is directly opposite a "Big Truck Alert" sign and just before the Laurel Summit Inn, a brown building. Make a left onto Laurel Summit Road which is paved.

Travel 2.2 miles on Laurel Summit Road. At this point there is a split in the road with a paved road to the right. Do not go right, but travel straight onto the dirt road. You are still on Laurel Summit Road. The dirt road along this stretch was mostly of a good surface during our visit (but it gets rougher past the campsite entrance if you travel through Linn Run State Park). Laurel Summit Road has numerous locations central to the trails that will suffice for day parking. A nice, long (shared use) lot is opposite the patrol house and Warming Hut (shortly after where Laurel Summit Road turns to a dirt road) which is big enough for equestrian trailers. This portion of Laurel Summit Road was dirt, wide, had plenty of shoulder, and was not heavily traveled (during the week and on the weekend), making for an equine friendly environment.

To reach camping Site #1, travel another 2.7 miles along the dirt road (a total of about 5 miles from Route 30), slow down, and you will come to an intersection of dirt roads. You'll need to make a right onto (the old) Rector Edie Road, now known as the JE Miller Road. However, at the time of our visit, the turn to the right was sharp and too tight for large rigs. *Again another location with a nice big parking or camping area but a tight entrance!* If it has not been enlarged by the time of your visit, you will need to be proficient with backing your rig to enter this road. We needed to pull past the road, back into the road opposite of where we needed to turn, and then pulled forward down the road on which we had wanted to make the right. While scouting the area, we did this several times, and we did not find it difficult, just inconvenient. *Of course that is easy for me to say, it wasn't difficult as John did the backing! I did mention this to the ranger with a suggestion that they widen it. He was very receptive so maybe by the time you visit, this may have been widened. Site #1 is brand new; we believe we were the first equestrians to try the site and a roomier entrance may not yet have been thought of or needed to date.* Once we backed up, we then could head down JE Miller Road. There is a "Rector Edie Road" sign. (At the corner of Rector Edie Road/JE Miller Road, there is a small overflow area for the campsite. Contact the office if you anticipate using it. The overflow area also has a tight entrance off of Laurel Summit Road but is easier to enter off of JE Miller Road.) We continued traveling down JE Miller Road. This is a rough, but solid, road with scatterings of flat rocks. If gravel or stone dust is added, it should be easier to travel for those hauling a rig. As you travel down this road, note the various trailhead markers to connect to the trails. They are simple to see and well marked. The road leads to a gate which is the one you need to confirm is unlocked prior to your visit. Continue; after traveling a total of 1.1 miles from Laurel Summit Road, there is a road to the left which leads to a clearing. Make a left into the open area which is Site #1. There is a sign and a marker.

While traveling to and from, be aware that fog is common in this region and motor travel may be best during mid day when the fog has burned off. Listen to the weather forecast. We experienced dense fog in the first two days, making road travel difficult.

*Note: regarding the day parking lots, all manure, hay, and bedding must be removed from the parking lots. Forbes State Forest specifically states it should be carried out and should **not** be scattered in the woods by these public parking areas. This is posted in the Forbes State Forest designated parking lots or day use areas which are shared with other types of trail users; please abide by it so we can continue to be welcome at these lots. Regarding camping areas, manure must be cleared from the camping area and scattered away from the site.*

THE TRAILS:
Forbes State Forest is an immense area. Within or nearby, there are several State Parks and Wild and Natural Areas. Overall, horseback riding is not permitted within the State Parks and is directed, instead, to the adjoining Forbes State Forest trail system. Generally, the rule is that horses are not permitted within Natural Areas and may or may not be permitted within Wild Areas. It depends on the Wild Area's terrain and the State Forest district. There are many clusters of trails at different locations. There are those in the northern section, such as the PW&S Trail network (south of Route 30 and north of I-76), the Mountain Streams Trail System (south of I-76 and north of Route 31), plus other nearby trails (south of Route 31). This chapter covers the Laurel Highlands Trail System and PW&S (the old Pittsburgh, Westmoreland and Somerset Railroad corridors) trails north of I-76. Looking at the green Forbes State Forest Public Use Map, reflecting the various tracts, this trail system is located in the northeast section of Forbes State Forest. The Mountain Streams Trail is covered in another chapter. We did not visit the section south of Route 31.

What a great time I had riding these trails! The area has such a remote feel and the scenery is beautiful. There are so many places to explore. Besides the beauty of these trails, one of the outstanding features (much to the credit of the folks at Forbes State Forest and the Pennsylvania Conservation Corps [an offshoot from the Youth Conservation Corps]) is that these trails are clearly marked and maintained. Low lying sections were covered in fine stone. Just about the time

127

we were unsure as to where to proceed, there was a sign to help us out. Each of the trailheads and intersections that we encountered were well marked. Red rectangles indicated cross-country ski trails; orange diamonds designated snowmobile trails. The trails looked inviting as the surface was usually very good, they were cleared and cut, and there were names for each of the trails which corresponded to the trail maps for this area. The map also has "MS" (map site) numbers so when you come to a point in the road, not only is there a road sign but there is a MS number sign and it corresponds with the map. If you prefer marked trails, you should like this destination!

During our visit, we rode in a clockwise loop (looking at the colored map). From camp, we made a right and headed in the direction of the gate. Just past the gate we made a left onto the Silvermine Trail. Immediately, we could see a lot of work was put into this trail as many surface improvements had been made. (Upon later talking to one of the rangers, we learned that the Pennsylvania Conservation Corps [PCC] and other volunteers work on these trails each year. They had done a nice job and we appreciated it.) The Silvermine Trail travels through some very picturesque areas. There are some rocky patches, some of which had already been improved by the PCC. Silvermine had more rocks than the other trails but we did not consider it to be a hindrance, and we found it passable and pleasant to ride. The other trails that we rode were more of a dirt surface. Every one of the trails that we rode was gorgeous and diverse. We came out by an open area and a gas well site to the left. At this point, we continued and took the dirt road ahead and slightly to the right in the direction of Lippo's Loop (see the map). We came out to another intersection and picked up the Towhee Trail. At this point, there seemed to be trails heading in all directions, each one looking interesting. We took the Towhee Trail, which was of a nice surface, through an attractive forest of tall ferns (must be very colorful in the fall). We followed the signs to Lippo's Loop and rode the loop. We then made a left on Bill Alberts Trail and picked up the Loop Trail. I liked so much about these trails, but one of **my favorite parts** was the mammoth rock formations along the Loop Trail riding toward the Warming Hut. As you ride by, notice the cave, the unique formations, and the interesting shapes from years of glacier activity. We continued to Laurel Summit Road near the Warming Hut. *Check out the nice bathroom facilities. There is a "his" and "hers" but we were wondering what the third door was for.* We continued our ride along Beam Run Road. It is not open to general motorized traffic. However, exercise caution in the event of logging activity. We continued along the Beam Run Road which was a leisurely ride. We did not see anyone or any vehicle the whole stretch. Beam Run Road converts to a trail. We rode this lengthy stretch through some very attractive woodlands. Periodically, there is a glimpse of the surrounding mountains; this is likely much more scenic when the leaves are off the trees. We came to another marked intersection (MS#2) and made a right onto Edie Road which becomes JE Miller Road. We then took JE Miller Road back to camp.

Avoid the Laurel Highlands Hiking Trail which is a hiking (only) trail. It is clearly reflected on the Laurel Highlands Trail System map and is marked by yellow rectangles. There are also blue rectangles indicating hiking trail connectors. They may join in with multiple-use trails and do not necessarily indicate hiking only. If there are snowmobile (orange diamonds) or X-C skiing (red rectangles) markers, you are on a multiple-use trail and should be okay. Always check the latest map and information from the office, along with recent postings of signs, as permitted usage can change due to weather and other factors.

There are so many trails in this area; we could not cover all of them in our visit. We know there are likely difficult ones as some are labeled as such on the map plus this is mountainous country. We chose to ride some of the trails that were recommended by the office as being mostly easy, leisurely, and scenic (and they gave us good advice). Obtain the PW&S colored map which describes the various loops and indicates which trails are advanced, steep, etc. Do avoid using unauthorized trails such as "hiking only" as I have been told citations and fines could be issued and applied. The map will help you stay on course. We passed many offshoots that had signs indicating they are "Expert" trails to notify mountain bikers and other users that they are challenging. We did not take these as some looked rockier than the regular trails. Overall, the terrain was incredibly tough and durable even after it rained. Most trails were well maintained and fine stone fill had been brought in for some sections to rectify low lying areas. There are periodic scatterings of rocks, a few sections had quite a bit, but the horses were able to step around them. *In spite of the area's existing and increasing popularity resulting in possible erosion around rocks and intersections, I am hoping the rocks will continue to be minimal in the future due to the exceptional maintenance already being performed on these trails on an ongoing basis.* It appeared this locale was not yet known to equestrians by the time of our visit, so remain alert for mountain bikers as many mountain bikers may not be used to seeing equestrians on the trails. We ran into several but they seemed to be experienced and savvy mountain bikers, and each knew to yield to the horses. They were also very friendly and we talked about our mutual enjoyment of these trails.

I wish we could have extended our visit to explore more of these trails; but we had others to visit and new destinations to introduce equestrians to. We already have plans to return again, but for now, we'll leave the fun of exploring the remaining ones to you. But don't forget the colored "Laurel Highlands Trail System" map with the PW&S Trail System as it will give much meaning and guidance to where you are riding. Enjoy!

EQUESTRIAN CAMPING:
There are several authorized motorized camping locations within Forbes State Forest. The map and directions to each of those can be obtained from the State

Forest office. Unfortunately, at the time of our visit, only Site #1 could accommodate large equestrian rigs. Additional sites were in process so more may be available in the future. When asking about other sites, don't forget to ask about accessibility, turn around room, grade, and tree tie line availability. Site #1 is ideally remote and central to the trails. Although the turn onto the entrance road is tight and requires backing, we could maneuver with our dually and 50+ foot rig. If not widened, super large freightliner types may not be able to access the entrance road and may have to ask the office for other accommodations.

Site #1 has plenty of turn around room. The surface is uneven so you'll need to proceed slowly. Steer clear of the outer perimeter of the site as that terrain is not as consistent in turf as the center of the parking area. It helps to unload the horses before finding that "right" spot. We unloaded the horses, let them graze, and then moved the rig without the extra weight. Heavy rain soon arrived and the ground remained solid along the entrance road and in camp. This locale had ideal horse turf! The camping area is grass, there are plenty of trees to tie line to, and room to set up a portable electric fence or corral. Several large rigs can fit at this camping location. The State Forest asks that, at no time should horses be tied where they can do damage to trees or shrubbery. All rope, string, or other materials must be taken out and not left. No nailing to trees. Basically, carry in and carry out applies. Clean up all manure, hay, and straw from the parking area and campsite. Manure is permitted to be scattered in the woods and should be at least 100 feet from the camping site. Don't forget the fly spray and fly cover; you will likely need them. Bring warm clothes and blankets. We visited the second week in August and we were wearing long johns! Water is available on trail or at nearby Linn Run State Park. Traveling out to Laurel Summit Road, bear right onto Linn Run Road, and look for the cabins and restroom area on the right side of Linn Run Road. You can see the spigot from the road. It will be easier if you disconnect and travel without the rig as Linn Run Road is bumpy and may not have ample room to pull off.

This quiet, remote campground was fantastic as it was situated far from any roads, cabins, or activity, and yet perfectly central to the trails. At night, when the mist and fog finally cleared, the sky was a beautiful blanket of stars. However, bring a good flashlight. At night, when the moon isn't out, the camping area is pitch black!

HISTORICAL INFORMATION:
Forbes State Forest derived its name from a British General, John Forbes, who played an important role in the early colonization of this area during the period of the French and Indian War in the mid 1700s. By the 1800s, this area was extensively logged by timber companies. Railroad tracks, built to transport lumber, crisscrossed the area and the paths are still visible today. The PW&S trails travel the former paths of the Pittsburgh, Westmoreland, and Somerset

Railroad. The PW&S was active at the turn of the 19th century into the early 1900s, and carried logs, coal, and bluestone which were used to pave the streets of Pittsburgh. Later, the railroad also transported passengers to the top of the mountain to enjoy the view. But sections of the railroad corridors were challenging and sometimes hazardous due to steep grades. Severe winter weather conditions also hindered operation. By 1909, the forest had become stripped bare and railroad cinders caused wildfires to erupt destroying remaining flora. The land had become a barren wasteland. From over hunting and environmental conditions, many forms of wildlife were almost nonexistent. Without timber to transport, the PW&S ceased operations.

In the early 1900s, purchases of the land were made by the state with the goal of replanting and restoring the woodlands. The Department of Forestry and the Pennsylvania Game Commission brought deer from other states, including New York, to help restore wildlife to the area. Although, today, Pennsylvania is still a leading source of some of the finest hardwood lumber, we have learned the importance of restoration, reforestation, preservation, and protecting the natural beauty of Pennsylvania's woodlands. Today's forests are home to deer, bear, beaver, turkey, grouse, pheasant, and a variety of other residents, including an interesting assortment of birds and waterfowl. *I had heard how the elk had to be brought in, but was not aware that deer had to be reintroduced to replenish our wildlife. It is tragic that so much of Pennsylvania's native wildlife was killed off as Pennsylvania once had its own herds of elk, deer, and bison.*

COURTESIES:
Many thanks both to Edward Callahan, District Forester at the Forbes District Bureau of Forestry, and Carol Brownfield, Administrative Assistant at the DCNR Linn Run State Park office, for being so thorough, and for providing so much useful and well detailed information. The organization of materials that you provided assisted greatly so that I could get a feel for this large area. It is a pleasure to correspond with helpful folks like yourself. Thank you to Rangers Paul, Chris, and Scott with the Bureau of Forestry office who were very friendly and informative. Ranger Chris stopped at our site and talked to us about the area. Also, I would like to express my gratitude to Terry Springer, a fellow equestrian, who corresponded with me regarding suitable trails for riding within Forbes State Forest. Thank you to Julie Donovan and the friendly folks at the Laurel Highlands Public Relations Office for sharing so much information on this region. Thank you to Barbie at the Laurel Hill State Park office, and also to Bob Hufman. My gratitude to the Loyalhanna Watershed Association along with the Bureau of Forestry for providing such a wonderful destination which equestrians can enjoy on horseback.

During my many discussions, one insightful recommendation was made. This is one which I thought horseback riders should seriously consider for all destinations. (This was echoed by some other park and forest representatives at

131

other locations that we visited.) Snowmobile enthusiasts are very active, organized, and visible in working with land management on the trails and attending meetings with the State Forest office. This has resulted in an excellent rapport between the two. I often hear that equestrians are not active or influential in this way. Equestrians need to make the time, and it usually doesn't take a lot of time, to be positively active and to be seen. Now is the time to influence the outcome as there are so many new trails opening and old trails which are still accessible. We can do this by contacting the Forest District or land management office to see if we can assist in trail maintenance. These days, many organizations are experiencing a shortage in staff. They welcome volunteer help, plus they feel appreciated in their efforts as it becomes a team effort. I checked with one ranger at this location if volunteers could be used and he indicated they are very much welcome. I know my personal goal, upon completion of this book, is to do just that with a few trail systems that are local to my home.

THINGS WE LEARNED THIS RIDE:

- After speaking with the ranger, I learned that in certain situations at this location, alternate camping areas can be opened up to accommodate large groups. That is a great idea to accommodate club visits.
- In the near future, camping permits may be applied for online and a confirmation number will be issued which will serve as a permit.
- I learned that, overall, the direction of the State Forests is toward uniformity in practices, increased trail construction, and designated motorized sites vs. the old practice of motorized camping at random locations within the State Forests.
- After visiting this destination, I was reminded that our State Forest and State Park land managers are very progressive. They manage to maintain the balance of preserving our beautiful State Forests and State Parks, while at the same time catering to the many needs of its diverse users. I have seen this personally while writing these books and remain grateful to DCNR and the Bureau of Forestry for their excellent work.

NEARBY:

- Laurel Highlands Visitors Bureau, Ohiopyle & Somerset (800) 333-5661, website: www.laurelhighlands.org. Ask about the interpretative area and observation tower at Mount Davis, Pennsylvania's highest summit at 3,213 feet.
- Mountain Horse Saddlery and Gift Shop (English, Western, and Australian tack, supplies, some handy camping equipment, feed +lots more), Route 711 just south of Route 31, Donegal (724) 593-8100, website: www.mountainhorsesaddlery.com.
- Diesel in Jennerstown along Route 30. Fill up without the trailer as there is insufficient room for trucks with trailers.

- Mountain Market Store, at the corner of Linn Run Road and Route 381 (just outside of Linn Run State Park), is a nice, handy general store if you forgot anything at home.

NEARBY AND SURROUNDING AREA STABLES:
- Double K Stables (guided trail rides, boarding, lessons, hauling services, sleigh rides), Somerset (814) 443-1510, website: www.doublekstables.com
- Stone Ridge Stables (boarding, "English" lessons, overnight stabling), Latrobe (724) 593-5665
- Mt. Vista Stables (boarding, training), Ligonier (724) 238-4117
- Seven Springs Mountain Resort (guided trail rides, sleigh rides), Champion (800) 452-2223
- Mountain Trails (overnight stabling, boarding, lessons), Donegal (724) 575-2788
- Camp Soles (guided trail rides, summer equestrian camp), Rockwood (814) 352-7217

NEARBY AND SURROUNDING AREA VET SERVICES:
- Laurel Highlands Animal Hospital, Somerset (814) 445-8971
- J. Sacksen, Somerset (814) 352-7515

NEARBY AND SURROUNDING AREA FARRIERS:
- J. Lynn, Ligonier (724) 238-0180
- M. Smith, Blairsville (724) 676-0319
- P. Talbot, Youngstown (724) 309-7257

18. The Mountain Streams Trail System
Forbes State Forest
BOF-DCNR
(Bureau of Forestry/Department of Conservation & Natural Resources)

Lasting Impression: "Horses in the Mist"... We arrived in a heavy fog and it felt like our whole ride was in and out of clouds. Even without the sun, the beauty of these trails was evident.

Location: Forbes State Forest consists of several separate tracts. We visited two separate sections of Forbes State Forest, one on the north side of I-76 (see the chapter on the Laurel Highlands Trail System & the PW&S Trails) and one on the south side (the Mountain Streams Trail System). You need to trailer from one to the other as the turnpike divides the trails. Mountain Streams Trail System is located south of the Pennsylvania Turnpike I-76 and north of Route 31 in close proximity to the town of Donegal in the vicinity of the border of Westmoreland and Somerset counties.

Length: *Day Ride or Weekend (or longer if you choose to ride nearby areas)*- An estimate of total trail miles is not provided. You can spend a day or two exploring the trails along the Mountain Streams Trail System and also the snowmobile trails south of Route 31. If you want to extend your stay, you can trailer to the neighboring north side of I-76 and ride the Laurel Highlands Trail System and the PW&S trails and adjoining areas. Or you can trailer to nearby Ohiopyle State Park. See those chapters for more information.

Level of Difficulty: The trails that we rode were mostly easy to moderate except for one steep section.

Terrain: The trail surface can vary greatly from wide, grassy, mowed and well maintained tracts, to logging roads, old railroad passageways, and State Forest dirt roads. There may be fresh ballast on some of the roads. There are various branches from the main trail which are often single dirt tracts.

Horse Camping: At the time of our visit, there were designated motorized camping sites within Forbes State Forest but not within close riding distance to the Mountain Streams Trail System.

Non-horse Camping: Yes

Carriage Potential: There are many double width tracts and dirt roads which should be good for carriage driving. Carriage drivers should assess the terrain first to determine if there are sufficient continuous links for their purposes. Contact the office for more information.

Maps and Info: To obtain maps, information, and camping application for Forbes State Forest, call (724) 238-1200 or write Forest District Headquarters, Bureau of Forestry, Forbes Forest District #4, P.O. Box 519, Laughlintown, PA 15655-0519, email: fd04@state.pa.us. More information can be viewed at the

DCNR website: www.dcnr.state.pa.us or by contacting DCNR, Bureau of Forestry, P.O. Box 8552, Harrisburg, PA 17105-8552. We did not see maps at the Mountain Streams Trail System parking area, so call for maps in advance. The maps for this sector do not have the detail like the Laurel Highlands Trail map for the northern section, yet they are still helpful for following the trail and road systems. Ask for the Forbes State Forest Public Use Map (green cover), the Laurel Highlands Snowmobile Trail Systems Map (22" x 17" blue and white map with red and green trail markings), the Mountain Streams Trail System Map (8.5" x 14" colored map), and the Forbes State Forest "Designated Motorized Camping Site" flyer (8.5" x 14") which includes directions to camping areas for motorized vehicles.

Activities: Hiking, Biking, Horseback Riding Trails, Fishing, Bird Watching, X-C Skiing, Snowmobiling, Camping, and Hunting

Fees for Trail Use: None

Permits for Day Trail Use: None

Permits/Fees Required for Overnight Camping: Permits are required for overnight motorized camping (no fee).

Comfort Station: Comfort facilities are available at the various State Parks within the Forbes State Forest. We did not see any at the parking lot or along the trail.

DIRECTIONS:

There are many ways to reach the Mountain Streams Trail System. Parking areas are located on Route 381 and Route 31. To reach the Route 381 lot, take Route 31 to the town of Jones Mill and turn onto Route 381 north. If traveling from the Pennsylvania Turnpike, take I-76 to Somerset Exit #110 and follow signs to Route 31 west toward Donegal. From the intersection of Route 31 and Route 381, take Route 381 north for .7 miles. The lot is on the right at the corner of Camp Run Road.

You can also reach the Mountain Streams Trail System from the north by taking Route 30 to Route 381 south (this intersection is between the town of Laughlintown and Ligonier) and continue as described below. Route 30 has many steep grade cautions; be careful of what approach you use. As we were camping on the north side of I-76, from Laurel Summit Road we took Route 30 west for 5.6 miles, made a left onto Route 381 south, took Route 381 south for 12.4 miles (south of the town of Kregor and just before Route 31) to the lot on the left at the end of Camp Run Road. *We were able to haul our large rig along Route 30, the stretch between Route 219 and Route 381, without a problem. Only attempt it if your vehicle has good pulling power.* If your vehicle has difficulty with mountainous terrain and you are traveling from the camping area described in the Laurel Highlands Trail System chapter, you are better off taking the Linn Run Road approach as follows. From Motorized Site #1, travel out the entrance road to camp and make a right onto Laurel Summit Road south. The road will turn from dirt to paved; bear right onto Linn Run Road. (The paved road was rough during our visit yet passable.) Take Linn Run Road through Linn Run State Park. *You will come to some cabins and a restroom; there is a water spigot by the restrooms if you need water.* Continue on Linn Run Road until the town of Rector (roughly 9 miles from the JE Miller and Laurel Summit Road intersection). Make a left onto Route 381 and head south. Travel about 9.5 miles; shortly after crossing the turnpike and the town of Kregor, you will see a lot on the left at the corner of Camp Run Road. (There is a bridge with a tight 'S' turn just before reaching the lot. We found it to look worse than it was and didn't have a problem.) The lot on the corner of Route 381 and Camp Run Road is a medium size lot with room for a few large rigs. There is also some pull through room. The trailhead is on both sides of the lot, one side is marked with a sign and the other (on the opposite side of Camp Run Road) has a brown post which may have had a sign previously.

There are additional parking lots in this vicinity. If you continue .7 miles and make a left onto Route 31, you will find three lots. One of these is a large lot on the left side toward the other end of Camp Run Road. This is a lot which has convenient access to the snowmobile trails on the south side of Route 31. If you ride the south side, follow the snowmobile paths and avoid the Natural Areas. You can see where the parking lots, trails, and State Forest roads are located on the Mountain Streams Trail System Map. *Note: the following is posted in the Forbes State Forest parking lots which are shared with other types of trail users; please abide by it so we can continue to use these lots: "All manure, hay, and bedding must be removed from the parking lots." The State Forest indicates it should be carried out and should not be scattered in the woods. Different rules apply to camping areas where equestrians can scatter manure in the outlying areas as long as it is a certain distance from the camping site.*

THE TRAILS:
The Mountain Streams section and adjoining areas offer a few days of enjoyment exploring trails on horseback. Horses are permitted on all trails and State Forest roads unless specifically designated as hiking (only) or closed to horses (i.e., sensitive terrain or flora). There are various markers along the trail as follows: orange diamonds-snowmobile trails, yellow rectangles-hiking only trails, blue rectangles-hiking connector trails, and red rectangles-ski trails. Horses are **not** permitted on the Laurel Highlands Hiking Trail (marked by yellow blazes), in the Roaring Run Natural Area, or in the Mt. Davis Natural Area.

At the time of our visit, there were three trail maps (see maps and info above) for this section south of the turnpike. There is the green State Forest Public Use Map; the large, two-sided snowmobile trail map (one side reflects the trails on the north side of I-76 and the other side of the map reflects the Mountain Streams Trail System south of I-76 and south of Route 31); and the Mountain Streams

136

Trail System Map. If you look at the snowmobile map, the red lines indicate snowmobile trails which equestrians can ride. The green dotted paths on the map are ski touring trails that sometimes equestrians can ride and sometimes they cannot (i.e., equestrians can travel certain ski touring sections in the Mountain Streams vicinity [north of Route 31] but horses are not permitted on the ski touring path which travels through the Roaring Run Natural Area [south of Route 31]). Also, the trail has red rectangles along much of its path (indicating cross-country ski trail) but are reflected as "snowmobile trails" on the map. There may be overlaps. Some of this I found confusing so I checked with a Ranger. I concluded that the best way to proceed was to simply follow the snowmobile paths, use judgment on the ski touring paths, avoid the designated Natural Areas, and stay off of any trails with yellow markings indicating it is the Laurel Highlands Hiking (only) Trail.

The Mountain Streams Trail System travels through what once was farmland, logging roads, and old railroad corridors which were used to transport lumber and coal. Some sections of this trail and nearby trails have only been acquired in recent years. The fabulous thing about Forbes State Forest is that they are on a continuous mission to improve and expand their trail system by acquiring old railroad right-of-ways and linking trails. This has resulted in the addition of the multiple-use (yes open to horses!) Pike Run Trail, the Mountain Streams Trail, and the Blair Brothers Railroad Grade Trail. At the time of this writing, the office indicated these were still under construction and bridges may not yet have been built.

This has been a favorite destination for equestrians for many years. There are a variety of types of trails that travel through scenic woodlands. We started from the parking lot on Camp Run Road at Route 381 and picked up the Mountain Streams Trail (there is a sign at the trailhead). This is a wide, leisurely, maintained trail through some very pretty forest land. Mountain Streams Trail is mostly flat until you come to one section. And as our guide advised us, make sure your girth is tightened and your breastplate is fastened. This is one climb that we found better ascending vs. descending. Looking at the map, think about riding in a clockwise direction. John said it looked like some alternates or switchbacking might be available at this one steep spot. *Our other guide mentioned she is scheduled to attend Trail Stewardship classes. She will likely return and have some good ideas on re-engineering this one. Plus, one of the rangers indicated the office welcomes volunteers. This, combined with our guide's interest in Trail Stewardship courses, should put these trails in good hands.* Other than the climb up the mountain, the established or official trails seem to offer easier, cleared, and maintained paths. If you branch off of the designated routes you may find a rougher and more demanding terrain. Throughout our ride there was plenty of water on the trail. There were periodic signs but not as many signs and markers as the trails on the north side of I-76.

There were lots of blazes on the trees to tell you that you were on an established trail; however, you'll need to utilize the map to know which direction to proceed at the intersections.

We traveled the Mountain Streams Trail which is a significant tract until we reached the Mountain View Trail. We made a right on the Mountain View Trail, a right onto Tunnel Road (dirt), and a right on Sky View Road (dirt). At this point we deviated a bit as the Mountain Streams Trail System does not provide a continuous loop back to the lot unless you ride the dirt road. Instead of riding the State Forest dirt road, our hosts thought it would be more scenic to digress and ride a side trail which leads into Hunt Springs (a.k.a. Twin Ponds or Double Ponds). Before heading back, we had lunch at the Hunt Springs locale and enjoyed the surroundings. This Hunt Springs/Twin or Double Ponds area has been popular with equestrians for a long time. It is a nice grass clearing and there is water available at the spring house. Bring your collapsible buckets which will come in handy to water the horses. If you take a walk around the pond, be careful at the lower part where the path is interrupted and the dam has broken through. This is an interesting location because at one time there was a private residence, whose owners built the pond. It used to be quite an attractive manmade swimming hole with a diving board, all situated in a scenic setting. Time and weather have taken their toll; only the spring house and the pond remain. One can only imagine what it was like in its time.

Throughout the ride, except for the one climb up the mountain, the grade of the established trails was gradual and not difficult. In fact, most of the trails were of an old logging road type and were leisurely. There are some signs to guide you; there are also many unmarked and unmapped branches that head off from the main trail. Since the Mountain Streams Trail System doesn't follow a complete loop, equestrians usually innovate to find their way back. We chose the path along the Camp Run River. There are also dirt roads and alternate routes that you can use to return to the parking areas. We had a very enjoyable ride and there were still many other areas to explore within this section. In retrospect, on our next visit, we plan to park at the other end of Camp Run Road and explore both the established trails north and south of Route 31, as the map reflects numerous loops at that locale.

EQUESTRIAN CAMPING:
At the time of our visit, there wasn't a large equestrian designated site with direct access to these trails. We, instead, camped north of the turnpike (see the Laurel Highlands chapter). However, I was told that there may be a motorized camping area suitable for large rigs established in the future. Check with the office for any developments. *Local equestrians: this would be a great opportunity to help with this, express your interest, and positively influence the outcome! This is a great*

group of people at this State Forest office who are willing to work with equestrians.

COURTESIES:

Thank you to the many individuals at the Laurel Highlands Public Relations Office, the State Parks in this region, and to the Bureau of Forestry for answering my many questions. Thank you to Edward Callahan, Carol Brownfield, Julie Donovan, and all the other folks I spoke with. Everyone was so professional, positive, and helpful. I would like to convey my appreciation to the Bureau of Forestry for allowing equestrians to enjoy this section of the Forbes State Forest on horseback. I have heard so many nice things that the BOF has done for equestrians including covering the metal open grate bridges with wood so they would be "horse friendly" and safer for equestrians. Please continue to remain patient with us equestrians as, through our increased awareness and knowledge of trail stewardship, we learn how we can return the many considerations you have shown us. I would like to express a special thank you to fellow equestrians Terry and Bill Springer, and Sandi Wadsworth for showing us these trails. It was great riding with you and we hope to visit again next year when we return to Forbes State Forest.

NEARBY:

• Mountain Horse Saddlery and Gift Shop, Route 711 just south of Route 31, Donegal (724) 593-8100, website: www.mountainhorsesaddlery.com. Emergency equipment needs or just feel like shopping? Check out this gorgeous, organized, well stocked tack shop. There is something for everyone including a fun gift shop. (You can bet I went shopping!) And there is an interesting wildlife park just behind the shop. Plus, if you have unhappy campers who prefer the comforts of home; there is a neighboring, attractive log cabin motel which is in close proximity to both the Donegal Exit of I-76 and the Mountain Streams Trail System.

• Laurel Highlands Visitors Bureau, Ohiopyle & Somerset (800) 333-5661, website: www.laurelhighlands.org

• Frank Lloyd Wright's Fallingwater, Mill Run (724) 329-8601, website: www.paconserv.org

NEARBY AND SURROUNDING AREA STABLES:

• Seven Springs Mountain Resort (guided trail rides), Champion (800) 452-2223

• Mountain Trails (overnight stabling, boarding, lessons), Donegal (724) 575-2788

• Double K Stables (guided trail rides, boarding, lessons, hauling services, sleigh rides), Somerset (814) 443-1510, website: www.doublekstables.com

• Stone Ridge Stables (boarding, "English" lessons, overnight stabling), Latrobe (724) 593-5665

- Mt. Vista Stables (boarding, training), Ligonier (724) 238-4117
- Camp Soles (guided trail rides, summer equestrian camp), Rockwood (814) 352-7217

NEARBY AND SURROUNDING AREA VET SERVICES:
- Laurel Highlands Animal Hospital, Somerset (814) 445-8971
- J. Sacksen, Somerset (814) 352-7515

NEARBY AND SURROUNDING AREA FARRIERS:
- J. Lynn, Ligonier (724) 238-0180
- M. Smith, Blairsville (724) 676-0319
- P. Talbot, Youngstown (724) 309-7257

The horses, with fly cover, at the nearby Laurel Summit Road campsite

19. Trough Creek
Rothrock State Forest
BOF-DCNR
(Bureau of Forestry/Department of Conservation & Natural Resources)

Lasting Impression: Wow, am I a fan of our State Forest systems and our Bureau of Forestry! Well done! Ride high above Raystown Lake on wide, leisurely trails with good terrain and abundant wildlife. This is a very clean and well maintained State Forest.

Location: Rothrock State Forest is located in central and southcentral Pennsylvania. Rothrock State Forest is composed of a few separate tracts which span Centre, Mifflin, and Huntingdon Counties. These tracts are a significant distance from each other and in completely different areas. You cannot ride from one to the other; you will need to drive about an hour or two. As a result, the Trough Creek Division (southwest section) is covered in this chapter and the Brush Ridge/Broad Mountain section (northern locale) is covered in a separate chapter. Each of these can be seen on the Rothrock State Forest Public Use Map obtainable from the district office. The Trough Creek Division of Rothrock State Forest borders Raystown Lake.

Length: *Day Ride or Weekend Destination*- Rothrock State Forest totals over 94,000 acres. The largest section is the northern tract which consists of about 80,000 acres (see the next chapter). Horses are permitted on all trails and State Forest roads except for areas specifically closed to horses such as Natural Areas and The Mid State Hiking (only) Trail. The Trough Creek Division, although mileage estimates were not provided, is best described as a locale where you can spend a few days riding and covering different trails, logging roads, and State Forest dirt roads.

Level of Difficulty: Mainly easy and leisurely; at the most lightly moderate

Terrain: Excellent terrain, usually double tract, durable surface, minimal rocks, maintained trails including downed trees cleared, stretches of high grass, no "on the edge" trails encountered

Horse Camping: Yes

Non-horse Camping: Yes

Carriage Potential: There is much carriage potential in the Trough Creek section of Rothrock State Forest due to the many State Forest dirt roads, the double tract logging roads, and farm lanes. Possibilities are extensive. Gates are at the entrance to many of the trails and arrangements would need to be made. As with the other locales we visited, interested carriage drivers should contact the office to introduce their interests and to obtain more information.

Maps and Info: For information regarding Rothrock State Forest, contact the Bureau of Forestry-DCNR at Rothrock State Forest, P.O. Box 403, Rothrock

Lane, Huntingdon, PA 16652, (814) 643-2340. *Note: many of the trails in the Trough Creek tract are handicapped accessible.* For info or maps on Trough Creek State Park, contact DCNR, Trough Creek State Park, RR1, Box 211, James Creek, PA (814) 658-3847, email: troughcreeksp@state.pa.us, website: www.dcnr.state.pa.us. We did not see maps at the parking area or along the trail, so call for maps in advance. Ask for the Rothrock State Forest Public Use Map (good overall view, but hard to view trail detail), the Trough Creek Snowmobile Trail Map, and the colored topographical map for the area you are riding (good for seeing trail detail). I received all of these from the office and they were very helpful as they reflected which were multiple-use trails and which were hiking only.

Activities: Hiking (including along vistas, along a suspension bridge, by waterfalls, and cliffs), Biking, Horseback Riding Trails, Picnicking, Swimming, Boating, Fishing, Bird Watching (including eagles), Snowmobiling, X-C Skiing, Camping, and Hunting

Fees for Trail Use: None

Permits for Day Trail Use: None

Permits/Fees Required for Overnight Camping: A permit for overnight motorized camping must be obtained prior to your stay (no fee).

Comfort Station: There are restroom facilities at the nearby State Parks including Trough Creek State Park. In addition, there are several water spigots in the vicinity of the picnic area at Trough Creek State Park. One is centrally located as you pass it on the left side opposite the picnic area and near the Paradise Furnace ruins as you travel to the Trough Creek equestrian camping site #8. There is also a dump station for those staying at the Trough Creek State Park Campground (fee). If you are staying on the State Forest land and not staying at the State Park campground (such as equestrians), contact the State Park office for permission to use the dump station and for information regarding payment for use.

DIRECTIONS:

From the north, you can take Route 26 south from Huntingdon for roughly 16 miles to Route 994 east and continue as indicated below. From the south, you can take Route 26 north to Route 994 east and continue as detailed below. (The ranger cautioned not to approach from Route 522 or Route 829 due to rough roads, steep grades, and 'S' turns.) From the turnpike, take the Pennsylvania Turnpike I-76 to Exit #161 Breezewood. *Fill up here, especially if you need diesel, as gas stations are sparse in many sections of the State Forest.* Go through the toll booth and travel about another 1.5 miles (on the turnpike access road) to pick up Route 30 west. Take Route 30 west for 8 miles and pick up Route 26 north. Route 26 north winds but is a nice road, and the section we drove did not have any steep grades. *Route 26 is also very scenic and travels through rolling hills nestled in a valley.* Take Route 26 north for 28 miles and watch for signs to Route 994 east. Take Route 994 east, continue over a bridge

142

toward the lake resort area, and travel a total of 5.2 miles. Make a left at the large brown Trough Creek State Park sign. (We did not see a name posted for this road but we believe it was a continuation of SR 3001 and, per the map, is called Hill Farm Road.) Go 1.7 miles to a stop sign and make a right. After making the right, continue straight; pass the large picnic area on the right and the historic kiln on your left. At this point, the paved road splits and you can either go right toward the picnic area or head straight up the hill (bearing slightly left) to an 'S' turn. Continue straight and travel up the 'S' turn. The 'S' turn isn't bad, it is a short distance of good surface and with ample room. We used the whole road to turn as we were pulling the 50' rig. However, it was not stressful as this section of the road wasn't busy on the Thursday afternoon of our arrival. (We also observed on the following Saturday that the 'S' turn was not busy. But, as always, proceed with caution and expect the unexpected.) This was the only climb we found while approaching this area and it was brief. After the 'S' turn, you will pass some Youth Forestry buildings on the right shortly after the road turns to gravel. You are now on Tar Kiln Road which can be seen on the map. You will see a sign that says Tar Kiln Road and you will come to a fork in the road where there are more signs. Bear right and stay on Tar Kiln Road. This is a nice gravel road of level grade. It is a two-way road but not very wide, so watch for oncoming traffic. During our stay we saw quite a few vehicles travel quickly along this section of the gravel road; fortunately, you can hear them coming due to the gravel. There are some places with sufficient shoulder if you do need to pass. *Having just arrived and thinking we were on a quiet road, John was driving while glancing to the right to look for wildlife and trails. Along came a vehicle traveling fast and the day almost became one we would remember for a long time. Luckily, when I sensed he was looking to the side vs. straight, I was watching the road for the two of us!* Travel a total of 3 miles from the stop sign and you will see a wooden gate (not locked) to the left and a post marker #8. Make a left into the camping area. There is a dip, so proceed cautiously. This location has a short entrance of a two lane grass path from the gate to a circular opening of medium size, and can accommodate about 4 or 5 rigs of medium to large size. You do need to work together to fit a few rigs and also will need to do some backing as the terrain is not graded and somewhat uneven. Check with the office to see if you will have the site to yourself or if you will be sharing the site, so you know how much space you can occupy.

THE TRAILS:
Rothrock State Forest covers an extensive area on separate, unconnected tracts that are a significant distance from each other. There are many areas to ride including the Trough Creek area (southwest section), Broad Mountain trails (northeast location), and also a variety of other trails including the ones in the northwest section. The Rothrock State Forest trails are marked by white blazes and a small round sign that says, "State Forest Boundary." The trails at Trough Creek have brown equestrian signs and arrows making the trails easy to follow.

These signs will help determine if you are on State Forest land versus other land, and also help you to stay on course. There are six designated Natural Areas and two Wild Areas in Rothrock State Forest. Horses are not permitted in the Natural Areas.

The focus of this chapter is the Trough Creek area which is on the tract located in the southwest section of Rothrock State Forest near Raystown Lake. There is equestrian camping at Trough Creek (Site #8 off Tar Kiln Road) and an extensive system of snowmobile trails, logging roads, State Forest roads, and double tract trails throughout. We knew absolutely nothing of these trails prior to our visit. What a wonderful surprise! There is some awesome riding, especially the lofty sector overlooking Raystown Lake, and a connecting system of easy and leisurely trails. On a hot day, depart early as the wide trails get a lot of sun. Head out for a nice ride then kick back in camp feeling like you have the place to yourselves!

We arrived on a Thursday and set up camp. We headed out early Friday morning before 8:00 am with plans to ride the outer loop and get a good feel for the Trough Creek area. Ride we did, almost 8 hours worth as we very much enjoyed the trails. We were off to a good start in that it was easy to hook up with the trails. We made a left out of camp on Tar Kiln Road (in the direction opposite of how we approached camp), rode a short distance on the gravel State Forest road, and came to two State Forest gates, one on each side of the road. We decided to make a left and head in the direction of Raystown Lake. Immediately, we were pleased to see the many markers to guide us, both snowmobile markers and equestrian markers. What a nice feeling to see the trail marked this way and done so well. It made us, as equestrians, feel very welcome. The trail stayed consistent! Do bring the map; we followed the signs and used the map when we came to intersections which can be a little confusing. We just tried to remain alert for markers at the intersections to make sure we stayed on the designated route. The brown signs with an equestrian image, along with arrows, made most of our travels very easy. This was a treat to follow a trail so well marked, we could just relax, enjoy scanning the woods for wildlife, and soak up the beauty.

We rode in a counter clockwise direction. We took the "Over There Trail" (nice, easy, double tract, old logging road/snowmobile path), to John Bum Road (a gravel road with a wide, mowed shoulder allowing room to get off the road if needed), to the Horse Knob Fire Trail (wonderful, scenic, wide, grassy stretches where we saw the most wildlife), to Terrace Mountain Road (a very scenic dirt/gravel road, one which I particularly enjoyed), back to John Bum Road (a dirt/gravel road with wide shoulder), to the Cleavon Trail (very pretty stretch through pine forests), and followed the signs past the Trough Creek State Park picnic area (very scenic ride down the park road). *Note: there wasn't much water along the trails so water the horses before departing.*

Just before the picnic area, we each took a turn (while the other held a horse) to dismount and view the ruins of the Paradise Furnace iron kiln on the left and the interesting historical information provided along the walkway. Do visit this site as it presents a very good explanation of the iron-making process. *Bring change as there is a nearby soda machine, located conveniently along the path at the park. A can of ice cold soda was quite refreshing on the hot day when we visited.* We took in a view of this area, which once was a CCC (Civilian Conservation Corps) camp, and then continued down the road past the picnic grounds. We were careful and considerate not to bring the horses on the side of the picnic grounds and, instead, traveled the far side of the road and followed the arrows. (Please be sure to dismount and scatter any manure along this section to help keep equestrians welcome along this historic route.) We continued to the next intersection and picked up Cassville Road (another State Forest road with plenty of shoulder), then followed the "Down Under Trail" (also nice) to the pipeline path (nicely mowed path with gorgeous views offering a variety of alternate paths), made a left on the pipeline path, a quick right onto Kendig Road (also very pleasing, more of a path or dirt logging road than a State Forest road), left onto Tar Kiln Road, and back to camp. Throughout we found the dirt/gravel State Forest road connectors to have lots of room (off the road if need be) making them pleasurable to ride. We encountered some vehicles while connecting between trails but we did not find it to be a problem due to the mowed, wide shoulder bordering the roads. Weekends may have more activity.

Our favorite part of the trail was the overlook along Raystown Lake in the vicinity of Horse Knob Fire Trail. This is a nice, easy, wide (not "on the edge") trail which gradually climbs to the top of the mountain. It follows the crest of the summit while traveling high above the gorge below. There are actually views on both sides of the trail. Although many vistas are obstructed by trees, there are also intervals where you can see just how high you are and also catch a view of the valleys and lake below. If you look in the direction opposite the lake, there is a great view of the surrounding mountains. The trail, the elevation, the lake, and the scenery on both sides are just spectacular. This is a don't miss section of the trail. We plan to come back and ride this section in the fall, when the foliage is in full color, and also when the leaves have come off of the trees.

At camp, the morning was quiet except for the chatter of birds. There is plenty of wildlife in this area evidenced by what you will see out on trail, the various prints in the mud, and the "droppings" along the trail. We could see from the evidence that berries were popular with the local bears. While riding the stretches of high grass we saw deer, and mother turkeys and their offspring. Then I had an experience of a different kind, a first for me. This could have been another memorable experience as I saw this cute, little short-legged creature with a snowy white type of fur immediately in front of me on the trail. It moved rather slowly and I just stopped the horse short of almost stepping on it. It had a furry tail all puffed up and almost looked like a white squirrel, but I couldn't quite see its face as its fluffed up tail and rear end were toward me. I couldn't understand why it didn't get out of the way quickly. All of a sudden John said, "That is a baby skunk." I did not know skunks came in that color but I didn't question it. I got "out of Dodge" in a hurry! My ex-reining horse did a quick roll back and we put plenty of space between us and that cute, but stinky, critter. After we laughed about my close (almost) encounter and when the coast was clear, I moved down the trail, again leading. Well we were farther down the trail, just about a mile or two, and sure enough, another skunk was directly in front of me in the center of the trail. But this skunk had more black and was more recognizable. Another roll back and then I let John lead for a while. It got to be almost a game as to what would pop up next. I soon relaxed and let my horse resume the lead as he has the faster walk. All of a sudden, something burst out of the high grass and into the air, with a whole lot of noise and commotion. This time I had come upon a mother turkey with several youngsters, camouflaged but scurrying all around me in the high grass. Right after this, there was another lone turkey which we could not see in the grass until we were directly upon it. After another surprise flutter, it then returned to being quiet for the rest of the course. As much fun as that was, I think both my horse and I were getting a little bit jumpy wondering what would happen next. *I am glad I read **after** our ride that copperheads and rattlesnakes are common to the area, as I really may have been concerned!* We viewed all this wildlife on the trail overlooking Raystown Lake. We didn't see one, but there is a chance of seeing an eagle soaring overhead by the bluffs over the lake. Also, throughout our trail ride there was an amazing amount and assortment of butterflies. Friendly little fellows, they would fly all around me and come quite near for extended periods. I joked that they were accompanying us while we rode; it felt like something out of the movie "Fantasia," as they formed colorful circles in flight. I haven't seen so many diverse colors of butterflies in a long time!

Throughout our ride there were many wide paths or old logging roads that headed in different directions, and looked like alternative areas to travel. In addition, the pipeline, with its groomed wide tracts of grass and seemingly endless expanse, looked very inviting and offered additional riding. During this visit, we stayed mostly on the main trail but we do plan to return and do some exploring in the future. We did not see any hikers, bikers, or other horseback riders throughout our entire ride. However, we did see manure and it looked like these trails had been visited by equestrians. They were very lightly used and there was little evidence of regular activity. We were wondering if many equestrians had heard of this destination. We hope to now share it so that it does get the maximum enjoyment it deserves.

Rothrock State Forest is large and diverse with ridges and valleys. I was told the trails were not maintained unless volunteers work on them. That appeared to be the case in the Brush Ridge and northern tract, but not at Trough Creek. The Trough Creek area looked so well kept that I would have to conclude that someone was doing a nice job, and the State Forest deserves much credit. The State Forest and the State Park were nicely maintained, clean, fallen trees were cleared, and everything from the trails to the mowed State Forest road shoulder (which provides room for equestrians, hikers, or bikers to get off the road if a vehicle approaches) reflected diligent work on the park's behalf. Thank you to all those that contribute to these beautiful trails!

After riding the trails, take a drive and check out some of the beautiful views along the road systems within the State Forest, especially near the lake.

EQUESTRIAN CAMPING:
Motorized camping is permitted at designated locations within the State Forest. Site #8 is the camping site situated in the Trough Creek Division and is ideally located near the trails. A maximum of 10 people per site is permitted. The camping area is set behind a wooden (not locked) gate just off of Tar Kiln Road. We put the gate back in place once we were within the site so that it added an extra barrier in case the horses got loose. There is a short entrance of two lane width to a medium size, circular, open area of grass. Based on the stumps on the outer perimeters of the site and the new saplings, this was an old logging staging area or base. It is now a grassy circle bordered by young growth and it can be challenging to find trees big enough to tie line to. Portable corrals or electric fencing would work if you do not need the parking area for your group (although some sections may be hard to drive a stake into as there is a tough surface of shale). We would have preferred to tie the horses (farther back) in the circle but we had found the only suitable trees toward the entrance. (It would be ideal if the State Forest put tie rails or tie posts at the rear of the circle, something like the convenient tie rails at the Broad Mountain day parking area would work nicely.) Since we were traveling alone, we faced our rig (out) to the entrance and hung our tie line from the large trees behind the rig, actually going across the entrance. (This entrance is not traveled by anyone other than those at this camping location.) We couldn't tie on the same side of the entrance as there was a rugged terrain of rocks and old stumps on the edge. By tying from one side to the other, across the entrance, the horses had a level, safe grass surface to stand on. One could also tie from the trailer to a tree to keep the horses from blocking the entrance path if additional rigs were coming. That wouldn't work for us as our horses would move the trailer all night and we wouldn't get any sleep.

The site was very quiet during our stay except for occasional cars passing down Tar Kiln Road. We found this to be a pleasant, peaceful spot and we felt like we had the woods to ourselves. However, there are quite a bit of flies, so do bring bug spray and fly protection.

HISTORICAL INFORMATION:

Rothrock State Forest derives its name from Dr. Rothrock who was a pioneer in forestry and who, in the late 1800s, had the honorable position of being the first forestry commissioner of the Division of Forestry (which developed and progressed into today's Bureau of Forestry). Dr. Rothrock established one of the first training centers for foresters. Like many other Pennsylvania forests at that time, the land was stripped and left devoid of all timber. The wood served various uses, especially to supply the nearby furnaces including the ones at Trough Creek State Park and Greenwood Furnace State Park. By the approach of the 20th century, some of the furnaces were no longer in demand and closed. Dr. Rothrock seized the opportunity to purchase the land. Over time, additional purchases were made. Dr. Rothrock deserves much credit for recognizing the need to obtain, restore and preserve this land that is Rothrock State Forest as we know it today.

In the mid 1930s, Trough Creek State Park was established on land that was formerly the Paradise Iron Furnace Company. There is an interesting display at Trough Creek State Park by the kilns (near the main picnic area) which explains the iron ore process. It also explains the types of workers needed to run the furnace. In the 18th and 19th centuries, wood was used to supply charcoal to fuel furnaces which made iron ore. Iron ore was critical and in much demand at this time in our nation's history. Iron masters of successful operations were affluent and considered high in society's communal order of the time. An example of an iron master's home is the Trough Creek Lodge which was built in the mid 1800s. (You can experience a bit of the life of an iron master as you can rent this home, a stone house, which was situated where the iron master could keep a close eye on the operations of the Paradise Furnace. The home has modern accommodations and is handicapped accessible. Look for this home by the 'S' turn as you ride past the kiln historical site.)

In the 1930s to early 1940s, Rothrock State Forest was used to house six Civilian Conservation Corps (CCC) camps. During this time, many of the Rothrock State Forest's and State Park's roads and facilities, including Penn Roosevelt State Park, were built by members of the CCC. Also of interest, legend states that when Edgar Allen Poe traveled in this region, he saw the ravens that made their homes on the cliffs near Trough Creek State Park. That became the inspiration for his tale, "The Raven."

COURTESIES:

I would like to express a very special thank you to Brian Pfister, Forester, Rothrock State Forest, for mailing such useful materials on Rothrock State Forest along with providing excellent directions and trail recommendations. You were a great help in making sure I found the right trails and the appropriate equestrian areas. I would also like to express my appreciation to the understanding staff at

148

the ranger station when we made some last minute camping changes to our plans. Trying to cover unknown territory with horses, finding the best trails, estimating traveling distance between camping sites and trails in mountainous country, along with hoping weather conditions cooperate, can be very challenging when trying to make plans and reservations. Thank you to all those folks at Rothrock State Forest (Bureau of Forestry-Department of Conservation & Natural Resources) for allowing equestrians to enjoy and share in this beautiful area.

THINGS WE LEARNED THIS RIDE:
• I learned that skunks can come in a different color, and also that I need to get out of their way quickly as they won't or don't need to get out of mine.

NEARBY AND SURROUNDING AREAS:
• Centre County Visitors Bureau (800) 358-5466, website: www.visitpennstate.org
• The Silver Stirrup tack store (nice folks, diverse tack selection, and handy trail items), off Route 764 in Duncansville (814) 695-4530
• Rockhill Trolley Museum, Rockhill Furnace (814) 447-9576, (610) 965-9028, website: www.rockhilltrolley.org
• East Broad Top Railroad, Rockhill Furnace (814) 447-3011

NEARBY AND SURROUNDING AREA STABLES:
• Hartslog Valley Stables (overnight camping and stabling, showers, guided trail rides, hookups, and stalls [near Raystown Lake]), Huntingdon (814) 644-0754
• Horsepower Farm (boarding, therapeutic program, lessons, camp), Huntingdon (814) 667-2497

NEARBY AND SURROUNDING AREA VET SERVICES:
• E. Bracken, Williamsburg (814) 832-2313, (814) 932-6893 cell
• M. James, Martinsburg (814) 793-3566 (use (814) 793-9226 only if he can't be reached at other number)

NEARBY AND SURROUNDING AREA FARRIERS:
• Chester Horton Horseshoeing, Alexandria (800) 993-SHOE, (814) 669-4652

20. Brush Ridge & The Northern Tract Rothrock State Forest BOF-DCNR

(Bureau of Forestry/Department of Conservation & Natural Resources)

Lasting Impression: There are numerous clusters of trails, old railroad paths, logging, and mountain dirt roads to explore in the northern tract of Rothrock State Forest. Some of these are already popular and well known with locals for day rides. Although in its early stages at the time of our visit, the initiation and development of designated motorized camping areas may now attract equestrians from afar. Each sector of trails has its own characteristics and many are unique in terrain from the others, making this an explorer's paradise. Some are easy and leisurely with gentle terrain; but travel to the next ridge and you'll find a more rough and challenging mountainous surface.

Location: The Brush Ridge and the northern tract of Rothrock State Forest are located in central Pennsylvania east and southeast of State College, and extend over Centre, Mifflin, and Huntingdon Counties.

Length: *Day Ride, Weekend Destination (possible potential for week-long destination)*- This chapter's main focus is the Brush Ridge Trail system and the northern tract of Rothrock State Forest. The northern tract is the largest block (approximately 80,000 acres) of Rothrock State Forest. There is no exact trail mileage as there are no specific, designated trails. The Brush Ridge Trail system itself makes for a nice day ride, but riding can be extended by exploring the miles and miles of other nearby and distant multiple-use trails and State Forest roads (dirt) within the northern tract.

Level of Difficulty: Easy, to moderate, to difficult; even impassable due to downed trees or rugged terrain

Terrain: The trails consist of single or double dirt tracts; durable, old logging or mountain roads; beautiful, wide, maintained grassy paths such as that of the Brush Ridge Trail; or short stretches in the valley that can be somewhat rocky, hold moisture, or have downed trees.

Horse Camping: Yes

Non-horse Camping: Yes

Carriage Potential: The Brush Ridge trails described in this chapter are mostly single tract and not suitable to carriages; however, the northern tract of Rothrock State Forest offers extensive State Forest roads to explore. The described camping area would be a functional locale for parking with a carriage as it adjoins the State Forest roads (see description of site below). We did not see any evidence of carriage driving, so carriage drivers would need to scout for suitability and check with the office for rules and regulations.

Maps and Info: For information regarding Rothrock State Forest, contact DCNR, Rothrock State Forest, P.O. Box 403, Rothrock Lane, Huntingdon, PA 16652, (814) 643-2340. Additional information is available at the DCNR website: www.dcnr.state.pa.us. We did not see maps at the parking or camping areas. Call and ask for the Rothrock State Forest Public Use Map (green), any snowmobile maps, and the large, colored topographic map (about 17" x 22") for the area you plan to visit. As there is no "trail map," few if any markings, and the area is very large, these will be very helpful. They also reflect where the Mid-State Trail travels so you can avoid it since it is off limits to horses. For State Park historical data, general information, or maps, contact Whipple Dam State Park, Penn Roosevelt State Park, or Greenwood Furnace State Park at (814) 667-1800 or via the DCNR website indicated above. For disability or other information, contact the above State Forest number or the Pennsylvania Bureau of State Parks (888) PA-PARKS.

Activities: Hiking, Biking, Horseback Riding Trails, Picnicking, Swimming, Boating, Fishing, Bird Watching, Snowmobiling (Rothrock State Forest claims to be second only to Potter County in snowmobiling), X-C Skiing, Camping, and Hunting

Fees for Trail Use: None

Permits for Day Trail Use: None

Permits/Fees Required for Camping: Yes, a permit is required (no fee).

Comfort Station: None (however, facilities are available at the nearby State Parks)

DIRECTIONS:

To day parking at Broad Mountain Road/Brush Ridge trail location: Take Route 26 to the town of McAlevys Fort. If traveling in a southeast direction from State College, take Route 26 south for about 16 miles (from the intersection of Business Route 322) to McAlevys Fort. *Note: Route 26 has a steep decline between State College and Rothrock State Forest. (It is not very long; just take it slow and proceed with caution. We did not have any problem and were able to haul back and forth a few times, but trucks will need to be able to handle the grade.) Also, we concluded traveling to Broad Mountain Road (by Greenwood Furnace) on Route 305 from Route 655 was even more challenging as it was steep, plus it has switchbacks. On another visit, we approached this area from the south at Raystown Lake and headed north on Route 26 toward McAlevys Fort. This approach was much more gradual and easier on the truck brakes.* Make a left onto Route 305 east and travel on Route 305 (following signs) into Greenwood Furnace State Park. You will pass through the park grounds. At 4.8 miles make a left onto Broad Mountain Road (a.k.a. Black Lick Road). This is the same turn as the Visitor Center. The gravel road starts off as a narrow, bumpy, winding road (you may wonder if you have the right road) and then it quickly improves and straightens out. Take Broad Mountain Road for 1.8 miles. You will see a gravel entrance to the left followed by another identical entrance a short distance past it. Both lead to the same small loop. There isn't a sign but once you enter it you will see tie rails and various one lane tracts entering the woods, along with "ski trail" signs. The lot is a small to medium, pull through lot which can accommodate about three large trailers and possibly four 2-horse, smaller trailers. We could see the lot and the trails have been used frequently by equestrians. *And we did not see one pile of manure in the lot; good job cleaning up!* Please note that, at the time of our visit, this parking area was to be used for day parking only, not equestrian camping.

To designated motorized camping site #3 at Pine Swamp Road north of Whipple Dam State Park: This is where we stayed while riding the Brush Ridge Trail and is the closest rig friendly site if you need to stay overnight. You can reach this from Route 26. From the town of McAlevys Fort, at the intersection with Route 305, take Route 26 north for 3.8 miles and make a right into Whipple Dam State Park. Or you can travel about 12 miles from the intersection of Business Route 322 in State College on Route 26 south, and make a left into Whipple Dam State Park. Follow the signs to Whipple Dam State Park. You'll see a sign for the park and a road sign for Whipple Road. There is a small grocery store and gas station on the corner where you turn onto Whipple Road. Make the turn onto Whipple Road and follow the park signs. Pass the park and picnic grounds. Continue for 4.5 miles (Whipple Road will become Laurel Run Road) and you will come to a small bridge on the left at the corner of Pine Swamp Road. Make a left and cross the bridge (we took our larger living quarter rig and had sufficient room). Make a right into the open, grass area after the bridge. As you pull in, bear left as there is a slightly low area to the right of the entrance which may be soft. The roads to this location were good, wide, graded, constructed of a tough gravel surface, and well marked. Unless you are familiar with the surrounding roads, do depart the same way you came to avoid roads which may be too narrow for big rigs.

THE TRAILS:
Equestrians are permitted on all trails and State Forest roads except for areas specifically closed to horses, such as the Mid-State Trail (hiking only). The Mid-State Trail is marked with orange rectangle blazes; side trails have blue rectangle blazes. There are many miles of trails and hundreds of miles of State Forest roads (most are unpaved). There are four State Parks in Rothrock State Forest: Greenwood Furnace State Park, Trough Creek State Park, Whipple Dam State Park, and Penn Roosevelt State Park. Equestrians should avoid picnic areas and the core of State Parks unless a road or location specifically permits equestrians, such as that at Penn Roosevelt State Park. The Thickhead Mountain region and Penn Roosevelt State Park (of the northern tract) provide additional miles of horseback riding along closed sections of forest roads. These trails can be seen

on the colored topographic map on the west side of Penn Roosevelt State Park. There are various multiple-use trails that network through and around that mountain range and adjoining areas. Equestrians have also frequented trails along some of the southwest sections of the northern tract such as the Tussey Ridge sections and Pine Hill outlying areas. The Rothrock State Forest system contains six Natural Areas; biking and horseback riding are not permitted in Natural Areas.

Broad Mountain/Brush Ridge location: We visited this locale twice. The first time, it rained and we were concerned the shaded, single path trails may have still been wet so we decided to postpone our ride. The second visit was after a period of a few sunny days but also several days after the remains of Hurricane Frances had visited the area; so we didn't know what to expect. We set out to the right on the trail (facing the back of the lot in the direction away from Greenwood Furnace State Park) and the surface looked good so we continued. (Heading to the left would lead to the valley trail; see below.) There were trails heading in all different directions, many crisscrossing loops. These trails were originally intended for use as ski trails but I was told they are actually more popular with equestrians. Initially, all the signs said the same thing ("ski trail") so it was confusing as to which way to proceed. Since this network of trails is visited frequently by equestrians, if we were unsure of where to go, we decided to just follow the hoof prints. That worked well.

We were told that these trails are maintained mostly by volunteers. We found some to be in good shape but there were also numerous trees down and it appeared they had been down for a very long period. It wouldn't take too much to clear these or reroute, so hopefully that will occur. We continued to follow the hoof prints which traveled around any obstacles; sometimes it was a bit challenging and took some navigating but we did not have a problem. Plus the trails have plenty of alternates, just backtrack or sidetrack and pick up another loop. There were some wet patches and rock clusters in the low lying land (horses should have shoes) but we continued to try different loops while trying to favor the high ground. Ultimately, we linked up to the Brush Ridge Trail which travels over the ridge of the mountain. As we turned onto this double tract, it immediately stood out that this trail was exceptionally maintained. The few mile stretch of the Brush Ridge Trail is a wide, mowed grass, double tract path of excellent surface and gradual slope. Brush Ridge Trail travels the crest of the mountain and offers glimpses of the surrounding mountains and valleys. *I would like to revisit this section when the leaves are off the trees and the visibility is not limited. Plus, it is my kind of trail as it is neither "on the edge" nor steep.*

The Brush Ridge Trail was **our favorite part** as it made for a very nice ride. We continued along this trail which approaches Greenwood Furnace State Park. Horses should keep to the outside of the State Park as there aren't equestrian trails within. We rode the full length of the Brush Ridge Trail and then took the trail back down to the valley by a sign saying "ski trail." At first it looked steep, but actually it was a nice trail of gentle grade. However, when we got to the valley, the footing became inconsistent with scattered rocks, some downed trees, and wet spots (understandable after the recent storms but this may be best visiting after dry periods). It became somewhat arduous as to where to proceed. We kept following the other hoof prints. Since there were cabins to the side, it looked like this was the only area available to complete the loop. However, the low lying areas could just use a wooden walkway or a few short bridges and some stone dust, and that would resolve those couple of bad stretches. It wasn't too long a ride in the valley and then we proceeded to higher ground which soon returned to the lot. Other than the section just described, the trails were very nice and the Brush Ridge Trail was exceptionally beautiful. Regarding that one inferior section, until improvements are made, I would prefer to backtrack along the Brush Ridge Trail, pick up one of the many side trails, and try returning to the lot from that direction. Or just ride the Brush Ridge Trail to the end and return via Broad Mountain Road (dirt/gravel).

We made a day trip to this locale and explored this section and connecting loops for about 5 hours. Your ride can be extended by many hours by hooking up to some of the nearby trails. The colored topographic maps reflect the trails on both sides of Broad Mountain Road and other trails in the surrounding areas. The trails we rode were mostly easy to moderate, but I have been told the opposite side of Broad Mountain Road may be more challenging. If you see other equestrians at the parking area or on trail, you may want to ask them what they recommend and what they found. Surprisingly, as these trails do get use, we did not run into any hikers, bikers, or horseback riders while riding them.

Pine Swamp Road campsite: We then drove to our campsite. As we were just staying the night, we did not have the opportunity to also explore some of the trails in the immediate vicinity of the Pine Swamp Road campsite. (We had chose to camp at the Pine Swamp Road location since there wasn't a motorized designated camping area that could accommodate equestrian rigs near the Brush Ridge trails where we planned to ride. So we traveled to this site which is about 16 miles from Brush Ridge. It is much closer as the crow flies but we stayed on the main roads.) Although we didn't get to ride the trails in this section of the northern tract and cannot comment on the terrain, we did check out how to access the trails. You can ride directly from Site #3 as there are trails which can be accessed via connectors, plus you can meander around the dirt and gravel State Forest roads. Looking at the topographic map obtained from the State Forest office, there is a network of trails surrounding the Thickhead Wild Area and throughout the Thickhead Mountain region. To reach these, ride out (in the direction away from the bridge which you arrived on) from the campsite and make a right onto the gravel road, continue down the road, cross a bridge, continue to a fork in the road, and make a right onto a dirt road (the road indicates it is a dead end). Based on the map, this dirt road becomes a double tract, multiple-use trail (appears to be one of the area's old railroad grades), heads north of the campsite, and connects to many single tract and multiple-use trails. The entrance to the rail-trail appeared of good surface but the connecting trails may vary significantly in terrain.

Other trails: There are also other trails throughout the northern tract which I was told equestrians frequent that are not described in detail in this chapter. Equestrians ride Pine Hill in the western section of the northern tract (although I did not see much in the way of multiple-use trails indicated on the map for Pine Hill; it may be that the State Forest roads and/or power or pipe lines are also ridden) and also trails near Penn Roosevelt State Park (this appeared worth looking into) in the northeast section of the northern tract. This State Forest is huge and diverse and offers much exploring.

I was sad to hear that, within two months of my beginning to research Rothrock State Forest, a few sections of trail had been closed to horses and bikes. I was told this was due to the surface not being considered strong enough to support horses and bikes. If you are local and frequent these trail systems, please connect with local equestrians, clubs and volunteers to stay abreast of developments and the maintenance of the trails. With both the surging popularity of mountain biking and trail riding, and the close proximity to State College, these trails will continue to get increased use and scrutiny. Increased use without careful trail management by all can result in the erosion of trails and their ultimate demise. It's important that all users practice good trail stewardship, and equestrians remain positively visible and are proactive to prevent closure.

EQUESTRIAN CAMPING:
At the time of our visit, there were eight designated motorized camping sites in Rothrock State Forest; only three of which we were told were suitable for large equestrian rigs. We camped at two of the three. Site #3 is described in this chapter, Site #8 in the Trough Creek Chapter, and Site #1 (which we did not visit) is located below the Pine Hill picnic area in the southwest section of the northern tract.

This motorized camping area at Site #3 is in a remote (there are some cabins nearby but this site had plenty of space between) and open grass area set high on dry, firm ground. We did not find soft spots but always check on foot before pulling onto a site in case of recent rains. There is room to park about 3 to 4 large living quarter type rigs. We had been informed by the ranger (in advance) that this site is not maintained, and we did find that it was quite overgrown. Where we pulled in was sufficient, but the surrounding area had very high grass and blueberry bushes. It's not too bad to just park there, but you do need to walk the horses through the knee high growth to the woods in order to attach them to the high line (one's legs get pretty wet with the dew of the morning). Backing is required; although, if the outlying grass and brush were cut there would be lots of room to pull through and room for more rigs. Bring strong fly spray and cover for the horses; there was a heavy population of flies on the warm days in early September when we visited. (We did not have any problems on trail, just at this campsite. Nor did we see any marshland. Possibly the overgrowth added to the abundance of flies.) If you find flies or insects to be the norm for this location, you may want to visit when it is cooler. If this is throughout the riding season, please provide feedback to the office; it may be that a different site is needed for equestrians. The year we visited was the first year for designated motorized sites and equestrians were not yet using them, so it may be just that the demand for equestrian camping has not yet presented itself and locations have not yet been tested. Of course it depends on whether the trails are good. When demand increases and sites are tried, enlargement, improvements, or relocations may be made. With an expression of interest, there is also always the possibility of equestrians requesting and being granted more suitable locations which are also central to the best of trails.

HISTORICAL INFORMATION:
If you enjoy history, make sure you visit some of the nearby State Parks, such as Greenwood Furnace State Park where you can view the huge furnace evidencing the area's heyday of iron making in the 1800s. Communities developed around this prosperous industry of its time; remains of some of the buildings and old homesteads can still be seen as you ride along the trails. Look for the ornamental trees and stone foundations. Many of the trails in the area were once created as a result of logging and railroad activities of the time. To obtain or view more historical information on the history of Greenwood Furnace and to view the furnace and blacksmith shop, stop by the attractions which are located along Route 305 just before you turn onto Broad Mountain Road. Please be reminded to avoid the busy State Park core activities or historical attractions on horseback. Unless the park specifies otherwise, these should be visited only on foot.

COURTESIES:
Thank you to Brian Pfister, Forester, Rothrock State Forest, for maps of this area and good directions. It would have been tough finding these trails without your support and assistance. Thank you also to Randy White who was very helpful and informative.

THINGS WE LEARNED THIS RIDE:
Importantly, I noticed a pattern in the State Forests while I was researching for this book that I had not seen while researching trails for "Ride Pennsylvania Horse Trails- Part I" in the eastern half of Pennsylvania. I asked a Forest Ranger and he confirmed my observations. The State Forests are now moving in the

direction of designating motorized locations vs. the old practice of allowing motorized vehicles to camp wherever within the State Forest, as long as they met the certain guidelines such as being a minimum distance from the streams, roads, etc. Although currently this is experimental, it does seem like the direction it is going. This is very significant to equestrians. This can be a positive in that large areas may be cleared so that we can fit our rigs in where maybe we couldn't find a place to park before. However, to equestrians, it is also a disadvantage in that we will lose the freedom to choose where we would like to camp (strategic to the trails of our choice and locations suitable for horses). For instance, a designated motorized area has not been created near the Broad Mountain Trails due to its close locale to Greenwood Furnace State Park campgrounds. So, to reach the popular Broad Mountain/Black Lick Trail System, equestrians must load up the horses and trailer to the trailhead. (A site has not been designated near Greenwood Furnace State Park so as not to compete with the State Park campground. Yet equestrian camping wouldn't compete with the State Park campground as they can't use it. This is where equestrians need to voice their needs and desires to the appropriate office. It may be as simple as just communicating that we need these areas strategic to certain trails.)

NEARBY:
• Centre County Visitors Bureau (800) 358-5466, website: www.visitpennstate.org

NEARBY AND SURROUNDING AREA STABLES:
• Hartslog Valley Stables, (overnight camping and stabling, showers, guided trail rides, hookups and stalls [near Raystown Lake]), Huntingdon (814) 644-0754
• Horsepower Farm (boarding, therapeutic program, lessons, camp), Huntingdon (814) 667-2497

NEARBY AND SURROUNDING AREA VET SERVICES:
• Centre Equine Practice, Centre Hall (814) 364-1921
• S. McAllister, Centre Hall (814) 234-7415

NEARBY AND SURROUNDING AREA FARRIERS:
• T. Siegenthaler, Spring Mills (814) 364-9534
• Scott Sims, Julian (near Port Matilda) (814) 353-1511

21. The Old Logging Trail
Raystown Lake
COE
(U.S. Army Corps of Engineers)

Lasting Impression: The views at Raystown Lake are magnificent and stunning. The Old Loggers Trail is situated near the west shore of the lake and offers many scenic glimpses of the lake and the boats anchored in its coves. Once a popular locale for horseback riders, this trail has become in need of maintenance (low hanging growth and downed trees) and a horse trailer parking lot at the time of our visit. When restored and reopened, this should provide a nice ride for those who like a challenging trail and rugged mountain riding. Plus, there is another neighboring trail which was under construction during our visit and should offer a more moderate terrain once completed. The very good news is that I found the U.S. Army Corps of Engineers to be wonderfully receptive to equestrians and multiple-users, and they are working on restoring and re-engineering this trail. But it is critical that equestrians express and show their interest in this trail system if they want to obtain adequate parking and improvement of the trails.

Location: Raystown Lake is located in southcentral Pennsylvania in Huntingdon County. Raystown Lake borders the southern tract of Rothrock State Forest.

Length: *Day Ride Destination*- The Old Logging Trail is only about 5 miles in length but a new adjoining trail will extend this by roughly 20 to 30 miles.

Level of Difficulty: The Old Logging Trail is an advanced trail and challenging due to steep grades. Horses need to be fit. The COE office spoke of rerouting a portion of the trail; if this occurs the trail will be less strenuous. The nearby multiple-use and bike trail under construction is planned to be of a gentler grade.

Terrain: There are nice, easy, wide logging paths, old mountain roads, and challenging single paths on the mountainside. The trails are not rocky, but there are sections which are extremely steep in the vicinity of markers 27 toward 23. (The "Steep Trail" is best ascended vs. descended; this is the section under consideration for rerouting.) Horses should have shoes.

Horse Camping: None (however, we camped with the horses at the nearby Trough Creek section of Rothrock State Forest and traveled to this trail system)

Non-horse Camping: Yes

Maps and Info: For information regarding Raystown Lake which is operated under the U.S. Army Corps of Engineers, contact USACE, Raystown Lake (814) 658-6810, website: www.raystown.nab.usace.army.mil. You can also contact U.S. Army Corps of Engineers, Box 222, RD1, Hesston, PA 16647-9227, (814) 658-3405. We did not see maps stocked at the parking area, so call for maps in advance. Although the trail is well marked, do request the colored brochure map of the Old Loggers Trail which is very helpful. During our visit, a map was not yet available for the new (adjoining) trail system. For information regarding equestrian parking, trail progress, or volunteer work contact Allen Gwinn, Park Ranger, (814) 658-6810, email: allen.gwinn@nab02.usace.army.mil.

Activities: Hiking, Biking, Horseback Riding Trails, Picnicking, Swimming, Boating, Fishing, Bird Watching, Camping, and Hunting (certain sections)

Fees for Trail Use: None

Permits for Day Trail Use: None

Comfort Station: None (there is a portajohn at the entrance to the Susquehannock Camping area, which neighbors the parking area)

DIRECTIONS:
This trail system can be reached via Route 26 to Seven Points Road or States Road by Hesston and proceed as indicated below. From the Pennsylvania Turnpike I-76, take the turnpike to Exit #161 Breezewood. Go through the toll booth and travel about another 1.5 miles (on the turnpike access road) to pick up Route 30 west. Take Route 30 west for 8 miles and pick up Route 26 north. Take Route 26 north for 28 miles and come to Route 994. Continue on Route 26 for another 7 miles (past Route 994) and make a right onto States Road. *I believe you can also continue a short distance to Seven Points Road and make a right. This access was completely closed during our visit so we did not clock from there.* Travel 1 mile on States Road and make a right onto Seven Points Road. Travel 2 miles on Seven Points Road. (There is a brief, but significant, climb and then it levels off.) You will come to a turn in the road; make a left toward Susquehannock. Travel about 1.5 miles and you will see the lot to the right. The lot is bordered by split rail fencing and is just before the entrance to the Susquehannock camping area and guard booth. There is a sign at the entrance. The entrance is uphill and the lot is at an elevated location. It was **not** yet suitable for equestrian parking. *Note: unfortunately, at the time of our visit, the lot was extremely small and tight; too small for most horse trailers. (We were hauling our large trailer and had to park at a different location which was not open to the public but, fortunately, under the circumstances, we were permitted to park there.) Even a two-horse trailer would have to do some tight maneuvering. We spoke with the office and they indicated they would work with equestrians to extend the existing lot to accommodate horse trailers if equestrians expressed an interest. The lot at the Old Loggers Trail could easily be expanded as there is suitable, flat land already adjoining it. The office asked for our feedback and we recommended the expansion. If you decide to visit this trail, check with the office in advance to determine if the lot has been expanded or another established to accommodate horse trailers. When I discussed this with the rangers at the COE, they were very receptive to our recommendations and were interested in attracting equestrians, along with other users, to these trail systems. Isn't that nice to hear! If you live near this trail system, go for it; make a difference.*

If you had not made the left toward Susquehannock, but instead continued on Seven Points Road, you would pass the COE Administration building on the left, the COE Registration Center on the right, and the Visitor Bureau/Ranger Station (check out the displays and the view from the deck behind this building) on the left. Also, along Seven Points Road is the second parking area, the Seven Points trailhead, for the Old Loggers Trail. It will be on the right side and you will see a painted walkway on the highway where you need to cross to pick up the trail on your left as you pull in. There is a sign on the left, "Old Loggers Trail." This trailhead is on the opposite side of the road where you park and you can see it once you are parked there. A large horse trailer can fit; however, it is not our preference for horse trailer parking as it is just a pull-off along a busy road. If you choose this location, horses need to be comfortable near traffic (including vehicles hauling boats on trailers). Also, if you find another more suitable parking area, ask the head ranger in the office if that location can be used for horse trailers. When we spoke with the various rangers, they were unfamiliar with equestrians' needs; nonetheless, they were interested in learning those and were also very professional, helpful, and receptive to recommendations and suggestions.

THE TRAILS:
Raystown Lake is about 30 miles long with 118 miles of shore, and is the longest lake in the state. The lake covers about 8,300 acres, and the recreation area is almost 30,000 acres and is surrounded by many natural areas ideal for hiking, biking, and horseback riding. The lake itself is a popular attraction for boating enthusiasts and fishermen. There are two designated equestrian areas in the Raystown Lake COE region where horses are permitted. There is the Terrace Mountain Trail (supposed to have many scenic views of the lake) which travels from the Lake Raystown Resort area to Weaver's Falls in the Saxton vicinity. This trail is an old road (not a loop), about 6 miles in length (12 round trip), and we were told is a wide path of moderate level of difficulty with some rocky patches. We did not ride the Terrace Mountain Trail. The second designated trail is a combination of the Old Loggers Trail and a connecting new multiple-use and mountain bike trail that was under construction during our visit. We rode the Old Loggers Trail which is about 5 miles in length but, due to steep climbs, takes extra time to cover. We were hoping to ride the Old Loggers Trail then ride the new multiple-use/bike trail which was not yet ready for use. There is not yet an exact estimate of the miles on the new trail, but it is supposed to be about 20 to 30 miles when completed and will link many local farm roads and logging roads making for a lengthy ride. Check with the office as to the status of this trail and where equestrians can park.

The Old Loggers Trail was created in the vicinity of Susquehannock and Seven Points and travels along remote sections of the lake shore. It links a network of old farm roads, logging roads, service roads, and various trail systems. As you leave the Susquehannock Old Loggers Trail parking lot (next to the Susquehannock campground entrance), the trail immediately descends down a steep decline (connector) for a short distance and then joins with a level, old logging road. We proceeded carefully down the entrance to the trail system. I didn't feel it was too bad but John felt this tract should be reworked to a switchback as a steep, straight trail approach is vulnerable to erosion especially if use is increased. An alternate, more gradual approach is to ride in the entrance of the camping area and make a right to pick up the logging trail. Either way, if you choose to ride the Old Loggers Trail, you should be at ease with steep terrain as this is only the beginning. On the opposite side of the entrance road to the camping area (opposite of where you link with the Old Loggers Trail and just down from the camp attendant's booth on the left) is the site of the new multiple-use trail that is under construction. This is planned to be more moderate in terrain.

Looking at the Old Loggers Trail map, we started our ride by traveling from marker #15 to marker #8. This stretch is an old logging road of easy, gentle grade and is leisurely. At this point I was wondering why they said this trail was steep. I soon found out.

We wanted to check out the Seven Points lot, so we rode from marker #8 to marker #1. There was water for the horses at marker #8. The stretch from #8 to #6 is a narrow tract along the side of the mountain and overlooks inlets of the lake where boats anchor to enjoy the tranquil scenery. This is a very scenic portion of the trail system with its teal colored water appearing almost surreal. But the trail is also precipitous and may have too much of a feeling of "on the edge" for some riders. I did like this section; however, it is not one for beginners and horses need to be comfortable with the boats in the water. Between markers number #6 and #2 we noticed that downed trees had just been cleared. But there was still a lot of overhanging brush and vines in this section which interfered with our head clearance. At the time of our visit, it wouldn't take much to improve that section (just some snipping and clipping) as the rest was fine. Although the Seven Points connector requires backtracking, I wouldn't want to miss this section as the scenery was gorgeous.

We then returned to marker #8 and headed toward marker #27. Near marker #27 the sign said, "Steep Trail." I was wondering what their definition of "steep" meant. We commenced our climb and then it seemed to level off. I smiled and thought that it was steep but not that bad; I was really enjoying this trail system. And then....we came to a section where the old logging road continued straight and the designated trail made a sharp left. John quickly pointed out that the logging road would have made a nice, gradual (better) trail than the trail on our left that we were about to ascend. It was a shame that the logging trail had become overgrown. We stayed with the markers and began our intense climb to

161

the top of the mountain. The designated trail climbs almost straight up the mountainside without switchbacks. This was hard on the horses and hard on the land. This sector would be an ideal project for trail improvement as there is plenty of area to reroute and switchback so that the approach is more gradual, and to minimize the chance of erosion. Once we got through most of the steep part, we encountered several downed trees and low brush between markers #25 to #19. We had to dismount and search for bypasses through dense forests at several locations. (We reported this to the office who had asked for our feedback. That same day, the head ranger personally cleared those trees! I was very impressed!) The trail, then again, became trouble-free and leisurely, and followed the logging trail between markers #20 and #14. Throughout, the trail was nicely marked with numbered posts and signs along the route. (In the eastern section of the trail system, a few signs were mischievously pulled and angled the wrong way. Double check your direction with the map so you are not fooled into proceeding in a different direction than you desire.)

This trail system was rough at the time of our visit but also very beautiful. With some work, it could again become a nice place to visit for an afternoon ride. Once the new trail is completed, there may be a significant amount of miles added to the trail network. Allen Gwinn, one of the head park rangers, indicated the current lot could be enlarged if equestrians expressed an interest. Folks who say there is nowhere left to ride, well here's your chance to make a difference. This is a gorgeous area with lots of potential along with good management who are receptive to input and welcome equestrians. Check with the head ranger before taking any action on your own. And, let's assist but also be sensitive not to wear out our welcome. This could become another fun destination like the U.S. Army Corps of Engineers' Blue Marsh trail system (covered in "Ride Pennsylvania Horse Trails- Part I").

HISTORICAL INFORMATION:
Raystown Lake was created in the 1970s for flood control purposes. Overseen by the U.S. Army Corps of Engineers (COE), it also serves additional water-related functions along with providing a popular multiple-use recreation destination.

COURTESIES:
The folks who oversee the Raystown Lake COE land were wonderful. I met several of the rangers; what a nice group of professional, positive, and willing individuals! They genuinely welcomed and considered my suggestions for improvements. I would especially like to thank Park Ranger Allen Gwinn for providing information on the U.S. Army Corps of Engineers land, and for being so receptive. Allen has indicated that folks who would like to volunteer or assist regarding these trails contact him at (814) 658-6810. Currently, the local mountain bike group has been a driving force in getting the new trail system put in place. They have been active but equestrians have not. This area is a beautiful

162

destination and the door has been left open for equestrians to provide their input and help with the trails. We couldn't ask for more; here is our opportunity. Local equestrians, please show a positive presence and get involved!

I would also like to thank the helpful and professional young man at the guard booth at the entrance to the campground. When we found the lot was too small for our trailer, he made several calls and helped us contact the appropriate ranger to locate a temporary parking area so we could still ride the trails. Thank you to Park Ranger Jude Harrington who informed us of where we could park. My gratitude to Judy Reed for contacting me regarding facilities she offers for equestrians, and for sharing her knowledge of the Raystown Lake vicinity.

THINGS WE LEARNED THIS RIDE:
I had the opportunity to talk with several of the rangers at the Raystown Lake COE office and was very appreciative of their flexibility and enthusiasm in working with equestrians. I was very pleased to see they welcomed equestrians and their input. As a result of our discussions and, importantly, if other equestrians express serious interest, I believe more modifications will be established in the future to accommodate equestrians on the trail.

NEARBY:
- Centre County Visitors Bureau (800) 358-5466, website: www.visitpennstate.org
- The Silver Stirrup (tack and trail items), Duncansville (814) 695-4530

NEARBY AND SURROUNDING AREA STABLES:
- Hartslog Valley Stables (overnight camping and stabling, showers, guided trail rides, hookups, and stalls [near Raystown Lake]), Huntingdon (814) 644-0754
- Horsepower Farm (boarding, therapeutic program, lessons, camp), Huntingdon (814) 667-2497

NEARBY AND SURROUNDING AREA VET SERVICES:
- E. Bracken, Williamsburg (814) 832-2313, (814) 932-6893 cell
- M. James, Martinsburg (814) 793-3566 (use (814) 793-9226 only if he can't be reached at other number)

NEARBY AND SURROUNDING AREA FARRIERS:
- Chester Horton Horseshoeing, Alexandria (800) 993-SHOE, (814) 669-4652

22. Sideling Hill
Buchanan State Forest
BOF-DCNR
(Bureau of Forestry/Department of Conservation & Natural Resources)

Lasting Impression: My first impression was that the view from the Summit Road vista at the Sideling Hill tract of Buchanan State Forest was just awesome. My lasting impression is that you can have fun exploring this area for days on horseback as there are trails that head in all sorts of directions. Although Sideling Hill is in its early days of equestrian planning and camping development, it already has some very nice trails and has the potential to be a top equestrian trail and camping destination.

Location: Buchanan State Forest is located between McConnellsburg and Breezewood in southcentral Pennsylvania and consists of various tracts of land that span Franklin County, Fulton County, and Bedford County.

Length: *Day Ride or Weekend Destination*- Buchanan State Forest consists of roughly 75,000 acres of State Forest land on several separate tracts. At this writing, there isn't a formally designated equestrian trail system or estimated trail mileage. Horses are permitted on all State Forest land and roads except for hiking (only) trails or where specifically prohibited. Even more trails should be available for equestrians in the future as the park office indicated they are in the process of developing equestrian trails and overnight camping locations. The Sideling Hill Tract currently offers, at least, a few days of riding. The Broad Mountain tract is covered in another chapter. We did not visit the Martin Hill tract. If you visit that area, ask to see the ATV map. Martin Hill has a popular designated ATV area which you may want to avoid on horseback during peak activity.

Level of Difficulty: The trails we rode at Sideling Hill were easy to moderate.

Terrain: Miles of gradual, wide paths or dirt roads through woods, grass or dirt surface, minimal rocks (except the Sciotha Trail which was rocky and steep)

Horse Camping: Yes

Non-horse Camping: Yes

Carriage Potential: There appears to be much carriage potential at the Sideling Hill tract. There are many wide double tract paths, old logging roads, and State Forest roads. There are gates at the entrances to many of the trails and the office would have to be contacted as to whether a key could be obtained or if they could be opened. (Obtain the maps; they often reflect where the gates are located.) I checked with the office and they indicated they had not yet experienced an expression of interest from carriage drivers. However, the office did sound receptive to the idea. If you are interested in carriage driving, contact the office.

Maps and Info: DCNR, Bureau of Forestry at Buchanan State Forest, 440 Buchanan Trail, McConnellsburg, PA 17233, (717) 485-3148, website: www.dcnr.state.pa.us, email: fd2.mcconnellsburg@al.dcnr.state.pa.us. We did not see any maps at the trailheads. Call for maps in advance; ask for the Public Use Map and snowmobile maps as they will be useful for following the trails and roads.
Activities: Hiking, Biking, Bird Watching, Horseback Riding Trails, Snowmobiling, Picnicking, Camping, and Hang-gliding
Fees for Trail Use: None
Permits for Day Trail Use: None
Permits/Fees Required for Overnight Camping: Permits are required (no fee).
Comfort Station: None (there is a dump station [small fee] at the Sideling Hill rest area off of the Pennsylvania Turnpike)

DIRECTIONS:
Sideling Hill Summit Road camping or day parking location: *We were directed to Summit Road as the Oregon Road lot was very wet. Before planning to camp at this site, check with the office that there are no special events scheduled for this locale such as hang-gliding. Yet it is important to note that hang-gliders may visit this site at any time the wind is right for flight. Being that ideal weather conditions cannot be planned, hang-gliding cannot always be coordinated in advance, with notification given to the office so that the office can alert equestrians. It should be noted that this location is also used as a heliport area for forest fires.* Take the Pennsylvania Turnpike I-76 to the Breezewood Exit #161. Go through the toll booth and stay in the right lane. Follow signs to Route 30 east (you will travel a total of 1.5 miles on the turnpike access road before reaching Route 30). Take Route 30 east toward McConnellsburg. *Note: be sure to get off at the Breezewood exit, not the McConnellsburg exit, as there can be some steep sections on Route 30 if you approach from the McConnellsburg direction.* Travel to the top of the hill; this is a bit of a climb but it is not bad after that. Go over the Pennsylvania Turnpike and continue on the other side. You will pass Route 915 south on the right and a gravel entrance to Oregon Road on the left. Continue on Route 30 east and follow signs to Route 915 north. Pass the Buchanan State Forest sign. After traveling a total of 4 miles on Route 30, slow down and look for a left onto Route 915 north. *Guys: don't get distracted by the "dance club" on the left, or you will miss your turn!* Make the left onto Route 915 north and travel a total of 2.3 miles. (While on Route 915 north, you will again cross the turnpike.) Look for Mt. House Road (to Hustontown) on the right and make the right onto Mt. House Road. Go .2 miles and make a left onto Summit Road (gravel). Take Summit Road 4.5 miles (it will feel much longer on this gravel road) to the high vista. When you reach a very large, open, level, cleared area on the top (lots of room and pull through space, including for large living quarter type rigs), you're there! The view is awesome. We visited on Easter weekend and there were no leaves to block the view. If you

choose a season other than summer, you'll want to pick a warm day to visit as you are at the top of a mountain and it is windy! To reach the trails, travel out the same section of Summit Road that you entered on. Travel down Summit Road and make a right on the Anderson Trail. Various trails connect from this trail.

Sideling Hill Oregon Road day parking and camping (by the old Forest Headquarters): Take the Pennsylvania Turnpike I-76 to the Breezewood Exit #161, bear right, and follow signs to Route 30 east as described above. Once you are on Route 30 east, proceed to the top of the hill, cross over the turnpike, go to the bottom of the hill and you will see Route 915 south (on the right) and a gravel road to the left. This will be about a total of 3 miles on Route 30; do slow down before 3 miles as you could easily miss the gravel road to the left which is somewhat nondescript. (The gravel road travels under the turnpike and joins Oregon Road.) Make a left onto this road and go through the underpass. Just after the underpass, make a right. You'll see the sign for Oregon Road. Travel 2.9 miles on Oregon Road. (As you pass the lake, note that there seems to be trails that travel toward the lake. We didn't have the opportunity to visit this section, but there may be some interesting possibilities for additional scenic exploration at this corner of the Sideling Hill tract.) *Oregon Road is a two-way road but of narrow width and not a lot of shoulder. If another hauling vehicle or lumber truck comes in the opposite direction, there may be a problem passing each other. You can, instead, choose to approach this lot from the direction of the old Forest Headquarters described below.* Go through an underpass/small tunnel under the old Pennsylvania Turnpike. *I checked with the office and this underpass is of standard height for clearance and the office indicated logging trucks travel through with no problem.* Immediately after the underpass is a field on the left with pine trees at the entrance. You can park or camp here. About 10+ sizable rigs could fit in this lot. Be careful of turning along the outlying areas of this field as the perimeters can be very wet in the spring and after rainy periods. You may need to avoid this section at those times or check with the office in advance as to the condition of the surface at the time you are planning your visit. This is a good location for day parking and camping. (See the note below regarding securing horses and nearby fencing.) Also, the office is just becoming familiar with equestrian camping so confirm these parking areas have not changed. Equestrian camping is in an early phase at Buchanan; as more equestrians express interest in Buchanan State Forest, I believe the designated parking and camping locations may be adjusted, possibly moved or even expanded as the sites become tried and tested. This office was very welcoming, receptive, flexible, and willing to consider all options.

Sideling Hill Oregon Road day parking and camping- other approach passing the Forest Headquarters: If you would like to avoid the narrow width of Oregon Road between Route 30 and the Oregon Road parking/camping lot, as an alternative, pass Oregon Road and instead follow the directions (above) to the

Summit Road lot on Route 915 north. But do not turn onto Mt. House Road; instead continue on Route 915 north for an additional 1.2 miles. Make a left onto Oregon Road. *Note: the turn is tight and the shoulder is limited due to drainage channels on each side of the road. I would prefer it be wider, but John assured me, if taken carefully, he could get our 50+ foot rig in. Smaller trailers should have a sufficient turning radius.* Once you have made the left onto Oregon Road, pass the old Forest Headquarters, and travel a total of 1.3 miles. The Oregon Road day parking and camping area will be on the right. Although the approach from this end requires a tighter turn to access Oregon Road, the rest of the road is roomier and has more shoulder to allow for two vehicles needing to pass. If the Oregon Road lot is not dry and the Summit Road overlook has hang-gliders, you will need to check with the office as to other parking/camping alternatives.

An area that we were told equestrians sometimes ride from, but we did not visit, is the area south of Route 30 by the Sideling Hill Tower. This too is worth looking into to. This is marked on the map and directions can be obtained from the Forest Headquarters.

THE TRAILS:
Buchanan State Forest consists of numerous, separate tracts of land. Two of the larger sections are Sideling Hill (covered in this chapter) and the Bear Valley Forest Division of Broad Mountain (see that chapter). Along with the Public Use Map (green cover), snowmobile maps are available from the office for these sections and can be helpful in providing points of reference along the trail. Snowmobile trails are open to horses and are marked with orange diamonds. Horses are not permitted on the hiking (only) trails such as the Tuscarora Trail and the Mid-State Trail. The Tuscarora Trail is near the Buchanan State Forest tract located on the Franklin/Fulton County line, and the Mid-State Trail travels through the Martin Hill area. Neither is located in or near the Sideling Hill and Broad Mountain tracts.

Sideling Hill is wonderful in that equestrians can ride on any trail. Of course riders still need to use good judgment, be courteous to other users, and avoid picnic and other group areas. We kept to the main trails and enjoyed a leisurely ride. The Sideling Hill area's trails are well marked with signs at intersections. Sometimes a sign was broken, but mostly they were present. The Sideling Hill trail layout is easy and, along with the map, we found it simple to follow. We visited in April, and camped at the Summit Road site. Since there were no leaves on the trees, the trails offered views in many directions even as we traveled through wooded areas. As for heights, if you strongly dislike high altitudes, you may prefer to ride the trails in the lower elevation of the Oregon Road vicinity. However, Summit Road is wide and spacious, and the trails and State Forest roads that we rode were mild, gradual, and away from the edge of the mountain.

If you do camp elsewhere, still try to take a drive up to the Summit Road vista and enjoy the view or watch the sun set. It is beautiful.

Because we camped at the Summit Road location in Sideling Hill, we accessed the trails from the Summit Road locale. If you camp at the Oregon Road site at Sideling Hill, you can access all these same trails from the opposite direction. In addition, the Oregon Road site offers close proximity to a larger selection of trails than the less centrally located Summit Road location. On the first day of our visit to Sideling Hill, we decided to take a short ride to get the horses settled in. We rode down Summit Road (gravel/dirt), in the direction toward Route 915, and hooked up with the Anderson Trail. We took the Anderson Trail, which is a wide and gradual trail, down the side of the mountain. We made a right on Hinish Trail, linked into Enid Road which connected to Summit Road, and back to camp. Many of these trails, such as the Hinish, were once either old logging roads or rail paths that the railroads used for transporting timber from the area. The Hinish Trail is a connector between many trail systems. It links Oregon Road and Route 915 to the northern tip of the park. On the map it doesn't appear to connect all the way to Enid Road, but it does. You can also explore the loop northwest of Enid Road as there are trails in that area. As well, there are various side trails that are all along the way and may provide the opportunity for exploring or traveling off of the road. The Summit Road loop, which is dirt and gravel throughout, was relaxing, easy to moderate, and with good footing. The Enid Road, at the end of the loop, is a road of tar and chip with lots of shoulder. We rode Enid Road, as we were riding on a weekday, and enjoyed the view that the loop around Summit Road vista offered. We could have taken a side trail but we did not encounter any vehicles on any of the connecting roads (but it was off season and during the week). On Saturday, there was more activity due to the hang-gliders. Had we ridden this route on Saturday we could have had a few vehicles pass us. If you don't ride it, do consider taking at least a drive around Summit Road and Enid Road. Try to visit when the leaves aren't on the trees, when the views are at their best.

On our second day, we traveled from camp down Summit Road to the Anderson Trail. We made the right on Anderson Trail, left on Hinish Trail, and crossed Route 915 to Oregon Road. We took Oregon Road, passed the Forest Headquarters, passed the parking/camping area (on the right) and, just before the underpass, we took a trail to the left which led to the old Pennsylvania Turnpike and the tunnel. We found the abandoned turnpike and tunnel to be very interesting and almost surreal. After visiting the turnpike and tunnel, we returned via Oregon Road, crossed over Route 915, picked up Hinish Trail, made a right onto Prop Trail, a left onto Sciotha Trail, and a right onto Ross Trail. We took Ross Trail back up to Summit Road where we made a left to head back to camp. All the trails we rode, except for one, were easy to moderate. They were wide logging roads, old rail paths, or State Forest roads. The only trail, of what we sampled, that was more difficult was the Sciotha Trail which was rocky and steep in sections. However, we did find it passable and did not experience any problems.

Throughout our visit to the Sideling Hill tract, the trails remained of good, firm surface and there were many places to water the horses. As for water availability, we did visit in April, and mid-summer may be different. There was a spring fed watering hole of decent size just off of the Anderson Trail on the right while we were headed away from Summit Road. With a few springs feeding it, I would think this would provide a good source of water year round. While riding these trails, you will see fenced areas to protect seedlings from local wildlife; exercise caution as some of these are electric fences. Intersections are well marked and correspond with the map. Although the main trails that we tried were easy to moderate and not rocky, the side trails can vary greatly and may present much more challenging courses. Be very cautious of riding off trail and trail blazing as there may be fencing or old debris presenting hazards. This is evident along the turnpike where fencing, from either the old turnpike or the WWII prisoner of war camps, still remains; see below for more information.

EQUESTRIAN CAMPING:
Although equestrians have informally ridden various tracts of Buchanan State Forest for decades, the office indicated that only recently have they been experiencing an influx of calls and inquiries from equestrians for horse trail and camping information. So much is still in its development stages.

<u>Sideling Hill Summit Road location:</u> Probably most equestrians will be directed to the Oregon Road site for camping. Since we visited in early spring and that area had not yet dried out, the Summit Road location was recommended (instead). This is about as high and dry as you can get. It is an absolutely beautiful location at the summit of the mountain offering a panoramic view of the valleys below. You can watch the sun rise and set over the mountains; simply gorgeous. There is a large clearing for parking with plenty of room for about 10+ rigs. Camping is primitive. There aren't any large trees close to the parking/camping area on Summit Road; you will need to walk down the north slope of the mountainside for a short distance to reach a suitable grove of trees to string a high line. There are not a lot of trees but there are clusters of small pine trees that are secure enough to tie a line to. Consider bringing burlap or other material for tree protection against chewers because the trees are situated close to each other. Water is not available at this locale and you need to bring your own. A minor drawback to this site location is that, to reach the trails, you must ride down Summit Road to pick up one of the trails as it is not as centrally located as the Oregon Road site. Even still, during our visit it was very relaxing; hardly anyone was on the State Forest roads, and riding up and down Summit Road offered views in all directions. We very much enjoyed our stay at this locale. There is one real disadvantage of the

Summit Road site in that hang-gliders sometimes and perhaps often (depending on the direction of the winds as they prefer northeast winds) meet at this open area to propel off the ledge. During these gatherings, it is likely that the Summit Road parking/camping area should be avoided with horses. (I have no idea what our horses would think of hang-gliders but I am sure we would not want to be camping at the top of the mountain while hang-gliders are jumping off the windy mountainside or hovering overhead.) We visited on an off-peak weekend with marginal weather and still a large group of hang-gliders showed up with their equipment in tow. Luckily, we were out on trail at the time they were by our camp.

Sideling Hill Oregon Road location: This is at a very nice location for primitive camping and is close to many different trails. There is a nearby stream to obtain water for the horses and a big, open area that could accommodate about 10+ large horse trailers. There is a pond too. (We did not visit during the summer months so I cannot comment if there are a lot of insects due to the water.) The one thing that we did not see at this location was a sufficient, secure area to tie the horses. There is soggy or soft ground in the outer perimeters so those locations would not be suitable, and there are few, if any, trees to tie to in the immediate vicinity of camp. (Reminder: the State Forests request we stay a certain distance from any water source, so do not choose the area near the stream or pond.) Since Buchanan State Forest is still new to dealing with equestrian campers and not yet familiar with their needs, I recommended to the office that tie posts be constructed in the near future to offer a secure tie area for the horses and also to protect the environment. Tie line posts or straight stalls seem to be the best option for this type of site due to the lack of (tie line) trees and due to the nearby sensitive terrain. Other than that, the Oregon Road location (or the "ball field" as the office calls it) is a lovely, remote setting, has convenient water for the horses, and has trails leading directly out of camp.

To reach the trails from the Oregon Road location, just ride out Oregon Road and make a right or left. To the right are the tunnel and the old Pennsylvania Turnpike. The turnpike was built in the late 1930s and closed by the late 1960s when an alternate route was built over the mountains. The tunnel and turnpike are interesting attractions as the old four-lane turnpike narrowed from four to two lanes at the tunnel; this feature had to have caused many an accident during its time. We rode a short section of the old turnpike to view the tunnel. Riding the turnpike is a different experience; you almost expect cars to come through at any moment. Please note: if you would like to ride to the turnpike to see the tunnel, do not cross the creek from camp. (When we crossed the creek by the Oregon Road camping area, we encountered old fencing that ran parallel to the old turnpike. The fencing was still standing in locations and in others it was down and camouflaged by leaves on the ground. In all cases, it presented a danger as it would be easy for rider and horse to become entangled. We questioned the origin of the fencing as it could be either due to the turnpike or due to the fact that this location was once enclosed with fencing when the CCC camp was converted to a WWII prisoner of war camp. At that time the area was surrounded by high fencing topped with barbed wire, which leads me to conclude that the fencing was from when this area was a detention camp. Either way, to ride to the old turnpike and to avoid the fencing, ride out the entrance of the Oregon Road lot, toward the underpass and, just before the underpass, bear to the left and you will see a path that goes out to the old turnpike. This access was clear and open when we crossed. But proceed cautiously in case any old fencing is still on the ground. We have notified the office of this danger and hopefully it will be removed.

You can also travel through the underpass along Oregon Road and back to the lake area. Many trails lead off of Oregon Road. Turning to the left as you ride out of the Oregon Road camp, you can ride Oregon Road, cross over Route 915 and pick up other trails including those to the Summit Road vista.

Please note: the office does remind equestrians that manure, hay, shavings, and straw must be either removed or scattered away from the parking and camping areas. If scattered, it should be at least 100 feet from the parking lots and the camping locations.

HISTORICAL INFORMATION:
The areas within and surrounding Buchanan State Forest are rich with history. As you ride or travel through this region, there are many traces of early settlers' homesteads, villages, and roads. Connectors were built by various sources, including British troops, traveling between forts during our nation's early period of colonization. Today, names of places still reflect some of the early settlers of the region. The State Forest itself is named after James Buchanan, a former President of the United States, who was born nearby. In the 1800s, rail corridors were built to accommodate the growing logging industry. Some of these old logging roads can still be seen throughout the forest system. Later, in the early 1900s, Buchanan State Forest was acquired by the State. The land had been timbered extensively and a period of regrowth and restoration was needed and initiated. During the Depression years, the government acquired substandard or unproductive farmland with the goal of helping the owners of these lands to move onto or "resettle" new, fertile farmland. These were called "Resettlement Lands" and the land was allowed to return to a natural state. Also, in the 1930s, under President Franklin Roosevelt, men were given jobs to work for the Civilian Conservation Corps (CCC) within the forest to build roads, trails, fire roads, picnic areas, park facilities, and other projects. At one time, there were over 90 CCC camps constructed in the State Forests of Pennsylvania, each having roughly 200 men per camp. Later, the CCC facilities in many of these camps were used to hold WWII German detainees. Some of the remains of the CCC housing can still be seen along the trails of the State Forest. Today, Buchanan State Forest is again

covered with forest growth and is once more an important source of lumber. Other products of this area have been natural gas and sandstone.

The State Forest contains other attractions such as the Kerper tract or Redbud Valley Nature Center (Fulton County) where the diverse flora, including wildflowers, attracts a variety of birds much to the delight of birdwatchers. The Buchanan State Forest region includes the Pine Ridge Natural Area (Bedford County), Sweet Root Natural Area (Bedford County), and the Martin Hill Wild Area (Bedford County). Information received from the office indicated both hikers and horseback riders can enjoy the Pine Ridge Natural Area which includes many of the "Resettlement Lands" mentioned above. *It's been my observation that Natural Areas are usually not open to horses; this Natural Area is probably of a durable or exceptional surface.* Within the Sweet Root Natural Area is a section of natural growth that has never been cut for timber. This section can be accessed by foot (only) off of Route 326. The Martin Hill Wild Area has preserved a section of land in an undeveloped and unspoiled state. This scenic area, which encompasses Little Pond and Big Pond, supports an array of wildlife including (much to my dismay) rattlesnakes.

COURTESIES:
I would like to express my gratitude to Bryan Wilford, Forester at Buchanan State Forest, for sharing information regarding this State Forest, for his excellent directions, and for welcoming suggestions from the equestrian perspective. Brian made us feel very welcome as he stopped by our campsite to check on how we were doing, and if we had any questions or recommendations. Thank you to Brenda Gottfried and her daughter Julie who so helpfully scouted out the area for us in advance. Thank you for the pleasure of your company during our visit. Brenda has contributed much to the trails and has worked with DCNR at the Michaux State Forest, including at least one of the equestrian campgrounds. Just recently, Brenda moved to this area; I am hoping she will also be representing equestrians' interests at the Buchanan State Forest and will contribute much to these trails and the establishment of designated equestrian parking and camping areas.

THINGS WE LEARNED THIS RIDE:
- If you are traveling in April, and especially if you plan to camp on the top of the mountain, bring a snow shovel. The weather can change at any time at that time of the year and at high elevations. We had 60 degree weather one day and the next morning, Easter morning, awoke to snow!
- We shared our camping/trail destination with a new (for us) type of multiple-user- hang-gliders! Hang-gliders are probably not the most compatible user to share space with horses. We returned to our campground to find a large group of hang-gliders had been using the overlook by our camping area to launch from. Luckily, we had not left any horses back at camp as they would

172

probably have broken loose and run from the hang-gliders and possibly have gotten hurt. We learned quickly that the Summit Hill camping location is popular with local hang-gliders.

- We also learned that even in the middle of a remote rural area, if you want good cell phone reception, head for the top of the summit!

NEARBY AND SURROUNDING AREA STABLES:

- Uncle Clems (guided trail rides, overnight pack trips, primitive overnight accommodations if traveling with one's own horse), Harrisonville (717) 485-9314, website: www.uncleclems.com
- Buck Valley Ranch (guided trail rides and many other activities), Warfordsburg (800) 294-3759. You can visit their website at www.buckvalleyranch.com. This locale is located south of Sideling Hill near the Maryland border, off of Route 70.

NEARBY AND SURROUNDING AREA VET SERVICES:

- A. Doherty, Needmore (717) 573-4569

NEARBY AND SURROUNDING AREA FARRIERS:

- T. Awckland, New Paris (814) 733-4996

23. The Broad Mountain Tract &
The Bear Valley Forest Division
Buchanan State Forest
BOF-DCNR
(Bureau of Forestry/Department of Conservation & Natural Resources)

Lasting Impression: This is a work in progress and has not yet been developed to its full potential. There are some very nice riding areas in the lower section of the snowmobile trails, and some very challenging but very scenic riding up the side of the mountain. But there are lots of possibilities so watch this one for developments or volunteer and make this one happen in the near future.

Location: The Broad Mountain tract of Buchanan State Forest is located east of Cowans Gap and northwest of Chambersburg in Franklin County.

Length: *Day Ride or possible future Weekend Destination*- There are two tracts of Buchanan State Forest that are covered in this book, Sideling Hill and the Broad Mountain tract of the Bear Valley Forest Division. Each is located separate from the other. This chapter focuses on the Broad Mountain tract which offers two trail loops designated as suitable to horses. Each of these two loops is a significant distance from one another at the top of Broad Mountain. You can ride one for a few hours or connect to the other and explore for several. As with most other State Forests, horses are allowed on all State Forest land and roads except for hiking (only) trails and areas indicated as closed to horses.

Level of Difficulty: Moderate to difficult or impassable

Terrain: You are riding a mountain. The terrain can vary greatly from gradual, leisurely, wide forest gravel or dirt roads, and easy grassy stretches to progressive mountain roads, and challenging climbs or descents along dirt and/or grass paths with rock-strewn stretches. Horses need to be fit to climb the mountain. Horses should have shoes as there are rocky sections.

Horse Camping: There is a recently designated motorized camping site at the top of Broad Mountain, at the northeast section of Broad Mountain Road near the pipeline (see below). Road widening and construction was in progress so we were unable to haul to or stay at this site.

Non-horse Camping: Yes

Maps and Info: DCNR, Bureau of Forestry, Buchanan State Forest, 440 Buchanan Trail, McConnellsburg, PA 17233, (717) 485-3148, website: www.dcnr.state.pa.us, email: fd2.mcconnellsburg@al.dcnr.state.pa.us. We did not see any maps at the trailheads. Call for maps in advance; ask for the Public Use Map and snowmobile maps as they will also be useful for following the trails and roads.

Activities: Hiking, Biking, Horseback Riding Trails, Snowmobiling, Picnicking, and Hunting
Fees for Trail Use: None
Permits for Day Trail Use: None
Permits/Fees Required for Overnight Camping: Permits are required (no fee).
Comfort Station: None

DIRECTIONS:
We rode the Switchback Trail in the eastern section of the Broad Mountain tract of Buchanan State Forest. We found the following to be a gradual approach to access the parking area at the foot of the mountain. Take I-81 to Route 30 west. Take Route 30 west for about 11 miles. (We were told not to take Route 30 east from McConnellsburg due to steep grades.) Make a right onto Apple Way Road toward the town of Edenville. (On the corner where we turned, there was a gray commercial building with the name Kurdziel, along with a thrift store, and an L&S Orchard fruit stand on the right side of the road. This intersection is 10 miles west of Chambersburg and 12 miles east of McConnellsburg on Route 30.) Take Apple Way Road for 3.7 miles, bear right, and continue for a total of 4.9 miles to Fort McCord Road. (At this intersection there is a street sign "St. Thomas-Edenville" on the right and a "Fort McCord" street sign on the left.) Make a left onto Fort McCord Road. Take Fort McCord Road 2.2 miles and make a left onto Mountain Road. Immediately, you will come to another stop sign. Make another left; you are now on Mountain Road. Travel 1.6 miles on Mountain Road and the road will turn to dirt. This is a one lane road serving two ways. (We did not see any activity along this short stretch during our visit but proceed with caution, especially around turns.) Continue for another .7 miles along the dirt road to the lot. (While on the dirt road, you will encounter a gate directly in front of you. Follow the dirt/gravel road to the left; do not go straight through the gate if it is open. Usually, it is closed as this is an entrance to the Letterkenny Army Depot. A little farther down, you will see a fork to the left with a gate at the end of it. Do not turn left; continue straight along the main gravel road.) You will reach a round, gravel parking area of small to medium size at the end of the road. This is where you can park. This lot can only accommodate 2-3 horse trailers comfortably; large groups could not fit in this lot. There is ample pull through room for most trailers and minimal, if any, backing would be required. Our friends had a 40+ foot trailer and we had a 50+ foot trailer, and both fit with no problems. The trailhead is at the back of the lot.

THE TRAILS:
There are two trail systems that are designated snowmobile routes and also serve as multiple-use trails considered suitable for equestrians. One is in the eastern section of the mountain near the Letterkenny Army Depot. This trail starts at the base of the mountain, travels in various, easy loops at the base, and then forms a switchback to the top of the mountain ending on Broad Mountain Road. The

other loop is roughly two miles down Broad Mountain Road and travels in loops along and around the Old Bear Valley Road. We rode the trails situated in the eastern section of the mountain (a.k.a. the "Switchback Trail"). We did not ride the Old Bear Valley Road system.

Upon arrival, the location has a remote feel. The trail starts out as an appealing, spacious State Forest road that travels through tall trees and woodlands. For a short while you can see a fence which divides the State Forest land and the Letterkenny Army Depot land. Do not attempt to ride on the Letterkenny Army Depot land. Soon the trail transforms from a dirt State Forest road (this section was closed to vehicles) into wide, green paths with high grass and assorted flora along its path. It hadn't been mowed recently but still the lower trails were leisurely to ride. There were a couple of trail branches that headed in different directions, one we tried but it either ended or had grown over. Once you enter this section, there aren't signs to direct you. The lower trails are nice and if you don't mind a shorter ride, you can choose not to head up the mountain and take it easy below. We wanted to head up the mountain and see what the trail and scenery had to offer. As soon as we were on the mountain trail, the terrain became more challenging as there were some downed trees. We managed to clear or bypass these and continue up the path. Surprisingly, there was water at various intervals (springs running down the mountain) even though we weren't in the valley. But the ground was firm and it was not muddy. We were glad to have water for the horses because they could use it going up this mountain. At first the switchback is gradual and of decent surface of mostly grass and greenery. As you ascend up the latter part of the switchback, the surface becomes irregular due to erosion and rocks. There was dirt between the rocks to aid footing but there was quite a length of challenging trail. *This probably wouldn't be difficult to fix as clearly other equipment had gone up and down these trails at some time.* The views quickly become spectacular and you are able to see in many directions. Along most of the route, the trail was wide and not "on the edge." Although, if you are afraid of heights, this might be too much for you as you are traveling to a high elevation on the side of the mountain looking out over the valley and surrounding countryside. You are right there! Also, if you or your horse are not seasoned or in good physical shape and used to mountainous terrain, do not attempt this trail up the side of the mountain.

In summary, we found the lower lying section of the Switchback Trail to be moderate and the upper section of the Switchback Trail to be an advanced or expert trail. We felt ascending was better than descending as descending would be much more challenging due to the upper sections being rocky and the footing not firm. Endurance riders might love this one as it has an easy warm up section below and then it provides a good workout in the last stretch up the mountain. A positive to this trail is that it had good width, was a switchback, and the wide expanse allowed the horses room to catch their breath.

We reached the top of the mountain and to the right was the designated motorized site. I had been told that work was being done on Broad Mountain Road and the site so it was not yet ready for use. The access road was currently being widened and the site was being cleared. The suggested camping area is an open, large locale that is situated along the pipeline. It is gravel with room for numerous rigs. There is a clear cut and scenic view of the valley below. Surrounding the lot there were plenty of places to tie or high line to, but equestrians should be cautious around the vicinity of the parking area due to bottles. We saw this in the lower parking area and at the parking lot at the top of the mountain. However, it appeared that these areas were being cleaned up and re-engineered to minimize possible loitering or littering. We did not experience any problems with bottles once on the trail. If you want to put up a high line, walk a short distance from the parking area where this should not be a problem. *This would be an area where equestrians could positively influence the outcome of camping areas and trails as this section is in progress and volunteer work is needed.* Since much construction work was being done on these roads and parking areas, hopefully, discarded bottles will not continue to be a concern. If you decide to camp at the top of the mountain, check with the office as to their recommended driving route. Remind the office representative that you are hauling and request a gradual approach (you may need to talk to the ranger in charge who is most familiar with this remote tract). Other equestrians advised us not to approach via Gilbert Road as it is steep for hauling.

At the summit, there are other trails with signs marking the trail. These can vary greatly in level of difficulty; exercise caution when exploring. There was construction at the entrance to many of these; so much is in process or rework. The trails we were told to avoid by local equestrians, due to extremely steep conditions, are the Greensprings Trail, One Mile Trail, Tiny Trails, and the Smith Trail. To come off of the mountain, we took a trail that was rough due to large rocks and growth, and we would not recommend it. You could either backtrack (not recommended in its current condition) down the switchback or ride the dirt road down (a long distance) to Gilbert Road and back to the road leading to the parking area. There may be other alternatives off of the mountain.

Although there is much beauty and interesting scenery, the trails seem to be either forgotten or in the early stages of development. I believe these trails have been ridden lightly by local equestrians over the years but really haven't developed into a well known or popular destination for equestrians hauling to this locale. It may be that few know about them, there is little information, maybe that there are very challenging sections (although I have seen equestrians flock to trails with much more aggressive and rugged terrain), or that the trails haven't come into their own yet. I debated whether to include them but I felt there are many very nice sections, and there is much potential. Plus, I found the State Forest office personnel that oversee this tract to be friendly, willing, and helpful. They were very professional during my many inquiries and I believe would welcome equestrians to work with them on this remote location. (Just the presence of equestrians at remote sections of other State Forests has been proven to reduce improper usage such as loitering or littering at secluded sites.) From what I could see along Broad Mountain Road, there was much ideal terrain that could be made into nice, moderate trails along the flat surface of the mountain. Thus, there are many possibilities. I believe this is one location that it is up to equestrians to start the process to make it what it could be; equestrians need to show the interest. If they don't use it, it will grow over. If they do use it and help with snipping and clearing, and rerouting around rocky sections where possible, it could blossom. Then the State Forest would see the interest and the justification for trail expansion, and it could develop into something more. The future of this one may be up to us equestrians to decide if we would like to make more out of it.

COURTESIES:
Thank you to Bryan Wilford, Forester at Buchanan State Forest, for answering my many questions regarding this area. Also, I would like to express a very special thank you to Brenda Gottfried and her daughter Julie for showing us these trails and for graciously allowing us to stay at their place so we could cover them. We really enjoyed visiting with them and look forward to riding with them again next season.

NEARBY AND SURROUNDING AREA STABLES:
- Idelhour (breeding, boarding), St. Thomas (717) 369-3412

NEARBY AND SURROUNDING AREA VET SERVICES:
- A. Hinton, Companion Animal Veterinary Services, Newburg (717) 477-8938
- T. Lartz, Mountain View Veterinary Services, Shippensburg (717) 477-8938

24. Northmoreland County Park
Westmoreland County Park

Lasting Impression: Northmoreland County Park, although not a long trail system, offers a nice, leisurely ride on well maintained grounds over attractive, rolling countryside. Be sure to ride the northwest section of the park which offers some of the prettiest views and remote parts of the trail system. If you don't have your own horse or if you can't trailer to these trails, there is a resident stable at the core of the park which offers guided trail rides and travels many of the same trails that we rode.

Location: Northmoreland County Park is located near the towns of Vandergrift and Apollo in Westmoreland County and is northeast of Pittsburgh.

Length: *Day Ride Destination*- Exact mileage wasn't available (different sources estimated between 5 and 10 miles) but there are at least a few hours of riding on the 548 acre property. The office indicated they are looking to establish more trails.

Level of Difficulty: We found the sections we rode, the northwest ("winter sports area" on the map) and eastern sections, to be easy with gentle climbs. However, sometimes you ride the edge of play areas and will need a horse that is well seasoned and adjusted to diverse activity for an enjoyable and safe ride.

Terrain: Maintained terrain of good footing, grass or dirt surface, not rocky, some park road crossings

Horse Camping: None

Non-horse Camping: None

Maps and Info: Westmoreland County Bureau of Parks and Recreation, R.R. #12, Box 203, Greensburg, PA 15601; (724) 830-3950 or (724) 830-3951 or (800) 442-6926 ext. 3950. (If you have difficulty reaching someone at the park, try the boathouse at (724) 727-3899.) A very helpful source of information for this region is the Laurel Highlands Visitor Bureau which can be reached at (724) 238-5661 or via their website: www.laurelhighlands.org.

Activities: Hiking, BMX Track, Horseback Riding Trails, Picnicking, Equine Complex (guided trail rides), Ball Fields, Fishing, Boating, Model Aircraft Field, Hunting, Winter Sports Area, and Other Game Activities

Fees for Trail Use: None

Permits for Day Trail Use: None

Comfort Station: Yes

DIRECTIONS:
There are many directions to approach this park. The park is off of Route 356 and you can either take Route 56 to Route 356 or Route 66 to Route 356 to reach the park. If you choose these or other approaches, call for further directions to

179

confirm they are rig friendly. We, instead, chose the following approach; this involved some backtracking but was suggested by the office as it was on major roads suitable to hauling. We approached from the direction of the Pennsylvania Turnpike and Route 28. To reach the park from the Pennsylvania Turnpike I-76, take I-76 to Exit #48 Allegheny Valley and follow signs to Route 28 north. About 1 mile after getting off I-76, you will link with Route 28 north. Follow the signs (there are two sets of signs back to back; the ramp is actually at the second one). Take Route 28 north for 12.5 miles to Exit #17. Get off the ramp, make a left. Follow signs for Route 356 south. (Route 356 winds but there are signs.) From Route 28, travel a total of 9.6 miles on Route 356 south. You will pass an intersection with Route 56 and see stores on the left including a Dairy Queen (a nice treat after you ride). Once you reach a total of 9.6 miles on Route 356, make a right into the park (there will be a sign) onto Park Road. Go 1 mile on Park Road (at the 1 mile mark, you'll need to make a right at the stop sign by the park sign) and you will come to the maintenance building and park office. (The office indicated that equestrians could park there. My concern would be that equestrians might be in the way; see below.) To reach the other lots, continue another .8 miles (total of 1.8 miles on Park Road) and make a very sharp right. This is before the stop sign and before the Airshaft Road sign and sculptures. Parking is limited and a standard 2-horse or 3-horse slant load trailer is the most that you would want to attempt to park. We would not bring our trailer with living quarters as there is nowhere to park a rig of that size. During special events, local riding clubs may receive permission to park at other locations. If you choose to visit with a large rig, call the park office and ask their recommendation. Do remind the office that you'll need sufficient turning radius along with no cement markers dividing the lot and blocking any backing.

When I checked with the office, they indicated three areas where equestrians could park. Equestrians can park near the maintenance building. This is a very small lot requiring maneuvering to turn around. You may need to back or park slightly on the grass to fit; the office asks that equestrians take care not to tear up the grass. On the weekday that we visited, I noticed that loaded trucks were pulling in and out; that may make some horses uncomfortable. If you would like to avoid the truck activity or be at a more remote location (assuming there are no ball games scheduled), there is a larger lot by Softball Field #4. This lot can fit a few standard size 2-horse or 3-horse slant load rigs if the spaces are not full due to a ball game. *Note: some backing and maneuvering are needed but shouldn't be too bad if the lot is almost empty.* The trail is just up the hill to the side of the field. We found this section of the trails to have some of the nicest views and some of the most remote sections of the park. The trail access can be seen from the lot. Do not ride or go on the ball field. Horses are also prohibited from any of the groves and playing fields. (However, equestrians can travel on the outlying borders and outskirts of the fields.) We asked if equestrians could also park in the parking area by Softball Field #5 as there was a larger parking area by this

180

field. They said it was a possibility; however, equestrians should pull to the rear, past the red gate (dependent on the gate being open) and stay clear of the ball field. This option would be only viable if no game was going on. Equestrians could drive around the back of the field, go through the gates, and would need to back into position to be able to exit back out. Probably, the best bet would be near Softball Field #4. But, in spite of the limited parking, don't let that deter you. This is a lovely park to visit and equestrians have a good rapport with the park office and are made to feel welcome. Wherever you choose to park, situate your vehicle that you can get out without difficulty in the event that the lot fills up later.

THE TRAILS:
This is a well maintained, groomed park, but it is a popular park. We visited on a Sunday and rode on Monday. Weekends are very busy in the central areas, picnic groves, lake area, ball fields, radio operated model aircraft area, and BMX areas. Horses are permitted in the outlying areas but you will want to make sure your horse is well seasoned considering the variety of multiple co-users. Horses should not go near the model aircraft field (there is a sign at the entrance). If your horse is on the nervous side, the northwest section of the park may offer a more leisurely, remote ride vs. the eastern and southwest sections. To connect from the northwest section to the eastern section of trails, ride out of the lot at Softball Field #4, cross by the pine trees, look for a ribbon, and you will come out by the stable. You can then link with the other side of the trails by riding past the stable entrance and past the maintenance building. *Please be careful not to step on any landscaping/garden work by the maintenance building so we remain welcome.*

To really explore the park, we preferred the weekday and had the park completely to ourselves. We could comfortably explore more areas while enjoying the quiet and scenic beauty of the park and surrounding landscape. Our spring ride was enhanced by the flowering wild cherry trees, honeysuckle, and also the dogwood trees. We rode the northwest section **(our favorite)** and the eastern section. There is additional riding (about 2 hours in the southwest section) south of the Northmoreland Lake. We did not include those lower trails in our visit but were told that it is a more challenging section. The trails that we rode were mainly easy with gradual climbs and gentle terrain.

Do bring a map for reference as this is not a well marked trail system. In many of the areas, especially by the stable, you can just follow the hoof prints. Along the way, there are a few signs and also some ribbons to guide you. With the various roads and event areas, and using the map, you shouldn't get lost. Also, bring water for the horses as there are no drinking locations along the trail system.

COURTESIES:

Thank you to Julie Donovan, Public Relations Manager for the Laurel Highlands Visitor Bureau and a fellow equestrian, and the folks at the Westmoreland County Parks & Recreation Department who helped me in obtaining information for this park. What a nice group of friendly people! Also, I would like to express my appreciation to Butch and the staff at the Northmoreland County Park office for providing information on the park and for making us feel very welcome. I was told that there is talk of adding more trails. *Local riders: please keep active and be helpful in making this happen!* I would like to express a special thank you to Danielle and Crystal of the Northmoreland Equine Complex (at the heart of the park) for guiding us through the park and sharing information on the trails. Also, thank you to their mother, Linda, for her support in our pursuit of information on these trails.

THINGS WE LEARNED THIS RIDE:

Have you ever had your horse trailer stuck in mud? Try to trailer an elephant off of the mountain when it has rained! Neither a common occurrence, nor one I ever gave thought to, but elephant transporters have their challenges! We were told that each year, on Labor Day, a circus comes to the park. Last year there was so much rain, the rest of the circus packed up when it was time to go except for the elephant; they couldn't get the elephant off of the mountain! They had to wait until the ground dried and firmed up sufficiently to support hauling. The way the rain was last year, they thought they would never get that elephant out of there. And we equestrians think we have problems! *You may not want to ride the trails when the lions, tigers, and bears of the circus are present or within smelling distance of your horse. Most horses would take great exception to passing those trail obstacles!*

NEARBY AND SURROUNDING AREA STABLES:

* Northmoreland Equine Complex at Northmoreland County Park (located in the park, guided trail rides, boarding, pony rides, birthday parties), Apollo (724) 727-1316
* McHenry's Horse World, Apollo (724) 478-4644, (724) 697-4030

NEARBY AND SURROUNDING AREA VET SERVICES:

* J. Leonard, Fox Run Equine Center, Apollo (724) 727-3481
* F. Haustovich, Mars (724) 625-9433

NEARBY AND SURROUNDING AREA FARRIERS:

* E. Castello, Curtisville (724) 265-0949, (412) 721-5965 cell
* R. Wilderoter, Glenshaw (412) 967-6099, (412) 298-2817 cell
* R. Laux, Worthington (724) 297-3001

25. South Park
Allegheny County Park

Lasting Impression: South Park is a pretty park with lots of hidden trails and nice places to ride. We had a guide show us these trails that can be a bit confusing for first time visitors to find and follow. However, with some designation, linking, and mapping of the trail systems, this attractive park would draw many more equestrians who are unfamiliar with the trails, and also preserve the remaining equestrian trails for future generations to enjoy.

Location: South Park, as the name indicates, is an Allegheny County Park located south of the city of Pittsburgh.

Length: *Day Ride Destination*- South Park has approximately 2,000 acres. Exact estimates of miles were not available. I had heard there were at least 20 miles of trails permitting horses; however, I believe that estimate was prior to when some of the tracts were paved for bikes and hikers. Basically, we concluded there are a few hours of riding.

Level of Difficulty: The trails we rode were easy to moderate. For an enjoyable and safe ride, horses need to be comfortable with the variety of types of multiple-use in this park including mountain bikes and active road crossings.

Terrain: There are nicely mowed grass stretches and rolling fields passing other recreation areas, single paths in the woods, gentle terrain, minimal rocks, some major, paved road crossings, and sections with heavy mountain bike use.

Horse Camping: None

Non-horse Camping: None

Maps and Info: For information, contact the South Park Administration, Buffalo Drive, South Park, PA 15129, (412) 835-4810 or 4809. You can also contact the Allegheny Parks Department, 211 County Office Building, 542 Forbes Avenue, Pittsburgh, PA 15219, (412) 350-7275, www.county.allegheny.pa.us/parks. We did not see any maps; request one in advance as it is helpful to have a map to be able to tell where you are when you come out from a trail and are near a road. We used the roads to identify our location as the maps do not reflect trail detail.

Activities: Hiking, Biking, Horseback Riding Trails, Picnicking, Ball Fields, Wave Pool Complex, Golf Course, Game Preserve, Horse Show Area, and Ice Skating

Fees for Trail Use: None

Permits for Day Trail Use: None

Comfort Station: There are comfort stations at various central areas throughout the park.

DIRECTIONS:

There are many ways to access this park. If you take a look at a map, you will see South Park is located south of Pittsburgh between Route 88 and Route 51, just west of Pleasant Hills. If you live locally, you can take Route 88 directly to the park. We were traveling from the north side of Pittsburgh and took the following route. To reach the park from this direction, take the Pennsylvania Turnpike I-76 to Exit #28 and pick up I-79 south. Take I-79 south for about 24 miles to the Bridgeville Exit #54/Route 50 east. Go to the end of the ramp; make a right at the end of the ramp following the Route 50 east sign. Travel a short distance to a 'T' intersection; make a left still following Route 50 east. Travel into the town of Bridgeville. After traveling a total of about .8 miles (total from I-79), make a right at the light. You will see the Orange Belt sign. Follow the Orange Belt for 8 miles to Route 88. The road has many bends and turns, and changes names along its route; be sure to follow the signs for the Orange Belt. Come to Route 88 and make a left onto Route 88/Library Road. Take Route 88/Library Road for 2.8 miles and then make a hard right onto Corrigan Drive. I was told by the office that it is okay to park at various locations throughout the park. The two usual ones are the lot before the Round Barn and the lot by the horse arena. Travel about 2 miles on Corrigan. You will see the Round Barn (by what looks like a large racetrack) on the right; equestrians sometimes park at this busy parking area. To reach the horse arena parking, continue and come to a 'T' and make a right on Brownsville Road. Travel a short distance to a light, and make a left on McCorkle Road. The horse arena is on the right. The advantage to parking at the Round Barn is that you cross just one busy road (vs. more if you park at the horse arena lot) to the opposite side, head for the cluster of woods as per the map, and hook up with the trails there. If you park at the horse arena, you need to cross a few busy roads and fields adjoining groves to reach the wooded trails. However, on a weekday when the groves are not occupied, the open fields and the back of the groves (do not ride near the groves) are a pleasure to ride as they are nicely mowed and maintained by the park. We were also told that equestrians could park by the ice skating rink (grid C5 on the park map) or by Grants Grove (#92, grid D4 on the park map). Looking back, I would prefer a different, less congested location than either the show grounds or the Round Barn, and would have tried these others. Although we did not visit these lots, they may be more centrally located to access the trails and avoid crossings. You may want to scout these prior to hauling and see what your preferred access is.

THE TRAILS:

I have fond memories of South Park as a place I came to as a child with my cousins who lived nearby in Pleasant Hills. It was interesting to revisit it at this stage of my life. From what I can remember, and not surprisingly, it is much more developed and has evolved into a very busy place with many diverse uses and many types of visitors to serve. If I recall correctly, I believe I did have a pony ride near the Round Barn where they still have pony rides today. There certainly is something for most everyone here from golf courses, skating rinks, ball fields, to a game preserve, etc.; I can see why it is a popular destination. And we were glad to see that, in spite of the growing population everywhere, they still have preserved portions of the park for those who want to enjoy it in its natural state such as the equestrians, hikers, and mountain bikers. There are still many lovely, large fields nicely mowed and many clusters of woods remaining throughout the park where this can be done. My one concern is that since there is no organized, defined area or system of equestrian and mountain bike routes that, without definition, the trails will dwindle and lose out. (I was told that the paved hiking and running areas were once part of a dirt trail system which equestrians could ride.) I am very appreciative that we are welcome at this pretty park and are allowed flexibility as to where we ride; I just hope that equestrians continue to remain welcome, and adequate room is reserved or considered for them as future changes occur.

This is not a remote trail system; instead it is a popular park destination located near some of the most populated suburbs of Pittsburgh. We found the most challenging part of riding the trails at South Park was crossing the busy park roads (paved). *Too bad they don't have the tunnels and bridges along the trail like they do at Fair Hill in Maryland.* It helps to know how to avoid some of the busier sections as our guide showed us.

Due to there being no specific trail markings, the following is a high level description of what we rode. (Sometimes there were white blazes on the trees but there were no signs, trailhead posts, nor trail markers corresponding with the map.) Our guide, Marianne, took us from the horse show arena lot, across McCorkle Road, along Sunny Slope Road, and then we worked our way via open fields within view of the groves and other areas (we avoided the actual groves as horses are not permitted at or on the grove sites). We rode toward the cluster of woods illustrated in the middle of the map, zigzagged through various trails in the woods, ultimately took a trail that traveled parallel to Texas Road, and anywhere we saw a path, we picked it up. Basically, we rode in a counter clockwise direction (on the map) and covered various sections. The wooded trails were nice and held up well in spite of the recent bad weather. Certain sections were more popular with mountain bikers, evidenced by the logs laid as a base for jumps. Riders need to go around or over these but we did not find any to be a problem. Also, there are many water crossings but we found all that we encountered to be easy. Riders will need to proceed cautiously through a couple of the small stream crossings due to flat rocks which were placed by mountain bikers resulting in the footing being awkward for horses. It's best to bypass these and look for a different route; there are many that travel through the woods. Overall, this was a minor obstacle. Really, the only challenging part we found was the road crossings; we were glad we chose to visit during the week versus a weekend. We did notice that some of the roads had four-way stop signs which were well placed and aided our crossing. It would also be helpful to have a horse crossing sign near some of the wooded areas as a safety measure and also to guide equestrians.

In my view, this may not be the kind of park to drive a long distance to as you may have to travel longer to get there vs. ride. It takes some back road driving to reach the park from many of the major roads. But is a very desirable and enjoyable park for folks in the area and surrounding counties. If you do choose to visit this park for the first time, try to ride with someone familiar with the park. Then, once you find the trails, it gets much easier to get your bearings and explore. Otherwise, your first visit could be confusing due to limited information or guidance.

HISTORICAL INFORMATION:

The Allegheny County Parks are a network of parks which are administered by the Department of Parks, Recreation and Conservation. There are nine County Parks within the park system totaling about 12,000 acres. The intention of these parks is to provide a recreational retreat in an unspoiled, undeveloped environment for the residents of Pittsburgh and the surrounding communities. The beginning of the development of this system of parks occurred mostly in the late 1920s to early 1930s, and again, later, between the 1950s to the late 1970s. When Edward Babcock first envisioned a need for an extensive park system north and south of Pittsburgh in the late 1920s, this area was mostly farmland. To develop the park into woodlands, one of the best park designers of the time, Paul B. Riis, was hired to design the parks' landscapes. This man had quite a resume as he was the same individual who designed the landscape and some of the buildings and the lodges for other well known national parks such as Yellowstone National Park. *Having personally traveled to so many of our national parks, until now, I never gave thought that one man may have had a hand in so many of these different destinations!*

Utilized as county fairgrounds (including a racetrack) in the 1930s, South Park became a very popular destination. For decades, the county fairgrounds flourished and attracted large crowds of visitors. By the 1960s, industry had arrived and the people were attracted to the park for a variety of industrial demonstrations and expos that took place. In these more recent times, people flock to the park for the wave pools and other outdoor recreation. But you can still enjoy the history of long ago at the Oliver Miller Homestead, the blacksmith shop, and the Visitor Center which houses a small museum of early settlers' life in this region.

The Oliver Miller Homestead is located in the central part of the park. For many years, spanning from the 1770s to the early 1920s, one family owned this land. In 1772, Oliver Miller and members of his family and in-laws settled in this region and a log cabin was built. However, western Pennsylvania, which had only opened for settlement in the 1770s, was still subject to Indian raids. Families would have to flee to the safety of forts when uprisings occurred. One could only imagine how brave these early settlers had to be to travel to and inhabit this new, unknown, and sometimes dangerous territory. However, the Miller family ultimately and successfully settled at this site and many generations lived at this homestead. The cabin was expanded over the years and eventually it was replaced by stone altogether. An interesting (free) brochure detailing information regarding the Oliver Miller Homestead and its history can be obtained from the park office.

Besides the early Indian raids, the generations of the Miller family witnessed and partook in many roles in our nation's early history, including the Revolutionary War and the Whiskey Rebellion. Oliver Miller's sons served in the Revolutionary War. In the 1790s, the Whiskey Rebellion arose and was an extremely important issue to the people of the time. Basically, federal law imposed a tax on all whiskey and also dictated that all stills be registered. At that time, home stills were abundant (estimates have indicated one out of six farms had a still) and were a critical means of making a living for farmers. Whiskey served many functions, including medicinal. It also was a major trading item so that settlers could purchase goods and ammunition. Whiskey of this region was called Monongahela Rye Whiskey. As there were no modern means of transportation, this important product was transported to points of sale in eight-gallon containers or kegs on the backs of horses over the mountains. Angry at the extreme taxes, fines, and still registration regulations being imposed, farmers united and rose in protest. These were called the Whiskey Rebellion years and represented one of the first times in our nation's history the newly created Federal Government had to intercede and restore peace. It was George Washington who sent troops to stabilize the area. Of significance, the timeliness, reliability, and willingness of the government to act eventually yielded a positive outcome of a more unified government and people.

In 1927, Allegheny County acquired the Miller family homestead. The home and surrounding land ultimately became what we know today as South Park. In the early 1930s, the stone house was dedicated as a National Historic Landmark. In the late 1980s, a log cabin was built in the image of the Miller's first home and is utilized as the Visitor Center where original artifacts of the Miller family and early American life can be viewed. In the 1990s, a blacksmith shop was built. The shop was constructed to reflect the typical blacksmith shop of the mid to late 1700s, and demonstrations are given at different times during the year. If you enjoy history, make sure you visit the homestead (open Sundays during certain seasons) and the Visitor Center when you are in the park. For hours and more information, check with the park office.

COURTESIES:

We enjoyed our visit to this park and the company of our guide, Marianne, who graciously showed us the trails and gave us a nice tour of the park. Even though already familiar with these trails, Marianne called the park office to double check where equestrians were permitted to travel and to obtain extra maps. Thank you Marianne! Thank you to Dick, in the park office, who made me feel very welcome and was helpful in providing information including good, detailed directions. Thank you to Dennis, with the pony concession, for sharing information regarding the trails in the park. Also, my appreciation goes out to the many individuals and groups, including local equestrian organizations, that have contributed to this park system and preserved this lovely area, and also to the early conservation pioneers such as Edward Babcock who had the foresight to preserve park land for all to enjoy.

THINGS WE LEARNED THIS RIDE:

• During our research for western PA, we often took two sets of trailers. (Our large one stayed at camp, and we used our 2-horse, day trailer to shuttle back and forth to the trails while doing research.) We were heading back from South Park with our 2-horse trailer to our "home base" and were traveling north on I-79. We passed a big horse trailer with a double blowout. We saw them too late to immediately stop, so we continued to an exit and backtracked, went down to the next exit, and made our way to the side of the road in order to help them. By the time of our arrival, help was already on the way and these folks were fine. We then got back on busy I-79. Having seen their emergency triangles behind the horse trailer, I asked John where ours were as we had two sets and I had just asked him to put them in the trailer before we left for this trip. He assured me they were "somewhere" with us. (Hmmm.....) Well as soon as this was said, we had our own blowout. We must have picked up a nail or something at that same spot where the other folks had a problem. Of course, where we had the blowout was a section of road with little area to unload a horse or even pull over safely. As I went to look for our flares, emergency equipment, and all our tools, I realized they must be back (where we were staying) in the other trailer, not the day trailer. Plus, we had recently cracked our plastic ramp so we didn't have that either. With traffic whizzing by, John and I rushed to find the instructions for where the jack was and how to work it, along with all the tools to pull a tire off. So much for being prepared. But we quickly innovated and rigged a ramp made out of some planks by the side of the road and were able to change the tire with the horses in the trailer and get out of there as quickly as possible. Luckily, I had some treats to keep the horses still while John changed the tire. But with or without the treats, the horses were extremely patient as the loud trucks roared by. Ah, trail horses! What I learned is for each vehicle and trailer to have a safety kit, a good jack, and a drive up ramp (metal/chrome that lasts longer), and to never take it out of the vehicle because, sure enough, you will come to need it when it is not with you.

- I learned the common, old sayings of the area, "You can't get there from here" and "The shortest distance between two points is under construction."

NEARBY AND SURROUNDING AREA STABLES:

- Pheasant Hollow Farm (boarding, lessons), South Park (412) 655-2199
- Morning Star Stables (boarding, lessons), South Park (412) 653-7750

NEARBY AND SURROUNDING AREA VET SERVICES:

- Dr. Fondrk, West Newton (724) 872-3530
- N. Loutsion, Canon Hill Vet Clinic Inc., Canonsburg (724) 746-4220

NEARBY AND SURROUNDING AREA FARRIERS:

- D. Bentrem, Burgettstown (724) 947-3411, (412) 580-4458 cell
- E. Moehring (724) 350-7355
- R. Buchko, Bridgeville (412) 498-5531 cell

26. Round Hill Park
Allegheny County Park

Lasting Impression: This is a lovely, clean, well maintained park offering a few hours of leisurely riding in loops throughout the park. As this is a popular weekend destination, riding the main part of the park is likely most enjoyable during the week when you have the quiet and beauty of the park mostly to yourself.

Location: Round Hill Park is located in Allegheny County southeast of Pittsburgh.

Length: *Day Ride Destination*- The park totals over 1,100 acres. An estimate of total miles of trails was not available; however, the park offers a nice day trip with a couple of hours of riding, plus there is additional riding on the opposite side of Round Hill Road.

Level of Difficulty: The groomed (main) park trails are easy with side trails ranging from easy to moderate. The opposite side of the road from the Exhibit Barn offers trails with more of a climb and is more challenging.

Terrain: The main trail paths on the north side of Round Hill Road are wonderful, wide, mowed, and well groomed tracts on level land or rolling hills with various offshoots that can vary in terrain. The south side of Round Hill Road does not have formal, maintained trails and offers more challenging, undeveloped, diverse, and hilly terrain. Riding in this section can be limited due to natural barriers such as downed trees or dense vegetation.

Horse Camping: None

Non-horse Camping: None

Maps and Info: Round Hill Park, County of Allegheny Department of Public Works Parks Division, (412) 384-4701, (412) 384-8555 or (412) 767-9200. Or contact the Allegheny Parks Department for information at 211 County Office Building, 542 Forbes Avenue, Pittsburgh, PA 15219, (412) 350-7275, website: www.county.allegheny.pa.us/parks. Ask for the map of Round Hill Park which is helpful in that it shows the lay of the land for a reference point while riding the trails. The main trail is shown on the map but there is additional riding on the offshoots, at the edge of the fields, and also on the south side. For information regarding the Round Hill Farm Programs, contact (412) 384-4701. For disability information, contact the Allegheny Parks Department above.

Activities: Hiking, Horseback Riding Trails, Picnicking, Ball Fields, and Exhibit Farm

Fees for Trail Use: None

Permits for Day Trail Use: None

Comfort Station: Toilets are located in the park in the central areas by the groves and the Exhibit Farm.

DIRECTIONS:

We approached the park from the north. However, if you want to approach the park from a different direction, you can reach the park by taking Route 51 to Route 48 north (probably a more direct route with less turns but we did not haul from this direction). Shortly after getting onto Route 48 north, you will see Round Hill Road. Turn right onto Round Hill Road and you will see the park on the left. We, instead, traveled from the Pennsylvania Turnpike (from the north) as follows. To reach the park from this direction, take the Pennsylvania Turnpike I-76 to Exit #57 Route 356. As soon as you go through the toll booth (it may be helpful to ask as it's easy to miss), follow signs to Monroeville, Route 48/Route 22 (a local route that brings you to Route 48). *We missed the turn and had to get off the next exit for Route 791, turn around, and backtrack.* Take Route 48 south toward McKeesport; you will also see the Orange Belt signs. Once on Route 48 south, you will travel a total of 18.5 miles to the park. Route 48 south has many curves and bends plus a few climbs. Still, large trucks travel this route so large rigs should be able to make the turns. (The park entrance may be tight for larger rigs and is more suited to standard 2-horse or 3-horse rigs vs. anything of significant size.) But there are signs to guide you; just be sure to keep an eye out for the signs and for the many sharp turns. You will also begin to see signs for the Round Hill Exhibit Farm. At one point the signs for the Exhibit Farm are beyond the intersection where you need to make a sharp right. We couldn't figure if they were (incorrectly) putting the signs after the intersection or if there was another approach. Stay with Route 48 all the way. After 18.5 miles, look for a left onto Round Hill Road. Make the left onto Round Hill Road and then make another left into the park at the entrance. There is a large sign. Enter the park, pass the duck pond, and bear left (Hereford Drive) toward the groves. There is another sign. Go a total of .9 miles in the park and you will see a lot on the right with a sign that says "Golden Rod" and "Wagon Wheel." The lot is a pull through area of medium size with room for a few rigs. Large groups would not be able to fit and would likely have to disperse to other lots. (Check with the office if special circumstances apply for organized rides.) At the rear of the lot, you can ride in two directions. You can either take the single path into the woods at the back of the lot (probably a better choice if it is the weekend and the nearby groves are busy) or you can ride in the direction of the groves (but not into the groves), while avoiding the picnic areas, keeping at the edge of the grove land, and hooking up with the trails to the right.

THE TRAILS:

We actually rode from the Wycoff Farm and Stables and entered the park grounds via the entrance of the park. We picked up the trail at the end of the first lot, came out along the white fencing surrounding the Exhibit Farm (check out that gorgeous tree line down the center of the white fencing), rode across the field toward a playground, continued to hug the tree line, and took a trail to the front. We came upon where the park borders with the back of a private property. We

191

rode the perimeter along a creek and were careful not to go too close to the soft ground as there are sink holes. At the end of this short stretch, we came upon a horse sign marking the trail and rode into the woods. Once within the woods there were various trails in different directions, both of single paths and double width, some of which were cleared by bush hogs. We then came out at the Wagon Wheel lot and rode to the right, up the hill to the playground, and back to the right to rejoin the main trails. This gentle section offered nice opportunities for a canter or a running walk, and had some of the prettiest trails in the park as there were many freshly trimmed, wide double tracts. From there we rode through open areas, back into the woods, toward the Exhibit Farm, and across the road at the back of the Exhibit Farm. On the opposite side of the road, the park land continues. We ascended the trail along the power line (this was a pretty good climb but we did not find it difficult and you could rest your horse along the way) until, at the top of the tree line, we saw a trail on our left that cut through the trees. We hooked up with a farm tractor trail, headed to the right and farther uphill. Then we rode to the back of the field and picked up a trail along a stream and again headed to our left. We traveled a short distance and encountered a large downed tree which blocked our passing. So we backtracked and rode around the fields. We then returned to the other side and did a little more riding on some of the nicely mowed trails. The mowed sections of the north side were particularly attractive due to the many dogwoods blooming. Along the way, some of the trails had signs to guide you and other times we did not see them. But this is not a large place so you should not get lost. Rather, we found it a relaxing opportunity to meander throughout. Just make sure you pick up the main section of trails in the vicinity of the Wagon Wheel lot. Once you find them, you can expand from there. More trails may be marked in the future as when I spoke with the park office, they indicated that they plan to establish more trails and would like to promote the trails with the local riding groups. *Sounds like a good opportunity to volunteer, help maintain the trails, and positively influence the establishment of new ones!* Periodically along the trail there are signs, but often there are not. As long as you stay clear of the logical areas like the picnic groves, ball fields, etc. and respect the grounds, there are many trails you are permitted to explore. There is one section along the road before the Wagon Wheel lot that says no horses; this short stretch was the only place we saw posted as off limits to horses. Please be careful to steer clear of this area.

The opposite (south) side of the road has much potential for additional trails to be added. On the south side, we rode around the border of the fields and power lines and had a nice ride. As we entered the woods, we had to limit our ride as there weren't many established trails, and some had been overgrown or trees had fallen. Although having lots of good potential, that section was undeveloped during our visit so clearing would be needed to truly explore or expand one's ride in that section. But there is probably not a lot of work to do to open or reopen them. (As I mentioned, the office indicated they were very willing to work with equestrians and also expressed an interest in both expanding the trails and attracting more riders. This section would be ideal for that. There are a few local riders that I know of who have already been friends to the park, and have been very helpful, concerned, and active with the trails. With some assistance from additional volunteers, this already nice park could be made even nicer by helping expand the trail system in this section.)

One important note, we asked if this park is usually busy on weekends. We were told it is. However, we found it ideal during the week. If you choose to ride on weekends, you will need to stay away from the more congested areas. I asked other riders of this trail if there is a lot of multiple-use traffic along the trail. They said that there isn't much activity and most bicyclists seem to prefer to ride the nearby Yough Rail-Trail rather than visit the park. We only encountered an occasional dog walker or hiker. Although not permitted, we were told you may encounter a four-wheeler on the south side (we did not see any nor did we see many tracks other than by the power line). A benefit to the south side of the park is that the south section is away from the main park activities and may offer solitude when planning to ride on weekends.

Good to see dogs on leashes at this park. In our travels we have seen where many dog walkers do not keep their dogs on a leash. The dogs may be unfamiliar with horses and charge them. Also, while riding in the main park area, we heard gun shots. There is a shooting range outside of the park but we were told it is quite a distance off. Depending on the wind, it can sound closer than it actually is. We did not hear it for long nor did we have any problems or form any concerns.

The brochure from the office encourages volunteers to adopt sections of the park including trails. If interested, call (412) 350-2455.

HISTORICAL INFORMATION:
This park was once a cluster of farms which were purchased to form the park. Central to the park is the Exhibit Farm which is a working farm and is open for tours. Visitors can enjoy the farm which is open during season. Farm life is the park theme evidenced by the grove names "Timothy," "Hay Loft," "Alfalfa," "Meadow," etc. For more information and special events, contact the office. The Wycoff Stables are located directly across the road from the park. The Wycoff family is part of the local history in that their family has had that farm for roughly 200 years!

COURTESIES:
We spoke with Jerry LaFrankie and another gentleman, Dave, from the park office. Both Jerry and Dave made us feel very welcome. Dave indicated he was very interested in letting equestrians know about the park's trails and also wanting to expand the park trails and promote the trails with local riding clubs. Let's get

the word out; this is the kind of thing we want to hear! So if you are in the area or live in the area, make sure you visit this park. If you can volunteer to assist on the trails, please do as this is already a really pretty park with nice trails, along with even more potential. The opposite side of the park is a place where volunteers could establish some additional riding areas to extend the ride in the park. Jerry stopped by to say "hi" while we were at the nearby Wycoff Farm and Stables and was very helpful and encouraged our suggestions. Hopefully, local equestrians will continue this nice relationship with the park personnel for its ongoing success. Please be reminded, to help keep equestrians welcome at wonderful locations like these, the park asks that equestrians stay away from the congested areas including the picnic groves. Besides being a health ruling it is best to avoid those central areas where activities or excited children may possibly spook a horse and result in a dangerous situation. Also, in a park that is as nicely groomed as this one, please be extra careful not to tear up the ground along the entrance roads so that it remains attractive for all to enjoy, and pick up manure and trailer debris at the lots.

Thank you to Melissa Clark of Wycoff Farm and Stables who rode with us and the folks at Wycoff Farm and Stables, Jim and Dorothy, for putting us in touch with Melissa. Melissa, on her handsome paint horse, showed us many of the park's trails. It was very enjoyable riding with Melissa and also hearing of her youth growing up in California. Melissa has many interesting stories including attending Sunday school with Dale Evans (of Dale Evans and Roy Rogers fame) who was her teacher. Melissa also had the fun experience of riding and exercising Dean Martin's (the actor and performer) horses. Also, thanks to Lisa who assists with the maintenance of the trails.

NEARBY AND SURROUNDING AREA STABLES:
- Wycoff Farm and Stables (boarding near the park with close access to the trails, fun shows), Elizabeth (412) 384-2123
- Fallen Timber Stables (boarding, lessons and training [on one's own horse] with a "Western" emphasis), Elizabeth (412) 751-9996

NEARBY AND SURROUNDING AREA VET SERVICES:
- Dr. Fondrk, West Newton (724) 872-3530
- G. Hurley, Coal Center (724) 239-5137

NEARBY AND SURROUNDING AREA FARRIERS:
- E. Campbell, Jeannette (724) 527-6446
- R. Buchko, Bridgeville (412) 498-5531 cell

27. Deer Lakes Park
Allegheny County Park

Lasting Impression: This trail system was a very pleasant surprise, one we had not heard about before our visit. Take an easy and leisurely ride along gentle terrain and enjoy the trails at this pretty park.
Location: The park is located near the town of Russellton, northeast of Pittsburgh in Allegheny County.
Length: *Day Ride Destination*- The Park is roughly 1,200 acres. We didn't find an exact estimate of trail miles; however, there are at least 10 miles plus connecting trails. This destination is a nice day trip as you could easily spend many hours exploring the trails.
Level of Difficulty: Mostly easy, some sections may be considered moderate
Terrain: The trails are mainly gradual, hilly, but not "on the edge". They vary from wide paths to single paths along generally wooded or canopied trails.
Horse Camping: None
Non-horse Camping: None
Maps and Info: Deer Lakes Park (412) 350-2455 or (724) 265-3520. You can also contact Allegheny County Parks Department, 211 County Office Building, 542 Forbes Avenue, Pittsburgh, PA 15219, (412) 350-7275, website: www.county.allegheny.pa.us/parks. For disability information, contact the above number. Note that the trails are not marked on the map. Plus the map that we received was an older map and did not always reflect the park layout as it is today. But still request a map as it provides points of reference. *Note: the office was short on staff during our visit; you may need to call early to obtain a map.* We did not see any maps stocked at the parking area.
Activities: Hiking, Horseback Riding Trails, Picnicking, and Fishing
Fees for Trail Use: None
Permits for Day Trail Use: None
Comfort Station: We did not see any toilets at the parking area; however, facilities are available at the more central areas such as the fishing areas.

DIRECTIONS:
There are many ways to access this park. The problem is that some of the roads are not suitable for hauling. While scouting for directions from Route 28 we encountered a narrow tunnel that was on a dangerous, blind curve. We heard that a tractor trailer had recently gotten wedged in it. We also found certain approaches were hard to describe due to lack of signs. We, instead, used the following approach for hauling and found it simple to reach the park. Take the Pennsylvania Turnpike I-76 to Exit #39 Butler Valley Exit. Take Route 8 north to Gibsonia. Travel 2.6 miles on Route 8 north and make a right onto the Red

Belt (see sign). Follow the Red Belt signs. After only .3 miles, come to a stop sign and make a right, still following the Red Belt sign. (At this point and after, be careful to follow the signs; we missed this turn the first time through.) You will pass two 4-way stop intersections along the way; continue following the Red Belt signs. Cross over the railroad tracks. After a total of 6 miles from Route 8, the Red Belt turns to the left. Do not turn left; at this point leave the Red Belt and discontinue following the Red Belt signs. Instead, travel straight. We did not see a sign at this point except for a small State Route sign SR1015. You will now travel beside the railroad tracks toward Russellton. Pass under a train trestle and head into a small town. After a total of 8.5 miles from Route 8, there will be a bank on the left and a small shopping center. Make a left. You will see an Orange Belt sign. Go a short distance and pass under another train trestle. At the Deer Lakes Park sign, make a left into the park. Travel .7 miles (passing the playground and fishing area). You will come to a sign that says "Deer Lakes Park Entrance No. 1." At this sign make a right; this is Cattail Drive. Go through the gates. *Note: if you arrive at the park before 9:00 am, they might not be open. Check with the office first if you plan an early arrival.* Travel .5 miles to the top of the hill. There is a loop to the right for parking and is located just before the dead end. You can pull through, no backing necessary. There is room for several standard 2-horse or 3-horse trailers. There is sufficient room for a few living quarter type trailers also. This is a nice, groomed lot. Don't forget to clean up the manure (including before you depart for the trail so it is not lying there all day).

THE TRAILS:
The map does not reflect the trails or a designated trail, and there are few, if any, signs so you will be on your own to explore. But there are lots of trails heading in all directions just off of the maintenance road at the back of the parking area. The trails vary from single paths through the woods, to wide, easy stretches, to tracts along the edge of the fields. From the parking area, we took a single path at the back of the lot into the woods; we crossed the maintenance road and proceeded up to an area called Rainbow Grove. There is a sign on the tree that says bridle trail. After making a left, we saw many trails branch from the trail we were riding. One of our guides, Cindy, said it is a maze and we had to agree. But it is a beautiful, relaxing maze. However, it is not one that is easy to describe where to go. There really isn't much in the way of signs. There are green marks on the trees along the trail which indicate you are on an established trail, but you can still go in circles as it's hard to tell the direction of where you are traveling.

We rode down the side of the maintenance road (in the direction away from the lot), made a left, picked up a trail which led to Mehaffey Road, crossed the road, traveled in a big loop to the left, crossed Crayfish Drive and Mehaffey Road, headed back into the woods, crossed Cattail Drive, looped around the lakes, and back to the maintenance road and our parking area. These looked like a few overlapping figure eights when Cindy marked them on the map for us. (Actually, Cindy does a very good job enhancing the maps; she would be a good candidate to update the park map with equestrian trails for the park office as she probably knows as much or more about these trails than anyone else.) If you are without a guide, it is best to just hook up with some of the trails, give it a go, and explore. Or, if you feel more comfortable with an escort, watch the local club publications for rides. There are guided trail rides or special events each year which are a good opportunity to be introduced to the layout. Contact one of the local organizations sponsoring a ride (see below) or just go and follow the paths. The trail is worn enough that you can follow the hoof prints. But this is not the kind of trail system where you are looking to reach a certain destination, rather this is one to just meander and enjoy the ride and soak in the scenery.

We visited this park in the spring and it was full of honeysuckle, dogwoods, and a variety of flowers. I particularly enjoyed the plant trivia that Cindy shared; she has a wealth of knowledge on many of the trails in this region and also on the local flora. Cindy taught me what squaw root and fairy candelabras are and about George Washington spice bushes and how their leaves, when crushed, give off a nice scent. Their berries are used in potpourri. We also enjoyed the opportunity to see an abundance of wildlife including a healthy population of deer. One thing we liked very much about these trails was that the ground was of solid terrain with very little mud in spite of recent rains. There is some water along the trail but it is best to bring your own. The park was very well kept, lawns were mowed, and the paths were cleared. I am told that the superintendent of this park, Mr. Harold Thompson, has the demanding responsibility of overseeing two parks, Harrison Hills and Deer Lakes. Both were excellently maintained much to his and his staff's credit. There are also trails on the other side which we did not visit. We were told they can be more challenging in terrain.

Please note that the park does ask that riders not ride the middle of the maintenance road as emergency vehicles can and may need to travel quickly down its path. They would also like riders to stay off the park roads, stick to the trails, stay clear of the picnic pavilions and grounds (this is a health ruling) and fishing areas, stay on the outskirts of open areas or to the side of farm fields, and not leave horses unattended. Other than that, there is a lot of flexibility once you are in the woods. Equestrians are also advised to stay clear of areas around the lake as the ground is soft and the footing can be dangerous. We heard that there is a significant horse community around Deer Lakes and they have a cooperative relationship with other trail users. Based on the good condition of the park and the friendly folks that we met, we can see why both the visitors and the park have a nice reputation.

HISTORICAL INFORMATION:
Deer Lakes Park is one of Allegheny County's parks. When Allegheny County Parks were designed, a study was made of the local areas. It was found that fishing was popular in the surrounding mining communities such as Curtsville, Culmerville, and Russellton. As a result, a few lakes were constructed to meet this need. They are spring fed and actually feed from the same water source. They are stocked with a selection of pan fish and the lakes are very popular as they provide an excellent environment and convenient locale for this type of recreation.

COURTESIES:
Thank you to Harry Thompson, the park supervisor, for keeping this park so nicely maintained and thank you to Nicki in the park office for sending us information on the park and its trails. I would like to express a very special thank you to Diane Hensel and Cindy Bower for personally showing us these trails. Diane took time from her very busy schedule to provide exact directions to the park from where we would be staying, and to also put the ride together with the four of us. Cindy provided great maps and shared her knowledge about these trails. Cindy is very involved in the handicapped riding program and judged trail rides in this region (watch for information in local publications about upcoming judged trail rides and events). What a great way to start out our research in the Pittsburgh region with such nice company. I wish we lived closer so we could ride together more often; it was truly a pleasure. Also, our gratitude to the Stony Brook Saddle Club who we were told helps with the trails in this area.

While visiting the Allegheny County Parks we stayed at the Kannadaford Farm in Gibsonia. This was a lovely boarding facility whose proprietors at the time, Tom and Hannah Fuller, were gracious enough to accommodate us along with our three horses during our travels, and who made us feel very welcome during our stay in this region. We really enjoyed their hospitality. Thank you also to the staff, including Jim, and the friendly boarders at the farm for helping us contact farriers when we were in need. And a very special thanks to those farriers for helping us out. It was also an interesting experience viewing the dramatic sky color over the farm each evening. During our visit, we saw more painted skies and extreme weather than we had ever seen in all our travels!

THINGS WE LEARNED THIS RIDE:
I learned to stay to the side of park maintenance roads even if they appear to be quiet, dirt roads since police and other emergency vehicles may use those paths.

NEARBY AND ALSO OF INTEREST:
- Judged Trail Rides at Deer Lakes, Harrison Hills, and other local parks (724) 845-9258 or (724) 224-8103

- The Pines Tavern, 5018 Bakerstown Road, Gibsonia (724) 625-3252. There is a wonderful, upscale restaurant nearby called The Pines Tavern. It was our anniversary and we decided to treat ourselves to some fine dining in a casual atmosphere. The appetizers, entrees, and desserts were all excellent and presented nicely. If you would like to indulge yourself, you may want to give this restaurant a try.

NEARBY AND SURROUNDING AREA STABLES:
- Honey Do Stables (boarding), Tarentum (724) 224-4870
- Bargee Farms, Inc. (boarding, lessons, show), Allison Park (412) 767-5348
- Highland Stables (boarding, lessons, trails), Gibsonia (724) 443-0740

NEARBY AND SURROUNDING AREA VET SERVICES:
- J. Leonard, Fox Run Equine Center, Apollo (724) 727-3481
- Dr. Neubert, Glenshaw (412) 767-9732
- F. Haustovich, Mars (724) 625-9433

NEARBY AND SURROUNDING AREA FARRIERS:
- E. Castello, Curtisville (724) 265-0949, (412) 721-5965 cell
- R. Laux, Worthington (724) 297-3001
- R. Wilderoter, Glenshaw (412) 967-6099, (412) 298-2817 cell

28. Hartwood Acres
Allegheny County Park

Lasting Impression: This destination is an enjoyable treat for a morning or afternoon leisurely ride, and can be combined with a tour of the Lawrence mansion, gardens, and stables.

Location: Hartwood Acres is located in Allegheny County just several miles north of Pittsburgh.

Length: *Day Ride Destination*- An exact estimate of trail miles suitable for equestrian use was not available. However, the length would be best described as several plus miles of leisurely riding on a beautiful estate.

Level of Difficulty: Easy

Terrain: Firm footing, little or no rocks, rolling landscape, some open fields but mostly wooded trails

Horse Camping: None

Non-horse Camping: None

Maps and Info: Hartwood Mansion & Park, 200 Hartwood Acres, Pittsburgh, PA 15238, (412) 767-9200 (guided mansion tours) or (412) 767-9966 (office). Ask for the Cross-Country Ski Trail map which reflects trails open to equestrians. Also available to visitors is a booklet detailing the history of the Hartwood Estate, including a description of the mansion and its architecture, antiques, works of art, and gardens. For information on this park or other Allegheny County Parks, contact the Allegheny Parks Department, 211 County Office Building, 542 Forbes Avenue, Pittsburgh, PA 15219, (412) 350-7275.

Activities: Hiking, Horseback Riding Trails, Mansion Tours (reservation and fee required), Cultural Events, Amphitheater, and Special Holiday Events

Fees for Trail Use: None

Permits for Day Trail Use: None

Comfort Station: Facilities are located near the mansion and the main grounds.

DIRECTIONS:
Take the Pennsylvania Turnpike I-76 to Exit #39 Butler Valley/Route 8. Take Route 8 south for 2.9 miles. Make a left on Harts Run Road (you will see a realty business on the left at the turn). Travel 1.7 miles on Harts Run Road. You will come to a stop sign. At the sign make a left onto Middle Road. Go .6 miles on Middle Road. (You will pass the field and gated entrances to Hartwood Acres on the right.) Proceed just past the field and make a right into the large gravel lot. The lot is in between the field and a school; it is not marked but you can't miss it. Many horse trailers and vehicles can fit in this lot including large living quarter type rigs. There is plenty of pull through room to turn around (assuming there is no vehicle blocking your turn). We visited on a Saturday in early May and the lot

was almost empty except for dog walkers. However, this was weather related and not the norm as we were told that this is normally a popular locale for various users including mountain bikers.

THE TRAILS:

There are some very pleasant hours of riding the trails on this lovely old equestrian manor. Ride the bridle trails and carriage paths which grace the property and were designed with equestrians in mind. Meander on the wooded estate grounds and come upon the beautiful Hartwood Mansion, former home of the Lawrences, and also the Hartwood Stables. Each is located in a separate section of the estate grounds. The setting of these stables is **a must see!** The stable compound, itself, looks like a castle. We would love to just live in the stable!

Although the weather was a bit misty and bordering on rain, it was still warm and pleasant during our visit. Likely due to the weather conditions, we were able to have the trails almost completely to ourselves. As this is a popular destination for many users including mountain bikers, either off-peak weekends or weekday riding is more likely to be the ideal time to visit as the woods would probably be as tranquil and peaceful as the day we visited. *We were told by a local equestrian that there is a good relationship with the mountain bikers and the equestrians, and that most of the mountain bikers she encountered knew to wait or give notice in advance when approaching the horses. This is great to hear. Of course, one still needs to be aware, especially around blind turns. However, we did not see one bike, just lots of bike tracks. We only shared the trails with some very curious deer.*

To help find your way around the loops, refer to the cross-country ski map (see contact info above) along with the Hartwood Acres grounds map. Horses are permitted on the cross-country ski trails. Looking at the map, we approached the trail system in a clockwise direction from the lot described above. We rode out of the back of the lot to the right, and picked up some trails which looked popular with mountain bike enthusiasts. This section was very attractive, wooded, and had some low branches and tight paths, but still was quite nice. Then we connected with some wider trails where there were hoof prints, and that section seemed to be visited by equestrians regularly. In all, we spent a few hours exploring the trails which varied from single tracts to old carriage paths of double width.

When you approach the center of the estate, there are multiple-use signs to guide you. There are many different loops of trails and side paths which travel throughout the grounds surrounding the estate that are framed with woodlands of mature beech, oak, and hemlock. Also, many sections of the trails are lined by and travel past a wonderful assortment of wildflowers and plant varieties. These are the benefits of riding an old estate! I always say the next best thing to having the resources to own a beautiful place like this is being able to enjoy the generosity of another where that individual, family, or organization has invited the public to visit and share in the pleasure of such a special destination. You can do that here; the friendly staff makes you feel welcome and this place has been beautifully preserved for all to appreciate. And of course this is a great destination because, in the tradition of its founders, they welcome equestrians!

Try to visit in the spring when most of the flowers are in bloom. Not surprisingly, there is beauty year round at this location including in the fall when the diverse variety of mature trees burst into vibrant colors. Such detail was given to the grounds that even cuttings from Georgia trees were brought in and planted so that trees would bloom in September. To keep the grounds in a natural state and in pristine condition, picnic areas have not been established on the grounds. Please be considerate and conscientious in helping maintain this wonderful destination so that it is preserved, and also so that equestrians remain welcome.

HISTORICAL INFORMATION:
Hartwood Acres is a beautiful destination and is an equestrian estate which stands as a fond memory of a time gone by. Both equestrians and non-equestrians will be in awe and find it hard not to envy the life of its original owners. Built in 1929, Hartwood was constructed for the daughter of William Flinn who made his fortune in industry. The stone mansion was built with an English and Elizabethan influence, and was styled with comfort in mind. However, expense was not spared as the home has many period pieces, custom work throughout by expert craftsmen, interesting gables, dramatic arches, gorgeous woodwork, plasterwork ceilings that are truly works of art, copper gutters (covered in lead to reflect the Elizabethan style of the home), and much incredible ornamentation throughout. Observe the outdoor motif of forest animals, roses, and grapevines in the small details throughout the mansion. Besides the awesome stables, the equestrian influence is apparent in both the artwork throughout the home and the details on buildings with emblems with the initials of the owners encircled by a horseshoe and a stirrup. The estate is set in a gently sloping landscape surrounded by gardens and paths that travel within its borders and the Allegheny mountain range. The setting is truly gorgeous.

During your visit, don't miss a tour of the home which contains much of the original collection of art and treasures owned by Mary Flinn Lawrence and her husband. There is so much to see; make sure you obtain the booklet describing the home. You won't want to miss the interesting interior which even includes a Chippendale table with fossils ingrained in its marble surface.

And ah, the stables! Of course, don't miss the stables. The house is set high and the stables are situated in the valley below. What a stable complex! The roof is slate, the courtyard is cobblestone, the windows are arched in Gothic style, the walls are paneled in wood, the hardware is polished brass, and the stalls have two doors which provide multiple purposes including serving as fire escapes.

The Allegheny County Parks were acquired with the goal of having a park system within a 30 minute drive from county residents. Hartwood was not one of the original planned parks; however, the county was very fortunate and delighted to be able to acquire this beautiful estate in the late 1960s. Mary Flinn Lawrence offered to sell Hartwood Acres to the county at an inexpensive price. This was especially generous as the mansion, property, and landscaping were in perfect condition and ideal for a park system with its already established trails. On occasion, the grounds are used for weddings and other events. During my last discussion with park management, there was a movie being filmed at the mansion.

COURTESIES:
I would like to thank Debbie at the Hartwood Acres office, a very nice and helpful person, for her generosity of time in providing information and for making us feel welcome. Everyone I spoke to at the office was very personable and accommodating.

THINGS WE LEARNED THIS RIDE:
We were reminded how precious these few unspoiled, undeveloped destinations are. Preservations of the past and locations such as these, especially near major metropolitan areas and spreading suburban sprawl, are becoming harder to find and hold onto. We hope this one remains for many future generations to enjoy as we have.

NEARBY AND SURROUNDING AREA STABLES:
- Honey Do Stables (boarding), Tarentum (724) 224-4870
- Bargee Farms, Inc. (boarding, lessons, show), Allison Park (412) 767-5348
- Highland Stables (boarding, lessons, trails), Gibsonia (724) 443-0740

NEARBY AND SURROUNDING AREA VET SERVICES:
- J. Leonard, Fox Run Equine Center, Apollo (724) 727-3481
- Dr. Neubert, Glenshaw (412) 767-9732
- F. Haustovich, Mars (724) 625-9433

NEARBY AND SURROUNDING AREA FARRIERS:
- E. Castello, Curtisville (724) 265-0949, (412) 721-5965 cell
- R. Wilderoter, Glenshaw (412) 967-6099, (412) 298-2817 cell

29. Harrison Hills
Allegheny County Park

Lasting Impression: Check out the awesome view along the bluffs overlooking the Allegheny River, and enjoy riding the network of leisurely, single, wooded paths of Harrison Hills.

Location: Harrison Hills is an Allegheny County Park and is located in western Pennsylvania. The park is located northeast of Pittsburgh near the town of Freeport at the northeast tip of Allegheny County.

Length: *Day Ride Destination*- The park consists of about 500 acres with trails comprising several miles. But what it lacks in length, it makes up for in beauty and panoramic views.

Level of Difficulty: Mainly easy, at most moderate

Terrain: We found the terrain to be of firm ground, not rocky, hilly, but overall not steep. There are a few side trails which are steeper and more challenging but there are alternate routes.

Horse Camping: None

Non-horse Camping: None

Maps and Info: Allegheny County Parks (724) 295-3570, website: www.county.allegheny.pa.us/parks/story/harrison.asp. For general or disability information, contact the Allegheny Parks Department, 211 County Office Building, 542 Forbes Avenue, Pittsburgh, PA 15219, (412) 350-7275. You can also call Deer Lakes Park at (724) 265-3520 for information.

Activities: Hiking, Horseback Riding Trails, Picnicking, and Ball Fields

Fees for Trail Use: None

Permits for Day Trail Use: None

Comfort Station: Yes

DIRECTIONS:
You can reach the park off of Route 28. To reach the park from the Pennsylvania Turnpike I-76, take the Pennsylvania Turnpike I-76 to Exit #48 Allegheny Valley and follow signs to Route 28 north. About 1 mile after getting off the turnpike, you will link with Route 28 north. Follow the signs (there are two sets of signs back to back; the ramp is actually at the second one). Take Route 28 north for 11.3 miles to Exit #16. Take Exit #16; travel down the ramp and make a right. (You will see a sign for the Red Belt.) Go .6 miles to the top of the hill (passing a Ford dealer) to a stop sign. Make a right. Go 1 mile and look for an entrance to the park on the left; there is a big sign. Go into the park, bear left, and go down the hill. It's the first lot on the left. The lot was specifically constructed for equestrians and is roomy. At least 10 rigs of average size (2-horse or 3-horse trailers) or a few large trailers with living quarters can fit. There is pull through

room; however, some of this can be limited if other cars are present (then some backing would be necessary). We visited on a Sunday and rode on a Monday in May and the lot was not busy. This is a nice lot in a remote setting, ideal for horses. To reach the trails, ride in the direction away from the entrance to the lot, past the restrooms, over a small gulley, past a large pine tree (locals refer to it as the "Christmas tree"), and travel either to the right or the left. One trail is directly along side the large pine tree and the other is on the opposite side of the road. If you look closely, you can see the path.

THE TRAILS:

Just a few hours of riding but well worth the trip! If you are traveling through the area, try this one just for the fabulous panorama overlooking the Allegheny River. Pack a lunch, ride to the overlook, and enjoy the view. But **do not miss** the view from the vista! Watch for eagles soaring overhead (we saw one). Plus enjoy nonrocky trails of gentle terrain. A map is helpful to follow the trails. Looking at the map, the left side of the map or northern section of the park is undeveloped and is perfect for riding. The right side of the map or southern section of the park has more groves and activities. Be sure to steer clear of the center of the groves with horses. Even still, when we visited, we had the park to ourselves and the surrounding area was quiet and peaceful.

There isn't a designated equestrian trail, per se, and the trails aren't marked by names or mileage but there are green blazes on the trees to give some direction as to what to follow for horse trail riding. With use of the map and an understanding of where to pick up the trails, it wasn't hard to stay on course. There are lots of side trails but if you get too far off, just backtrack and pick up the main trail. These trails are used by local equestrians so it's easy to follow the hoof prints. (They are used but not overused, which is nice.) You can meander around the trails in the north and northeast sections for quite some time. They are mostly single path, wooded tracts. There are places to water the horses along the way.

To reach the scenic bluffs, depart from the lot, head in the direction opposite the entrance of the lot, cross the small bridge, and you will see the large, single pine tree to the right (you can pick up the single path trail that travels alongside the tree to ride this in a counter clockwise direction). We decided to pick up the trail on the opposite side of the big pine tree and ride clockwise (north, then east to the bluffs, then south along the ridge, and then west back to the lot). We followed the hoof prints. There are various spin-offs in different directions. As there aren't signs, be careful to get your bearings and ride east toward the overlook. If you ride toward the road on the north side, backtrack, and find the main trail again. We ventured off in the wrong direction due to a downed tree, but once we rejoined the main trail it was easy to get back on course. *Note: throughout the park there are old bridges which are not suitable for horse crossing. Some have soft terrain around the edges. We found these passable by going around them and did not need to turn back.* We rode to the top of the woods by an anchor fence and an open field of old jumps. We crossed this field heading in an eastern direction and headed toward the bluffs. We then picked up the overlook or bluff trail following other hoof prints and green blazes, and rode in a southerly direction. Along this section the view was wonderful. You look out over the Allegheny River and can see for miles. It is likely even better when the leaves are off the trees as there is quite a bit of foliage which can limit the view in many sections. But there are cleared areas where you can see, so bring a camera. There is also room at the top to stop and have lunch, and take in the surroundings. We followed the ridge trail (while steering clear of the narrow hiking trails that veer off the main trail to the edge) and rode to the Watts Memorial Overlook (see map; also see below). When we arrived at the open field, just short of the overlook which is framed by white fencing, we made a right. We passed an old downed flag pole, rode a short distance of the border of the open area (marked by 4 and 4A on the map), and picked up the wooded trail to our right. There was a herd of deer observing us as we continued down the trail. The remains of another old flag pole bordered the trail. We descended the main path. Throughout this expanse, the air was full of the sweet smell of honeysuckle in bloom. Ultimately, we returned to the large pine tree and parking lot where you can extend the ride by connecting to the southern section of the park. Unfortunately, a nasty thunder storm rolled in so we were not able to explore other sections of the park. However, we were told to reach those trails, continue down the service road and look for the trails in the region marked by numbers 8 through 16 on the map.

HISTORICAL INFORMATION:
Allegheny County Parks has nine County Parks, many of which permit horseback riding. Harrison Hills is one of them. A gentleman by the name of Mr. Watts contributed much to the surrounding area by watching and reporting polluting violations of the river. As a result, he was entitled to one half of all fines assessed. However, much to his credit, he continued to contribute to the environment by returning any amounts received to the County toward the continued effort of keeping the waters unpolluted. The trail passes a section with a tribute to Michael Watts at the overlook.

COURTESIES:
Thank you to Cindy for mapping out the trails for us. During our visit to this destination, we swore that our friend Cindy had just placed fresh green markers along the path to guide us. Cindy, who is very familiar with these trail systems, had just given us a wonderful tour of Deer Lakes Park the day before. She became sort of our trail guardian angel, sending very detailed and helpful maps, and was determined that we see the prettiest parts of the trail systems. Cindy had wanted to guide us on this ride but couldn't make it on the day we visited. However, each time we weren't sure which way to proceed, there seemed to be a

fresh green marker to guide us. It just seemed too coincidental. Thanks Cindy, we know you were with us in spirit!

Thank you to the Stonybrook Saddle Club who maintains many of the trails. Also, my gratitude goes out to Mr. Ray Harbison; I was told he was very good to the equestrians by establishing a parking lot with sufficient room to park the trailers. Also thanks to Harry Thompson, the current park superintendent, for answering my many questions and for doing a very good job maintaining the grounds and the trail paths throughout two Allegheny County Parks, Deer Lakes Park and Harrison Hills.

THINGS WE LEARNED THIS RIDE:
Just because it sounds like thunder, doesn't mean a storm is rolling in. Upon entering this trail system, we heard a loud boom. With marginal weather and a storm looming, we thought we might not be able to cover the park this particular day. We rode a short distance tentatively, but did not hear any more. So we continued riding for a few hours. We were happy to cover some of the most scenic portions of the trail before the storm and, luckily, when we were at the high overlook it was still calm and quiet. Only until we returned to the lot vicinity did the actual storm roll in. Later, we wondered what the first loud rumble was only to find out that it was construction blasting. This was a one time thing, actually occurring some distance from the park property and trails, but we just happened to be in the right place at the wrong time where the sound carried. Amazing that the horses didn't even flinch at the time! I think it was because we all thought it was thunder.

NEARBY AND SURROUNDING AREA STABLES AND B&B:
- Armstrong Farms (B&B), Saxonburg (724) 352-2858
- McHenry's Horse World, Apollo (724) 478-4644, (724) 697-4030

NEARBY AND SURROUNDING AREA VET SERVICES:
- Dr. Neubert, Glenshaw (412) 767-9732
- F. Haustovich, Mars (724) 625-9433
- J. Leonard, Fox Run Equine Center, Apollo (724) 727-3481

NEARBY AND SURROUNDING AREA FARRIERS:
- E. Castello, Curtisville (724) 265-0949, (412) 721-5965 cell
- R. Wilderoter, Glenshaw (412) 967-6099, (412) 298-2817 cell
- R. Laux, Worthington (724) 297-3001

30. Mingo Creek Park
Washington County Park

Lasting Impression: Mingo Creek Park is a picturesque park with quaint covered bridges nestled in a lovely setting of rolling farmland. At the time of our visit, the surrounding area still seemed untouched by sprawling suburban development. This is a nice, lengthy trail system that has lots of potential.

Location: Mingo Creek Park is located in southwest Pennsylvania, near Route 136, about 12 miles to the east of the town of Washington in Washington County.

Length: *Day Ride Destination*- Mingo Creek Park consists of about 2,600 acres and there are approximately 17 miles of trails open to horseback riders.

Level of Difficulty: Moderate to challenging

Terrain: The terrain varies greatly from attractively mowed, open grass stretches along rolling hillsides to single, shaded, dirt paths through diverse woodlands. This trail system, which is mostly under a dense canopy of shade, retains moisture and is best visited after a period of dry weather.

Horse Camping: None

Non-horse Camping: None

Maps and Info: For maps, permit and other information, contact Washington County Parks and Recreation, 100 West Beau Street, Suite 604, Washington, PA 15301, (724) 228-6867. The map does reflect the horse trails and is very helpful. For disability information, contact the above number.

Activities: Hiking, Biking, Horseback Riding Trails, Picnicking, Ball Fields, and Special Events (such as the Covered Bridge Festival, Weddings, Fishing Tournaments, Bike Races, and Running Races). *Perhaps this would be a nice destination to plan a wedding on horseback!*

Fees for Trail Use: None

Permits for Day Trail Use: Permits **are** required (no charge).

Comfort Station: None at the equestrian parking areas (facilities are located at various other locations throughout the park and are reflected on the map)

DIRECTIONS:
Parking for the equestrian trails is at two locations, one in the southwest section of the park at the west entrance off of Sichi's Hill Road and is indicated on the map, and the other at the east entrance and is also marked on the map. There are various ways to reach the park. From I-79, take Exit #43 Route 519. (Or take the Pennsylvania Turnpike to Exit #28 and pick up I-79. Then take I-79 south for 35 miles to Exit #43 Route 519. If traveling from this direction, make a right at the end of the ramp onto Route 519 south.) Take Route 519 south toward the town of Eighty Four. This is a winding road; be careful to follow the signs. Stay on Route 519 south for 7 miles and make a left onto Route 136 east. Take Route

136 east for 4.5 miles and make a left onto Sichi's Hill Road. The turn is directly opposite the Mingo Creek Inn. Sichi's Hill Road is a rough, paved road so take it slow. Go down the hill and come to a stop sign. Make a right onto Sugar Run Road. Travel about .1 miles and, before the creek, make a right into a large gravel lot which is the "west" lot. There is a horse trailer parking sign at the entrance. *Note: on your return trip, there is a significant short climb back up Sichi's Hill Road. We did not have trouble but we also brought our smaller 2-horse trailer, not our larger trailer. Due to the tight turns both approaching and through the park, this location is more suitable for a standard size, 2-horse or 3-horse slant load trailer, but not anything bigger or heavier.* The gravel lot is very large with plenty of room for groups and plenty of pull through room. Backing isn't necessary. The trailhead is at the back of this lot. You can either go to the left and cross the stream, or to the right and head up the hill into the woods. The shoulders of the stream can be difficult to cross (a bridge is needed), and the entrance to the woods briefly travels through a wet, low lying area before it heads up the hill. We chose to ride in a counter clockwise direction (if looking at the map) and headed up the hill into the woods. Before you decide on counter clockwise or clockwise, observe the creek crossing and decide which direction you prefer to cross it. It may be easier to ride clockwise and head across it; we found it very difficult (on our return trip) to cross the creek from the other direction due to a deep, soft edge along its banks.

Originally, we planned to park at the east lot but a large tree had fallen across the park road and it would be some time until it would be cleared, so we opted for the west lot. To reach the east lot, travel past the west lot, go over the bridge, and make a right onto Mingo Creek Road. Bear right, following Mingo Creek Road which, as its name indicates, travels along the creek. (The nice thing about driving along Mingo Creek Road is that you get to see many sections of this beautiful park that you cannot see from the horse trails. You can use this time to check out the two picturesque covered bridges which are kept in excellent condition.) We traveled 1.7 miles on Mingo Creek Road and then made a right onto Parkview Road. We took Parkview past the ball fields on the left, past the Henry Covered Bridge on the right, and then we could go no farther due to the very large downed tree across the road. We do know the east lot was just down the road on the right. We later rode to it and it was a nice size lot for standard size trailers. I felt it was in a prettier setting than the west lot; however, the west lot has more parking area as it is a large gravel lot. Although a good size lot, the east lot has a tree in the middle which may limit turning radius, but there is still plenty of room and this should not present a problem for standard size rigs. One of the two trailheads at this location is the single path on the opposite side of the road. It travels up the hill and is easy to access. The other end of the trailhead is behind the parking area on the opposite side of the stream. Since we did not park at this lot, we approached it from the stream side (opposite from the lot) and had to search for a place to safely cross. At its lowest, there is an abrupt drop of a few feet between most of the trail and the stream. A bridge is also needed at this stream crossing.

THE TRAILS:

Over time I had heard many wonderful things about Mingo Creek and was anxious to visit. And with good reason as this is a very nice park in a lovely setting with some very friendly and helpful park personnel. Although the weather was good the day of our ride, we quickly learned that recent storms had played havoc on these trails. Most of Mingo Creek Park equestrian trails are single paths that travel through the forest, do not get much sun, and thus hold the moisture. Shaded trails are ideal on a hot day but one disadvantage is that it makes it hard for the trails to dry out even when precipitation has not been heavy. This was very evident in the section leading out from the west lot in the opposite direction of the creek and also in some of the northern sections of the park. However, in spite of the rain, there were many sections in the park that seemed to have a tough undersurface and, although moist on top, were solid under foot. But the landscape is diverse and can quickly change. There are elevated stretches of trail and there is low lying land. The low lying sections were more challenging to travel across as mud could be significant. Some of the low lying areas are in the northern section of the park and we noticed that riders who were familiar with the trails bypassed those wet areas and traveled the remote border of the open grass fields where the footing was high, solid, and dry. They would then rejoin the trail at later intervals.

The trails are mostly narrow tracts through old and new growth woods. The old growth woods are in the southern section, had good footing, and there were some beautiful old trees to behold. We passed one huge beech tree with an enormous girth indicating it had been on this earth a long, long time. Many sections of the trails also travel over wide, mowed paths across open fields. The fields are very scenic and there are lots of them. Along the field sections, the trail path was freshly mowed and the surrounding (off-trail) sections had high grass. The paths through the open fields were nicely maintained by the park (much to their credit too as it probably wasn't easy to maintain with the uncooperative weather). We stopped to talk to the park personnel regarding questions we had on the trails, and they were very approachable, helpful, and delightfully conscientious about the condition of the grass paths. It's good that they maintain those as you'll need the mowed paths to follow some sections of the trails. Throughout the grassy areas, the footing seemed to be solid making it leisurely and pleasant to cross the fields. There are many climbs and descents along the path and plenty of water for the horses to drink while out on the trail. The trails are well marked with blazes (that correspond to the color of the trail on the map) along the way and signs to help guide you. This is an excellent feature of the park. Just watch for sudden turns and keep an eye out for the blaze color that you are trying to follow. We almost missed one sharp right turn and really needed to look around at the intersections. Do bring the map as you will find you need it the first time through.

The trails travel through the outer borders of the park and, although we visited on a Saturday, we had them mostly to ourselves. However, some local riders told us that these trails are popular with mountain bike enthusiasts so riders will need to be alert for approaching bikes. Along the trail, there are some wonderful views of the rolling countryside along with picnic tables which were strategically placed to enjoy these views. These are nice places to stop and have lunch. During our visit, there were multitudes of daisies and other wildflowers in bloom in the surrounding fields and beside the trail where the sun could reach. Along the path, we did not encounter any "on the edge" riding. But do watch for a few spots that have significant erosion from the weather. There was one particular challenging crossing shortly after leaving the west lot which had old discarded farm tires nearby. *It should be noted that we did find the trails and park to be very clean; there was just this one spot in the outer most section of the park trail system where tires had been abandoned.* A stream ran through a ravine and a small section on the side of the trail had caved in. This is not that uncommon on trails after severe rains; ravines get washed out. But you need to keep an eye on the footing until it is repaired. A plus is that these trails are not very rocky. One trail starts out from the east lot and is rocky going up hill. But this is only for a short distance and we found it passable and soon the rocks end. There were only a few places with clusters of rocks. The various paths were easy to follow; besides following the colored blazes, you can follow the hoof prints. The map will help with intersections as sometimes the trails travel in a few directions where it can be confusing where to proceed. There are some pipes along the trail in the southeast section of the park, but only for a short distance. Pipes or pipelines are not unusual in western Pennsylvania, but we were glad to see they were very minimal at Mingo Creek Park. Also, riders should be aware that there is an airfield in the eastern section of the park which is marked on the map. This section can be avoided as there are many other loops throughout the park. During our visit, there had been much overgrowth along the trails. We noticed this on other trails in this region also and, considering the recent rains, it wasn't surprising. It's easy for the greenery to begin to cover a single tract within a matter of days after it rains. I am sure the folks that maintain these trails were having a tough time keeping up with maintenance this particular spring.

Learning that nature had not provided us with ideal conditions prior to our visit, and wanting to give the trails a fair commentary, we inquired with other riders who regularly frequent the park. They told us that the trails normally are not muddy, and instead are usually very good. Based on this, we felt the trails were probably, overall, at most "moderate" to ride under normal weather conditions. Even still, there are a couple of challenging sections requiring attention. These areas are where fill or a bridge is needed such as by the river crossings (both parking areas) and in areas of erosion along the trail. Also, the clearance of some downed trees (which have been left for some time) is needed. If the paths are widened or overhead growth trimmed so that the sun can reach the surface, water retention could be minimized. The addition of a few small wooden bridges, walkways, and stone dust fill in vulnerable areas would greatly enhance and equip this attractive and desirable trail system to endure against the elements.

The equestrian trails travel the tranquil outer edges of the park and avoid the center of the park where the hub of activities transpires. The park requests that equestrians do not ride on the roads or across the covered bridges within the park. Before or after your ride, be sure to take a drive through the center of the park to see and take a picture of the two covered bridges. The covered bridges that you can view within the park are the Henry Covered Bridge (circa 1881) and the Ebenezer Covered Bridge (circa unknown). Weddings have taken place by the covered bridges and they are also used as a backdrop for other special events including the Covered Bridge Festival. Vehicles can cross the bridges but there are weight limits which must be observed. We passed the bridges but did not cross while pulling the horse trailer.

HISTORICAL INFORMATION:
Mingo Creek Park is located in Washington County and derived its name from an Indian tribe. The park area was once farmland, similar to that of the land that surrounds it today. In and around the park, there are many areas of historical interest including 30 covered bridges that span both Washington County and nearby Greene County. There is a wonderful Washington & Greene Counties Covered Bridge Driving Tour Book that can be obtained from the Washington County Tourism Promotion Agency, (800) 531-4114, website: www.washpatourism.org for free. The complimentary booklet details the location, history, and characteristics of these bridges. If you have the time, take a drive and visit some of these bridges.

Washington County is home to The LeMoyne House which is the first National Historic Landmark in our state as it served as a location for the Underground Railroad. Washington County was also once the site of the Whiskey Rebellion as many of its farmers depended on whiskey as a source of income.

COURTESIES:
Thank you to the staff at Mingo Creek Park for your help and assistance. Also, I have been told the Mountain Valley Trail Riders have contributed to the preservation of this trail system. Thank you to those folks and all those who helped create these trails for all to enjoy.

THINGS WE LEARNED THIS RIDE:

If a deer looks like it is constipated for an extended period of time, it may be giving birth. We passed a deer that remained in a squatting position even as we passed it. At first we did a double take and couldn't figure why it didn't move away or what its problem was. Then we realized she was getting ready to drop a fawn. We quickly left that section of the trail so as not to cause her any additional stress.

NEARBY:

- Washington County Tourism Promotion Agency (800) 531-4114, website: www.washpatourism.org

NEARBY AND SURROUNDING AREA STABLES:

- Mingo Creek Farm (boarding, training, lessons), Finleyville (724) 348-7479
- Coventry Equestrian Center (boarding, lessons, Dressage), Washington (724) 223-9692, website: www.coventryequestriancenter.com

NEARBY AND SURROUNDING AREA VET SERVICES:

- Dr. Fondrk, West Newton (724) 872-3530
- G. Hurley, Coal Center (724) 239-5137
- N. Loutsion, Canon Hill Vet Clinic Inc., Canonsburg (724) 746-4220

NEARBY AND SURROUNDING AREA FARRIERS:

- E. Moehring (724) 350-7355
- D. Bentrem, Burgettstown (724) 947-3411, (412) 580-4458 cell
- R. Buchko, Bridgeville (412) 498-5531 cell

31. Brady's Run Park
Beaver County Park

Lasting Impression: Brady's Run is a picturesque park with diverse terrain. We rode just a few hours and were enjoying ourselves, but then had to curtail our ride due to recent storm damage. One of the main trails was completely blocked by a large tree or group of trees that had recently fallen. We will have to return some day to explore the rest.

Location: Located in western Pennsylvania near the Ohio border, Brady's Run Park is a Beaver County Park and is situated along Route 51, just two miles north of the town of Beaver.

Length: *Day Ride Destination*- Brady's Run Park consists of approximately 2,000 acres. Exact mileage wasn't available; however, the trail system offers a few hours to possibly several hours of riding on varied terrain. We were told that there are plans for trail expansion.

Level of Difficulty: Moderate to advanced; some paths are difficult (sections of these trails are not for novice riders as there are some steep climbs, narrow paths on mountainous terrain, and a few challenging water and ravine crossings)

Terrain: Mostly single or double dirt tracts, some rocky patches (but passable), and remote, paved park road and inactive road connectors

Horse Camping: None

Non-horse Camping: None

Maps and Info: For information on Brady's Run Park, contact Brady's Run Park, 526 Brady's Run Road, Beaver Falls, PA 15010, (724) 846-5600. For information on the use of the horse arena, contact the Beaver County Recreation and Tourism Department, (724) 846-5600. Information on Beaver County Parks can also be obtained from the website: www.co.beaver.pa.us or by contacting the Recreation and Tourism Bureau at (724) 891-7030. We did not see maps at the parking area, so call for maps in advance. The maps reflect the trails but do not indicate the level of difficulty or permitted use. (If the maps are updated, it would be very helpful if the terrain is rated as the land can vary greatly on this trail system.)

Activities: Hiking, Biking, Horseback Riding Trails, Picnicking, Ball Fields, Fishing, Sledding, Horse Arena, Skating Arena, Boating, Horse Shows, and Other Activities such as the Maple Syrup Festival (Beaver County Parks do not permit hunting; always exercise caution during hunting season as nearby areas may permit hunting.)

Fees for Trail Use: None

Permits for Day Trail Use: None

Comfort Station: There is a building housing multiple outhouse-type toilets by the horse arena. *The bathroom is handy but women, be forewarned, there is not much*

privacy. Although the men and women enter different portions of the building, there are (intentionally) no doors to the outside of the building (just a partial wall, and not much of it) or doors to the stalls within the ladies room!

DIRECTIONS:
There are various ways to approach this park and different ones are listed on the website. From the south, take Route 65 north to Route 51 north to the park entrance. We approached this park from the north. If approaching from the north, take the Pennsylvania Turnpike I-76 to Exit #10 Route 60 south. Take Route 60 south (toward Beaver) for 5 miles to Exit #29 Chippewa. Get off the ramp and make a left. There is a sign. Take Route 51 south. You will see signs to the park. Go 2.8 miles to the light and the park entrance. Make a right onto Brady's Run Road. Pass the recreation facility on the left and go a short distance until you see a sign for a one lane bridge and the horse arena. Make a left and cross the bridge. Parking for the trails is at the horse arena grounds.

THE TRAILS:
The trails travel along the mountainside and there are several steep sections. If riding on a slope bothers you, this might not be the one for you. If you like a challenge through some very pretty scenery, or if you would like your horse to have a bit of a workout, you may want to give this a go. I was informed that new trails are being cut of a gentler grade by the Wildwood Trail but that was the section we were not able to ride due to the downed tree blocking the central route.

Upon reading the map, John noted that they recommended mountain bikers head in a clockwise direction to take advantage of some downhill sections. We decided we preferred to travel up the hill in case it was steep and, instead, chose to ride in a counter clockwise direction. We started out for the trails along the South Drive Trail, which is really an old road that is indicated as no longer being open for motorized use. This was a quiet, easy stretch on the day of our visit. However, our horses were quickly awakened from their sleep (walking) as they observed the large stainless steel containers along the old road. As our horses never saw anything like this before, they were quite concerned. It took some convincing for them to walk by these shiny, alien-like containers. We weren't sure what they were for until our friend and guide, Heather, told us these are for collecting maple syrup. Maple syrup is big in this area and the park is famous for its yearly Maple Syrup Festival in the early spring. *Too bad we missed that as I love maple syrup!* But our horses soon adjusted and we continued down the road to meet up with the trail. The South Drive Road leads up to a trail on the left. You can easily see it as it is a well used dirt path that climbs the side of the mountain. This is called Brady's Run Trail South. This trail presents a rapid climb (knowing it was steep, this was the section we intentionally chose to climb vs. descend). It then becomes a single, narrow path through the woods on the slope of the mountainside. The woods along the trail are dense; there are lots of pine forests, and the trail travels through a lovely, remote setting. The Brady's Run Trail South tract is full of great views looking down into the valley. The path is very scenic but it is also tight and may be too "on the edge" for some. There were a few places where I kept an eye on my horse's footing vs. looking around or down below. If heights concern you, some sections of this trail system may not be your preference. In actuality, there is plenty of forest below which can help provide a mental and physical buffer. The trail continues winding on the mountainside and crosses some ravines with streams. They can be challenging to cross and you may find your horse feeling the need to jump over them vs. walking through them. We visited on a clear day and, although the surface was mostly good, the trails and ravine crossings had retained moisture from recent storms. To maximize enjoyment, consider visiting when the ground has been dry for an extended period of time. If this was closer to where we live, we would definitely re-ride this in the near future during ideal conditions with solid footing to fully enjoy the views.

Most of the Brady's Run Trail South, although narrow, was kept clear in spite of the recent bad weather. At one point we did encounter some blockage (a small tree down), but we sidetracked to the adjoining farmland and went around the obstacle and rejoined the trail. We did note that this trail seemed very popular with mountain bikers based on the tire tracks and the jumps along the trail. We did not run into anyone but it was a weekday. It is likely that weekends are much busier. I did give thought that many of the sections of ridge trail that we just traveled had insufficient passing room and no areas to pull over. If you run into a mountain biker or other horses, it may be a problem. *Maybe some trails should be one-way only. Although, this could be a major issue as equestrians would probably prefer to go up this trail, and mountain bikers would likely prefer to go down it. We were actually traveling in the opposite direction of what was recommended for mountain bikers!* Do proceed with caution. Ultimately, the trail connects back to Picnic Area #1 (old #10) where we rode down the access road and made a right to pick up the Wildwood Loop Trail. About this time, we heard the all too familiar sound of one of our horse's shoes which had become loose. John was sure he loosened it while trying to cross the last ravine. We didn't have the tools to take it off (we have since included them in our saddlebag) so we decided John would head back to the trailer, and Heather and I would cover the Wildwood Loop Trail. The Wildwood Loop Trail looked very inviting as its entrance is a wide, leisurely path of gradual grade. We had only one concern as there is a section (on the map) where the trail is labeled "Descent of Death." Well, with a name like that, we didn't know what to expect. We figured we would still give it a try and climb vs. descend it. Maybe it wouldn't be too bad, plus this trail looked so nice at the entrance, much wider than the previous trail, and seemed to have very good footing along the path. I was ready for a more level ride since the ground (we just rode) was still slick in some sections from the recent bad weather. Plus, if the trail changed dramatically, we could always turn back. However, immediately after starting down the trail, we encountered a major obstacle. Much to my disappointment a large tree had recently fallen and was blocking the whole trail. Although I gave it a good try, there was no getting around this due to the abrupt slope and rocky surface of the adjoining land. We were forced to head back. It was very unfortunate that we could not take this trail as we were told it is a nice one and we were looking forward to it.

Challenges like this were not unusual this riding season and the prior year. Heavy rains and severe storms, both in the spring and summer, for two consecutive years had wreaked devastation on so many of the trails that we visited in western Pennsylvania. This limited some of the places we wanted to cover and also our complete enjoyment of the trails. We had made several long trips to western Pennsylvania to cover the trails. But on this one particular trip we had more than our share of challenges. After finally reaching our destination, we arrived to have it rain and thunder every evening while we were there. This was accompanied by extreme gusts of wind. Somehow we had some luck in that we never had a full blown thunder storm while we were on trail, only in the evening. But the storms seem to be always just at our back. Well we didn't get to cover as many of the trails at this park as we would have liked; however, we did get to ride a few hours. Regarding the Brady's Run Trail South, in spite of the continued ground saturation, there was a pretty good surface on the trails and it was not soupy. There are some rocky sections, especially where you leave the South Drive Trail/Road and enter the Brady's Run Trail South, but we did not have any problems. *I do believe that it is better to plan your ride to go up this hill vs. down as it is steep. We found the traction better heading uphill.* There were also several water crossings, some over awkward or difficult ravines making it more challenging. Again, to enjoy this trail one needs to feel comfortable with this type of terrain as this is not a beginner's trail.

We were later told that there may be trail expansion on the south side and also equestrians may be able to ride on the other side of the road. If you live in the area, you may want to keep abreast of developments and possible trail expansion. And while visiting the park, take a drive down Brady's Run Road and view the waterway and adjoining areas; it is very scenic.

HISTORICAL INFORMATION:
Beaver County actually was part of Washington County and Allegheny County before the 1800s. In the mid 1700s, this region was a hub of Indian, English, and French trade activity. George Washington conducted French fort inspections and survey expeditions in this area and stories of his travels are abundant. By the late 1700s, this area was just being opened up for settlement as it was still Indian territory. The land was rich in resources resulting in farms thriving, the development of waterways, and eventually the mining of natural resources such as coal, sandstone, and limestone. Due to various factors the population was,

initially, slow to grow. Upon the arrival of the railroad in the mid 1800s, residents flocked to the area and the economy began to thrive.

Beaver County operates the following three County Parks: Brady's Run Park, Old Economy Park, and Brush Creek Park. Old Economy Park is located in an urban location and is less suitable to horseback riding. Brady's Run Park and Brush Creek Park permit horseback riding.

COURTESIES:
I would like to thank Heather Volkar for joining us on this ride and for making a trip to obtain a park map for our ride. We wish we could have had a longer ride, but even still it was a nice ride. Also, I would like to thank the friendly folks at the Penn State Cooperative Extension in Beaver County for answering my questions.

THINGS WE LEARNED THIS RIDE:
- At this park and several other County Parks in the surrounding region, I was approached by several park personnel resulting in many interesting conversations with maintenance workers and park managers. It was quite an education on my part as I encountered factors at play that I had not come upon previously in my travels. The discussions were random and usually occurred after I made my normal, well-intended inquiry with park personnel regarding equestrian use of the trails and whether they needed volunteers to assist in the maintenance. I learned that certain County Parks have more complex dynamics than the other parks that we have visited. A typically welcomed, simple question of how equestrians and other multiple users can help the park didn't have a simple answer or just a positive reply. I was told this County Park system has union employees and that there are sensitive issues at hand including that there have been many cutbacks on personnel. The point was that volunteers could be perceived as hurting job security. (I believe when trails are maintained on an ongoing basis, most routine trail volunteer work probably would not even comprise one part-time job. Equestrian trail volunteers snipping low hanging branches or putting trail markers along the trail really shouldn't significantly infringe on the type of functions the park personnel perform. I would think equestrians and other trail users could actually help park personnel by reporting problems. Plus, trail users have access to locations that park personnel do not regularly frequent, so they can react more timely or help keep the park informed.) I do appreciate and am sensitive to the various perspectives, but I know delays or red tape can greatly discourage well-intended volunteers and hurt the ability to use the trails, maintain them, preserve them, and attract those who are the customers of the park. I hope in these situations there can be a better way with fewer complications so everyone can align, work together, and make progress. Preservation of these beautiful parks for all to enjoy should be a

top priority or everyone, including trail users and the employees, loses in the long run.

- I was in the tack room on the other side of the trailer when a group of several dog walkers approached the vicinity of our trailers. Knowing this was a large area with plenty of room to pass by, and thinking these were adults who should have known better than to approach a horse's hindquarters with their dogs, I didn't guard the horses as they walked by. I soon noticed they were lingering; I walked around the trailer to check on the situation and was shocked to see that two of the dogs were being allowed to sniff the horse's hind legs while he was tied to the trailer. This was an accident waiting to happen. Luckily, my horse handled it better than I would have imagined and he stood quietly. I asked two of the women to pull their dogs away; I then explained the danger to the dogs, themselves, and my horse. Amazingly, I could see they still didn't get it! Going forward, I will not assume anything and if anyone, especially non-equestrians, is within close distance of my horses, I will be more protective and proactive.

NEARBY AND SURROUNDING AREA STABLES:
- Garden of Eden Stables (boarding, lessons, possible overnight stabling), Cranberry Township (724) 775-4470

NEARBY AND SURROUNDING AREA FARRIERS:
- B. Heckard, Beaver Falls (724) 846-0982
- K. Heinsberg, Fombell (724) 453-0380
- S. Keith, Harmony (724) 453-0747

32. Raccoon Creek State Park
DCNR
(Department of Conservation & Natural Resources)

Lasting Impression: Very nice! We were lucky to have beautiful weather while riding this very nice trail system through the woods and along waterways, while catching a beaver surfacing and submerging along the way. This is beaver country and it is full of beaver dams, along with the appearance of blue heron and an assortment of other birds and waterfowl.

Location: Raccoon Creek State Park is located in western Pennsylvania in southern Beaver County near the border of northern Washington County, west of Pittsburgh.

Length: *Day Ride Destination (however, if horse camping is permitted, also a weekend destination)*- The large park sprawls over 7,300+ acres and surrounds the 100+ acre Raccoon Lake. There are designated multiple-use trails (including horseback riding) of 16+ miles in the western part of the park. We met with a ranger and he informed us that some of the equestrian trails have been extended toward the eastern section. This number may have increased or will be increasing in the future.

Level of Difficulty: Mainly easy, at most moderate

Terrain: The terrain varies from flat to hilly, has gentle climbs, no "on the edge" paths, and consists of mostly good footing.

Horse Camping: The office shared with me that equestrian camping was "in the plans." So there is a possibility. I hope that the local equestrians nurture this idea, assist in the process, and influence and expedite a positive outcome. This is a beautiful location and could offer a nice weekend get-a-way.

Non-horse Camping: Yes

Maps and Info: DCNR, Raccoon Creek State Park, 3000 State Road Route 18, Hookstown, PA 15050, (724) 899-2200, website: www.dcnr.state.pa.us or www.state.pa.us, email: raccooncreeksp@state.pa.us. We did not see maps at the parking area, so call for maps in advance. The newest maps, which have a color cover, are of good quality and are helpful for staying on course. Also, ask for the "Western Section Map & Trail Guide" which is helpful for following the equestrian trails. For disability or other information, contact the Pennsylvania Bureau of State Parks (888) PA-PARKS. For information on Beaver County, contact the Beaver County Recreation and Tourism Department at (724) 891-7030, website: www.co.beaver.pa.us. To become a volunteer, contact the park office at the above number or call (724) 899-3611 or visit www.friendsofraccoon.com. If volunteering, don't forget to mention you are an equestrian!

Activities: Hiking, Biking, Horseback Riding Trails, Picnicking, Swimming, Boating, Fishing, Ice Fishing, Ice Skating, X-C Skiing, Sledding, Snowmobiling (designated roads), Group Tenting, Cabins, Camping, and Hunting
Fees for Trail Use: None
Permits for Day Trail Use: None
Comfort Station: Not at the trailhead or on trail (see map for other locations)

DIRECTIONS:
The equestrian trails are in the western part of the park. If traveling from the north, take the Pennsylvania Turnpike I-76 to Exit #28 and pick up I-79 south. Take I-79 south for 17.7 miles to Exit #60B. Take Exit #60B. (If traveling from the south, take I-79 north to Exit #60B.) Exit #60B will connect with Routes 60, 30, and 22. Follow signs to Route 30 and Route 22 west. (There is a small stretch of Route 60 before it becomes Route 30.) From I-79, take Route 60/Route 30 west for 7.1 miles. At this point Route 30 travels to the right. Do not go to the right on Route 30 (and ignore the Raccoon Creek State Park sign that takes you to the east side of the park); instead continue straight on Route 22. From this point, continue on Route 22 for another 10.9 miles to Route 18. (Basically, it's 18 miles from I-79 to Route 18.) Get off the ramp, make a left, and take Route 18 north for 4.5 miles. You will come to Route 168 on the left. Take Route 168 north for about 4.4 miles, slow down, and look for the lot on the right. There is a sign for equestrian parking. (If you see Pumpkin Hollow Road or Route 30, you have gone too far.) The gravel lot is a pull through with a separate entrance and exit (no backing necessary *if no vehicles are there* for those who do not like to back their trailers). A few large living quarter types or several average or standard 2-horse or 3-horse trailers can fit. There is a mounting platform and a tie rail. The trailhead is there and clearly labeled "Appaloosa Spur." That will lead you to the trails. As with all destinations, confirm all directions with the office prior to departing in case of any trailhead changes or rerouting.

THE TRAILS:
Raccoon Creek State Park has a 100 acre lake in the eastern section. At the time of our visit, the horse trails did not travel near the large lake, but were located around smaller waterways in the western and more rural section of the park. Yellow blazes mark the equestrian trail. The horse trails are multiple-use and shared with hikers and mountain bikers. Equestrians do use these trails regularly, but we did not see a lot of activity during our visit. The trails have names: Appaloosa Spur, Appaloosa, Nichol Road, Buckskin, Palomino, and Pinto Loop. There is much evidence throughout the park of old homesteads; while traveling through the west end of the Appaloosa trail, look for the remains of an old homestead site with its spring house nearby.

The designated equestrian trails are mainly easy. Some stretches may be considered moderate due to hills, but we found them to be predominantly easy and leisurely. This was relaxing too as we visited on a weekday and had the trails mostly to ourselves. The trails are very well marked and the map is easy to follow. Much of the trails have a canopy of shade making for a cool ride on a warm day. The terrain was very good throughout, except for the Appaloosa Spur which receives more traffic as it is the entrance to the trails. *There was a muddy stretch for a short stretch; but it could very easily be rerouted around those wet spots by just moving the trail over as the surrounding terrain is level with good bypasses. As this link is easily accessible, it could also be topped with fine stone dust which would resolve the mud.* We rode the Appaloosa Spur Trail to the Appaloosa Trail. There are yellow markers along the way which signify the equestrian trail path. We crossed over an intersection and made a left onto the Appaloosa Trail. The Appaloosa Trail was a scenic and serene trail through the woods and lead to a quiet, forest dirt road called Nichol Road. You will come to a mailbox and trail registry on the trail. Do stop and sign in. *This is a good chance to practice opening the mailbox for trail class; just don't let the horse spook and knock it over!* These sign-in lists monitor and reflect that there is an interest in the use of the trails. They can also provide support for funding for these trails as they indicate demand for the trails to the park management and the state. After the mailbox, we made a left onto Nichol Road and crossed a small wooden bridge where I (he was so fast no one else got to see him) was surprised by a beaver at work on his dam. He quickly submerged himself and took cover. After the bridge, we continued on the gravel/dirt forest road to the right and up the hill. We took the Palomino Trail loop to the left, which was very nice, then came back to the forest road, made a right, passed a totem pole, and continued back on Nichol Road to the small wooden bridge and beaver sighting. Continuing straight on Nichol Road, we picked up the Appaloosa Trail and headed back to the lot. The roads that we mention are dirt roads or service roads which are closed to motorized vehicles (other than DCNR patrol or emergency vehicles) and also function as trails. We did not see any activity on these roads except for one DCNR vehicle. The roads are of mostly dirt surface and narrow width and offer a trail like feel. We found them quite pleasurable. But don't be mistaken, you are not riding all roads. The roads provide links between the trails. There are also many wonderful single tracts that loop throughout the forest.

Raccoon Creek State Park's trails are wonderful as they travel through cool, dense forests winding around the rolling landscape. Some sections offer nice views and would most likely be very colorful in the fall due to the variety of plant life. I imagine they would also offer excellent views of the surrounding countryside when the leaves are off the trees. We rode these on a spring day and were treated to the scent of fragrant honeysuckle throughout the trail system.

Varied flora and fauna are abundant. Riding through the woods full of oak, pine, hickory, and other colorful foliage in the fall must be a treat. Throughout the year bird watching is popular; not only near the wildflowers, but throughout the park as there are many varieties of birds and waterfowl. While riding the trails, also look for grouse, pheasant, mink, opossum, red fox, skunk, turkey, heron, deer, and even bear. And look for the beavers; this is "Beaver County!"

Not within the equestrian network of trails, but one section that is of interest to visit without the horses, is the Wildflower Reserve and Interpretive Center in the eastern section of the park. This section is known for having one of the most unrivaled, diverse assortments of native wildflowers in the western half of Pennsylvania. Also within the park, is the Frankfort Mineral Springs locale; this was once a well known site in the 1800s, where folks traveled long distances to bathe in the mineral water for its alleged healing powers. The mineral springs are located in the central part of the park and can be viewed along the Mineral Springs (hiking) Trail. Also of interest, the Heritage (hiking) Trail travels along some of the early settlers' wagon roads.

HISTORICAL INFORMATION:
While traveling along Route 168 to the equestrian trailhead, you will pass the King's Creek Cemetery located in the southwest section of the park. Many of this area's settlers are buried in this cemetery. In the 1700s and 1800s, this region was once a wilderness where early settlers made their home and farmed the land. In the 1800s, the area also became attractive for its mineral springs. For generations to come, many sections remained farmland and open, undeveloped space. In the 1930s, some of the farmland was acquired by the National Park Service with the goal of preserving the land and for public enjoyment. Early construction of public use areas was achieved through the efforts of the Civilian Conservation Corps (CCC) and the Works Progress Administration (WPA). In the 1940s, this land was conveyed to the state. The Commonwealth of Pennsylvania now managed it, a dam was built, and Raccoon Lake was born. The area was developed into a State Park offering the variety of activities listed above. Raccoon Creek State Park is one of Pennsylvania's largest State Parks.

COURTESIES:
The folks at the Raccoon Creek State Park office were very helpful and we had very pleasant conversations. Thank you to Joe Hamilton, Eugene Hart, and also to a ranger by the name of Patrick who stopped to talk to us. Joe mentioned there is a good relationship with the equestrians that maintain the trail and the park. This park has a designated equestrian lot indicative of the positive rapport between its equestrian visitors and the office. I asked what we could do as equestrians and if there was any area for improvement on our part. I was told the one area of concern was that some sections of the trail were wet, and I was asked my opinion as how to resolve it to prevent further deterioration. Both John and I thought about this as we rode, and felt rerouting would be easy and inexpensive as it was only a few stretches that had a problem and the adjoining turf offered alternatives. It looked to us that the trail just needed to be moved over in most

cases, and there were only a few spots where some trail stone might need to be added for drainage and firm footing. It appears that this would be a good opportunity for the local riding groups to volunteer to assist.

On this trail ride, we had the pleasure of riding with our guides, Heather Volkar and Laverne Shearer, who joined us along with their horses, one a Puerto Rican Paso Fino and one a Tennessee Walker. Each horse was unique, very well behaved, and both an attractive representation of their breed. Our horses mixed well with them adding to an already very enjoyable ride at a lovely destination with good company. Our thanks to Heather and Laverne for joining us and for sharing this trail experience with us.

THINGS WE LEARNED THIS RIDE:
When riding in a county, pay attention to its name. It's for a reason, such as there being elk in Elk County (I knew that one), beaver in Beaver County, etc. When I was so excited over how many beaver I had seen while riding the trails at Raccoon Creek State Park, I was reminded I was riding in Beaver County. Oh yes, I felt quite "blonde" at that moment!

NEARBY AND SURROUNDING AREA STABLES:
* Rockytop Stables (boarding), Clinton (724) 375-6667

NEARBY AND SURROUNDING AREA VET SERVICES:
* J. Harthorn, Avella (724) 345-3350
* N. Loutsion, Canon Hill Vet Clinic Inc., Canonsburg (724) 746-4220

NEARBY AND SURROUNDING AREA FARRIERS:
* D. Bentrem, Burgettstown (724) 947-3411, (412) 580-4458 cell
* T. McClain, Clinton (724) 899-2135
* R. Buchko, Bridgeville (412) 498-5531 cell

33. Hillman State Park
DCNR

(Note: this is a Department of Conservation & Natural Resources State Park; however, this park is unique in that it is managed by the Pennsylvania State Game Commission.)

Lasting Impression: Wonderful! There is much beautiful primitive riding here with lots of potential. With an abundance of solid ground with a tough surface, it is very suitable for equestrian use, even after wet weather, and would be an absolutely ideal area for equestrian camping. I hope that this becomes a more established equestrian destination as I really enjoyed exploring this area.

Location: Hillman State Park is located just north of Route 22 on Old Steubenville Pike/Old Route 22 near the towns of Florence, Bavington, and Purdy in Washington County.

Length: *Day Ride Destination (possible weekend destination if there was camping)*- The sign at the entrance indicates the park consists of 3,653 acres. As this is undeveloped land in its primitive state, there is no estimate on miles of trails. But there are at least several hours of riding.

Level of Difficulty: Mostly moderate

Terrain: The terrain consists of rolling hills, meadows, woodlands, scenic pine forests, knoll after knoll of picturesque countryside, and exceptional footing even after heavy rains

Horse Camping: None, although this location and terrain is well suited to equestrian camping.

Non-horse Camping: None

Carriage Potential: There may be some carriage potential at this destination due to the dirt roads and wide open areas. Investigate first without the carriage to determine if this would be desirable for carriage driving.

Maps and Info: These trails aren't marked as this land has been preserved in its primitive state. Initially, I did have some trouble locating a map for Hillman since it is undeveloped and unique in its shared management. There was a little bit of confusion with the local offices as to who should provide information for Hillman due to it being a State Park that is managed by the Pennsylvania Game Commission. However, since Raccoon Creek State Park oversees Hillman State Park, you should be able to obtain a map from this source. Contact DCNR for Hillman State Park, care of Raccoon Creek State Park, 3000 State Route 18, Hookstown, PA 15050-1605, (724) 899-2200, website: www.dcnr.state.pa.us, email: raccooncreeksp@state.pa.us. When I called the Raccoon Creek State Park office, they referred me to the Pennsylvania Game Commission, Southwest Region Office, (877) 877-7137 or (724) 238-9523. The Game Commission did not have further information on the State Park but they did confirm that equestrians were permitted on the State Park land. (In the interest of time, I went another route to obtain a map but, by the time this goes to print, you should be able to obtain it from one of the above numbers.) If a suitable map isn't yet available when you plan to visit, try a local topographic map or some of the online mountain bike websites which offer maps. Do obtain the map in advance; a map will be helpful for following the trails and orienting via the road system.

Activities: Hiking, Biking, Horseback Riding Trails, and Hunting

Fees for Trail Use: None

Permits for Day Trail Use: None

Comfort Station: None

DIRECTIONS:
If traveling from the north, take the Pennsylvania Turnpike I-76 to Exit #28 and pick up I-79 south. Take I-79 south for 17.7 miles to Exit #60B. Take Exit #60B. (If traveling from the south, take I-79 north to Exit #60B.) Exit #60B will connect with Routes 60, 30, and 22. Follow signs to Route 30 and Route 22 west. (There is a small stretch of Route 60 before it becomes Route 30.) From I-79, take Route 60/Route 30 west for 7.1 miles. At this location Route 30 travels to the right. Do not go to the right on Route 30; instead continue straight on Route 22. From this point, continue on Route 22 for another 10.9 miles to Route 18. (This is the same approach as Raccoon Creek State Park; it's 18 miles from I-79 to Route 18.) Get off the ramp, make a left and take Route 18 north. Travel about a half mile to Old Steubenville Pike/Old Route 22 and the town of Florence. (Take note of a convenient ice cream stand on the corner. If you are riding during the summer, it will hold a welcome refresher from the heat upon your return.) Make a right on Old Steubenville Pike/Old Route 22 and travel 2 miles. Travel slowly as it is easy to miss this left. Just past a brown and beige mobile home, make a left onto a dirt and gravel road labeled with a brown sign, "Hillman Park, Pennsylvania State Gamelands." (If you travel and see a building with "Knowlton" on the right, you went too far.) After making the left, proceed about .1 miles. The road is very rough so take it slow. At the fork, make a right and travel a short distance (about .2 miles) to a loop at the end of the road. It is a large clearing with plenty of turn around and pull through room where many rigs (20+) can fit including large living quarter types. The ground was solid even though there had been recent rains. There are numerous trails heading out in all directions from this lot. We chose a few paths to explore.

THE TRAILS:
Hillman State Park is an undeveloped area in a primitive setting. It is unusual in that the land is owned by DCNR but DCNR has an agreement with the Pennsylvania State Game Commission where the Game Commission manages the land. It is important to distinguish that this tract of land is a State Park where equestrians are permitted and a separate unit from the nearby Bavington State Gamelands (owned by the Pennsylvania Game Commission) where horses were

not permitted at the time of our visit. The State Park is a large area; it's helpful to obtain a map in order to see the boundaries.

From the lot, there are many areas you can ride. One loop that was recommended to us leads to the northwest section of the park. We rode out of the lot in the direction we entered from, made a right, rode another 100 yards, made an additional right, and rode down hill on the old potted road. We rode about .5 miles and came to another road and made a left onto Sharon Road. We headed straight out this road, crossed over Haul Road, continued, and came to a bridge with wood planks. We traveled over the bridge, crossed Five Points Road, and traveled straight past two posts marking a trail entrance into the woods. Probably due to a wet spring, this was extremely overgrown during our visit and had almost closed. Making for a challenging section, the narrow path had retained water from the recent rains resulting in a muddy surface. (This connector trail was the only wet and difficult section that we encountered at Hillman State Park.) If this short stretch is trimmed, it should be much easier to ride, plus the sun could reach it and dry it. (There are many other ways to visit these trails; so you can avoid this section if the opening doesn't look like it has been improved.) We would have turned around; however, it was a brief stretch which opened up to a wider, very nice trail... so we kept on. After that one tract, the trails just kept getting better and better. (We also deviated to an attractive but narrow bike trail, but we had to turn around as we concluded it was too narrow and more suitable to bikes. Nevertheless, it did look very interesting and scenic as it wound through tall pines. The rest of the trails, paths, and old dirt roads were fine, wide, and had good footing. However, if you explore, you are bound to find a little bit of everything as there are so many different users of and purposes for these trails and dirt roads.) We continued bearing right and traveled through a wonderful pine forest and enjoyed a nice, wide, leisurely trail. We came to a Pennsylvania State Gamelands parking lot (it can be confusing as you are within the State Park boundary but you may see State Gamelands signs. I kept checking the map that we were still where we should be.) At the lot, there are two paths to take, one to the left which leads to open fields and one to the right which travels by a pond. We took the left and enjoyed the wide, mowed paths that travel through the rolling hills of the State Park. I particularly enjoyed the scenic landscape along this section and it reminded me of the trails at Elk County. There are numerous areas where one can explore as there are paths heading in different directions. We meandered around this locale and then took Haul Road and worked our way back to the parking lot along Haul Road. We found Haul Road to have a nice, wide shoulder and little, if any, traffic.

Having enjoyed the stretch of grass meadows in the northwest section so much, I convinced my co-riders to extend our ride and visit the eastern section of the park. I knew there would be a more horse friendly approach than the first one we took; and sure enough, there was. In fact, there were two at the lot. There is one wide path which travels a small embankment at the back of the parking lot (opposite from where you head in) which leads to open fields and rolling countryside. There is also a wide path we had seen to the right as you enter the lot. We decided to take the trail on the right side of the entrance. This was a nice, mowed grass stretch which linked into more rolling knolls with trails heading out in numerous different directions. Some of the grass had been mowed sometime within the past few weeks and other grass growth had become belly high. Surprisingly, it was very easy going as the ground was good and we still found it a pleasure to ride. John asked, "Wouldn't it be wonderful if there were more mowed stretches?" Perhaps, but even how it was, I found it relaxing and enjoyable. We just watched our step and enjoyed the scenery. I couldn't believe how good the ground was in spite of the very wet weather this particular spring. Toward the end of riding this section, we encountered two other riders. Until this point, we had only seen people in the lot and it was mostly mountain bikers. Upon our return to the lot, additional equestrians had arrived. This seems to be a popular place to ride for local mountain bikers, equestrians, and riding clubs; however, the large area seemed to absorb everyone very well. Much to their credit, it seemed that the bikers and riders were off to a good start. We shared trail information with some mountain bikers and, based on the friendly "hellos" in the lot, everyone seemed to get along very well.

Note: there is some water for the horses along the trail, but not much. Bring water with you as in the summer it can get quite hot riding in those open fields. If you choose to travel some of the more narrow paths vs. the open fields, watch out for thorn locust trees. Chaps may be well advised. In addition, there is the Miller Airport just outside the park in the northwest section and also there is a fenced grass field for model airplane flying. Neither impacted our riding nor did we encounter either in our travels.

COURTESIES:
Thank you to Elsie Hillman; I have been informed that her contribution of this land was the reason that today equestrians and others are able to enjoy it. Thank you Elsie; the land that I was told was once rough from strip mining is now a beautiful landscape of rolling hills and greenery! Thank you so much for preserving and sharing this land! Also, thank you to Matt Beaver for helping me obtain a map of this State Park which was very useful. Thank you to both DCNR and the Pennsylvania State Game Commission for your patience in sharing information on Hillman State Park during my many calls, and for your joint and cooperative effort in overseeing this land. And importantly, thank you for your continued support in welcoming equestrians on this land. I wish I lived closer to assist or volunteer where needed as this is truly a lovely destination with so many possibilities.

A very special thanks to Heather Volkar who we now consider part of our "Team Ride Pennsylvania." Heather was the person who introduced me to Hillman State Park, and rode with us at this trail destination along with many other trails in the area. Thank you for the pleasure of your company and for making us feel so welcome in your neck of the woods. Thank you to Jack Welch and Doug Bentrem for answering my many questions. They are affiliated with a local riding group, the Mountain Valley Trail Riders, which frequents these trails. You may want to watch for published scheduled rides which are open to the public as they could provide an introduction to the lay of the land at Hillman State Park.

NEARBY AND SURROUNDING AREA STABLES:
- Rockytop Stables (boarding), Clinton (724) 375-6667

NEARBY AND SURROUNDING AREA VET SERVICES:
- J. Harthorn, Avella (724) 345-3350
- N. Loutsion, Canon Hill Vet Clinic Inc., Canonsburg (724) 746-4220

NEARBY AND SURROUNDING AREA FARRIERS:
- D. Bentrem, Burgettstown (724) 947-3411, (412) 580-4458 cell
- T. McClain, Clinton (724) 899-2135
- R. Buchko, Bridgeville (412) 498-5531 cell

34. Bear Run
Moraine State Park
DCNR
(Department of Conservation & Natural Resources)

Lasting Impression: Bear Run offers a few hours of mostly easy riding through woodlands of pine and dogwood, along with an assortment of flora and wildlife plus numerous views of Lake Arthur.

Location: Moraine State Park is located in Butler County in northwest Pennsylvania near where I-80 and I-79 meet. Moraine State Park allows equestrians to choose between two different scenic trail systems, Bear Run and Swamp Run. Each is independent of each other, and requires you to haul to the different locations. There isn't a connecting trail between the two and they are actually located a good distance from each other. Bear Run is on the west side and Swamp Run is on the east side. This chapter is about Bear Run.

Length: *Day Ride Destination*- The Bear Run network of trails is roughly 8 to 9 miles, with some possible additional riding on connecting trails and dirt roads.

Level of Difficulty: Mostly easy, leisurely, gradual terrain, and scenic (some challenging sections due to deep mud, particularly in the section south of Porter's Cove in the Beaver Run section)

Terrain: Mostly of firm surface and overall not rocky (there are a few stretches that retain water so this is best visited after periods of dry weather)

Horse Camping: None

Non-horse Camping: Camping is not permitted within the park other than two designated, organized group areas.

Maps and Info: DCNR, Moraine State Park, 225 Pleasant Valley Road, Portersville, PA 16051-9650, (724) 368-8811, website: www.dcnr.state.pa.us, email: morainesp@state.pa.us. We did not see maps at the parking area, so call for maps in advance; a map will be helpful for following the trail and road system. For disability or other information, call (888) PA-PARKS.

Activities: Hiking, Biking, Bike Rentals, Horseback Riding Trails, Picnicking, Swimming, Sand Beaches, Fishing, Boating, Boat Rentals, Windsurfing, Sledding, X-C Skiing, Ice Skating, Ice Boating, Ice Fishing, Snowmobiling, Cabins, Organized Group Camping, and Hunting. There is a separate paved path on the north side of the park for bicyclists between the Bike Rental Building and the Marina Restaurant, and also a rugged mountain bike trail on the north shore. Hikers and bikers can also share some of the equestrian trails; however, we did not see any other users during our visit.

Fees for Trail Use: None

Permits for Day Trail Use: None

Comfort Station: Yes

DIRECTIONS:
Moraine is conveniently located near the intersection of I-79 and I-80. It is also near Route 422 and Route 528. To reach the Bear Run trails in the southwest section at Porter's Cove, proceed as follows. From the north, take I-80 to I-79 or just take I-79 and continue as indicated below to Route 488 east. We traveled from the south and the Pennsylvania Turnpike. From the Pennsylvania Turnpike I-76, take Exit #28 I-79 north. Take I-79 north for 19.5 miles to Route 488 east. You will see the Moraine sign. Get off the ramp and follow the sign to Route 488 east. However, as soon as you get off, make the first left onto Badger Hill Road (there will be signs for Moraine State Park and for Bear Run campground). Take Badger Hill Road 1.4 miles to a clearing adjoining the lake. *You will pass a nice tack shop on the right which has quite a bit of handy items if you forgot something or just want a fun place to shop with good prices. Even John had fun shopping with me as he picked up a nice pair of boots for a reasonable price.* You will come to the end of the road; basically, you'll know you are there as the road travels into the lake and you can't go any farther. There is a small lot to the right and down to the left which is shared with boat trailers. Both gravel lots would require some backing with a horse trailer but are doable. In the gravel parking area, only a few horse trailers can fit. We used it to turn the trailer then parked on the side of the grass. However, there is quite a bit of room for several trailers, including larger rigs, if you drive past the gravel area and park on the open grass area. It's a bit awkward as the grass area is on a slant, so proceed with caution and watch for soft areas. But the folks we met had no problem maneuvering around that turn and had plenty of space where they parked. You can pick up the trail by the picnic area and beyond the gate.

THE TRAILS:
Moraine State Park is a large area and surrounds Lake Arthur, which is over 3,200 acres and has about 40 miles of shore. There are two multiple-use trail systems at Moraine State Park, Bear Run and Swamp Run. There are not many trail markings but there are periodic lilac or purple trail markings to guide you. (This was a different color and stood out from the usual assortment of trail blazes.) The best way to find one's way around and see the most scenic sections is to ride with some folks who are familiar with the trails as we did. However, since the trail system is not huge like a State Forest system and with the map as reference, it should not be easy to get lost.

Bear Run offers a few hours of gentle riding beginning from Badger Hill Road at Porter's Cove. Porter's Cove also serves as a boat launch, although there are also numerous other boat launch locations on the lake. We visited during the week and it was quiet in this section; it is likely more hectic on the weekends. Motorized boats of 20 hp or less are permitted, along with sailboats, kayaks, etc., so horses need to be comfortable with the sight and sound of boats on the water. But the lot is a good size and there is some land buffer between the lake. Plus we only saw a boat or two in the lot and the trails in this section head away from the lakeside. None of the horses had any problem with the boats but, if your horses are sensitive to boats, you may want to park nearer to the gate and away from the launch, or ride the inland Swamp Run trails and stay clear of the lakeside. The park gate and access to the trails are located to the left as you enter the parking area. (There are picnic tables next to it.) Before heading out from Porter's Cove, observe that Badger Hill Road (the entrance road) heads into the lake and reappears on the other side. After traveling through the gate and heading to the right or in a northerly direction, you will want to come out on the other side where this road resurfaces. That should help you get your bearings as that road is the key connector. Once you rejoin the road, make a left and take the road which will lead you to the various loops in the northern section of the Bear Run trails. (The northern section of this old road is really not a "road" anymore and was not active with park vehicles or any motorized traffic during our visit.) This portion is clearly reflected on the map where the solid line indicating Badger Hill Road is interrupted by the lake and reappears as a broken line (indicating a multiple-use trail) on the opposite side of the lake. We headed north in a counter clockwise loop (we mostly kept to the trails on the map and a few of their arteries). You'll see many single paths headed in different directions. The first offshoot that we tried to take was closed due to mud from heavy rains throughout the spring season. However, we were able to head down the road and pick up other trails. We rode the loops in this section and, although it could be tricky, it was not easy to get lost as they return to the main road or trail as reflected on the map. One scenic loop leads to an attractive overlook by an orchard. Other than the sound of the highway in the distance, it was a very pretty section and felt very remote. We took several of the side single paths that looped off of the main dirt road. *Note: you can run into mud in some of the lower sections; we found these passable but some were challenging.*

We then headed south along Badger Hill Road to pick up the southeast section of the equestrian and multiple-use trails. This travels just below Porter's Cove and can be seen on the map. Shortly after entering this sector of the trails, there is a wonderful section of marshland trail with good photo ops and interesting waterfowl sightings including Osprey. Although this is lowland, fill had been brought in to elevate this section so you could continue on the trail. On this stretch, there is a nice sandy surface to ride and it is excellent. The trail path is surrounded by reeds and the cove. The area, which is ideal for wildlife, offers the opportunity to see a variety of animals both airborne and land-based. I loved the views in this short stretch. Shortly after this section, as you approach the wooded branch in the vicinity north and west of Pleasant Valley Road, we ran into a stretch of deep mud. This could be partially due to our visit being in spring, the recent rains, and the fact that this section is in the lower lying areas. However, I am hoping that if the stretch of deep mud is there throughout the year, it can be improved like the wonderful section before it. It wouldn't take much to improve it and it is really needed as the mud acts as a "shoe sucker." If the same fill could be extended just down the trail and for a few other muddy areas, the ride could be very good and easy throughout. (An inexpensive surface of broken up pavement and other clean fill was used already in the adjoining section, with crushed fine stone/sand added on top. This worked very well. A wooden walkway could also be laid as other parks do with low lying areas. I believe this too would be an easy fix.) If you choose to cross the mud, there is a nice loop of trails traveling along higher ground just beyond it. However, the muddy sections are few in regard to the overall trail.

We enjoyed our ride at Moraine as it is a lovely area, easy to get to, and has many views of the lake. There is also a very friendly local riding club, the National Horse Lovers Association, that has contributed to these trails, equestrian parking areas, and picnic grounds. You may want to watch for group planned rides and maybe lend a hand with the maintenance.

HISTORICAL INFORMATION:
Moraine State Park is named after the word moraine meaning the various types of earth and other sediment that collected from glacier activity long ago. Once, glaciers occupied this region contributing to its interesting and diverse landscape including the formation of lakes, creeks, and gorges. Deposits of soil, minerals, rocks, and the remains of whatever became lodged below the glacier comprise the foundation and terrain of Moraine State Park. There are rolling hills and woodlands that surround the lake. Native Americans were attracted to this location for its rich hunting grounds. When the early settlers occupied the region, the land was altered and converted into farms and for other uses. Its natural resources were tapped and the state of the land was greatly altered to meet the settlers' needs of the time. Components of the land including limestone, clay, shale, gravel, sand, coal, and natural gas were stripped resulting in deterioration and contamination of the landscape. By the late 1800s, Moraine natural resources were depleted and the area had become an unsightly landscape of coal mines, debris, and open wells. Fortunately, in the 1900s, interest was taken in restoring the area. Frank Preston and others formed the Western Pennsylvania Conservancy to repair and preserve the land. The Pennsylvania Department of Mines and Mineral Industries along with the Department of Forests and Waters also joined the restoration project and contributed greatly to undo the damage to the land and restore its former beauty. In the late 1960s, a dam was created resulting in Lake Arthur. By 1970, the transition was complete and Moraine State Park was officially opened and dedicated. Today, the surrounding land has been beautifully regenerated through the work of the above organizations and as a result of the contributions of many.

COURTESIES:

Thank you to all those individuals, groups, volunteers, and organizations who did such a beautiful job restoring Moraine to its natural landscape after mining and other operations had destroyed its former beauty. And of course, thank you to DCNR, including Obie Derr, for permitting equestrians and for making them feel welcome to enjoy this wonderful park on horseback. A very special thanks to Punch and Laurel Murphy and Sandy and Lee Benninger who personally joined us to ride and show us the trails. They are active members of the National Horse Lovers Association. Much to this club's credit, they have been involved in the maintenance and promotion of these trails. We really enjoyed our ride with this very nice group and are looking forward to meeting up with them again on future trail rides.

NEARBY:

- Terry Luster's Saddlery (located on Badger Hill Road on the way to the Bear Run parking lot), Portersville (724) 368-9483 (I went shopping here and later wished I had bought more as they had many nice items for reasonable prices.)
- National Horse Lovers Association, Butler (724) 865-3011

NEARBY AND SURROUNDING AREA STABLES:

- Reich Stables (boarding, located adjoining Moraine State Park), Portersville (724) 368-3092
- Anvil's Ring (boarding), Mars (724) 625-2682

NEARBY AND SURROUNDING AREA VET SERVICES:

- Silver Spring Equine, Portersville (724) 924-1402
- F. Haustovich, Mars (724) 625-9433

NEARBY AND SURROUNDING AREA FARRIERS:

- K. Heinsberg, Fombell (724) 453-0380
- R. Wilderoter, Glenshaw (412) 967-6099, (412) 298-2817 cell
- R. Laux, Worthington (724) 297-3001
- K. Heinsberg, Frombell (724) 453-0380
- S. Keith, Harmony (724) 453-0747

35. Swamp Run
Moraine State Park
DCNR
(Department of Conservation & Natural Resources)

Lasting Impression: Swamp Run is located in a remote section of Moraine State Park and offers diverse woodland riding that passes old homesteads, along with providing a nice area to take a lunch break and enjoy the view of Lake Arthur.

Location: Moraine State Park is located in Butler County in northwest Pennsylvania near where I-80 and I-79 meet. The Swamp Run Trail is on the east side of Moraine State Park.

Length: *Day Ride Destination*- There isn't an exact trail mileage listing for this area but you can ride the main trail which is estimated at about 9 miles plus additional branches and connectors. Swamp Run is the larger of the two trail systems at Moraine State Park due to there being many more miles of adjoining areas to explore and extend one's ride.

Level of Difficulty: There are dirt forest roads which are easy, and single paths that spin off from the main dirt road which can vary from moderate to challenging due to overgrowth, mud, or rocks. However, we found these sections passable and enjoyable as the trails led to some nice overlooks and views.

Terrain: The terrain is gentle. The main double tract path was mostly of solid surface; the single paths could vary due to a few clusters of rocks or mud after wet weather.

Horse Camping: None

Non-horse Camping: Camping is not permitted within the park other than two designated, organized group areas.

Carriage Potential: There is a large parking lot along with wide, dirt, park maintenance roads that also serve as the main trail and would likely make a nice carriage surface. Check with the office for more information.

Maps and Info: DCNR, Moraine State Park, 225 Pleasant Valley Road, Portersville, PA 16051-9650, (724) 368-8811, website: www.dcnr.state.pa.us, email: morainesp@state.pa.us. We did not see maps at the parking area, so call for maps in advance. A map will be helpful for following the trail and road system. For handicapped or other information, call (888) PA-PARKS.

Activities: Hiking, Biking, Bike Rentals, Horseback Riding Trails, Picnicking, Swimming, Fishing, Boating, Boat Rentals, Windsurfing, Sledding, X-C Skiing, Ice Skating, Ice Boating, Ice Fishing, Snowmobiling, Cabins, Organized Group Camping, and Hunting

Fees for Trail Use: None

Permits for Day Trail Use: None

Comfort Station: None at the parking area or trailhead

235

DIRECTIONS:

The Swamp Run trails are in the eastern section of Moraine State Park and are located north of the Propagation Area on the map. These trails can be accessed from a few directions. From the south, take the Pennsylvania Turnpike I-76 to Exit #39 Butler Valley/Route 8 north. Take Route 8 north to Butler (about 19 miles). Continue north through Butler on Route 8 to Route 422. From the intersection of Route 8 and Route 422, continue on Route 8 north for another 5.7 miles. Make a left onto Swamp Run Road. (If you are traveling from the north, take Route 8 south and turn right at Swamp Run Road.) Travel 1.5 miles on Swamp Run Road and you will come to a fork in the road. Do <u>not</u> go to the right which is Chestnut Ridge Road. Stay on Swamp Run Road which now becomes a dirt road. There is a park sign. Take the dirt road a short distance to a large clearing. There is plenty of pull through room and turn around room. Groups of rigs can fit, including several large living quarter type rigs or 20 or so smaller horse trailers. The trails lead off to the right side of the road (as you drive in), both at the lot location and via the dirt roads. The propagation area is on the left past the lot and is off limits to horses as it contains wet areas and lowlands.

THE TRAILS:

To pick up the trails, we rode in the direction opposite the entrance and picked up a single path to the right. It was not marked, but was easy to see. There is a main trail which is a dirt park maintenance or access road which travels throughout the Swamp Run location and is reflected on the map. It also serves as a snowmobile trail in the winter. It is marked by orange diamonds. The dirt park road or double tract offers mainly easy riding, is wide, clear throughout, and is easy to follow. We did not see any park maintenance vehicles along this double tract, or any other activity. There are many single path offshoots along the way that travel in loops and offer a variety of interesting riding. However, they can be challenging due to overgrowth as the woods were very dense during our visit. A few portions needed to be cut back and cleared; sometimes it was so thick and narrow it was hard to see where the trail proceeded. But it was spring, rain had been abundant, and everything was bursting out; this was one year where it was hard to keep up with the growing flora. With some trimming, it wouldn't take much to reopen the trails which are well worth maintaining as these branches travel in some of the prettiest portions of Swamp Run. This may not be an issue later in the riding season during the fall and winter.

The offshoots are not marked and basically have just evolved over the years. Most are not difficult to follow as they usually just branch off, travel in a loop, and rejoin the main dirt, double tract. The paths are lightly worn but with a little looking are usually recognizable. Still, in case the trails have become weathered or grown over, it is helpful to travel with someone who knows the trails to avoid taking a wrong turn or missing some of the more scenic sections. As for the terrain, the main dirt road was mostly good. There were a few areas in the offshoots that were muddy or rocky but we did not find either to be a significant problem. We took our time and the horses were able to pick through those few sections that did have rocks. We rode in several loops traveling around the main dirt roads. One of these loops is particularly scenic as it leads to a grove of picnic tables which overlooks the lake and views of the various watercraft traveling its course. It is a nice place to stop and have lunch. Throughout our ride, we did not see any other trail users. In fact, the only place we saw anyone was on the watercraft. Ultimately, we returned to the lot via the main dirt park road. I liked the Swamp Run trail system as there were many interesting, old home sites, evidenced by a remaining chimney, stone wall, ornamental trees and/or a spring house along the paths. The trails are in a remote section and some of the views along the lake are both beautiful and tranquil.

Some of the dirt park roads or double tracts may have potential for carriage trails. Carriage folks may want to look into this and contact the park office if they are interested. Throughout the park, stay clear of the beaches as pets and horses are not permitted near this area for sanitary and safety reasons. As certain trails travel within view of the lake, horses should be comfortable with a variety of boats sailing or cruising by.

COURTESIES:
Thank you to Obie Derr and DCNR for welcoming equestrians at Swamp Run. Also, thank you to our guides, Punch and Laurel Murphy and Sandy and Lee Benninger, along with the rest of the helpful and friendly members of the National Horse Lovers Association.

THINGS WE LEARNED THIS RIDE:
The folks that we rode with told us an interesting story of how there was a scenic location on the lake that was ideal for taking a break and enjoying the view, but there was nowhere to sit. They wanted to put picnic tables at that spot but had no way to get them there. So they decided to innovate; they built a makeshift raft with barrel floats, and shipped the picnic tables to this area that was not otherwise accessible. They were successful and now there are tables for all to use. (We lunched at that picnic area and it offered a lovely location to take in the view of the lake.) Where there's a will, there's a way!

NEARBY:
- Terry Luster's Saddlery (located on Badger Hill Road on the way to the Bear Run parking lot), Portersville (724) 368-9483
- National Horse Lovers Association, Butler (724) 865-3011

NEARBY AND SURROUNDING AREA STABLES:
- Reich Stables (boarding, located adjoining the Bear Run section of Moraine State Park), Portersville (724) 368-3092

- Anvil's Ring (boarding), Mars (724) 625-2682

NEARBY AND SURROUNDING AREA VET SERVICES:
- F. Haustovich, Mars (724) 625-9433
- Silver Spring Equine, Portersville (724) 924-1402

NEARBY AND SURROUNDING AREA FARRIERS:
- K. Heinsberg, Fombell (724) 453-0380
- R. Laux, Worthington (724) 297-3001
- R. Wilderoter, Glenshaw (412) 967-6099, (412) 298-2817 cell
- S. Keith, Harmony (724) 453-0747

Signs of beaver activity along the trail

36. The Babcock Division
Gallitzin State Forest
BOF-DCNR

(Bureau of Forestry/Department of Conservation & Natural Resources)

Lasting Impression: This is a work in progress in a pristine setting. Currently, there is a lengthy tract that offers hours of pleasant, leisurely riding. This trail is like a rail-trail in that it travels in one direction; but there are plans for the construction of loops. The stretches that we rode were gorgeous, maintained paths. I didn't mind backtracking as it was a different scenic perspective each way; but once the loops are completed, this will be an even nicer trail system.

Location: The section of the Babcock tract where equestrians can ride is located north of Route 56, just west of the town of Ogletown. It is situated on the Appalachian Plateau in mostly Somerset County.

Length: *Day Ride Destination*- Gallitzin State Forest totals roughly 18,000 acres and there are a few separate tracts which are in Bedford, Indiana, Cambria, and Somerset Counties. The largest is the Babcock Division, comprising over 13,000 acres, which is located in Somerset County. This chapter will focus on that division. At the time of our visit, the ride was about 14 miles round trip; there are plans to add at least 5 miles of additional loops or connectors.

Level of Difficulty: The trails we rode were easy to moderate. (You do need to know how to correctly connect with these trails to avoid one difficult rocky section. This rocky section is a short stretch at the beginning of the Lost Turkey Trail at the Babcock lot. Equestrians should not ride this section, but instead follow the road to the left to connect with the multiple-use trails. From there the trails are very nice and mainly easy.)

Terrain: Ideal terrain, durable surface, grass covered wide paths, only periodic scatterings of rock

Horse Camping: None

Non-horse Camping: Backpack camping is permitted.

Maps and Info: DCNR, Bureau of Forestry District #6, Gallitzin State Forest, P.O. Box 506, Ebensburg, PA 15931, (814) 472-1862, email: fd06@state.pa.us, website: www.dcnr.state.pa.us. Kudos to the folks that maintain these trail systems as there were well stocked maps at the parking area and along the trail. Also, there were interesting pamphlets telling the history of the area. In case the maps are out, call in advance for a map. Although the maps need to be much more detailed (road names, map site markers, etc.), they are still helpful to visualize the lay of the land and the snowmobile trails. Ask for the Public Use Map for Gallitzin State Forest (green cover), the large Lost Turkey Trail Map, and the snowmobile trail map. Much of the Lost Turkey Trail is hiking only. But within the section of Gallitzin State Forest on the north side of Route 56 to the northern boundary of the State Forest on the Babcock tract, there is a portion of the Lost Turkey Trail which is shared with multiple users, including equestrians. Do not cross into the State Gamelands unless you receive permission from the State Gamelands office.

Activities: Hiking, Horseback Riding Trails, Picnicking, X-C Skiing, Snowmobiling, and Hunting

Fees for Trail Use: None

Permits for Day Trail Use: None

Comfort Station: None (there are facilities at the picnic area opposite the lot where you park; however, do not bring horses near the picnic grounds or south of Route 56)

DIRECTIONS:

The trailhead is opposite the Babcock picnic grounds on Route 56 between the towns of Ogletown and Windber. To reach the parking area, take Route 219 to Route 56 east. Head east on Route 56 toward Ogletown. Follow signs (where available) and proceed 7.9 miles on Route 56. You will see the Babcock picnic area on the right and an area on the left with split rail fencing at the entrance. We found the entrance a little tight for our long rig, but the lot had plenty of room once you were past the entrance. *Again a narrow entrance and a big lot!* The lot can fit several rigs assuming no other users are blocking the lot. There is a sign, along with a well stocked map and information pavilion. As you face to the rear of the lot, do not proceed to the right which is a short stretch of very rocky trail (labeled The Lost Turkey Trail), instead travel to the left (there is a snowmobile sign) to a dirt/gravel road and make a right onto the shoulder of the dirt/gravel road heading in the direction away from Route 56.

THE TRAILS:

Gallitzin State Forest includes the Clear Shade Wild Area, the Charles F. Lewis Natural Area, and the Clark Run Gorge which is very scenic and has a multitude of waterfalls. The tract that we rode is in the Babcock Division which is north of Route 56. The Lost Turkey Trail, which is a lengthy and mostly hiking trail, travels through Gallitzin State Forest, State Gamelands, some private lands, and ultimately to Blue Knob State Park. There is also a snowmobile path that joins the Lost Turkey Trail for much of its path. Equestrians must be very careful to stay on the trails where they are permitted within the State Forest, and not to travel outside the borders of the State Forest or onto State Game Commission land unless they have permission. When I contacted the Gallitzin State Forest office, they were very specific about where we could ride and where we could not. Gallitzin State Forest has a cooperative agreement with the neighboring land managers; please do not exceed these borders so we remain welcome. Equestrians can only ride from the lot to the area of the 17.6 mile marker on the Lost Turkey Trail map and then must turn back as that is the boundary of the State Forest. The map which reflects this mark can be obtained along the trail or from the office. (State Forest boundaries are marked by white blazes on the trees but that can be confusing as we have seen State Gamelands also use the white marker. Sometimes an emblem indicating whose territory it is accompanies the white blazes.) The State Forest office did explain to me that the trail was not a loop; however, they also said connectors are planned for loops to be established. So this would be like riding a rail-trail in that one would do some backtracking. The John P. Saylor trail system is on the south side of Route 56. The John P. Saylor is a hiking (only) trail network as it travels through some environmentally sensitive areas and bogs. *Unless bridges have been constructed or improvements have been made, the word "bog" always alerts me that the area is likely not one for attempting to bring a horse.*

We proceeded out of the snowmobile lot and followed the snowmobile signs. At first, we headed to the right (facing the back of the lot) by the sign which says "Lost Turkey Trail." Immediately, the trail went from a nice single, dirt path to one of large clusters of rocks. Do not approach the trail from this entrance; we found out later that this short section is really for hiking and it is rough. We turned back. After having to turn back so quickly, we weren't sure what to expect of the terrain and we pondered where we would ride. Then we decided to head out the left of the lot (facing the rear) by the snowmobile sign. We crossed the road by some logging operations and hooked into some wide, grassy paths of good, durable surface. We thought we had found some nice trails and that these paths would go somewhere as they were maintained in the beginning. But unfortunately, from what we could tell, it was straight out and straight back and not for a long distance. So we returned to the dirt road and continued down its path. (This road does permit motorized vehicles and is active, so exercise caution. There is usually plenty of shoulder to move to in the event of traffic.) We came upon a gate to the right. There wasn't a sign indicating this was the trail but we thought we would try it as there was an inviting, wide, grass covered trail. We took this and headed in the opposite direction from the parking area. This was just farther down and past the rocky section that we encountered earlier. It turned out that the one rocky section was not an extremely long section, so all you need to do is bypass that one short stretch of rocks. (Since every other part of the trail was of exceptional quality, that brief section could be easily converted to multiple-use as all it needs is a little clearing and fill so multiple users can travel directly from the lot and avoid any roads.) We then were in our glory as the trail became perfect. It was a tough and durable surface of grass and dirt, perfect for horses, mostly gradual, nicely maintained, and scenic as it travels along some high points at the top of the mountain. We couldn't fully appreciate the view due to the leaves on the trees but it must be even more spectacular in the late fall.

We continued along this trail for quite some time. There were places to water the horses along the trail. Throughout (other than the one rocky section) the turf remained consistent in quality. It wasn't muddy, there were only a few rocks, and

241

the terrain was solid. Some of these sections were where trains once hauled timber off the mountain and teams of draft horses pulled heavy logs over the surface throughout each day. The ground for the old railroad corridors, and logging and mountain roads had to be a durable surface to stand up to the extreme weight being hauled along their paths.

The trail descends the mountain and this was really the only (perhaps) moderate section that we encountered. It wasn't steep or "on the edge." In fact I found it easy to continue. (Later, on our return trip, the climb necessitated periodic breathers for the horses but we didn't find it to be an extreme ascent.) Ultimately, we encountered a road where the trail continued on the other side. We knew we only had a short section to ride before we reached the State Forest boundary and would soon have to turn back. We made a right on the dirt road wondering if there was a connector but there wasn't one. We rode a short distance and saw an attractive private property with log cabins surrounded by a very high wire fence. The unusual fencing, along with the beauty and interesting log cabins, aroused our curiosity. We checked our maps and brochures, and upon reading them we realized this locale had historical significance. This property is owned by the Babcock family for which this portion of Gallitzin State Forest is named. The Babcock family began their lumber business in the late 1800s. The Babcock lumber business grew and was soon operating in several states. They had a reputation for quality and were highly successful over the years, so much so the company is still in existence today. *How's that for good management!* Interestingly, this same company once owned the land which is now Great Smokey Mountain National Park, Cherokee National Park, and other popular public destinations. Fortunately, they sold these lands to the federal and state governments and we have them today to enjoy. The fenced locale that we had just observed is the remaining private property of the Babcock family. As we rode down the road, we enjoyed seeing the original log cabin structures including the lodge or social hall. Since this is private property, you cannot visit or approach the grounds. However, you can view it from a respectable distance as you travel the trail.

About the time we saw the Babcock compound, we weren't really sure where to continue our ride. Brenda and I discussed how we wished we had the phone number of a mutual acquaintance who knows these trails. (His name is King and he is a local equestrian and trail boss for the Chestnut Ridge Club rides). If we had his phone number, he would surely be able to tell us how to proceed. Just at that moment, and I kid you not, out of the woods rode King on his white horse. It looked like something out of a movie and was perfect timing! Well we chatted with King and learned which way we needed to go. King set us straight and we headed back along the trail. (Thank you King!) You can continue and cross the road to ride a short section of trail beyond this point, which makes a loop and returns back to this road. Be extra careful not to leave the State Forest border at this locale. We now needed to backtrack as there wasn't a connector. However, I always say that backtracking through scenic areas offers a different perspective. One can see things they didn't see before. I was right as the trails were just as beautiful and as interesting riding in the opposite direction. Once we came to a few branches of trails, we thought we had chosen a nice grass stretch to continue back to the lot. But unfortunately, it led to the rocky section we wanted to avoid. To avoid this happening to you, bear right on the trail and head toward the main dirt/gravel road as you return to the parking area.

We enjoyed this trail system and are grateful that the Gallitzin State Forest welcomes equestrians. We are looking forward to the creation of the new multiple-use loops. I am sure they will be nice as there are many sectors with good terrain that would have easy access to extend the trails via loops.

HISTORICAL INFORMATION:
There is a Prince Gallitzin State Park and a Gallitzin State Forest which are at two different and separate locations. This chapter is about Gallitzin State Forest. Gallitzin State Forest derives its name from Prince Demetrius Gallitzin who, in the late 1700s, founded a mission in the vicinity of the Cambria County tract. Prince Gallitzin was born in 1770 into wealth and nobility in what is now the Netherlands. His father was a Russian nobleman of the highest echelon of his time and his mother was the daughter of an officer who served under Frederick the Great. Prince Gallitzin was afforded a life of privilege, travel, and the best education of his time. His family had resided in many parts of Europe including Paris. As a result of the French Revolution's immobilizing effect on the nobility in Europe, it was resolved that Prince Gallitzin would travel to America. His interests turned to religious training. Under the first Archbishop of Baltimore, he became the second American ordained priest. Fulfilling an assignment in the Allegheny region and recognizing the need for a Catholic missionary, and with a desire to attract more Catholics to the area, he bought up land in the Alleghenies to sell at reduced cost. His choice of faith was not met with approval by the Russian government and he was cut off from his inheritance. He had chosen to forsake all of his inheritance for his religion and also chose to live without comforts in a small log structure in the Allegheny Mountains. There he remained and preached for over 40 years, even throughout many years of grave illness, until his death in 1840 in Loretto. Demetrius Gallitzin was and is considered by many to be a great Apostle of his faith as he is credited for bringing over ten thousand Catholics to this region.

There is also the story of the lost children of the Alleghenies. In the mid 1850s, two small children had wandered off from their home and were lost. An extensive search was undertaken but not successful. By the time they were found they had succumbed to the elements. There is a monument to these children in the vicinity of Hog Back Ridge along the Lost Turkey Trail near Blue Knob State

Park. Over a century later, two adults were also lost in this region. But this story had a happy and humorous ending. In the mid 1970s, the Youth Conservation Corps was assigned the task of constructing what would come to be known as The Lost Turkey Trail. When the leaders of the project, the manager and director, ventured out on trail, they became lost. Partially to blame, someone had misplaced a marker. When they finally made their way back, news spread, and the youth of the camp expressed, "The two head turkeys were lost on the trail." The name stuck and the trail was called "The Lost Turkey Trail."

COURTESIES:
Many thanks to Julie and Brenda Gottfried for joining us on this ride. Julie and Brenda have joined us on a few rides and it is always a pleasure. Also thank you to Nancy Gable who told us about these trails and whose father, long ago, rode many trails in this vicinity. Nancy shared some of the tales of the area including the story of the lost children of the Alleghenies.

NEARBY AND SURROUNDING AREA VET SERVICES:
- Dr. Knepper, Windswept Equine Center, Berlin (814) 267-5617
- H. Croft, Stahlstown (412) 593-6111
- M. James, Martinsburg (814) 793-3566 (use (814) 793-9226 only if he can't be reached at other number)

NEARBY AND SURROUNDING AREA FARRIERS:
- J. Lynn, Ligonier (724) 238-0180
- T. Awckland, New Paris (814) 733-4996

37. Other Trails, Trails in Progress, & Possible Future Equestrian Trails

This is a list of current trails or future possibilities. Please note: we rode all locations listed in detail in Chapters 1 though 36 of this book. We were unable to ride some of the following due to uncooperative weather or they were not yet established. You can contact the listed numbers or addresses for more information, or do a search on the web for the latest information.

Hell's Hollow, McConnell's Mill State Park (existing trail system):

Hell's Hollow doesn't sound very pleasant in name but it is supposed to be a very nice trail system. We had this locale in our trails to be covered for the book. But, unfortunately, this location experienced extreme weather conditions for an extended period of time prior to our visit. This had taken its toll, and the terrain had not had the opportunity to dry out. In the interest of not adding stress to surface areas, we had to forgo our visit. However, we have heard some nice feedback regarding this location and are providing the following information if you would like to visit when circumstances are more favorable.

Location: McConnell's Mill State Park is located near the intersection of Route 422 and Route 19 in Lawrence County near the Butler County border. This is close to Moraine State Park but is a separate tract.

Length: Mileage wasn't available but we were told there are at least 4 or 5 hours of riding.

Maps and Info: Moraine/McConnell's Mill State Parks Complex, 225 Pleasant Valley Road, Portersville, PA 16051-9650, (724) 368-8811, email: morainesp@state.pa.us. When I first inquired, the individual I spoke with was not familiar with where equestrians are permitted to ride. If this occurs, just ask to speak to someone knowledgeable with the trails at Hell's Hollow, or ask to speak to Obie Derr. *I have corresponded with Obie and he was always very helpful.*

Permits/Fees for Day Trail Use: None

Directions: As we did not ride this locale, these directions were provided to us, courtesy of the National Horse Lovers Association. From Ellwood City, take Route 65 north for about 4 miles. Make a right at Frew Road (you will see a church at the turn). Take Frew Road to a stop sign; make a right, and then another quick right. You should now be on Center Church Road. You will pass a 'Y' in the road. Do not make a right onto Hogue Road, but rather continue straight or bear left which is Heinz Camp Road. Take this a short distance, travel up a hill, and you will see a lot on the left. Ask the office for a copy of a map or brochure of McConnell's Mill State Park. This approach is reflected on the map. You can also contact the National Horse Lovers Association, who frequent these trails, for more information; members can partake in their rides at this destination. Membership applications can be obtained by calling (724) 865-3011 or by watching local publications for more information.

Courtesies: Thank you to Obie Derr who has been wonderful in making equestrians feel welcome at this location. Also, thank you to Don Cramer for providing map information and directions. I wish we could have visited this locale before this book release but we do expect to visit with you in the future. Thank you also to the National Horse Lovers Association for providing information about and directions to this locale.

Brush Creek Park, Beaver County Park (existing trail system):

We planned to visit Brush Creek but, due to the extreme weather conditions in western Pennsylvania, we were told that the grounds would likely be very soft or muddy. We did not want to risk damage to the trail surface so we had to cancel our ride. Hopefully, we will have the opportunity in the near future to visit this locale as we were told it is a very nice area.

Location: Beaver County is located in western Pennsylvania near the Ohio border. Brush Creek Park is a Beaver County Park and is situated near the towns of Hazen and Ellwood City in the northeast section of the county.

Length: Brush Creek Park is the smaller of the two Beaver County Parks that permit horses and contains about 600 acres. The park only lists a few miles of trails but adjoining trails lengthen the ride. Other sources indicate up to 14 miles of trails.

Maps and Info: For information on Brush Creek Park, contact Brush Creek Park, 526 Brady's Run Road, Beaver Falls, PA 15010, (724) 846-5600 or (724) 846-3509, website: www.co.beaver.pa.us/parks/brush.htm. For disability information, contact (724) 891-7030.

Activities: Hiking, Horseback Riding Trails, and Picnicking (Beaver County Parks do not permit hunting)

Fees for Trail Use: None

Permits for Day Trail Use: None

Directions: Please note: these directions were shared by the park office as we did not ride this trail system. To reach Brush Creek Park, from Ellwood City, take Route 65 south, make a left onto Route 588. If you are traveling north on Route 65, make a right onto Route 588. You will head east on Route 588 into the park's main entrance. For a visit during the week, the office recommended parking at Lot #1. Lot #1 is on the right and can be seen on the map. On weekends, this lot is not to be used due to soccer games and various events at that location. Also, during the week, another location mentioned by the office is Lot #7. Enter the park; continue all the way around the park drive to Lot #7. This is near the covered bridge and playground. You can park at Lot #7 and pick up the trail on the other side of the bridge. This lot is suggested only for during the week as the covered bridge is a popular wedding location on weekends. For weekends, the office recommended parking at Lot #8. To reach this lot, travel all the way around the park on the main park road. You will see sign #8. Pass the bridge, go to the top of the hill, see the sign, and make a left. We were told this lot can only accommodate smaller 2-horse or 3-horse trailers. Local riders indicated the trails travel through some very scenic areas.

North Park, Allegheny County Park (existing trail system):

Location: North Park is located north of Pittsburgh in Allegheny County.
Length: North Park comprises about 3,000 acres. Horses are only permitted on designated trails which totals a few to several miles.
Level of Difficulty: The trails are not difficult; but the road crossings can be. We rode this but did not cover this trail in detail in a chapter in this book as horse and rider need to be experienced and comfortable with crossing busy park roads (paved). This is not a destination that will suit all riders. At one time you could connect easily throughout the park and between crossings, but changes within the park and external development now limit options. Yet there remain some very nice areas within the park with old growth woodlands, and local equestrians still ride these trails. If you do not mind a shorter ride and want to just park at the show grounds and meander throughout a limited area, this can make a nice ride. As sections of the park interrupt the trail, try to go with someone familiar with the park so you know where to pick up the trails and how to safely cross the roads. Exercise caution at all crossings. If you travel on your own, bring the map. It is not detailed but it will help you as the trails have minimal or no markings.
Terrain: The trails are single and sometimes double width dirt tracts that travel through wooded areas and are of a good surface.
Horse Camping: None
Maps and Info: County of Allegheny, Parks Department, 542 Forbes Avenue, 211 County Office Building, Pittsburgh, PA 15219-2496, (724) 935-1766
Activities: Hiking, Biking, Horseback Riding Trails, Golf, Picnicking, Swimming, Fishing, and Ball Fields (The largest of the nine Allegheny County Parks, North Park contains one of the biggest man-made lakes in the region with over four miles of shoreline, offering a prime destination for fishing enthusiasts.)
Fees for Trail Use: None
Permits for Day Trail Use: None
Comfort Station: Yes, at the show grounds parking area and other locations
Directions: Take Route 8 north from I-76. At Route 910, make a left or head west on Route 910. You will come to a four-way intersection. Make a left onto Pearce Mill Road and follow signs into North Park. Look for a right by Kummer Road (located before the skating rink and before you enter the core of the park). Take Kummer Road, proceed up the hill, and follow signs to the show grounds. Parking is on the right. There is plenty of room to park and maneuver a rig. Once at the arena, to link with the trails, either travel across the road in the direction of the golf course and make a right into the woods (not marked), or stay

on the side of the show ring and circle around the entrance to the development next to the show grounds. The trail is just beyond and along a wooded path which parallels Kummer Road for a stretch. There is also a trailhead at the opposite end of the lot. Ask for the "Trails of North Park" photocopy 8.5" x 11" map which shows an overview (not detailed) of the equestrian trail.

The Allegheny Passage, Youghiogheny River Trail, a.k.a. the Yough Trail (existing multiple-use rail-trail):

Several trail groups, including the Allegheny Trail Alliance, have joined together to establish this amazing, long rail-trail that is part of a planned system to connect with the C&O Canal towpath in Maryland, resulting in a continuous path from Pittsburgh to Washington. The Allegheny Passage connects from Pittsburgh to Cumberland, Maryland totaling over 200 miles. Once joined with the C&O Canal towpath, the total linked system will exceed 300 miles.

There are different names for different sections of The Allegheny Passage and are reflected on The Allegheny Passage map. The Youghiogheny River Trail is part of The Allegheny Passage and is located in the middle section of the trail system. Hikers and bikers are permitted throughout the length of trail but equestrians are requested to travel the more rural areas such as the middle link (on the grassy shoulder) between Boston and Connellsville, and the southeast tract (grassy section) between Rockwood and Garrett. *If you visit the heart of Ohiopyle, you will see why some sections are not suitable to equestrian use (see the Ohiopyle chapter). Ohiopyle is one of the most popular sections of The Allegheny Passage, but is in a hub of activity, much too congested for the average horse and rider. Just check out the huge trestle which crosses the river at Ohiopyle as an example of what one could encounter at certain locations along this rail-trail. If you like to hike or bike, this section is a must visit. Even just a drive into town (without the rig) is well worth it to enjoy its beauty, partake in its activities, and see its sights.* We visited sections of this trail on foot but did not cover this trail on horseback for this book.

I asked the Allegheny Trail Alliance for directions to a lot suitable for equestrians in the section between Boston and Connellsville. They indicated the West Newton lot is popular with equestrians and can be reached by taking the Pennsylvania Turnpike I-76 to the New Stanton exit and taking Route 70 west. Take Route 70 west to Route 31 north into West Newton. Travel through town, there will be a steep hill (the office indicated equestrians do use this approach), a bridge, and then the lot is on the left. There is also a large lot in Boston and Connellsville. Before using any approach, check for grade and suitability. In regard to the lower section between Rockwood and Garrett, I was told the lot in Garrett is sufficient to accommodate horse trailers. Watch for possible news of an equestrian friendly campground in the lower region between Rockwood and Garrett.

For more information and a map, contact the Laurel Highlands Visitors Bureau at (800) 333-5661, website: www.laurelhighlands.org. Information can also be obtained from the Allegheny Trail Alliance (ATA), email: atamail@atatrail.org, website: www.atatrail.org, or contact (888) 282-2453. We plan to visit this rail-trail in the near future. I would like to thank Sandra Finley (at the ATA office), the Allegheny Trail Alliance, the Fayette County Horseowners Association, and all the other individuals and groups who support and maintain this rail-trail, and also all those who have welcomed equestrians on portions of this trail.

Note: it is requested that equestrians stay on the grassy sections of the trail. I have been told that, recently, equestrians have been riding on fresh laid gravel. Doing so can quickly cause disfavor with other users and land management. Please abide by the rules, and only ride where designated so that we may remain welcome on these trails.

Rock Run (formerly the K&J Coal Company grounds), Cambria/Clearfield Counties (in process, future trail system):

Rock Run is located near the border of Cambria and Clearfield Counties. There are about 6,000 acres, and plans are to divide the area into an ATV section and a non-motorized, multiple-use section (including horses). Initial grants and funds have been secured to begin this project. The K&J Coal Company ceased operations and this area has remained vacant for several years. The Cambria County Conservation and Recreation Authority acquired the land and will oversee its transition into a recreation area. For more information, watch for developments via their website: www.ctcnet.net/cccra or by contacting the Cambria County Conservation and Recreation Authority, 401 Candlelight Drive, Suite 234, Ebensburg, PA 15931; or visit www.dcnr.state.pa.us. Thank you to the Cambria County Conservation and Recreation Authority for considering equestrians in your plans, and to Laurel Murphy for sharing news of this developing trail system.

Susquehannock State Forest, Northwest Section (possible future trail):

There is talk of a new trail system to be established in the northwest section of Susquehannock State Forest. For information, call (814) 274-3600 or contact Susquehannock State Forest, 3150 East Second Street, PO Box 673, Coudersport, PA 16915-0673, or email: fd15@state.pa.us.

Settler's Cabin Park, Allegheny County Park (possible future trail destination):

This one was interesting and the only one of its kind that we visited. I had numerous conversations with various representatives before our visit confirming that horseback riding was permitted at Settler's Cabin Park, along with directions regarding where to park. This locale is 8+ hours from our home so we couldn't just stop by beforehand to see what was available. Although we drove an additional 1½ hours from camp, fortunately, we decided to check it out in advance and did not haul the horses from camp. We arrived to find the recommended lot (alongside the maintenance building) to be too small for even a short horse trailer, and no sight of any trails. We then drove to the park office and learned that, technically, horses are permitted, but there were no trails. It was unclear as to whether there were ever some sort of trails. Okay... anyway, after we spoke, the friendly and well-intended manager at the park office indicated that equestrians were welcome, but trail work and development would need to be done. I asked if he could use volunteers. He explained they were short staffed but, due to this being a union based workforce, volunteers would need to coordinate all efforts with the park management.

Volunteering at this destination may be more complex (as tasks must not conflict with union regulation) than working with the average park; however, Settler's Cabin Park is a very nice park with potential. If you are a local equestrian, ambitious, and would like to organize a group to establish trails, contact the manager of Settler's Cabin Park to initiate and coordinate the clearing of trails so that equestrians can share in the enjoyment of the park. Roughly 1,600 acres, Settler's Cabin Park would provide an opportunity for equestrians to develop a nice day ride trail destination.

Location: This is an Allegheny County Park situated west of Pittsburgh. Located south of Route 22 and west of Route 79 (accessed via Exit #60 west), its location can be viewed on the "Pittsburgh and Its Countryside" Laurel Highlands Pennsylvania Outdoors Discovery Map from the Allegheny County/Greater Pittsburgh Convention & Visitors Bureau, (412) 281-7711.

Info: Allegheny County Parks Department, 542 Forbes Avenue, Pittsburgh, PA 15219, (412) 350-7275, website www.county.allegheny.pa.us. You can also contact (412) 787-2750 for more information.

38. State Gamelands

The destinations in this book are not Pennsylvania Game Commission lands; however, these destinations often border State Gamelands. In order to determine if one can extend their ride into State Gamelands, equestrians must contact the applicable office to determine what type of use is permitted. Each State Gameland has its own regulations, limitations and authorized uses; some may be open to horses (and will be posted as such) and some may not. Trail usage may be limited to certain times of the year (not during hunting season). I have heard of groups or specialized rides obtaining permission to ride on the State Gamelands. Usually, organizers of the group rides must file their planned route with the office. If riders are traveling main dirt roads or sturdy ground, they will stand a better chance of obtaining permission. Check with the local office for the State Gamelands that you are interested in visiting. It may be that they permit multiple-use or that there may be exceptions such as the group rides.

For information regarding State Gamelands, the large map of the state with the location and corresponding number of the State Gamelands, or a detailed map of a particular State Gameland, contact the following:

For general trail info:
Pennsylvania Game Commission, 2001 Elmerton Avenue, Harrisburg, PA 17110-9797, (717) 787-9612; state headquarters (717) 783-8164; website: www.pgc.state.pa.us

For land management: (717) 787-6818

For additional info on Pennsylvania State Gamelands:
Northeast region (877) 877-9357
Southeast region (877) 877-9470
Northcentral region (877) 877-7674
Southcentral region (877) 877-9107
Northwest region (877) 877-0299
Southwest region (877) 877-7137

For a State Gamelands map: Call (717) 783-7507 (small fee if mailed) or access the State Gamelands website: www.pgc.state.pa.us.

39. Our Trail & Horse Camping Questionnaire

When we visit a new locale, I ask my list of questions so that I have a feel for the destination and what to expect. I included this list in Ride Pennsylvania Horse Trails- Part I and have again included it as I believe it can be helpful for both new and seasoned campers.

Name of contact person, address, phone, website, email address?
How many miles of horse trails? **Ask for maps and information on the trails.**
Terrain and difficulty of trails? (i.e., rocky, sandy, unmarked, well marked, narrow, wide, on the edge, any road riding, trail obstacles, etc.)
Are the trails multiple-use, if so what type of use? (i.e., bike, motorized, ATV)
Timing of visit? Ask for recommendations for best times. (Considerations: ideal temperatures, trails not muddy, insects [flies, mosquitoes, ground bees], flowers in bloom, fall foliage, not crowded, hunting seasons, any special events taking place that would interfere with trail enjoyment, recent severe weather affecting trails, downed trees, etc.)
Do they have horse camping? **Cost of camping, permit required, stalls?**
If no horse camping, any nearby places to camp with or to board a horse?
Can the trails be accessed directly from the camping area or do you have to drive to the trailhead? **Is road riding required to reach trails?** **How busy are the roads?**
Can the facility accommodate a large rig? State full size of your unit. How many feet are the sites? Are the sites pull through or is backing necessary?
Are there hookups? **Are sites primitive?** **Do they have water?** **Is it potable?** **Is there shade?**
Is a farrier or veterinarian available if needed?
Are box stalls available? If you choose box stalls, mention you will bring your own buckets and ask for their buckets to be pulled prior to your putting the horse in the stall. Horses using community buckets can catch various ailments. Check with your vet as to recommended vaccinations. We bring both a spray disinfectant for areas the horse may have contact with, along with an anti-chew spray to discourage or minimize nose contact with surfaces. Sometimes stalls are not as nice as they sound on the phone, or transmission of ailments can happen at the best of places due to transient traffic. Often, our preference is to tie line or put them in an open corral. If there are no stalls, and if traveling with an extra horse, ask if there is anywhere an extra horse can be left securely. Check that other horses can't gain access to your horse. **Hay and bedding available?**
Tie/high lines or portable electric fences permitted? **Tie stalls?** **Are they covered?** **Do they have full dividers between horses?** (Can unfamiliar horses bite or kick each other?)
Coggins needed? **Health certificate needed or any other item?** **If dogs are permitted, rabies or other info required?**
Toilets, showers, dump station? (Can your size camper reach the dump station?)
Any (additional) nearby horse trails? **Ask for any other info & maps to be mailed.**
Ask for specific directions to campground and trailheads. (Remind them you are hauling and need sufficient clearance. Ask about any extreme climbs, tight turns, construction, or rough roads.)
Do they take reservations? **Deposit required?** **Cancellation policy?**

40. Packing For Equestrian Travel

Necessities and Handy Items:

Horse Trailer/Camper:

- Fire extinguisher, safety road kit (with reflectors, flares or emergency triangles)
- Jack, wrench, spare tire, flat tire ramp (also good for getting the trailer level on uneven terrain)
- Maps, directions, overnight trailering guides in case of a breakdown
- Portable waste water caddy for campers, 5 gallon water refill containers
- Folding table, folding chairs
- Buckets, feed trays, or feed bags
- Hose, water, feed, hay (we always bring extra hay if there is room)
- Hay bags to hang from tie line (preferably material/canvas kind, not string bags as horses' legs can get caught in those especially if tied low)
- Bungee cords- we like these as our horses are less likely to get tangled; however, horses can cause them to spring and snap. We do not use the emergency release kind for tie lining as we find they release too easily.
- 'No chew spray' for bad behavers (useful around stalls, fences, tree wraps)
- Manure fork, broom, manure bucket or portable wheelbarrow
- Tie line (1+ inch thick nylon rope, allow 25'/horse, 100' helps if trees are spaced far apart), burlap to wrap around trees to prevent damage from horses chewing the bark
- Ladder to place tie line high in trees and "come along" pulley to secure line
- Wood shavings or straw bedding for horses (straw helps in wet weather, and helps prevent erosion to the tie area)
- Saddles, bridles, saddle pads, girths, breast collars, helmets, chaps, spurs, crupper
- Lead ropes, halters, brushes, hoof picks
- Waterproof horse blankets, fly sheets, fly masks, fly spray, human insect repellent, bee spray
- Leg wraps, shipping boots
- Horse papers, Coggins, dog papers (if applicable) including rabies certificate, etc.
- Propane (or charcoal), grill, wood for fire
- First aid items including bute, mineral oil, gall salve, iodine, medicated ointment, eye wash
- Poultice, mineral ice (for you and the horse) or liniment
- Standing bandages, gauze, thermometer
- Disinfectant spray (if stalled or if public buckets not removable)
- Large containers of water, if water is not available when camping (we always travel with a few 5-gallon jugs in case of breakdown or traffic jam)
- Check horses' shoes- we bring 2 extra shoes, made up ahead of time, for our one horse who has a unique style of shoe, so it can be matched in the event of losing one. We also use borium. For quick fixes, we keep a used shoe for each horse as a spare.
- Paper goods, towels, dish detergent, camping utensils, stove, etc., as needed
- Flashlight, citronella candle, lantern, radio, 3 prong electric outlet adjuster
- Small crow bar and tool kit (for when you back up and snag your mud flaps which are now cutting into your tire), WD-40

Along with other clothes items:

- Sunglasses, hat, helmet, riding shoes
- Swim wear

For cold or bad weather:

- Muck or rain shoes-muck shoes are easy on/easy off if needed in a hurry if a horse gets loose
- Long johns, sweatshirts
- Jacket, raincoat, and umbrella
- Wool sweater, warm socks
- Riding gloves

For the saddlebags:

- Horse identification such as a business card to stay on the horse in case your horse decides to depart without you. Bring extra cards; they come in handy.
- Collapsible water bucket (for when the water is so close yet so far)
- Trail map and extra copy, compass, topographical map, GPS
- Glasses or magnifier to read that map, pen, paper, and chalk to mark trails
- Cellular phone
- Extra layer of clothing (I scrunch up long john tops which condense nicely), gloves
- First aid kit including any prescription medication if applicable, antibacterial crème, iodine, alcohol swabs, Band-Aids, bandages, tube of electrolyte paste, Banamine (consult with your vet first), bee sting/insect bite lotion, small can of insect repellent spray, moist antiseptic towelettes, tissues, and Benadryl or allergy medication. (If you run into ground bees, allergy medication can be very helpful. Check with a physician first.)
- Canister of bear pepper spray
- Water, snacks, extra food in case you take a wrong turn on the trail
- Extra lead and halter to tie horse, Chicago screws if applicable
- Extra strands of leather or latigo in the event equipment breaks
- Trail marking tape. (We prefer orange. We also use a few strands to block off danger zones on trails and warn others of bees.)
- Sunscreen, rain coat, camera, film, camcorder (especially in Elk County)
- Vet wrap, bandanna (handy for many uses)
- "Easy Boot," duct tape to secure the boot, hoof pick, knife (many carry belt knives which can be useful in an emergency)
- Treats for the horses (can be used as a coercion or reward)
- Small flashlight (if you get lost and are returning at night)
- A bell if you are riding during hunting season *(John hates when I put the bell on the horse!)*. I also pack a paper thin, orange vest that folds tightly so it's handy when needed for good visibility.

41. Blooper Recap

Ah, did we have fun and challenges doing this book. We were definitely up against the tests of our endurance, perseverance, and patience. In fact, we never thought of ourselves as endurance riders, but the last two riding seasons sure felt like it. We rode the best of trails and we rode the worst of trails. We drove the best of roads and we drove the worst of roads. We had the best of weather and we had the worst of weather. Early in our research we encountered one trail which became so narrow one couldn't turn around and had to proceed forward, only to encounter where the ground caved in from recent storms and the horses had to jump the ravine while you hoped you didn't miss and slide down the steep gorge. That was a mountain goat trail, not a horse trail. (No, that trail is not in this book.) Another trail was so steep that John's horse began to tumble head first with him on his back. Fortunately, John pulled his head up and they got through by sliding down on his horse's haunches (didn't make the book either). And how about that trail with the hidden barbed wire that we almost didn't see, which hung at neck height and was left over from when it was a WWII prisoner camp? Or the time we rode back to camp to find out that, while we were gone, a large hang-gliding gathering had taken place with our camp in the middle of it. Imagine a horse's reaction to those monster, bird-type apparatuses flying overhead. And that time it took us eleven hours to reach western Pennsylvania (from eastern Pennsylvania) due to I-81 shutting down; all three horses amazingly remained patient throughout. There are those memories of the 4th of July when an unexpected fireworks display occurred directly over our horses' heads while they were tie lined. Then there's the rattlesnake who laid camouflaged in the autumn leaves and waited until my horse was about to step on him to raise his head and rattle his tail. My horse could have beaten any reining horse spin on that day. Then there was this cute little white ball of fur in front of my horse's nose which I couldn't make out because of his white, fluffy tail which blocked my seeing his head. Didn't know skunks came in that color! Another winning reining spin. And there was that porcupine who refused to budge from the trail; just wouldn't get out of our way and was not about to let us pass without incident. But then there was the time when we were face to face with a bear and the horses, amazingly, didn't even flinch but walked quietly along causing the bear to run from us. Perhaps our horses have seen it all or at least most of it. And to keep me on my toes, the lonely, well-stacked elk that snuck up behind me to come and visit me face to face as I sat and watched the sun set behind the mountains (see the back cover).

And our vehicles and equipment took a beating. The steep roads; the miles of washboard surface dirt roads; rugged back roads with no overhead clearance, no room to pass other vehicles, branches scratching the sides of the truck and trailer, jagged rocks cutting into the tire sidewalls, and nowhere to turn around down dead end roads. On our last trip we took two vehicles as we often did while researching. One was left at camp and the smaller trailer we used for day trips. While climbing those mountains with two rigs, we burnt out brakes on both trucks and returned home to a very expensive brake bill.

Oh the weather; I can't forget the weather. You name it, western Pennsylvania had it and we experienced the effects. There were tornadoes, micro bursts, hurricane remnants, hale, snow on Easter morning, trees torn from the ground in every direction blocking our path on road and trail, along with wicked electric storms every afternoon for days on end. During one trip, three days straight, each of our three horses lost shoes due to the moist weather. Upon the onset of a sudden micro burst, John was trapped in the truck while I was trapped in the trailer as it rocked from side to side while the wind gust twisted and tore our hardware and awning. (I stood in fright holding my little gray dog, I felt like Dorothy with Toto.) Somehow the trailer hung in there and was fine as it faced the wind, but the awning departed our company. We put on a new one, never even got the trailer back out and another storm hit. Each time the awnings were on a slant for runoff; it wasn't enough. We are now on our third awning in one riding season. We had to replace the new portable gas grill too. Something about a large dog urinating on it while the owner looked on without even offering to clean it. Either way, it just wasn't the same! Then the dog proceeded to do the same to our chair. Hmmm, not the way to get along with one's neighbor.

And how many times can one's husband back up onto his mud flaps and bend the heavy metal frames to the point they are piercing the tire walls, until he realizes that long mud flaps aren't practical on uneven ground? (Ever see a beautiful show horse's long tail tear as the rider is asked to back their horse? Same kind of thing.) John, how many sets of those have we gone through now?

And then there is the day we stopped to help some fellow equestrians on busy I-79 near Pittsburgh. They had a double flat tire with horses on board and were at a dangerous location on the busy road. We couldn't get directly to them, passed them, and turned back to help them. After stopping to help, we departed and headed down the road a few miles, only to get a nasty blowout ourselves. We were at a bad spot and no one was around to help us. Plus, we left most of our tools and our flares in the other bigger trailer. Two horses on board, no ramp, no jack; we quickly innovated. But hey, that's okay about the flat tire; we had to replace all the tires on both trucks and trailers anyway when they went in for their new brakes. I guess you could say we had covered the "Wild, Wild West" of Pennsylvania!

BLOOPERS

ALONG THE TRAIL: old dynamite storage caves, Allegheny National Forest (top) and springhouse, Susquehannock State Forest (bottom)

ALONG THE TRAIL: the old man in the tree, Two Mile Run County Park

A good, seasoned trail horse can provide children with a positive introduction to the world of horses (Grayson [top photo] and Reed [bottom photo] on Tabasco).

U.S. STABLING GUIDE
U
Eleventh Edition

Order Now!

A Selection of the Equestrian's Edge™ Book Club

U.S. STABLING GUIDE
U
Eleventh Edition

THE COUNTRY'S COMPREHENSIVE GUIDE FOR HORSE
TRANSPORTATION IN THE UNITED STATES AND CANADA

THE BOOK YOU NEED WHEN TRAVELING WITH YOUR HORSE.
Contains over 1000 state-by-state listings of stables and
B&Bs that will board your horse after a long day on the road.
Plus other useful information for the horse owner.

$26.95

800-829-0715

THE BOOK YOU NEED WHEN TRAVELING WITH YOUR HORSE.
Contains over 1000 state-by-state listings of stables and
B&Bs that will board your horse after a long day on the road.
Plus other useful information for the horse owner.

$26.95

**Check out Smucker's
for all your harness & equine needs.**

Smucker's Harness Shop, Inc. has a complete line of tack and equine products, and also performs repairs on the premises.

42. Please Provide Your Comments!

Note to the Reader: trails are always changing. If you find that any of the described trails have significantly changed, new trails have opened, or you know of Pennsylvania trails not covered in this book, please notify the publisher at the address below. Any comments will be considered in future editions of books and for website updates. Thank you in advance for your input.

Also, watch our website for other developments.

Send to:
Hit The Trail Publications, LLC
P.O. Box 970
Cherryville, PA 18035

Or write us via our website:
www.ridepennsylvania.com OR **www.patrail.com**